Selling Opportunity

ALSO BY MARY LISA GAVENAS

Color Stories:
Behind the Scenes in America's
Billion-Dollar Beauty Industry

Selling Opportunity

The STORY of MARY KAY

MARY LISA GAVENAS

VIKING

VIKING
An imprint of Penguin Random House LLC
1745 Broadway, New York, NY 10019
penguinrandomhouse.com

Image credits can be found on p. 417–418.

Book design by Daniel Lagin

LIBRARY OF CONGRESS CATALOGING-IN-PUBLICATION DATA
Names: Gavenas, Mary Lisa author.
Title: Selling opportunity : the story of Mary Kay / Mary Lisa Gavenas.
Description: New York, NY : Viking, [2026] | Includes bibliographical references and index.
Identifiers: LCCN 2025047273 (print) | LCCN 2025047274 (ebook) |
ISBN 9780670015412 hardcover | ISBN 9781101621318 ebook
Subjects: LCSH: Mary Kay Cosmetics. | Ash, Mary Kay. |
Businesswomen—United States—Biography. |
Cosmetics industry—United States. | LCGFT: Biographies.
Classification: LCC HD9970.5.C674 M37243 2026 (print) |
LCC HD9970.5.C674 (ebook) | DDC 338.7/66855092—dc23/eng/20260123
LC record available at https://lccn.loc.gov/2025047273
LC ebook record available at https://lccn.loc.gov/2025047274

Printed in the United States of America
1st Printing

The authorized representative in the EU for product safety and compliance is Penguin Random House Ireland, Morrison Chambers, 32 Nassau Street, Dublin D02 YH68, Ireland, https://eu-contact.penguin.ie.

Dedicated to

The Leon Levy Center for Biography

CONTENTS

Selling Opportunity

INTRODUCTION

Seminar, July 1992

A girl grows up during the Depression and gets married too young. When she is not cooking or cleaning or taking care of the kids, she peddles cleaning products to other housewives. The work has no salary and no security. She keeps at it anyway, through divorce and disappointment.

In 1963, after she has been divorced three times and widowed twice, she sets up her own company, selling second chance and self-invention for the price of a skin care showcase. Her timing is perfect. Generations of girls have had educations that left them stuffed full of ennobling rhetoric and eager to pursue their American Dreams. They are primed for the promise of a career with no cap on earnings and hours that can be arranged around the needs of husbands and children.

By 1969, she is remarried and giving out keys to pink Cadillacs while women around her weep with gratitude. She recruits hundreds, then thousands, then hundreds of thousands of women. She turns shift workers and stay-at-home moms into millionaires. She becomes the most famous saleswoman in the world. Maybe the most famous ever. Dolly Parton has the script in development.

She signs up women of all ages, sizes, and colors, then praises them to the skies and crowns them with rhinestone tiaras. Magazine covers ask, "Why do so many women feel tired?"; she tells women to hire a housekeeper. She runs sales contests with prizes like mink coats, diamond bracelets, and what she calls "Cinderella gifts . . . the things that we wait around for that guy on the white horse who never shows up to bring us."

Thus Mary Kay Ash, a woman with no great aptitude for numbers, becomes the first woman to chair a company on the New York Stock Exchange. She stands shoulder to shoulder with titans of industry and heroes of sport to receive the Horatio Alger Award for "triumph over adversity," then racks up scores of other accolades, most of them preceded by "the first woman" or "the only woman."

If the economy slumps, her profits go up. This summer, as Montgomery Ward shutters its remaining stores and Sears braces for the largest loss in American retail history, her consultant count is hitting a new high. While Macy's files for bankruptcy protection, the company she named after herself is about to debut on the Fortune 500. World domination is next. Moscow offices are under construction. Mainland China is in the works.

Each year, she celebrates these successes at Seminar, the annual gathering that starts as an awards dinner with home-cooked chicken on soggy paper plates and soon grows into a three-day, multimillion-dollar extravaganza. When not even the humongous Dallas Convention Center can accommodate all the women who want to attend, she adds a second Seminar that starts as soon as the first one is over. Then she adds a third. Now she is up to four in a row. All are sold out.

This morning, well before Seminar start time, eight thousand women are in their assigned seats in the center's main arena while, across town, a spillover crowd fills the Great Hall of the Dallas Apparel Mart, waiting to watch on closed-circuit TV. Some are first-timers from as far away as Australia and Taiwan. Most are repeats. Every one of them has paid an attendance fee close to $100 plus her own transportation, food, and lodging to be here. Since about 70 percent hold full- or part-time jobs, most have taken time off work too. They've also had to find child-care, get husbands sorted, and show up wearing full rig in the near-hundred-degree heat of a Dallas summer.

The business analysts will tell you that none of that makes sense. This work still has no salary and no security. Company-wide reps average sales of $2,400 a year, and the percentage who become "Mary Kay millionaires" is minuscule. That doesn't seem to bother the women here, though. Ahead of them are three full days of hearing that they are beautiful and that they can make their dreams come true. In between expos, motivational talks, and razzmatazz song-and-dance numbers, they will watch women who look just like them claim a share of this year's $6 million prize hoard. Big winners, women with six-figure sales incomes, will stand onstage, point at the nosebleed seats, and say, "A couple of years ago, I was sitting right where you are."

And now it's starting. Mary Kay Ash is due onstage any second. "When Mary Kay comes out, you can hear a pin drop," says a woman who never misses Seminar. "There is always a hush." Purses click open. Cameras come out. She is never late. She is not today.

Here she comes, in her heels, her diamonds, one of those big white-blond wigs she always wears. At seventy-four, she still looks the same as she did when she went toe-to-toe with Morley Safer on *60 Minutes* over a dozen years ago. When the audience jumps to its feet at the sight of her, she stands at the podium and blows kisses until they calm down and take their seats. Then she begins talking as if eight thousand women are sitting across from her at the kitchen table.

To this audience, nothing she says is surprising. They expect to hear the company catchphrase—"You can do it!"—and they do. Everything else is an elaboration. "If you think you can, you can. If you think you can't, you're right." "Fail forward to success." That unhurried, almost-uninflected way of speaking makes an old saw like "It's not where you start, it's where you finish" seem inarguable. Every so often, with that same dry delivery, she slips in a one-liner like "What does she have that you can't have fixed?" and gets a laugh.

There is no fire and brimstone, no podium thumping. "She is not the rah-rah cheerleader type," says a consultant. Mary Kay tells them, "You can have anything in this world you want—if you want it badly enough and you're willing to pay the price," but she does not make it sound easy.

CHAPTER ONE

The Change-of-Life Baby

In the spring of 1918, Mary Kathlyn Wagner was the fourth and final child born to Alexander Edward Wagner and Lula Vember Hastings, hardworking people who had reason to hope they were done with infants and diapers.

As parents, Alex and Lula were not the type to fuss over a third girl baby. Ten days after her birth, she appeared in the records of Harris County, Texas, as a "healthy white female" not yet named. Younger than her closest sibling by over a decade, she later described herself as a "change-of-life baby," even though her mother was probably only thirty-four when she was born. In the Texas of that time, the last-born would often grow up spoon-fed and spoiled. This one would not.

The Wagners didn't waste time on that kind of thing. Although Lula's lineage went as far back as any old-money family's, the Wagners were as far from leisure class as white people could be. Before Mary Kay's birth, they moved around Southeast Texas working as rice farmers or picking up jobs in small towns. They never seemed to own land, never seemed to be working for themselves. Scheme after scheme ended with banks and business partners suing for garnishment. One year, when the Wagners lived in the southeast corner of Harris County and were farming someone else's spread, they did well enough to have three or four laborers around the place. That didn't last. Living in boomtown Beaumont when Texas gold was gushing out of the ground, they watched people all around them grow fantastically wealthy. They didn't make a dime.

Failing to strike oil or make their fortune farming, the Wagners took jobs at a hotel in Cypress, a whistle-stop twenty-four miles from Houston. There, in 1907, wildcatters drilling for oil hit 108-degree hot springs instead. The sulfurous water turned hair stiff as a block of wood and stank to high heaven. But it also turned tough, weathered Texan complexions soft as a baby's bottom. Sooner or later, everybody got used to the smell.

A decade later, the Hot Well Improvement Company was still trying to recruit investors for its plans to transform two cement pools of smelly water, thirty acres of weedy land, and one rickety barn of a building into a destination spa. Headed by an Ohio-born wheeler-dealer named Frank Connable, the Hot Well Improvement Company had switched up operations more than once. Thus far, its greatest success had been luring Houstonians out to Cypress on Sundays with advertisements of a fifty-cent chicken dinner. The plan was for Lula to take over the chicken dinners along with other cooking and housekeeping. Her husband would act as jack-of-all-trades and on-site manager. According to Connable, who operated out of the Commercial National Bank Building, Houston's first skyscraper, this was a crackerjack, can't-fail proposition.

On paper, it seemed promising. Texas was dotted with resorts like Wizard Wells, Sour Lake, and Sulphur Springs, where health seekers put down good money for miracle cures. Up in Palo Pinto County, Mineral Wells sustained two sanatoriums, supported more than forty hotels and boardinghouses, and shipped three million bottles of "Crazy Water" a year. Closer by, Marlin—town tagline "If You're Ailin' or Your Health Is Failin'"—profited from that nasty-tasting stuff burbling out of the Municipal Hygeia behind the courthouse. Advertised for ailments ranging from tobacco addiction to female complaints, Marlin's water possessed proven power as a laxative, sufferers could expect relief within the hour. Baseball teams came to train in the offseason. Conrad Hilton built a hotel.

In Cypress, Connable was aiming for an establishment to rival the Hot Wells Hotel and Spa, a resort near San Antonio that attracted the likes of Sarah Bernhardt and Teddy Roosevelt. Discovered in 1892 when the Southwestern Lunatic Asylum drilled for drinking water and hit a sulfur spring instead, its mineral water was judged too hot and smelly for the lunatics but just right for locals, who, being of German and Central European extraction, were known to enjoy such things. A spa was built, burned down, then rebuilt. Backed by Yankee investors, the improved Hot Wells had a bowling alley, telephones, electric lights, natatoria, and an ostrich farm that provided plumes for ladies' hats and ostrich-race betting for ladies' husbands. French filmmaker Gaston Méliès, enraptured by its unclouded skies, vowed to make Hot Wells the world capital of cinema. Setting up next door, he cranked out over seventy movies in under sixteen months before decamping for the unclouded skies of Southern California. By then, his departure made no difference. Hot Wells had 190 rooms and was turning away customers.

Surely the potential of Cypress was greater still. Its hotel was surrounded by over a hundred acres that the Hot Well Improvement Company planned to split into plots for resort homes, enticing prospects with a $1 share in the spa company for every $10 spent on land. Already the venture was blessed with proximity to a fast-growing port flush with oil money, a name near identical to the world-famous Hot Wells Hotel, and a steady trade in chicken dinners. Nor was Cypress one of those teetotaling Baptist burgs. Directly behind the depot, Juergen's Saloon did booming business; Tin Hall, a dance palace the size of a cow pasture, had been going strong since 1889. The Wagners were told that all it would take was some good hard work on their part, plus a short wait until expanded amenities were in place.

Forecasting a future as "the health and pleasure resort of South Texas," Connable announced that future guests would be deposited at the hotel's front door, just as soon as the Houston & Central Texas Railway installed a spur line. Potential investors were assured that the as-yet-unbuilt bottling plant would soon be shipping Cypress's mineral water far and wide. Imminent improvements—roller coaster, skating rink, tennis court, bowling alley, chute-the-chutes, "and other contraptions for the amusement-loving public"—were advertised. Any day now, the Hot Well Hotel would be the pleasure spot of the South. Big money would start rolling in.

Until then, the Jacksons, an African American family consisting of a widowed laundress with five children, lived on the place to help with the heavy work. For the time being, the chief adornment of the Hot Well Hotel was the painted tractor tire in the front yard, where baby Mary Kathlyn was posed for a photograph in 1919. Because business was best on weekends, when people came up from the city, the Wagners got used to working seven-day weeks. They'd learned not to expect much else.

Early childbearing, backbreaking labor, and bad luck were family traditions.

On her mother's side, Mary Kay's ancestors were Englishmen who emigrated to Maryland in the late 1600s and remained well below what became the Mason–Dixon Line. A few fought as Loyalists in the War

The Hot Wells Hotel near San Antonio, circa 1910.

The Hot Well Hotel in Cypress, which advertised "Buildings Modern in Every Respect."

of Independence. Generation by generation, they moved south, working small farms in Tennessee, the Carolinas, Alabama, and Louisiana. Davy Crockett was a distant relative.

When Mary Kay was born, that past was still present. Family who were not farmers, farmwives, or farmhands followed trades like blacksmith or harness maker. Mary Kay's maternal great-grandfather, James Dimmitt Cross, born on a small Tennessee farm during the presidency of Andrew Jackson and come to Texas to settle Falls County in the mid-1800s, was still working his farm and collecting the $15-or-so quarterly pension that the state doled out to destitute veterans of the Confederate Army. "Common whites," as opposed to slaveholders, he and Great-Grandmother Julia Parton Cross told stories of Civil War days, when he spent four years as a barefoot infantryman in Flournoy's Regiment, taking at least one furlough long enough to start the seventh pregnancy in her eventual total of thirteen but otherwise leaving Julia to run the farm, raise the kids, and get by on state relief.

Compared with them, the Wagners were newcomers. Texas was full of sturdy German farmers who survived the Mexican-American War, the Civil War, and the state's frequent epidemics of yellow fever. But Mary Kay's father was not one of them. He was an outsider. Born on a small farm in Cook County, Illinois, Alexander Edward Wagner was the seventh living child of Prussian-born Martin Wagner and his Prussian-born wife, Catherine, who had her first baby when she was seventeen and her last when she was forty-five. Later, Mary Kay's father would sometimes list his birthplace as Missouri, where his parents also farmed for a while. Sometimes he would change his birth year. In Cypress, he sometimes went by "Alec" instead of "Alex." That would change too.

Eventually, a few Wagners wound up in Texas. Alex and his brother Conrad found work as farmhands in Port Arthur, a recently settled stretch of the Gulf Coast, arriving right before the Great Galveston Hurricane of 1900, soon to be known as the worst natural disaster in U.S. history. The brothers were just in time to see the hurricane ruin the rice crop, ravage the seaport, turn the town to tinder, and set off floods and fires that killed at least eight thousand people.

When Mary Kay's mother and father met, Alex was dark haired, thin as a rail, considered a catch if you didn't mind that he was Roman Catholic or that his ears stuck out. Lula was the kind of girl who looked like a good cook: short, sturdy figure, mousy hair that had once been blond, and the pale, pretty complexion that her youngest daughter would inherit. The two were married by a justice of the peace on January 4, 1902, when Alex was about twenty-two and Lula was around seventeen or eighteen. Nine months later, their first child, Dealia Cozzette, was born. Cecil DeWitt followed in May of 1905, Daisy Yvette in July of 1907.

After they had been married a couple of years, Alex and Lula had their elopement convalidated by the big Catholic church in Beaumont and had Dealia baptized the same day. When Cecil was born, he was baptized Catholic too. No Catholic baptism of Daisy was recorded. Before long, Dealia Mary went back to being Dealia Cozzette; Cecil Joseph was Cecil DeWitt again. When Alex found work in a stretch of Harris County with no Catholic parishes, the family went back to being Baptist.

Marrying with no savings and no homestead, Alex and Lula had done what their families had always done. Alex's parents had resettled at least three times since emigration. Lula's father had been born in Mississippi, moved to Texas, and worked his way up to owning land in Liberty County, where he served on Democratic committees and made a failed run for alderman. Aside from that, neither side of the family had much to boast about in the way of acquisition or accomplishment. Neither showed much interest in education. Both parents knew their letters, their numbers, their Bible. Neither aspired to more. Neither attended high school. Nor did their first three children.

In Texas, high school was not for the likes of them. The legislature had fought tooth and nail to keep public high schools out of the state. Such institutions were thought to make the working class too uppity and unhappy with their lot in life. Hence, Texas was ranked near worst of all U.S. school systems, only slightly better than the miserable education available in nearby Louisiana.

Even getting elementary schools had been a battle. Conservatives fought public education—"Away with free schools; let every man educate his own child!"—declaring it outrageous to ask any taxpayer to contribute to the education of another's children and invoking a God Almighty who gave them the right to rule their own offspring. The fight continued until 1915, when Texas became one of the last states to require compulsory schooling, easing its citizens into the idea by requiring only sixty days' attendance when the law took effect the following year. In 1917, its minimum increased to eighty days, before settling at one hundred days in 1918. But no one went out of their way to enforce it, and the absentee rate at rural schools ran upward of 40 percent.

When Mary Kay was born, those rural schools made up the majority of the state school system. Sentimentalized by city people who never had to attend them, Texas's one- and two-room schoolhouses generally featured a water pump in the yard, kerosene lamps on the wall, and a reeking outhouse out back. The curriculum was "reading, 'riting, and 'rithmetic" to prepare pupils for lives as farmers and farmwives. The teachers were homesick fourteen- and fifteen-year-old girls forced to board with trustees and share bedrooms, and usually beds, with female pupils. Miserly salaries were paid months late. Schoolmarms often left after a year. Many didn't last that long.

In Cypress, Mary Kay's sisters and brother were assigned to Big Cypress School No. 2, a one-room schoolhouse two miles down the Old Shell Road. There, a lone teacher coped with children of assorted ages in a single room notoriously hot in spring and fall, virtually unheated in winter, and not well ventilated at any time of year. Books and desks were shared when either was available. Mercifully, the school year was short. The closest high school was in Addicks, over a dozen miles away. Almost no one bothered.

In places like Cypress, everybody had suffered through the same education. Everybody's parents and grandparents had gone through it too.

For the new baby, all that would be different.

She was born at the Hot Well Hotel late in the evening of Sunday, May 12, 1918, after Lula had finished cooking and serving the

Big Cypress School No. 2.

chicken dinners. Mary Kay told people that she was a blue baby and that to goad her into gasping for oxygen, someone dunked her in the water, still warm and full of pinfeathers, used to scald that day's chickens. Later, the doctor filling out the birth certificate wrote "Houston Hot Wells" in the space provided for a town, which Mary Kay usually abbreviated to "Hot Wells," a local name for the place. If people confused it with the town in Hudspeth County, or assumed that she meant the resort outside San Antonio, she did not correct them.

By the time their fourth child came along, Alex and Lula had no need for the broods of farmhands their families had bred. This blue-eyed, blond baby could only be seen as one more girl to clothe and feed, albeit one who arrived before the summer season got underway. Houston had banned alcohol within city limits, which ended short of Cypress, so Houstonians would be flocking their way. Tin Hall and Juergen's Saloon expected land office business. Even the Hot Well Hotel expected an uptick.

But the Wagners' bad luck was soon back. Strikes wrecked local shipping and, with it, the local economy. By August, the rest of the country was in a recession too. Splashing around in smelly water had come to seem a preposterous pastime. In the fall, Spanish influenza found its way to Houston and the mayor outlawed public gatherings. Thousands sickened; hundreds died. Restaurants and dance halls shut. Bathhouses were labeled centers of contagion.

In November, the Great War ended. Although no one in the Wagner family served—Cecil was too young, Alex was overage and blind in one eye—everyone in Cypress suffered when the army announced the closure of Camp Logan, shipped its free-spending soldiers home, canceled supply contracts, and left locals with little or no work. The outside world intruded again when, in early 1919, the Eighteenth Amendment passed. Within a year, Cypress would be dry. Even Juergen's Saloon would go out of business.

Things went from bad to worse. In a legal feud begun years before, the Hot Well Improvement Company went bust. Cypress mineral springs would remain a feature of Houston life for the next four decades, but no luxurious resort would materialize. No investors would put up resort homes. No railroad spur would be built. The pandemic put paid to the fad for taking waters, and spas would never regain their prewar popularity. During Prohibition, watering places like Hot Springs, Arkansas, would gain renown as gangster playgrounds. The Hot Well Hotel would not.

Soon the Wagners were out of work again. In January of 1920, a census taker found the family still at the Hot Well Hotel. The three oldest children still attended the one-room schoolhouse down the road. The Jacksons were still on the place as servants; twelve-year-old Mamie, who had already left school, was probably the one minding Mary Kathlyn. The hotel's only customers were a cattleman and his wife. Within weeks, all that would change.

Looking back, the birth of the new baby had been a turning point. Soon after she arrived, senility forced Great-Grandfather Cross off his land. When he died the next year, the family applied for a Confederate mortuary warrant for the money to bury him. Then Great-Grandmother Cross, who had raised a dozen children and drudged through a lifetime of farmwork, became a charity case by making her mark on a form certifying that she was an indigent, illiterate Confederate widow. A year later, she died too, taking with her the family witness of the Texas frontier and the Civil War.

Cotton prices plunged. Nobody seemed to be taking up farming anymore. The life was too hard and, in Texas, the price of entry was too high. Lula's brother, Boman "Doc" Hastings, who had been a blacksmith, found a job making tanks for an oil refinery and moved to Houston.

He wasn't the only one. That year, as America's population shifted from rural to urban, the Land of Opportunity became a land of city dwellers. Along with so many others, the Wagners decided that there was no future in farming or country life. No matter how bad things got, they would never go back to it.

At the start of 1920, the Wagners moved again: this time, twenty-four miles south to Houston's Sixth Ward.

CHAPTER TWO

"You Can Do It!"

In Houston, no one's prospects were preordained. Millionaires were minted by the minute, improbable ambitions realized daily. Defying jinxed geography that sited the city fifty miles inland, Houston made itself into one of America's premier deepwater ports. As the Wagners closed the door on the Hot Well Hotel, plans were afoot to make the Houston Ship Channel even deeper, even bigger, even busier. All around, oil refineries and cotton processing plants were going up in gleeful anticipation.

Impatient to move past regional renown as railroad hub and cotton exchange, the city was willing itself toward ever greater glories. Boosters claimed Houston was the fastest-growing city in America. True or not, it was the biggest city in the biggest state, with a population doubling each decade. Awash in oil money from surrounding strikes, Houston was funding a slew of civic improvements that included a school system intended to bring national bragging rights. The Dow School, a state-of-the-art institution practicing the latest in self-directed, John Dewey–inspired pedagogy, was only two blocks away from the Wagners' new home in the Sixth Ward.

An enterprise extolling hard work and high ideals could hardly have found a better spot. North of the city's center, the Wagners' new neighborhood had repeatedly reinvented itself since its start as a cluster of cozy "Sunday homes" where German farm folk stayed over when they came to town for Saturday shopping and Sunday church. When Houston became known as "the city where seventeen railroads meet the sea," the Sixth Ward filled with neat bungalows for families of the gandy dancers, yard rats, and car knockers working at nearby Grand Central Station. Now, after the Great War, the Ward was changing again, becoming a village within city limits, a cross section of class and circumstance crammed into a few square blocks.

Fathers had all kinds of jobs—minister, bus driver, baker, factory boss—and a few made it into the Blue Book, Houston's social register. Peck Kelley, still years away from being called "the finest white jazz pianist of all time" but already a popular bandleader, lived over on State Street. Mexicans were starting to move in among the Germans, Irish, English, Polish, and Italians. Jews already lived there. Of the dozen families living nearest the Wagners, two spoke Yiddish at home: One hailed from Jerusalem, another from Russian Lithuania.

At the end of the Wagners' block stood a brick mansion with stained-glass windows and Corinthian columns. Kitty-corner sat the shed that served as neighborhood grocery. Of the ward's dozen churches, Tabernacle Baptist was only two blocks east, St. Joseph's Catholic another two blocks beyond. On its south, the Sixth Ward was bordered by Buffalo Bayou, a winding waterway lined with cypress and river birch; on its north, by Washington Avenue, a straight-shot thoroughfare soon to be lined with car dealerships.

And into the midst of all this moved Alex and Lula, who, in Cypress, could go for days without speaking to another soul besides the Jacksons, who worked the place. Both had a sixth-grade education. Neither had negotiated a mortgage. The slickers must have smiled when they saw them coming.

Alex agreed to pay $3,650 for a two-bedroom house on Kane Street that had sold for $950 five months before. Built in 1890, it was what people called a shotgun cottage, because its three main rooms lined up so straight that you could supposedly sit on the front porch and shoot chickens in the backyard. Like most buildings in that part of Houston, 2111 Kane had no basement. Like lots all around, its tenth of an acre was barely big enough for a house with a small shed in back and a strip of grass between front door and sidewalk. Unlike gingerbread-trimmed Victorians up and down the street, its box construction was so basic that a later owner assumed it had been built as a barn. Alex made his down payment, promised a balloon payment later that year, and signed for an 8 percent mortgage that amounted to $40 a month, roughly half his income. With everyone chipping in and up to five people working full-time—plus the occasional boarder—that mortgage would take seventeen years to pay off.

But at least they had escaped the stink of sulfur and were on their way to owning a place in town. Here, on Houston's humid nights, everybody sat out on the front porch after supper. Yards were so small that kids played in gangs up and down the gravel streets. Houses were so close together that you could hear everything through screen doors and

Houston's Main Street: Foley Brothers, where Daisy worked, at left; Colby's Rooms, where Lula worked, at bottom right.

the open windows. Peck Kelley had to use a stringless piano so he wouldn't vex the whole neighborhood with his practicing. Everybody knew everybody else's business.

Surely the Wagners could not fail to prosper here.

Houston had employment enough for everybody. Daisy, turning thirteen, became a cashier at Foley Brothers, the downtown department store. Cecil, turning fifteen, became a clerk at the grand South Texas Commercial National Bank, famed as one of the most beautiful buildings in the South. Dealia, the oldest, started as a saleslady at a general dry goods emporium, then moved to Emporium Millinery, the kind of place that sold ladies' furs in a city where temperatures rarely dipped below sixty degrees. Lula became a cake baker at Colby's Rooms downtown, still in a kitchen but now in a kitchen on the busiest stretch of a big city's Main Street.

Alex, who henceforth would use Edward, his middle name, for business enterprises, had the grandest plan of all. His years at the Hot Well Hotel had given him a taste for being called "proprietor." This time, though, there would be no men in fancy suits making big promises. He would run his own show: the Kings Trail Auto Repair Company.

He had a promising start. Leasing a double lot at 1821 and 1823 Washington Avenue to accommodate all the business bound to come his way, he announced "Automobile and Machine Works" with "E. A. Wagner, proprietor." On call seven days a week, twenty-four hours a day, Kings Trail specialized in radiator repair but was willing to tackle just about anything. Advertisements bragged of its inventory of Ford parts, pledging: "We employ only experienced mechanics and guarantee all work"—one of those mechanics being brother-in-law Doc, who moved to 2111 Kane Street with the Wagners.

Kings Trail seemed sure to forever change the family fortunes. In 1921, with Houston soon to boast the highest rate of car ownership in the country, Alex was canny enough to concentrate on Fords and get a good location on one of Houston's major corridors. A hundred years later, that same stretch of Washington Avenue would still be lined with car showrooms, used-car lots, repair shops, tire dealers, and gas stations.

For all that, his enterprise lasted barely a year. By 1922, he had sublet its big brick-framed bays and ceded his specialty, radiator repair, to someone else. Uncle Doc headed elsewhere. By 1923, Kings Trail had other proprietors. Soon after, the name was gone too. During the next decade, both business and name would be revived, but no one in the Wagner family would work there again.

For the next four years, Alex disappeared from city directories as completely as if he had vanished into thin air. By 1925, Lula was advertising for boarders. As soon as she found them, she sued for the divorce granted in April 1926, when Mary Kay was seven. When Mary Kay was ten, her parents remarried and her father returned to Kane Street, never to leave again.

Later, Mary Kay would say that he spent three, sometimes she said four, years in the State Tuberculosis Sanatorium outside San Angelo, an institution so big it was treated as a town called Sanatorium, with its own hog farm, school, and post office.

Even in the 1920s, three years was an extended treatment, given that Sanatorium patients were restricted to a six-month stay and denied readmission. To this day, Sixth Ward scuttlebutt says he was a drunk.

Lula plowed on.

She kept her job at Colby's Rooms, going from cake baker to cook. In 1926, she left to cook at Blanchard's, another downtown restaurant, before leaving to waitress at yet another. By Texas law, only Alex had been allowed to make major financial decisions, such as the house purchase. As her husband, Alex controlled community property, her earnings, and any property she might own. When he returned, Lula was allowed to support him.

Eventually, seeing no way to support him, herself, or anyone else on women's wages, Lula opened a greasy spoon. When Mary Kay was ten, Lula leased a run-down store at the corner of Washington Avenue and

White Street for $50 a month, christened it "Wagner's Café," and began dishing up grub that would fuel railroad men through shifts at Grand Central Station. There would be no fifty-cent chicken dinners here. The specialty was waffles. The rest of the menu ran to cornbread, black-eyed peas, barbecued pig ribs, and a chicken-and-dumplings plate that was more dumplings than chicken. Walls were covered in stamped metal. Floors were pine. Both were easy to scrub clean. Its attraction was its location; Wagner's Café was within walking distance of both the train station and the family home at 2111 Kane Street.

Not that 2111 Kane Street had turned out to be much of a family home. Not with so many people moving in and out. Uncle Doc was gone by 1922. Alex disappeared soon after. In 1923, Dealia married a man who worked for Humble Oil and settled near San Antonio. Boarders came and went. Cecil, still clerking at the bank, turned twenty-one, married seventeen-year-old Ruby Massey, and moved out in 1926. The next year, Uncle Doc, putting his blacksmith experience to use as a body builder for the Ford Motor Company, moved back to 2111 Kane Street with his wife and two children. Soon they were gone again, and other boarders took their place. Those boarders, in turn, lasted less than a year. In 1928, Daisy was the last to escape: marrying a Californian, settling in San Francisco, and staying there even after the marriage fell apart. Mary Kay, too young to move anywhere, had her own job by then: taking care of her father.

There would be no more proprietorships in Alex's future, due to what was later called his "crippling illness." The official story, the one that Mary Kay would use in interviews, was that tuberculosis turned him into an invalid. Even though, during a decade when the disease killed so many children, anyone Mary Kay's age was supposed to be kept well away from a TB patient. Even though Alex sometimes worked—never for very long, never earning very much—as a salesman at places like the Blue Bird Creamery or L. B. Price Mercantile. Even though he would sometimes pile goods in his car and try to sell them door to door.

Running what Mary Kay called "Wagner's Wonderful Waffle Works," Lula was home less than ever. With a mother working sixteen-hour days and seven-day weeks because, as her daughter explained, "she couldn't make as much money as a man," Mary Kay became what would later be called a latchkey child.

She learned to get by on little sleep. Since her mother got up before dawn to open the café, Mary Kay got her father's breakfast and her own. At lunchtime, she hurried two blocks home to fix his food, then raced back to Dow, sometimes wolfing her own lunch as she walked. After school, she made his dinner, made her own, then did the housework. Because her mother would not reappear until well after the café closed, Mary Kay waited up to tell her mother what she had done and hear how she could have done it better. With her father, things were easier. He let her do everything for him and seemed satisfied.

In 1994, a company biopic portrayed this part of her childhood by showing a woebegone little girl taking a tray of food to an invalid father. When the father says that he wants some potato soup, the little girl runs to the telephone to beg her mother to come home. The answer is a hurried "I know this is hard, but Mother knows you can do it. I love you. Bye-bye." Click.

Maudlin maybe, but essentially accurate. During daytime, Mary Kay talked to her mother by telephone. From whatever kitchen she was in, Lula let Mary Kay know what needed to be done. "You can do it!" Lula told the little girl as she gave directions for some chore. "You can do it, honey!"

And Mary Kay obliged, without resentment or resistance. A childhood friend said, "She was extremely capable of taking care of any type of thing even from first grade." Lula told her, "You can do it!" So she did.

At school, the little Wagner girl entered another world.

Hell-bent on catching up with the rest of the country, Houston's city fathers used three multimillion-dollar bond issues to stake the Houston Independent School District as a potential world-beater. By the mid-1920s, the Dow School had advantages undreamed of by its pupils' parents. Or by brothers and sisters the ages of Dealia, Cecil, and Daisy.

The Dow School at 1900 Kane Street.

While children on the edges of Harris County were still riding mules to one- and two-room schoolhouses, Dow had separate teachers for each grade, classes half the size of the seventy-five common in rural schools, and classrooms with lined blackboards and individual, child-size desks. Its school year stretched to nine months, not the one hundred days customary in Texas. Instead of a stinking outhouse with a hand-cranked pump, Dow had child-size lavatories with hot and cold running water. Hot meals could be served in its cafeteria. Ascending to this heaven via steep front steps, students entered a place where high ceilings tempered the Gulf Coast heat, steam radiators buffered winter damp, and huge double-sashed windows allowed them to look down on the rest of the Sixth Ward.

When Mary Kay first climbed those steep front steps, Dow was in its heyday. Founded on the edge of Houston's business district in 1885, it had started as a school that squeezed 171 white children into two rooms. Renamed to honor district superintendent Justin E. Dow and relocated to a six-classroom building in the Sixth Ward, the school expanded again in 1912, when it moved to a new, sixteen-room brick building at 1900 Kane Street.

But no matter how fast its schools grew, Houston grew faster. During the Wagners' first five years there, the city swelled by 150,000. Schools lacked places for at least 7,500 children; many were on a half-day schedule. Dow was not. An ambitious principal somehow managed to add a free kindergarten. Then, in 1926, Dow expanded again.

The resulting twenty-six rooms became a showplace, rated second highest of all fifty-five elementary schools in the huge Houston Independent School District. The old teachers' entrance, where faculty hitched horses and mules, was converted to proper stabling, storage, and an automobile garage. The awe-inducing entry, parapets, and differentiating red mortar of the original school were augmented by facilities uncommon even in high schools and colleges, among them an auditorium with a proscenium wreathed in plaster laurels where Dow students could practice public speaking.

Yet the grandeur of the building was nothing compared with the high-minded goings-on inside. Houston's schools had initiated sweeping changes beginning with the 1924–25 academic year, redefining their curriculum to include "civic education" and "ethical character," then importing Dr. Herbert Bruner, a colleague of John Dewey's at Columbia University, to consult on further advances. Gone was the "three R" curriculum—the rote reading, 'riting, 'rithmetic—that generations of Mary Kay's family endured. In its place, students would be trained in what education officials called "the habit of success," which they interpreted as an endless quest for self-improvement. To ensure proper means of civic discourse, Dow hired Miss Leyla B. Scott, a newly minted graduate of the Rice Institute, to train its scholars in the art of oratory. Education was to be the grand and glorious guarantor of American ideals.

At Dow, Lula and Alex's youngest was the equal of anybody, a point proven on her first day of school, when she became instant best friends with Dorothy Gladys Zapp, who looked like a blond princess straight out of those bedtime stories that other people's parents read to their children.

An only child, Dorothy was the apple of her father's eye. Like Mary Kay, she was tiny and smart as a whip. Unlike Mary Kay, she had a father who was a steady earner and a mother who was always home. The three lived in a two-story house on the corner of Hemphill and Decatur Streets, a big place shared with neither boarders nor extended family. The Zapps had a radio and listened to it every night. The Wagners did not.

Dorothy's mother played bridge, baked cookies, and sent Dorothy to school in starched pinafores with her long golden hair coaxed into Mary Pickford curls. Mary Kay went to school in cheap cotton dresses that she bought and washed herself, her mousy brown hair mowed into a no-maintenance bob much like the sugar-bowl cut used at the Faith Home for orphans down in the Fourth Ward. "Mary Kay's circumstances were pretty grim. It wasn't just that she was poor; she had problems that transcended money," a member of the Zapp family declared decades later. "Mrs. Zapp took her in because it needed doing."

Or Mrs. Zapp may have done it because she had not had an easy girlhood herself. Augusta Koltermann Zapp survived a hardworking childhood on an isolated Colorado County farm followed by a stint teaching at one of the state's notorious rural schools—escaped only when she made her future husband promise that their married life would be lived within the sound of traffic. A redhead with the kind of personality that her descendants described as "indomitable," Mrs. Zapp was appalled to see Mary Kay eat a bowl of cereal for dinner. Soon she was having the little Wagner girl come to the house each morning to pick up Dorothy for the walk to school. As Dorothy dawdled over her warm toast and homemade preserves, Mrs. Zapp pretended not to notice that Dorothy was slipping most of that breakfast to Mary Kay. Because Mrs. Zapp poured milk over ice to tempt her finicky daughter into drinking more, Mary Kay drank hers that way for the rest of her life.

When they included her on the ninety-mile trip to the farm where Mrs. Zapp had grown up, Mary Kay got to ride in their beautiful car and encounter a grandmother who was nothing like Grandma Hastings. Because the Zapps also included her on summer excursions to the Galveston shore, the world-famous Mary Kay Ash would tell reporters that she took her children to Galveston each year. In old age, she would sit in her tinselly $100 million headquarters and reminisce about the homemade ornaments and the strings of popcorn on the Zapp Christmas tree. Without saying much about what went on at the Wagner house a block away.

Praising her for good grades, Mrs. Zapp told Mary Kay that the family was happy to have her as a role model for Dorothy. In Mary Kay's mind that meant, "If Dorothy made an A, I had to make an A+, because the only way I could really be close to Dorothy was to be there and try to outdo her." Then, when the girls were about eight, Dorothy's father earned a promotion. The Zapps moved to the other side of town.

Mary Kay's life went back to normal. Acting pleased as punch, she got on the streetcar each Saturday and went downtown by herself. Took the money her mother gave her and bought her own forty-nine-cent cotton dress. Treated herself to a movie. Sat at the lunch counter of S. H. Kress & Co., the big dime store down the street from where her mother worked, and savored its Palm Beach Sandwich, a pimento cheese on toast.

Years later, when she was in her forties and starting her own company, she would make a ritual of going to the shopping center's coffee shop every Friday to order that same pimento cheese sandwich. As that company became more and more successful, she would recall her early years more and more often: bragging of her childhood self-sufficiency, hosting Dorothy Zapp at Seminar when the two schoolmates were well into their seventies. She would quote Lula's "You can do it!" to the thousands of saleswomen she called her daughters. It would work on them just as well as it worked on her.

During these years, Mary Kay had plenty of family nearby. Both sisters had gone, but her brother had a job at the Armour meatpacking plant, and he and his wife had no children of their own yet. Grandma

Tax assessment photo of 2111 Kane Street in the 1970s, before additions.

Hastings, the sort of good Christian woman who would not allow a deck of cards inside her house but had no qualms about letting a little girl fend for herself, lived thirty-five miles away. Uncle Doc had moved out again without getting very far; his family ended up two doors down on Kane Street. His wife, Aunt Birdie, worked as a cashier in a bakery, and they kept a boarder, but cousins Lois and Deward were four and five years older than Mary Kay, a good age to mind the little girl or take her on outings. They didn't, though. They had chores of their own.

With the Zapps gone, Mary Kay tagged along after Tillie Bass, an older girl who lived across the street. Mary Kay would remember Tillie's mother teaching her to bake biscuits and do "all the little things nobody was at home to teach me." Otherwise, nobody worried much about Mary Kay. Compared with the rest of her family, she had it easy. She lived in a big city and went to a nice school. No one hired her out as a maid or farmhand. In 1920s Texas, with so many families barely removed from a farm tradition that put children to chores as soon as they could walk, eleven- or twelve-year-olds could still be hired for forty-eight-hour weeks, even if laws prevented parents from sending out the really little ones—age nine and under—unless it was farmwork like picking cotton. Besides, by the time Mary Kay ascended to the top floor of the Dow School for junior high, the Depression had started.

Now, as Mary Kay reached the age when her sister Daisy started a full-time job, bias against child labor spread, although in Texas that may have had less to do with child welfare and more to do with the number of grown men begging for work. By 1930, the census count of "gainfully employed" children between the ages of ten and fifteen was less than half what it had been in 1920, the year that Mary Kay's brother and sisters found jobs. And that number was less than half of what it had been for Lula and Alex's generation.

The Depression hurried other changes too. More Sixth Ward families had boarders. More fathers had problems finding and keeping jobs. After Uncle Doc moved his family to a new neighborhood, his name soon appeared on the roll of tax delinquencies, which took up page after page of the newspaper. The name of Mary Kay's future in-laws was there too.

The Wagner name was not. Lula's taxes and mortgage and insurance were paid. Mary Kay earned good marks at Dow and moved on to subjects like algebra and plane geometry, which would have been considered above her station only a few years before.

She was not alone. Houston's entire school system was aspirational. "Probably it is not generally known that every boy and girl in the Colored High is taking Latin. Such a condition does not exist anywhere else," an apoplectic official wrote, complaining that, for a population expected to earn a living by manual labor, "classical education is being stressed almost to the exclusion of vocational courses."

At Dow, where many pupils left school after junior high, the Depression-era curriculum prescribed foreign language and world history. Handwriting and diction were expected to be top-notch. Everyone got practice in public speaking. Girls were given the opportunity to study career-track subjects like Typewriting and Office Procedure.

Mary Kay shone at school. Coached by Miss Scott, she entered extemporaneous speaking contests that required her to pull a subject out of a hat and declaim on that subject like an expert. In seventh grade, she speechified on Stone Mountain, Georgia, a place that she had never seen, and won second place in the entire state of Texas. She practiced typing until she was the best in Mrs. Davis's class. Lula got her a Woodstock typewriter—Depression be damned—so Mary Kay could do typing drills at home.

She learned to excel without acting uppity. She read *Little Women.* She performed in the junior high's "scarf dance" ensemble. She molded herself to the Houston Independent School District's definition of an A student: one able to prepare "with little or no assistance from the teacher"; one who maintained an attitude "promoting the best interests of the group."

On Sunday mornings, after her mother had gone to work, she did her chores, ironed her dress, and got herself to Tabernacle Baptist for Sunday school. Back home, she helped out with the young couple and their toddler son who were Lula's latest boarders. Did everything she was asked. And then some.

Even in hard times, there were ways for a young person to get ahead. Ways that guaranteed reward for effort. Especially if that young person was not afraid of a little hard work.

"Mail This Card Today—*Now*!"

All she had to do was send a penny postcard ("Send no money—we trust you") to join thousands of other kids who were authorized agents for Cloverine Salve. Undreamed luxury awaited.

Mary Kay already had plenty of practice selling. Not a week went by that there wasn't a raffle, bake sale, or May Fête fundraiser. This time, though, she would be a certified representative of a nationally prominent company. Everybody knew Cloverine Salve.

An all-purpose ointment first concocted on the kitchen stove of a small-town doctor, Cloverine Salve was considered a sovereign remedy for chapped lips, chilblains, burns, and maladies ranging from nasal catarrh to "itching piles." Countrypeople used it for just about everything, including doctoring animals. Tributes to Cloverine's curative powers and inventive overuse abounded, like the Ozarks tall tale of a sawed-through hound dog stuck back together with a slathering of the salve.

But the ingredient most responsible for the salve's success was the free gift that came with it. In 1895, shortly after starting commercial manufacture, the inventor's son, George Wilson, came up with a selling scheme any child could master. With no money down, each agent received twelve tins of salve to sell, along with twelve oversize art pictures to give away.

At two bits for the salve plus the picture, it was a good deal. Parlors and back bedrooms all over America were decorated with Cloverine's color lithographs: a guardian angel hovering as two children cavorted near a cliff edge; a small boy and large dog kneeling for bedtime prayers; a Protestant version of the Our Father prayer framed by roundels illustrating all of the Ten Commandments.

Authorized agents, identifiable by the button proclaiming Cloverine "Best on Earth," had only to collect from eager customers and remit the resulting $3 back to Wilson Chemical, making them eligible to select a prize from a catalog full of toys and gifts. As a business model, this worked so well that the town of Tyrone, Pennsylvania, grew prosperous on the proceeds, with hundreds of locals employed at a factory built to look like a fairy-tale castle.

For children of a certain class and culture, selling Cloverine Salve was a rite of passage. Around the time that Mary Kay signed on, at least 60 percent of its quarter million or so authorized agents were children between the ages of eight and fourteen. In theory, those children had the option of taking a cash commission by subtracting their earnings from the amount they mailed back to the Wilson Chemical Company. In practice, almost none did. Not when the sellers' premiums were so splendid: the world-famous Daisy air rifle, "the rifle for youthful Americans"; Betty, "the prettiest girl dolly you ever saw"; a solid gold imitation diamond ring; a tarnish-proof Platinum Chromium–finish watch. Top sellers could help their families with a radio, a portable phonograph, or a set of china. At the peak of the sales pyramid, a young person who

As a buyer's premium, Wilson Chemical offered a color lithograph free with each tin of Cloverine Salve.

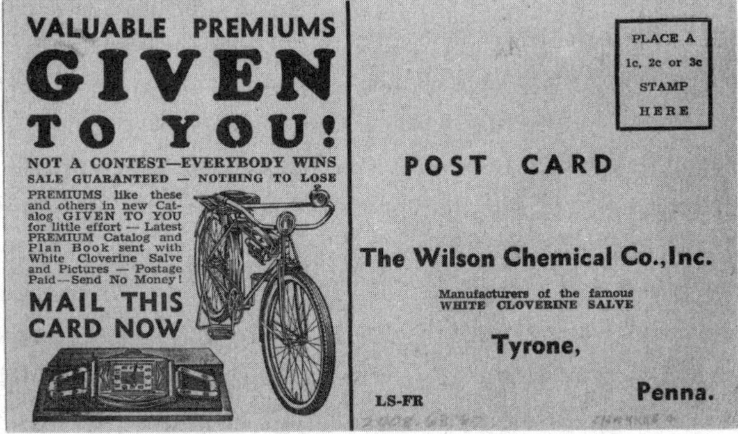

As sellers' premiums, Wilson Chemical offered toys and gifts.

sold 420 packages of salve could select "A Real Live Pony," sent express, charges collect, saddle and bridle not included.

Mary Kay did not win any ponies. Like most of Cloverine's underage sales force, she probably flooded her market. Or, as company literature implied, she might have done better if she had only tried harder. In any case, her sales career did not have a spectacular start.

Nor were there other signs of future success. As her years at Dow wound up, Mary Kay's name failed to appear on lists of class officers. She was not an officer of the Girl Builders, who vowed to do their best for God and country at their Monday afternoon meetings. She was not the girl wigged and costumed as Martha Washington in the George Washington bicentennial pageant. She was not Miss Dixie, Miss Houston, or the Miss Columbia escorted by Uncle Sam. That spring, Dow won no interscholastic competitions, no speech tournaments, no citywide spelling contest, no play competition. Mary Kay was not queen of its May Fête.

On May 12, 1932, as she prepared to leave Dow, her name did not appear in *The Houston Post*'s coverage of her graduation pageant, only in its "Birthday Club" column misspelled as "Mary Kathryn Wagner" alongside the names of other children whose birthdays qualified them for a free movie ticket to the local Loew's. Birthday or no, there was nothing waiting for her at home; Lula would be staying late to close the café. That night, news came that the remains of the Lindbergh baby had been found. People hurried to houses with radios to hear the gruesome details, leaving Mary Kay's fourteenth birthday forgotten.

Then, at last, something wonderful happened.

Mary Kathlyn Wagner got one of the grandest prizes to be gotten. By secret ballot of Dow classmates and faculty, she was voted the girl with the highest scores in honor, courage, scholarship, leadership, and service, and thus worthy of an American Legion School Award. Standing onstage at the Houston Chamber of Commerce, saluted by Principal Elrod and the membership of Max Autrey Post 377 in full Legionnaire regalia, Mary Kay heard rhetoric remarkably like the rousing speeches she would someday hear at sales rallies. Here, hard work counted for more than innate ability: "The pupil who is industrious and works hard over his lessons deserves more credit than the pupil who . . . gains a higher grade with less work." Here, in the form of a bronze medal coveted by every eighth and ninth grader in the country, was proof that effort would be rewarded.

Begun as a way for Legionnaires to promote the "can-do" spirit that won the Great War, the American Legion School Awards was a prestigious national program by 1932. And nowhere was it more prestigious than Houston. Living in a city that espoused the can-do spirit with fervor bordering on fanaticism, local Legionnaire Alwin Farrior decided that award winners were the makings of an elite who would shape the country's future. Not long after Houston's Legion posts made their first awards in 1928, Farrior, a member of the Legion's National Americanism Committee, took it upon himself to organize an honor society called Lambda Sigma Alpha, with membership composed of former medal winners.

By the time Mary Kay won her medal, Lambda Sigma Alpha had a chapter in every Houston high school and was on its way to becoming a statewide society. Members were expected to become standouts in high school and college, then conquer the wider world. John H. Reagan Senior High School, where Mary Kay was headed next, had one of the largest chapters in the United States.

Praised to the skies as an exemplar of Houston's can-do spirit and tipped for future greatness, the little Wagner girl was headed to one of the finest high schools in the state of Texas and, by extension, the entire country. Not as just another sophomore but as a proud member of Lambda Sigma Alpha. One of the elite.

College and a brilliant future were bound to follow.

CHAPTER THREE

Confidence

In the fall of 1932, Mary Kay entered John H. Reagan, newest and grandest of Houston's five high schools, themselves among the grandest in the state of Texas. In Houston, an education that went all the way from first grade through high school was an eleven-year proposition. Mary Kay planned to graduate in 1935, when she would be seventeen.

Born any earlier or almost anyplace else in Texas, she would have left school in seventh or eighth grade like the rest of her family. The year she was born, the state's former superintendent of schools was still arguing that high school encouraged "a growth of fungus aspirations and aims that had no soil," because it encouraged the working classes to harbor ambitions they could never hope to fulfill. In 1932, plenty of the old guard still considered secondary education a sure route to a sad end. Pure folly for a female.

Mary Kay's sisters and brother never really had the chance. Houston did not have a freestanding secondary school until 1895, when, eager to convey Houston's consequence, city fathers built a showplace that boasted fifty-six classrooms, took up an entire block, and billed itself as "the largest high school building in the South." Postcards were printed to document this wonder. Then, just before Dealia, Daisy, and Cecil Wagner moved to town, it burned to the ground.

John H. Reagan Senior High School.

But precedent had been established. Houstonians rebuilt on the site, then added four more high schools, issuing bonds—$3 million in 1924, $4 million in 1926, $4 million in 1928—to fund the spree. By the time the Depression came along, the city was invested in its own mythology. Houston was the place where dirt-poor farm boys grew up to be filthy rich oil barons. Here, anyone could make it if they worked hard enough. By 1932, over fifty-seven thousand children were learning that in over a hundred Houston schools.

Back in the Sixth Ward, Lula was putting in 112-hour weeks at the café, temporarily rechristened "Wagner's Waffle Shop." Mary Kay's father was listed on city rolls as coproprietor; it would take another year or two before Lula found him separate employment again. The telephone was gone, unnecessary and unaffordable with nobody working but Lula. To help make ends meet, Lula took in a nice young Catholic couple as her next boarders. That lasted until October, when the husband was convicted of check forgery and sent to the state penitentiary in Huntsville.

John H. Reagan Senior High School was a couple of miles away from all this in Houston Heights, an adjoining neighborhood that was considered uptown in a way that Mary Kay's neighborhood was not. The Heights manifested more amplitude and ambition than the Sixth Ward. Bisected by a boulevard with a sixty-foot esplanade, it could be traveled by streetcar. Its lots were bigger, the houses on them more elaborate. Civic boosters touted its pine trees as "so high they tickle the toes of the angels." It was also too far away for Mary Kay to hurry home and fix her father's lunch.

Reagan was a place where anything seemed possible. Built in 1926, it had been designed by none other than John F. Staub and William Ward Watkin, Houston's finest architects. Inside a complex the size of a small college were a spacious library, a state-of-the-art gym, and twenty-seven classrooms that included one for shop and another for typing, a skill at which Mary Kathlyn Wagner excelled. Its auditorium was grand enough to have a balcony, its grounds expansive enough to be called a campus.

Students boasted of themselves as the Bulldogs and were ferociously proud of their athletic teams, clubs, newspaper, and yearbook. Boys had the option of enlisting in the Reagan Cadet Corps and learning "the lessons of leadership by first learning the habits of obedience, loyalty, self-sacrifice, and respect for constituted authority." For girls, the counterpart was a drum-and-bugle corps called the Red Coats, founded by assistant principal Mrs. Byrd Creekmore, who was known to take no guff from anyone and who looked a bit like a bulldog herself.

Fleeing the same sort of bad luck that beset the Wagners, Mrs. Creekmore moved to Houston around the same time. Back in Oklahoma, she had married a widower who died four months after their wedding, stranding her with his three young sons and no means of support. Determined

A Red Coats field display spelling the school's initials.

to get the boys educated, she set her sights on the free tuition and demanding curriculum at the Rice Institute, "the Harvard of the South," and packed her bags for Houston. "She worked them pretty hard," a relative recalled, and all three, including future *Houston Chronicle* publisher J. Howard Creekmore, ended up as Rice graduates. With that, the Widow Creekmore considered herself confirmed in her methods.

Red Coat practices were no joke. The main feature of the uniform was a fancy, frogged, high-necked wool jacket that cost $35, more than a week's wages for someone like Lula Wagner. Mary Kay's was bought used. Worn with a flannel skirt and kepi, the jacket furthered the girls' tendency to faint from heat exhaustion, requiring a designated "first aider" with smelling salts to be on standby. Because the Red Coats also specified white oxfords as part of the uniform, some girls were seen wearing them to school every day, usually a sign they were the only shoes they owned.

Every Red Coat followed the same rules. Every Red Coat suffered through the same one- or two-hour drills before the start of the school day and sometimes another hour at its end. "The drilling was just like what men do. There was nothing frivolous about it," remembered a contemporary of Mary Kay's named Libby Weatherford. A Red Coat knew better than to complain. The five-foot-six-inch Weatherford went without lunch so often that she graduated from high school weighing less than one hundred pounds. "The Depression was on. Nobody said a word about things like that," she explained. "A Red Coat was a high-type person. There were no failures in the Red Coats. You cared about your grades. You cared about your appearance. You didn't do anything but your best effort."

Tall, dark haired, and striking, Weatherford would lead the Red Coats as drum major: "My size and height were an advantage to get in. They really liked the tall ones." Short girls got stuck in the back—happy to be there because being even a rank-and-file member of the Red Coats was enviable. As Weatherford put it: "We were lucky to come to school. Being a Red Coat was the cream of the crop."

Fourteen-year-old Mary Kay was not tall or dark haired or striking. She got herself into the Red Coats anyway, becoming one of the girls who marched in formations that spelled out the school's initials or made a human outline of the map of Texas. She traveled. She strutted in parades. She pitched in at bridge parties, fundraising dances, and outings for crippled children. Hand to the brim of her smartly cocked kepi, she saluted the lighting of the municipal Christmas tree.

Immaculately turned out and impeccably disciplined, the Red Coats and their rival drill teams were among the wonders of the city of Houston. Across town at Sam Houston High School, her friend Dorothy Zapp became a major leading the "girl soldiers" in the sateen and oilcloth uniform of the Black Battalion, a squad that had marched at the Chicago World's Fair and taken part in a concert conducted by John Philip Sousa himself. By virtue of its founding in 1927, the Black Battalion boasted of being the world's first all-girl drill squad, making it forerunner and rival to the Red Coats, the cowgirl-clad Carlton Cadettes of Jefferson Davis High, and the serape-draped Golden Gauchos of San Jacinto High.

That year, though, the Red Coats seemed to surpass them all. Reagan's football team went all the way to the state semifinals, and 160 Red Coats went along for every game, intimidating other schools with the power and precision of their drills; cheering the Bulldogs through battles that brought fans to the brink of tears; and supporting a championship bid so sensational that when coach Arnold "Post Hole" Krichamer left to become an assistant district attorney, his new job was considered a step down.

Mary Kay got good grades. By virtue of her American Legion School Award, she was automatically admitted to the Lambda Sigma Alpha honor society, one more organization under Mrs. Creekmore's wing.

She was there at the Shriners' Crippled Children's Ball when the Red Coats and Black Battalion set aside their rivalry and strutted into City Auditorium to the claps and hoots of a sold-out crowd. That night, in a city where double-feature movie tickets could be had for a nickel, the Shriners sold over twelve thousand tickets at an average of a dollar apiece. Two orchestras and the Arabia Temple's own band played until well past midnight as dancers spilled from the foyer onto city sidewalks. The next day's *Post* reported, "More than a hundred little twisted tots were given a new hope for an equal chance in life." Heady stuff for the little Wagner girl.

She entered interscholastic competitions. While boys vied in slide rule or Latin contests and other girls entered home economics contests like House Planning or Baking Powder Biscuits, Mary Kay brought high honor to the typewriting team. Working her Woodstock, she turned herself into a whiz-bang typist, the fastest at Reagan.

Which got her nowhere. In a yearbook photo taken at the end of that first year, Mary Kay seems both younger and sadder than the teenagers standing next to her. In another photo, she grins as eagerly as an orphan hoping to attract a family, an impression enhanced by a polka-dot dress that looks like a hand-me-down from someone larger. Under five feet tall, she was the thinnest she would ever be. Almost waiflike. Her chest as flat as a child's. Her name misspelled as both "Mary Kathryn" and "Mary Catherine." Her ugly dress worn with white oxfords.

When that first year of high school failed to yield the glories fore-

Mary Kay front and center with Lambda Sigma Alpha in 1933.

told by her American Legion medal, Mary Kay learned that she had only herself to blame. Taking up where Lula had left off, Mrs. Creekmore advised pluck, hard work, and, most of all, confidence. All over Houston, the "You can do it!" that Mary Kay heard at home was being condensed to a single word—*confidence!*—and touted as America's answer to any problem, up to and including the deepening Depression. CONFIDENCE IS URGED AS WAY TO RECOVERY read a front-page headline in the *Post.* At Reagan, the yearbook opened and closed with endpapers blazoning a capital-lettered CONFIDENCE across the Capitol Dome, the Washington Monument, and the American flag. Every page in between read as a rebuke to Mary Kay's lack of faith in herself. It was all up to her. She could do it.

Already a girl who gave her all to a good self-improvement scheme, fifteen-year-old Mary Kay set out to show her mettle. She dressed differently and wore makeup. She smiled her way into more extracurricular activities, skipped her junior year, and promoted herself into the senior class. Under the stern eye of Mrs. Creekmore, she became "reporter" of Lambda Sigma Alpha, the honor society's lowest-ranking officer but an officer nonetheless. As a Red Coat, she once again stepped smartly into the formation that spelled out J. H. R. at football games, marched miles in the Armistice Day parade, and spun in the social whirl that culminated with the Red Coat Spring Dance.

Mooting lofty topics, she joined the school's inaugural debate club, gaining a reputation as a girl who could think on her feet. Oratorical contests were fiercely contested in Harris County, where high school debaters were still being swept along by the swell of self-promotion that a young speech coach named Lyndon Baines Johnson brought to his job at Sam Houston High School in 1930. Johnson had, within a year of arrival, taught his team enough swaggering and speechifying to clinch city and district championships and come close to capturing the state title.

Reagan's team came nowhere near that, placing third out of five in that year's citywide contest. Boys and girls debated on different teams anyway, and Mary Kay competed primarily as an extemporaneous speaker, a "declaimer," ever ready to persuade with answers, examples, or anecdotes. Her training with Miss Scott showed. When her turn came, Mary Kay was poised and earnest. Relishing the attention, lapping up any applause that came after.

She joined the debate club on weekly trips downtown to deliberate topics of civic interest on KPRC, the *Post* affiliate that took its call letters from the city's nickname of "Kotton Port, Rail Center." Speaking on the

Mary Kay (*front row, third from left*) took second place in typewriting in the 1934 Interscholastic League Contest.

KPRC airwaves sent her to seventh heaven. She adored anything to do with the radio.

She shone in interscholastic competitions too, winning the title of second-fastest typist in the city of Houston. By the time yearbook photos were taken at the end of that second year, the sad-sack look was gone. She wore lipstick. She penciled her plucked brows like a movie star. She posed with crossed legs, wearing a stylish sweater, skirt, and dark stockings. Plus the white oxfords.

Determined to prove she could pull it off, fifteen-year-old Mary Kay was on track to graduate a year ahead of schedule.

In 1934, she was one among hundreds of Houston teenagers leaving school early. After years of frenzied growth, school enrollment stalled; only students sneaking in from surrounding areas, where small-town schools had cut back, consolidated, or closed, kept district numbers up. Students blamed the Depression: 1933 had been the worst year yet. Most students found it easier to drop out. Mary Kay took on extra work and hurried through.

In an autobiography published forty-seven years later, she wrote: "I would have liked to be my class valedictorian. But I decided to finish high school in three rather than four years and graduating from summer school ruined my chances." But even allowing for her ghostwriter's misinterpretations, that would have been wishful thinking. There were no awards waiting for Mary Kay.

Houston had done away with valedictorians by 1934. If it had not, the honor would have gone to Doris Seibert, the kind of girl who was book smart and looked it. Other prizewinners were just as predictable. The daughter of an executive would lead the Red Coats. A bubbly brunette was elected "most popular." Through the spring, *Post* society pages filled with pictures of high school girls in pretty clothes attending graduation parties and tea dances given by doting parents.

Mary Kay had spent a decade in Harris County schools, hearing that her prospects were bright, that opportunity was hers for the taking,

1934 yearbook portrait with her name misspelled as "Mary Kathryn Wagner."

and that she was the equal of anyone. As graduation and her sixteenth birthday neared, that no longer seemed to be so. Reagan's demon declaimer, whiz-bang typist, and proud Red Coat was headed to a future of scrubbing floors, waitressing, and working the waffle iron at her mother's greasy spoon.

Before that happened, there would be one last hurrah.

On Friday night, June 1, all 1,784 graduates of the city's five white high schools and white junior college—the largest graduating class in the history of Houston—staged a joint commencement at Buffalo Stadium. Diplomas had been distributed that afternoon, so the evening ceremony would be pure pageantry. No one wanted to miss this. Despite the start of a heat wave that would set records lasting into the next century, Buff Stadium was packed beyond its twelve-thousand-person capacity. Hundreds stood sweating in the outfield.

No one would be disappointed. At 8:00 p.m. sharp, the sky darkened, floodlights flashed, and the First Band, composed of Houston's finest high school musicians, struck up the grand march from *Aida.* Entering behind an ROTC regiment in immaculate uniform, eight double lines of graduates in identical gray caps and gowns assembled in center field. An eager audience joined them in singing "America" as a plane zoomed overhead. Assembled thousands bowed their heads for the invocation prayer, shed a tear or two as Senior Boys' chorus of Reagan High sang inspirational selections, and cheered the superintendent of schools' announcement that Pollyanna Eggleston, a senior laid low by appendicitis only the week before, had survived her ordeal and was attending the ceremony on a stretcher.

Spurning concession to the heat, University of Texas President Dr. H. Y. Benedict took his place at the podium wearing full academic robes over his suit and tie. Grand as a prophet, intoning inspirational phrases that had yet to become clichés, he delivered a commencement address full of fine talk about bright futures and high ideals. When, at last, he ended, Houston's First Band struck up John Philip Sousa's "The Thunderer" and the graduates marched toward the bright futures that they had just been promised.

There was no stopping her now. While the kids with money looked to college and the kids without money looked for work, sixteen-year-old Mary Kay outdid them all.

Six weeks later, she got married.

CHAPTER FOUR

Sell Ten, Get One Free

Mary Kathlyn Wagner was all of sixteen when she highballed it fifty miles out of town to elope with Julius Ben Rogers, who had just turned nineteen himself.

That summer was the hottest and driest anybody could remember. The Friday of their wedding, July 20, would go down in history for having some of the worst weather of the Dust Bowl decade. Later that seemed like an omen.

Proud to have gotten her groom to the altar of Wharton's First Baptist Church, Mary Kay barely noticed. To hear her tell it, the elopement was the Texas version of Romeo and Juliet running away to be married by Friar Laurence. Decades after the marriage dissolved, she remained coy about its start—letting listeners believe that she was at least seventeen, not naming the town, never giving the birth date of her first child—so that some people assumed she was yet another pregnant teenager who had to get married.

She was not. She was yet another teenager with big dreams. Her groom had been on the radio. He was dark haired, thin as a rail, attractive if you didn't mind that his ears stuck out a bit. Some thought he had his bride beat in the looks department, although everyone said she was the one with the pluck and personality. Like Alex and Lula, the two wed quickly and quietly. Other parallels to her parents' marriage would follow.

While Mary Kay later made no secret of her bitterness toward the boy who went by "J. Ben" or "Ben" Rogers, she also made no secret of the fact that the marriage was her idea. The Mary Kay Ash of the 1980s would blame the marriage on her "competitive nature." Describing her dreamy, guitar-playing groom as "the Elvis Presley of Houston," Mary Kay later recalled him belonging to a group called the Hawaiian Strummers, part of the craze for Hawaiian music that supported two music schools and at least half a dozen specialty acts around Houston, although Rogers couldn't make a living at it before, during, or after their marriage.

When they wed, he had no property, no prospects, no savings. His parents were barely scraping by. He smoked. He'd left school after eighth grade and had yet to settle into anything that could be called a good job, much less a career. Mary Kay called him "a tremendous catch."

Those turn-of-the-century Texas legislatures turned out to have been right: Going to high school had only given this daughter of the working class ideas beyond her station. That American Legion School Award and two years of Lambda Sigma Alpha left her feeling entitled to more education. She was now a sixteen-year-old stuffed full of slogans about Courage, Confidence, and Opportunity. She had poise, public speaking skills, and ambition aplenty. But there was no place to use any of it. Not for a girl. Not in Texas. Not during the Depression.

College was out of the question. Red Coat or not, no girl could join the ROTC programs that got so many boys through college; women would not be eligible for another forty years. Staying at Reagan would have only delayed the inevitable: Mary Kay's exact contemporary Libby Weatherford stayed until 1936 and, despite graduating as Red Coats drum major and glee club president, spent the next two years caged in a department store elevator, ferrying moneyed girls and their mothers up and down all day. She considered herself blessed to have any work at all

Jobs were hard to find. Good jobs almost impossible, even for able-bodied young men. Rogers became proof of that.

Both teenagers adored glamour and good times, without having much experience of either.

Like Mary Kay's, some of Rogers's people had come to Texas from Tennessee. Like Mary Kay, Rogers was the youngest in his family by several years. Like her parents, his had farmed without owning their own land. The Rogers family had moved around the emptiest parts of the state—Madison County, Wood County—chasing lucky breaks and golden opportunities. Like Mary Kay's father, Pleasant Frank Rogers had been a jack-of-all-trades, sometimes eking out the family income with work as a harness maker. Rogers was born when his parents were nearly forty and his family was living in Normangee, a whistle-stop on the Houston and Central Texas lines. In that part of Texas, the name Rogers was everywhere. Land for miles in every direction was known as the Rogers Prairie.

Yet the Rogers family somehow ended up with no land and not much of anything else. When he was a little boy, Rogers's parents moved to downtown Houston, where his father picked up what work was available, his mother took in boarders, and his big sister Ruby contributed her earnings from a beauty parlor. Rogers grew up in the catchment for San Jacinto High School, where rich girls featured on *Post* and *Chronicle* society pages went to school, but dashing as he seemed to a girl like Mary Kay, he would never be the type who escorted debs.

No product of progressive education, Rogers seemed unaffected by the sloganeering and capital-letter civic virtues that got his bride so worked up. People regarded him as feckless—a member of the Zapp family was later heard to declare, "See the father and see the husband"—but Mary Kay was convinced that she had Courage and Confidence enough for the two of them. She could create her own Opportunity. At sixteen, she was radiant with the romance of being grown up and having her own husband.

That didn't last.

Like her father, her husband was soon listed on city rolls as working at Wagner's Café. Replacing Lula's latest boarders, the newlyweds moved into the front room of 2111 Kane Street. Meanwhile, Mary Kay's father started work at Standard Mercantile, across the street from the café, where Lula could keep an eye on him. By fall, as her former classmates returned to Reagan, Mary Kay was pregnant.

Rogers did not spend much time around the house, so Lula took in a signwriter named T. J. "Tiny" White and his wife, Sarah, as her next boarders. Waiting for her baby to arrive, Mary Kay cooked and cleaned and helped out at the café. Hugely pregnant, she celebrated her seventeenth birthday, escaping chores when, just before midnight on May 17, she gave birth to Marylyn Yvonne Rogers at Memorial Hospital, the city's hospital of choice for forward-thinking young matrons like Mrs. Julius B. Rogers, as she then styled herself. Two days later, Reagan's

Dorothy Zapp, 1936.

class of 1935, which should have been her graduating class, held its commencement ceremonies.

Mary Kay considered herself way ahead of them. By virtue of her birthday five days before, she was a mother at seventeen. In a family with a tradition of early childbearing, her competitive nature had led her to equal or outdo her sisters, mother, grandmothers, and great-grandmother. On baby Marylyn's birth certificate, Mary Kay was listed as a housewife, her husband as a musician on a radio staff. On the county registration, someone wrote "Do Not Record" for the father's name.

That September, her friend Dorothy Zapp matriculated at Rice Institute, known to accept only about twenty women a year. On Kane Street, the little Wagner girl, acclaimed as an exemplar of honor, courage, scholarship, and leadership only three years before, drudged her days away with a husband, a baby, boarders, and all the cooking and cleaning that came with them. That year, the Department of Agriculture estimated that American homemakers spent at least fifty-one hours a week on housework, a statistical sampling that included college graduates and women with paid help. For women like Mary Kay, with babies but without modern conveniences, the USDA put the estimate at sixty or seventy hours a week.

And pretty soon another baby was on the way. That fall, just before Mary Kay's due date, the uninsured homestead and all the worldly goods of her Hastings grandparents went up in flames. Two weeks after that, a heavily pregnant Mary Kay cooked Thanksgiving dinner. Two days later, Julius Ben "Bubba" Rogers Jr. was born. Like his eighteen-month-old sister, this new baby was the image of his father, now a pump jockey at a nearby service station. Since that wasn't much of a job or a salary, Bubba joined his sister and parents in the front room of 2111 Kane Street.

The next year, Rogers got work at the Buccaneer Grill downtown, a favorite of gamblers, dope dealers, and the vice squad. But that wouldn't last either. The gambler who owned the Grill soon sold up, then got himself gunned down. For the women in the house, life was more predictable. Lula worked seven days a week and, in 1937, made the last of nearly $9,000 in mortgage payments on a house valued at $2,000. Mary Kay cooked, cleaned, worked at the café, took care of a baby and a toddler in the days before disposable diapers or automatic washing machines, and continued her search for ways that a mother of two young children could earn money. The Elvis Presley of Houston spent more and more time away.

Soon her father was gone too. In 1938, on a mid-July day when Houston's temperature hit a humid ninety-six degrees, Mary Kay's father had a fatal heart attack. His *Post* obituary, paid for by Lula, made no mention of the Hot Well Hotel, Kings Trail Auto Repair, or any of his other ambitions, only of his service at Standard Mercantile, which Lula listed as his place of death. His name was given as "Edward Alexander," not the "Alexander Edward" he had favored earlier. His age was given as fifty-seven, not the sixty he probably was. The newspaper listed seven surviving siblings scattered across the United States, plus his four children, six grandchildren, and widow. As the son, Cecil handled most arrangements, organizing a Baptist service for his Catholic father, then burying him in Resthaven, a mostly Protestant cemetery, under a Catholic-looking headstone complete with crucifix.

Rogers stepped into his father-in-law's job at Standard Mercantile. Then soon stepped out again.

Like her mother, Mary Kay could get only "female" jobs. These paid next to nothing.

Women's suffrage became federal law the year that the Wagners moved to Houston, but the right to vote had not changed much for women like Lula and Mary Kay. Male or female, nobody in the family voted. Nobody registered. Neither did most of the Sixth Ward. Voting wouldn't change the fact that men got the good jobs because they had to provide for their families. That was the way things had always been.

In her rush to become Mrs. J. Ben Rogers, Mary Kay did herself no favors. The Depression had only hardened prejudice against hiring married women. When relief programs started, most barred married women from paid work. Section 213 of the Economy Act of 1932 banned spouses of federal employees from paid federal employment, which meant that the wife was the one to go. Most school systems would not hire married women. Most insurance companies, banks, and utilities barred married women. If they did get hired, their unmarried sisters were usually the first to protest.

Americans agreed that the U.S. should join Mussolini and Hitler in keeping women out of the workforce. In 1936, when *Fortune* magazine surveyed 4,500 Americans to ask, "Do you believe that married women should have a full time job outside the home?" the poorest respondents disapproved the most. Overall, 79.4 percent of women and 85.2 percent of men were against married women working, with nearly 54 percent of men contending that a married woman should never work, no matter how much she needed the money. *Fortune* summarized its findings as "Women agree with men that married women should not have jobs; feminism retreats toward home and babies."

Married or not, when a woman found work, she didn't have it easy. When the average annual wage for men was $1,027, the average annual wage for women was $525, even if the woman was doing skilled labor and the man was not. For that, at least half of the women worked a week fifty hours or longer. A 1937 Department of Labor report admitted that unions had not been an equalizing force, since "the customary low wage rates for certain women's jobs have been continued even in some union agreements." That same report documented the widespread belief that legislation lessened opportunity: Women were afraid that asking for equal pay and regular hours would take away the precious few jobs available. Domestic work was unregulated but paid less. Nobody would have hired Mary Kay for that anyway, not when Houston was bursting with Mexicans, African Americans, and desperate Dust Bowl refugees who could be worked harder for longer hours and less money.

Piecework didn't pay much either. In places like Pennsylvania, the Department of Labor and Industry found half of its homework families reporting weekly earnings of $3.54 or less. Moving south, pay got lower. In 1936, a survey in Texas found "a skilled worker on embroidered and lace-trimmed children's dresses" working thirty-four hours to make $1.75. She was one of the lucky ones. Two sisters, also in Texas, worked a full week of skilled machine and hand sewing for a total of three dollars, or $1.50 each—less than a fifth of the going rate for a man's labor.

Sure, there were plenty of moneymaking schemes around. Almost all involved some kind of peddling. Not a day went by that some salesman didn't knock on the door to pitch some gadget. Most called themselves "independent contractors" and got merchandise through a combination of cash and credit; most were men willing to work without wages, benefits, or any kind of guarantee. It wasn't so different from selling Cloverine Salve. Some companies filled salesmen with fine words about limitless opportunity. Some handed salesmen a sheet of instructions for sending in orders and left it at that.

But everyone knew that women couldn't sell door to door. The weaker sex couldn't carry a sample case. They were known to have no head for figures. God alone knew what trouble they would get into. At the very least, they would be fending off untoward advances. At worst, they might face rape or arrest for prostitution. There was no way that any respectable national outfit could take a chance on that kind of thing. The success of firms like Jewel Tea, Fuller Brush, Real Silk, Electrolux, and a new venture called Stanley Home Products attested to the wisdom of relying upon an all-male, full-time sales force.

Two big firms, J. R. Watkins and the California Perfume Company, allowed women to work on a part-time basis. Selling spices, liniments, and the like through 7,200 dealers at the start of the 1930s, Watkins recruited part-timers with brochures that showed respectable widows. Under the man-bites-dog headline WOMEN WATKINS DEALERS was the reassurance that "many Watkins Women Dealers have found it the means of earning a satisfactory income and taking care of their home at the same time." Literature aimed at recruiting full-timers showed clean-cut young men and touted high earnings.

Likewise, the California Perfume Company, closing in on twenty thousand dealers by 1932, used female part-timers as sellers and men as full-time managers—a practice that would continue long after the company renamed itself Avon Products and began promoting its "Avon Ladies." Both companies had their greatest successes in small towns and on rural routes, where perfumes, spices, and the like were in short supply, opportunities to socialize were similarly scarce, and representatives could capitalize on the kindness of neighbors willing to help out a poor widowed lady. With that kind of customer base, neither company was going to argue for women to work full time.

On occasion, women also could be seen selling Bibles, educational tracts, or printed matter of an equivalently improving nature. But as the likelihood of making a living increased, so did the percentage of men. What women sold didn't pay enough to support anyone. In the early 1930s, a Department of Labor study of "business girls" documented the ways they supplemented "pitifully low wages." Along with overtime and outside typing, they sold crackers, underwear, stockings, soap, and writing paper, "exacting a considerable toll of their physical strength." All the extra work averaged an extra $1.68 per week, equal to about $47 in today's money. At any rate, there was something about trying too hard that was admirable in a man and unbecoming in a woman, something unseemly about a woman going door to door.

Lewis B. Quarles, Tabernacle Baptist Church.

So the former star of Reagan's typewriting team ended up in the office of Tabernacle Baptist Church on Kane Street. During the Depression, Tabernacle had watched attendance wane and tithing cease, until Pastor Lewis B. Quarles took a well-known wile of Mammon and turned it to the service of the Lord. Instituting premiums, Quarles promised that anyone who attended for thirteen straight Sundays would get a small white Bible for free. In no time at all, pews were crammed with true believers.

Half a century later, known nationwide as a pillar of the Southern Baptist Convention, Mary Kay would make much of the Quarles connection, without mentioning that it was probably a part-time or temporary job, since the city directory still listed her as a waitress at her mother's café. In 1979, she would tell *The New York Times*: "The fundamentals of various promotional and organizational techniques that I learned from Mr. Quarrels [*sic*] proved invaluable to me when I later embarked on my direct selling career."

Not long after, that direct-selling career got its start.

In a 1995 interview, she recalled being home late one Friday afternoon when a weary-looking widow named Ida Blake came to her door peddling what Mary Kay remembered as Grolier Books' *Child Psychology Bookshelf*, a multivolume set of moralizing tales intended to improve children's behavior. It was just common decency to invite the woman in and listen to her. It also made a break in the daily round of diapers and drudge work.

Targeting families who could not afford its products and did not do much reading, Grolier sold on the installment plan. In the late 1930s, the Federal Writers' Project profiled one of its customers, a housewife struggling through the Depression with the help of two boarders and a milk cow tethered in the backyard. Each month, she paid $4 toward Grolier's $80 *Book of Knowledge Encyclopedia*, which her three children were too young to read. As her prize possessions, the Grolier books were stored in their shipping box in her bedroom, where she showed them to the visiting interviewers, who considered them absurdly overpriced for "bad print and worse reproductions."

On that afternoon in the Sixth Ward, Mary Kay was flattered by Blake's appeals to maternal ambition and talk of psychology. Mary Kay loved anything to do with psychology. Pretty soon she wanted those books. Then she heard that they cost $50. Of course, she told the saleswoman that she couldn't afford them. Of course, the saleswoman sympathized. Kind as could be, Blake said she was too tired to tote the books home and offered to leave them at Kane Street over the weekend.

It was an old gambit, known since the days of *Sam Slick*, an 1830s picaresque about peddlers and their crafty ways. "We can do without any article of luxury we have never had, but when once obtained, it is not in human natur' to surrender it voluntarily," title character Sam declared over a hundred years before. Back then, Americans clucked at the cunning of a canvasser who left his pricey wares with simple countryfolk for a few days. The rubes fell for it every time.

So did Mary Kay. Especially after Blake told Mary Kay that anyone who managed to sell ten sets would earn a free set for themselves.

Blake's "sell ten, get one free" brought out the competitive nature that had made Mary Kay the wife of a tremendous catch at the age of sixteen. Exploiting access to the telephone and Sunday school roster at Tabernacle Baptist, Mary Kay spent the weekend cold-calling parents and "telling them about the best books I'd ever seen." She may not have been able to show them the merchandise, but "I got so excited that the women got excited too."

When Blake came back on Monday, the ten sets were sold.

CHAPTER FIVE

Acres of Diamonds Within Reach

The little Wagner girl exceeded expectations again.

Her success with those books should have been the start of something big. It was not. And would not be for years.

Direct selling had a long tradition in America, but not a good one. The Yankee peddler had been, by reputation, a wily and indomitable scoundrel who dealt in wooden nutmegs and oak leaf cigars. That such a resourceful, avaricious creature flourished in this new country seemed to say something about America's national character, even if the rest of the world was not sure what that might be. Scotsman Thomas Hamilton, in his 1833 *Men and Manners in America*, reported: "The whole race of Yankee pedlars, in particular, are proverbial for dishonesty. These go forth, annually in thousands to lie, cog, cheat, swindle. . . . Their ingenuity in deception is confessedly very great. They warrant broken watches to be the best time-keepers in the world; sell pinch-beck trinkets for gold."

As the nineteenth century progressed, that reputation got little better. In 1879, *How 'Tis Done*, American author Bates Harrington's "thorough ventilation of the numerous schemes of wandering canvassers," sold through several printings by debunking frauds ranging from "wind whistles" (unloaded on farmers who didn't realize their pricey thingamabob only worked on windy days) to patent medicines. Even as other forms of salesmanship were standardized by executives like John H. Patterson of the National Cash Register Company, door-to-door selling was slow to shed its whiff of the small-time and shady.

When Mary Kay started selling, that was finally beginning to change. A trade association formed in 1910 was accruing members who vowed to make the profession respectable. Then, in 1929, the Federal Trade Commission issued resolutions for house-to-house selling that decried misuse of the word *free* and censured all manner of misrepresentation: "All members of this industry shall protect the consumer not only as far as is required by law, but as required by good morals and the best ethics of business." Published, republished, and roundly ignored, those FTC resolutions did little to improve the behavior of the average peddler. That happened because of Fuller Brush.

The company that would dominate direct selling during the Depression had its inauspicious beginnings in 1903, when teenage Alfred C. "Uppie" Fuller, the eleventh of twelve children, left the family farm in Nova Scotia to join brothers and sisters living near Boston. His mother forbade him from taking up brush making, believing it had contributed to his brother's death from tuberculosis. Fuller then tried and failed at almost everything else. He was fired for derailing a trolley that he was not supposed to be driving. He was fired from the two jobs that followed. Finally, he went to his deceased brother's partner and proposed to perform the "clean, outdoor work" of selling brushes door to door. On his first day, he earned $3: "If I could just get into the house, and put on a demonstration to show what the brushes could do, they would sell themselves. I did not need the gift of gab."

Fuller cleaned, swept, and scoured to put his product across. If a dozen prospects slammed the door in his face, he perked up and plodded onward, reasoning that his next prospect was that much more likely to buy. With no line of patter to counter customer resistance, he made careful notes, which gave him ideas for product improvements. Saving $375 in his first year as a salesman, he set up a workbench and secondhand vise in his sister's basement, consulted his notes, and began selling his own brushes in 1906. By year's end, he had moved to Hartford, Connecticut, grossed $6,000, and was looking for salesmen to take over door-to-door drumming. He found plenty, but turnover was constant. Then, in 1913, twenty-eight-year-old Fuller met another former Nova Scotia farm boy, thirty-four-year-old Frank Stanley Beveridge. That year, sales went from $40,000 to $140,000.

Beveridge saw selling as a "door of opportunity," the most American of professions, where all men were created equal and no one could limit their earnings or ambitions. Recruitment literature soon teemed with Horatio Alger heroes, triumphs over adversity, rags-to-riches stories, and aphorisms like "Remember that American terminates in 'I Can' and Dough begins with 'Do'!"

Beveridge specialized in recruiting college boys: the kind of hardworking, honest young fellows whom people wanted to invite into their homes and speed on the road to success. That's how he got his start.

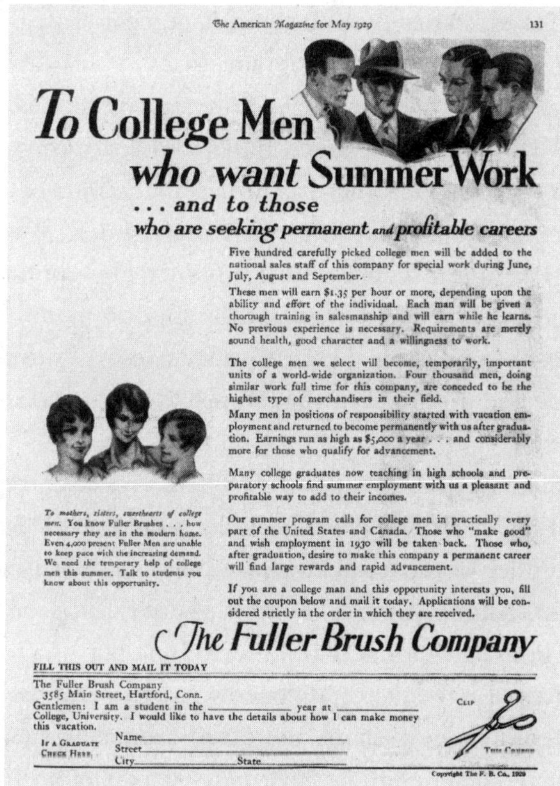

Fuller Brush recruiting ad, 1929.

That's how thousands of others, including Reverend Billy Graham, an exact contemporary of Mary Kay, would get theirs. "The trainers told us always to try to get our foot in the door and hold it there so that the customer couldn't close it," Graham recalled. "I came the hard way to learn the meaning of 'footsore.'" The future evangelist also learned that, at a time when $20 was a good weekly wage for a white man, his knack for converting prospects could earn him as much as $50 to $75 a week. By then, Fuller Brush had turned "a foot in the door" from slang for an aggressive sales technique to a synonym for the first step toward a goal.

Beveridge's push for college men, which did much to counter prejudices against peddlers, set an industry standard. Real Silk, a hosiery company that advertised itself as having ten thousand representatives in the mid-1920s, when it probably had closer to two thousand, trained college students to sell during school vacations. After graduation, their careers were fast-tracked, so that by 1930 about 41 percent of Real Silk executives were veterans of its college program.

None of that applied to women, though. No such programs existed for them. Real Silk, which peddled ladies' lingerie and stockings, did not allow women to sell until 1923, then did its best to discourage them with sales tests that men did not take. Like their sisters at J. R. Watkins and the California Perfume Company, Real Silk's female representatives were supposed to earn pin money, not the kind of money that paid tuition or rent. The professional door-to-door salesman was to be confident in attitude and dignified in appearance. Clean-cut. Godly. Square-jawed. Male.

Except in African American communities. There, female entrepreneurs were succeeding with strategies that Fuller would take decades to discover. While Fuller was still teaching himself to make brushes in his sister's basement, Annie Minerva Turnbo Malone had scores of women selling her Poro hair products and was well on her way to becoming a millionairess. By the 1920s, Malone was also operating Poro College, a thriving cosmetology school, and riding around St. Louis in a Rolls-Royce. Other companies might have dangled a diamond pinkie ring as a prize for salesmen, but it was Malone who cut direct selling's high turnover by guaranteeing a diamond ring to every saleswoman who stayed with her for five years.

One of her best left anyway, long before getting the ring. The first in her family not born enslaved, Sarah Breedlove had a formal education that ended after three months. Orphaned, she was supporting herself as an itinerant washerwoman at age seven, a career she continued as a fourteen-year-old bride, then as a widowed teenage mother. Inspired by a short stint with Poro, the woman who became known as Madam C. J. Walker quit doing white people's dirty laundry and, at age thirty-seven, used her savings to move from St. Louis to Denver. From there, she went on the road to sell her own hair products. Less than five years later, her beauty empire encompassed a factory, a beauty school, and a national network built by outtraveling and outworking all comers. Along the way, Walker leveraged a talent for self-promotion that left the likes of Fuller in the dust.

Decades before a diamond-decked Mary Kay got behind the wheel of her first pink Cadillac, a diamond-decked Madam C. J. Walker gained national notoriety for extravagant prizes and a personal style that ran to feathered hats, showy cars, a Harlem mansion, and a thirty-four-room villa opulent enough to be written up in *The New York Times*, a newspaper for white people.

"I had to make my own living and my own opportunity. But I made it!" Walker told the women who sold her products. "Don't sit down and wait for the opportunities to come. Get up and make them!"

Ida Blake was far from the first salesperson to knock on Mary Kay's door.

Just before World War II, roughly six thousand firms had about 1.75 million full- or part-time salespeople knocking on about five million doors a day—at a time when there were roughly thirty-five million households in the country. Blake was one of a few women selling door to door and, within that subset, one of fewer still pushing a high-ticket product.

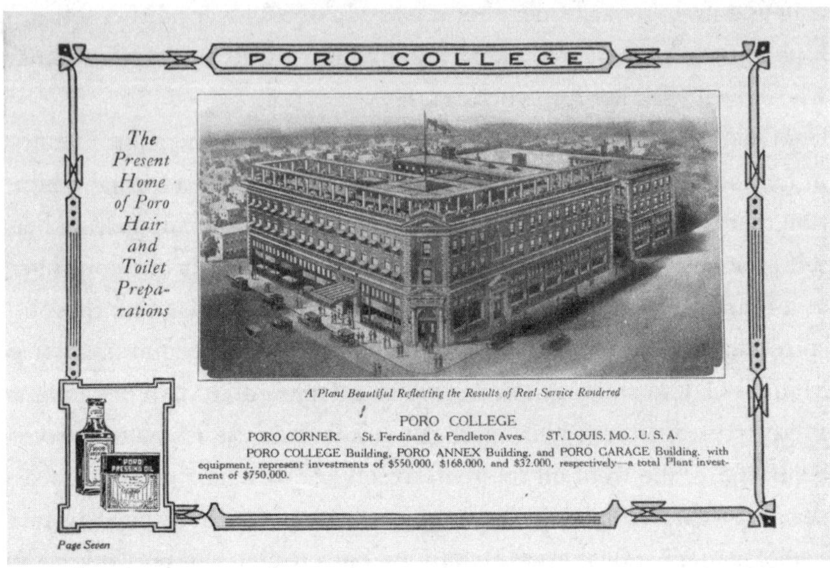

Poro College in 1922.

Convention of Madam C. J. Walker agents at Villa Lewaro, 1924.

The kind of product that, in theory, could yield a decent commission.

Recruiting Mary Kay was not difficult. Groomed by life with Lula and schooling under the stern eye of Mrs. Creekmore, Mary Kay was conditioned to think that any worthwhile endeavor entailed impossible odds and absurd amounts of work. Without shirking a single chore at her mother's house or her mother's café, Mary Kay did everything Blake asked.

When Blake told her to get behind the wheel of a car, Mary Kay obeyed, despite not knowing how to drive. When Blake directed her into the middle of Houston's rush-hour traffic, that's where she went. Decades later, she would turn that story into a parable so consultants could laugh at her long-ago terror and be persuaded that their own fears would soon be forgotten, that their own payoffs would prove as liberating.

Making the rounds with her mentor, Mary Kay decided that knocking on doors was a lot of work for little return. She had better ideas. Selling like she was out to prove something, she stormed through a ready-made list of prospects at Tabernacle Baptist.

Badge from the National Convention of Madam C. J. Walker's Agents, 1917.

Nine months later, she had used up her contacts. In modern marketing jargon, she had saturated her sales base. Then the complaints started. The books looked shoddy. The paper was thin. The ink was smudgy. The psychology didn't work. They weren't worth the money. Later, Mary Kay would say the problem was the product. To make money in direct selling, she liked to explain, it helped to have a "repeater." Encyclopedias were a onetime sale. So she stopped. At least that's the way she sometimes told the story. Other times, she would say that she was embarrassed by the quality of the product. Or she no longer believed in it.

During an interview in 1995, Mary Kay said that she sold $75,000 worth of books, a claim worthy of Parson Weems, the evangelical bookseller who came up with the legend of the young George Washington chopping down a cherry tree. During the 1930s, a 30 to 40 percent commission on that kind of sale would have put Mary Kay on easy street. Instead, she and her children were still on Kane Street.

Mary Kay was convinced that selling could lead to great things. She just needed a way to get started.

So did lots of other people. Mary Kay was among the third generation of Americans raised on *Acres of Diamonds*, the sermon that Baptist minister Russell Conwell published as a pamphlet, took on the Chautauqua circuit, read on the radio, and delivered over six thousand times before his death in 1925, when the torch was taken up by thousands of like-minded clergymen, politicians, and Rotarians. Conwell's parable taught that the keys to success were within each man. All that and heaven too, since "to make money honestly is to preach the gospel." According to *Acres of Diamonds*, acquisition of wealth was "your Christian and godly duty."

Making money was patriotic too. At Reagan, Mary Kay had learned that prosperity was available to anyone who was willing to work for it. All it took was faith in yourself, a readiness to abandon habits that inhibited success, and a capacity for good hard work. Direct sales sounded like the ideal venue. Maybe the only venue.

Men who would have scorned door-to-door selling in better days were now vying to work for Fuller Brush and Real Silk. Everyone else took what they could get. Most people who were doing door-to-door selling had no better option, and their customers knew it. In one Depression-era study, "pity" was the prime reason that people bought from canvassers. Claiming to despise the high-pressure sales tactics, resent the interruptions, and prefer local retail, nearly 70 percent admitted to buying from direct sellers.

In the early 1930s, the number of Americans going door to door had become so high that the profession was perceived as a national nuisance. Nonprofessionals by the tens of thousands were trying it too. Farmers went house to house hustling eggs, milk, meat, Thanksgiving turkeys, Christmas trees, and anything else with cash or barter value. Underage peddlers, over and above the 300,000 authorized agents of Cloverine Salve, pushed homemade toys, candies, or whatever came their way. "Salesmen of the doorbell variety have increased like grasshoppers and they appear at the average door at the rate of several a day," a small-town mayor complained. "Short of sheer brutality, the housewife cannot get rid of the unwanted caller in less than half an hour and possibly not that soon."

Thus, on November 16, 1931, when cold shoulders and hard words didn't do the trick, the town of Green River, Wyoming, enacted Ordinance Number 175, the prototype for what would become known as Green River ordinances: laws that curbed direct selling by restricting hours, mandating licenses, or ruling that unsolicited calls qualified as trespassing. In Green River, railroad men who worked the night shift found their daytime sleep disturbed by incessant door knocking and bell ringing. Proclaiming that "an emergency exists," Green River declared each disturbance a misdemeanor liable to a fine of $25 to $100. Soon GREEN RIVER ORDINANCE STRICTLY ENFORCED signs were going up all over America.

That in itself was nothing new. Towns had been passing statutes to discourage peddlers since the early 1700s. Demanding licenses. Levying fines. Changing nothing. Few could resist the likes of the doughty and determined Joseph Bloom of Consolidated Home Equipment, who sealed his status as a sales legend when, tossed in the hoosegow for selling without a license, he spread his wares on the cell floor and sold scatter rugs to the sheriff's wife.

But as the country grew more peddler plagued, opposition to direct selling hardened. When Fuller Brush had a district court enjoin the town of Green River from enforcing its ordinance, the town fought back. A circuit court of appeals upheld the validity of Green River's ordinance, as did subsequent courts in subsequent appeals. Fuller Brush pressed on regardless. Conceding that other companies' canvassers could be vexing, Fuller Brush argued that its salesmen approached in "an orderly manner" and ordered a milquetoast named J. L. Bunger, a defendant in previous cases, to get himself rearrested so Fuller Brush could take its case to the United States Supreme Court. Where, on March 1, 1937, it was dismissed a final time.

After all that, losing the three thousand inhabitants of Green River as customers made little difference to Fuller Brush profits. As the case wound its way through the courts, the company's sales climbed, reaching $10 million in 1938. The real trouble was the way the long legal battle had publicized Green River ordinances. Thanks to that Supreme Court dismissal, antipeddling statutes were now more enforceable. The problems of door-to-door peddling began to multiply.

Mary Kay's next venture sidestepped some of those problems.

When J. Ben lost his next job, young Mr. and Mrs. Rogers tried selling aluminum cookware. A staple of direct selling since the turn of the century, aluminum pots and pans were lighter weight and twice the price but otherwise not noticeably different from other pots and pans. To pitch them, canvassers played up their supposed power to cook vegetables with little or no water and thereby produce tastier, healthier fare. Wear-Ever Aluminum issued charts so that salesmen could show customers that the old method of boiling foods reduced 48 percent of body-building iron, 31.9 percent of tooth- and bone-building calcium, and 44.7 percent of "nature's laxative," magnesium. Confronted with the pseudoscience of the salesmen's charts, customers passed on Wear-Ever Aluminum at the peril of blood, bones, and bowels.

To demonstrate its merits, sellers of aluminum cookware—future celebrity pastor Norman Vincent Peale among them—were encouraged to arrive at a prospect's home with a bag of groceries. "The idea was to persuade some popular housewife, well-known for her cooking, to invite several neighborhood women to a luncheon at which time you would give them a sales talk on the advantages of the cooking utensils," Peale explained. To encourage a hostess to invite friends, she was promised a little gift, maybe aluminum salt and pepper shakers. Yet even the author of *The Power of Positive Thinking* found it hard to stay positive through the relentless rejection of canvassing: "But that cold house-to-house selling! Believe me, that called for extra courage, perseverance and super-enthusiastic persuasion."

Mr. and Mrs. Rogers were instructed never to use the word *buy*. Instead, they must use *adopt, invest, place in your home*. To counter price resistance, they were told to say, "The health of your children is worth more than the price of a few miserable pots and pans." Fronting the money for food, they enticed prospects with the promise of a delicious free meal. Because aluminum companies preferred a male sales force, Mary Kay did the cooking and her husband did the spiel. If there was food left over, the Rogerses had it for dinner. If not, they went without.

Most of the time, they went without.

For her next try, Mary Kay decided to go it alone.

In 1939, a direct-selling company called Stanley Home Products started admitting women to its sales force. Within a year, sales doubled. The next year, they came near to doubling again.

Up until then, there had been little remarkable about Stanley. As vice president at Fuller Brush, founder Frank Stanley Beveridge had dreamed up that company's most-copied customs and created a culture where all was optimism and incentive, ambition and affirmation—until 1928, when Fuller promoted Frank W. Adams, an accountant with no sales experience, to the company's number two spot. Adams's elevation was a slap in the face to Beveridge, who called Adams a bean counter. Things went downhill until fifty-year-old Beveridge was forced out in October of 1929. A week later, the stock market crashed.

Beveridge, known to all as "Mr. Bev," did a stint at Real Silk before starting his company in 1931, a time when even Fuller Brush seemed to be failing. Unheeding, Mr. Bev hewed to what he knew best. Like Fuller Brush, his company would sell brushes door to door via a full-time, all-male sales force that bought the products wholesale and resold them at fixed prices, receiving neither salary nor commission. Like Fuller, he sited his headquarters in New England, albeit in a ramshackle tobacco barn in rural Westfield, Massachusetts, and not on a snazzy campus in downtown Hartford, Connecticut.

A lot of the old Fuller Brush crowd joined up. Catherine O'Brien, Mr. Bev's secretary at Fuller Brush, improvised an office in the barn, flattening cardboard boxes to cover holes in the floor and rigging washing machines to mix batches of cleaner. Albert F. "Reggie" Regensburger, one of Fuller Brush's star salesmen, sent in the company's first $1,000 order almost as soon as he arrived. Even so, there could have been few worse times to start his company. Mr. Bev was taking on the top direct-selling company on its home turf; he was reentering the overcrowded direct-sales industry; and he was doing it with brushes, a category that had been in decline for a decade.

In what twenty-first-century entrepreneurs would have called an undercapitalized start-up, Stanley's staff worked in overcoats because there was no heat in the barn. Because the company could not afford to carry inventory, orders were rushed to the brush maker on the second floor the minute they came in. After two years, Mr. Bev had to borrow against his life insurance to keep the venture going. Then, just as business was getting better, New Deal work relief kicked in.

Although the Depression had given direct selling its pick of young men, most moved on as soon as a salaried job opened up. Now those men had another enticement. "The WPA [Works Progress Administration] is paying 40 to 68 cents an hour," Mr. Bev noted in an internal memo. "If a man leaves WPA and is forced to return he has to re-register and waits a couple of weeks or more for re-instatement he is therefore afraid to give up his WPA job for one with no stipulated salary." If war came, things would only get worse. More jobs would open. The supply of desperate young men would dry up. On the other hand, programs like the WPA paid women less and barred most married women. That made them ripe for recruiting.

At the same time, Mr. Bev had reason to rethink his sales techniques. In Maine, a new salesman under the supervision of Henry Harrison was writing some of Stanley's largest orders by co-opting the aluminum cookware companies' strategy of selling through parties, dinners, and group demonstrations. Jewel Tea, a direct seller of coffee, tea, and groceries, had started doing the same thing in the 1920s and was still reaping the profits. The promise of free refreshments proved a lure to housewives, while the social setting got them to pry open their purses. Adopting such demonstrations company-wide, Mr. Bev considered, would also get around Green River ordinances while improving recruiting and retention—perennial problems in an industry where annual turnover averaged upward of 300 percent.

His decision to adopt what he called "party plan selling" would forever change direct selling and, with it, the economic status of women and the social history of postwar America. But before any of that happened, it would change the fortunes of his small and struggling company. In 1938, prior to the party plan, Stanley Home Products posted an unspectacular $642,296 in retail sales. In 1939, a partial rollout of the party plan was enough to make sales jump 64 percent. In 1940, the first full year of the party plan, sales were up another 165 percent and Stanley had to add a distribution station in the Midwest. By 1941, sales were $3.6 million and about to increase another 150 percent.

The next year, Stanley made a push into Texas, dispatching direct-sales veteran C. B. Eckman as its new, Dallas-based area manager. As he had during stints at Fuller Brush and Electrolux, Eckman recruited dealers by placing blind classifieds in local papers. This time, though, his promise of "pleasant, profitable part-time or steady work" applied to women as well as men.

Next to ads like "white girl wanted to work in sandwich factory," Eckman's offer sounded better than good. His description of work that might pay $35 or more a week for men or women "able to speak in public" stated a preference for "women with knowledge of tidy housekeeping."

Perfect for Mary Kay.

With dreams of glory, she put $2 down on a $30 sample case to sell Stanley.

CHAPTER SIX

An Alligator Bag

Mary Kay was off to a bad start.

She was averaging only $7 a party—and those parties were few and far between. It didn't look like she would last any longer with Stanley Home Products than she had with the Child Psychology Bookshelf. Or with waterless aluminum cookware. Or with any of the other surefire moneymakers.

The company expected each party to bring in a $20 order. A $7 party meant that Mary Kay's share of the take was only a couple of dollars. Before expenses. A $7 party was a disaster.

At that rate, each time she tried to sell Stanley, she would have gotten deeper in the hole. Whenever she sent in an order, Mary Kay was supposed to send Stanley another $2 toward the cost of her demonstration case, until the entire $30 was paid off. She had no hope of earning the $35 a week mentioned in that classified ad.

As it was, she wasn't clearing enough to subsidize the dry mop and split duster she was obligated to give her hostess for throwing the party, finance the silver pastry server she was supposed to provide as an enticing door prize, add lagniappe like a Keytainer or percolator brush, and still make any profit for herself. She wouldn't have been able to pay cash up front to get a 5 percent discount or place a bulk order to net more commission. She wouldn't have qualified for the free merchandise earned by surpassing $50 a week in prepaid orders. She wouldn't have made easy money off reorders either, since she wasn't getting orders in the first place.

And because the size and snazziness of the Stanley hostess gift increased in proportion to the amount of product sold at the party, nobody was going out of her way to host a second party for Mrs. J. Ben Rogers. Nobody wanted to go through all the work of rounding up friends and feeding them refreshments if they weren't going to get anything out of it. Stanley parties were turning out to be like everything else: Stage a few that weren't successful, and people started to run the other way when they saw you coming.

This had been going on for a couple of weeks when Mary Kay heard about an upcoming Stanley rally and decided to go. Since there was no way her sales record justified the trip, this would be further proof that the little Wagner girl didn't have any better business sense than her father. Selling Stanley was already like carrying water in a sieve.

Going to the rally would mean upping "L.O.," salesmen's slang for money laid out with little likelihood of return. She would have to shell out a $12 fee, travel all the way to Dallas, be away at least two nights, lose any chance of making money for three days, and talk Tillie Bass into minding the kids again. She would be forking over yet more money to Stanley. She would be headed there knowing she wasn't going to win a thing. She would be a young woman traveling alone to a sales convention and staying with strangers in a hotel, which was no place for a respectable matron who might soon be asking for more typing work from Tabernacle Baptist.

Wild horses couldn't have kept her away. Wasn't getting out of a mental rut and having "new thoughts, new visions, new ambitions" the first point in Dale Carnegie's *How to Win Friends and Influence People*? Wasn't Carnegie always on the radio talking about how Aimee Semple McPherson had been a young and impoverished mother of two? Or how Greta Garbo had to leave her salaried job at a hat store to become Hollywood's "Swedish Bird of Paradise"? The trip to Dallas was just the kind of journey that Carnegie's titans of industry might take. True, she had demonstrated no aptitude for selling. But Stanley sales literature assured her that didn't matter. Gumption was what counted.

Instead of staying in the Sixth Ward and reading about moth crystals in *The Stanley Standard*, she would meet dealers who proved that Stanley could change lives. She would be there when company founder Frank Stanley Beveridge, "the Great Encourager" himself, told everyone: "You can achieve anything you want to achieve. You can achieve any goal that you set for yourself. You just have to keep working toward it."

As Mary Kay remembered it, she finagled the $12 from a friend after enduring a lecture that those dollars should be used for children's shoes instead of attending a "wicked convention like men go to." Then she emptied her Stanley demonstration case, a cheap metal box painted to look like a valise, packed her other dress, and added a pound of cheese and a box of crackers because she didn't know if the attendance fee included meals. Arriving at the Adolphus, the city's swankest hotel, she stiffed the bellboy who carried that case to her room. She didn't have a cent to spare.

For as long as she lived, Mary Kay would tell and retell the story of her first Stanley rally until it became a kind of hero's journey, a pilgrim's progress that compelled her to leave home, spouse, and children behind as she set forth on her path to redemption.

"Those three days changed my life," she would say later. By the time she said it, she would be staging Seminar, her own three-day sales convention, in the same city and following the same format of song, sermon, and ritual that she first experienced in the 1940s.

Even then, the format was nothing new. The length and rhythm of the rally would have been familiar to her Alabama- and Tennessee-born forebears, since camp meetings had been conducted the same way for over a century. For three days, souls would gather from far and wide. Some fleeing toil and craving transcendence, others reaffirming a faith long professed. Convened to hear testimonies of perfection, the congregation would sing. Then the speakers' exhortations to excellence would build in emotional intensity until women began to weep and the meeting erupted in spontaneous pledges to set new personal bests. At that point, the next crusade would be announced. The difference was that, at Stanley, it was a sales crusade.

"Rally! Rally! Rally!" a Stanley executive explained. "Kept 'em excited. Workin' toward the goal."

Four decades after, she would recall more than "a thousand people at that convention," a description that conveyed its importance to an overawed Mary Kay rather than its actual number of attendees. Even referring to it as a national convention was an exaggeration, since any Stanley get-together in Dallas would have been a regional rally with, at most, a few hundred salespeople.

Calling it a national convention made for a better allegory, though. As did some other edits she made, creating a story about her first Stanley rally that combined characters and events until it was as long on moral, short on specifics, and easy to remember as a parable. In years to come, she would attend dozens that followed the same format.

With dealers assembled, proceedings started with a sing-along. By company mandate, all weekly sales meetings kicked off with at least "two appropriate songs" and closed with at least one more. Many branches had a designated song leader, and some had groups practiced enough to pull off harmonies and rounds. At rallies, singing started from the stage, then the audience joined in. That got everybody over their shyness. "They'd get excited, you see. Take people out of themselves," a Stanley executive explained. "When you sing with a group, you realize you're not alone." Set to tunes deeply familiar and conveniently out of copyright, Stanley sang the same old songs with new lyrics.

Everybody did, everywhere from school assemblies to union rallies. Fuller Brush had dozens of songs about selling—which Stanley was able to use by substituting "Stan-ley" for "Ful-ler." To the tune of "I've Been Workin' on the Railroad," Mary Kay would belt, "I've been selling

Stanley products, all the livelong day." To "Jingle Bells," dealers would sing, "S-T-A-N-L-E-Y, Stanley all the time." A favorite like "Little Brown Jug" went:

Ha! Ha! Ha! You and me
We're chuck full of pep and glee.
Ha! Ha! Ha! You and me
Boost the Stanley Com-pa-ny.

Stanley had a songbook full of these, some spirited, some spiritual. The tune of "Tramp, Tramp, Tramp, the Boys Are Marching" could go either way. One version had a chorus boosterish enough for a Rotary meeting:

Sell! Sell! Sell! For Stanley products
Keep those orders rolling in—rolling in.
And we'll show the factory bunch that the sales force has the punch
And the Stanley crowd is bound again to win.

Another version used a chorus that could have come from a tent revival:

Yes, you bet that we can do it.
Cast all alibis away, away, away,
And the purpose firm and true we are out to win and do,
We can do it if we only follow thru.

After that rollicking sing-along, the rally rotated through recognition of top salespeople, more singing, motivating talks from managers and Mr. Bev, more awards, more praise, and more singing.

Throughout those three days, selling was never addressed in the language of Mammon but in the language of "the Stanley Opportunity." Mary Kay could have no doubt that selling was an ennobling endeavor, since God Himself seemed to be endorsing it. Assembled dealers were told that success was to be found only by placing trust in Him.

Mr. Bev was not a man given to distinctions between church and state. From the start of Stanley, he encouraged dealers to enlist church organizations in its "club plan," a precursor to the party plan that allowed organizations hosting Stanley demonstrations to share the profits. As Stanley became successful, he made generous contributions to Catholics, Jews, and Protestants alike. In 1943, he introduced the official Stanley Prayer, his redaction of a prayer written by Mary Soulsby: "O Lord, grant that each one who has to do with me today may be the happier for it. Let it be given me each hour today what I shall say. . . . Help me to enter into the mind of everyone who talks with me."

Even when the Lord's name was left out, Stanley speeches sounded like sermons. Stanley dealers were not in cutthroat competition for filthy lucre. They were in competition with themselves, often in ways that made Stanley sound more like a center for personal growth than a Berkshires brush manufacturer. The company motto, "To better your best," made individual success and company success one and the same.

Never was Stanley presented as primarily profit seeking. Mr. Bev would say, "We seek to share through our goodness and helpfulness. Take that out of Stanley, and you'll have just an ordinary, cold-blooded business organization." The Golden Rule was on-the-books company policy.

Throughout the rally, almost no mention was made of product: not by Mr. Bev and not by dazzlingly glib national sales manager Albert F. Reggie Regensburger. Mary Kay recalled that one executive disclosed the secrets of success as "Hitch your wagon to a star," "Get a railroad track to run on," and "Tell somebody what you are going to do." Those could have come from Regensburger, but they sounded more like area manager C. B. Eckman, who was notorious for spouting slogans. Copying them carefully, Mary Kay took his catchphrases as commandments.

An upcoming launch might be mentioned, but products were only means to an end. "They know how to sell window cleaner. You're not going to go into that. That's old hat," said a Stanley veteran. "Instead you talk to them about their reason for being in sales. What is their goal? Not just in sales but in life."

At Stanley, it was never too late. To try harder. To do better. To reinvent yourself and redeem your life. The English folk saying "Failure is the road to success" was a particular favorite. Mr. Bev took Robert Louis Stevenson's flowery rephrasing, "Let him try as he please, he is still sure of failure; and it is a very old and a very true saying that failure is the only high road to success," and rephrased it himself as the pithier "Try as hard as you will, you are bound to fail. But failure is the high road to success." Then attributed it to Stevenson anyway.

There were slogans upon slogans: "Fortify in '40," "Get Things Done in '41." Linking one snappy saying to the next, Mr. Bev could go on for hours, a technique perfected with "talk cards": a fistful of file cards with scribbled cues to proverbs, poetry, allegories, and song lyr-

Frank S. Beveridge using his "talk cards."

ics, which he reshuffled before each speaking engagement, thus guaranteeing that Stanley dealers heard the same message over and over but never the same way twice.

Mr. Bev knew his audience. Ralph Waldo Emerson, long-winded champion of self-reliance, was edited into easy-to-remember epigrams; thirty-one words from Emerson's 1841 essay "Compensation" redacted to a pithy "Every act rewards itself." Henry Wadsworth Longfellow, champion of morality over materialism, was granted authorship of the motto outside Stanley headquarters—"There is an honor in business that is the fine gold of it; that reckons with every man justly; that loves light; that regards kindness and fairness more highly than goods or prices or profits"—although the only Longfellow associated with that sentence was Walker–Longfellow, a Boston advertising agency that used the sentence in a 1914 pamphlet. No matter. Mr. Bev stamped it on stationery and everything else he could, while the misattribution passed into business history.

Charles Dickens, Sir Francis Bacon, and Abraham Lincoln were all fair game. As was poet Robert William Service, whose "Song of the Wage Slave" included the verse "I've done their desire for daily hire / and I die like a dog in a ditch."

An active Rotarian and pillar of the Westfield community who decorated his office with plaques reminding him to do more good more often, Mr. Bev was an early adopter of *associates* as a euphemism for *workers* and thought *employer/employee* sounded too much like *master/servant.* He spoke with a nonroyal *we* because he considered himself one of the Stanley workforce, whom he described as "ordinary people with extraordinary ambitions and talents" and thought of as family.

He was the perfect father figure: dependable, genial, the same age that Mary Kay's own father would have been. So supportive and evenhanded that his sales force played off his initials to nickname him "Fair and Square Beveridge." He looked the part too: stout, bald, thick glasses. In one-on-one conversations, he focused on faces with the concentration of a man who was deaf as a doorpost.

He was also, in contrast to the deceased Alexander Edward Wagner, lavish with prizes. During the Dallas rally, Mary Kay watched scores of salespeople parade to the podium to receive recognition for selling the same products from the same demonstration case that was upstairs holding her cheese and crackers. Sitting in the back of the audience, she gawked as a tall, slim brunette named Laveda O'Brien, a housewife from Corpus Christi, was crowned Queen of Sales with an actual crown. Then she watched as Queen Laveda was applauded by other Stanley sellers and presented with an alligator handbag.

That was too much. Seeing that Queen of Sales onstage, she said, "I decided on the spot that next year I would be Queen." Here were goodness and greatness and glory to be had.

Here too was the ideal sales incentive. Because even more than she coveted that crown, Mary Kay coveted the bag that came with it. "An alligator bag at that point was as far out of my reach as anything could be," she remembered. That was what movie stars had.

On the spot, Mary Kay began applying the advice in her notes. Deciding that this would be a way to "hitch your wagon to a star," she marched up to the winner and congratulated her, flattering the Queen of Sales into reenacting a "dem," as dealers called demonstrations, in her hotel room. If she could observe, she might be able to figure out what she had been doing wrong.

Apparently plenty. O'Brien, who would spend over a decade as a Stanley branch manager, was more than happy to show how things should be done. In the end, Mary Kay took nineteen pages of notes, interrupting with so many questions that the session took three hours, and writing down every bit of queenly patter with the intention of reciting it like a script when she got home to Houston. This would be her "railroad track to run on."

Two down, one to go. Eager to put "Tell somebody what you are going to do" into practice too, Mary Kay marched up to Mr. Bev and gushed, "Next year I am going to be the Queen."

Gallant as ever, Mr. Bev stared at her and replied, "You know, somehow I think you will."

Mary Kay knew a "You can do it!" when she heard one.

Armed with her nineteen pages, she headed back to Houston. In those days, Mr. Bev urged his sales force to memorize spiels, a technique that his hero, John H. Patterson, had used to double sales at the National Cash Register Company. The lesson was not lost on Mary Kay, who memorized Queen Laveda's patter word for word, then had her first $28 party. Four times her old average. Right off the bat.

At least that's what she said later. Whenever Mary Kay talked about this time in her life, she spoke only of selling opportunities. Addressing consultants, she would refer to herself as a single mother and tell her story with pauses that gave her audience enough time to imagine the frustration of being stuck in that shotgun cottage and tied to a two-timer who could not provide. Then she would segue into an anecdote or aphorism that illustrated how such impediments could be overcome. Selling gave you a chance. Selling got you money and recognition and support from other women. Anyone listening to her already knew that housework and wiping runny noses did not.

Whenever she could, she booked one or two parties a day, three or four if she was lucky. Day in, day out. Week in, week out. The etiquette of a Stanley Hostess Party decreed that the dealer arrive half an hour before party time. Leaving her demonstration case in the car—if she was lucky enough to be driving—Mary Kay knocked on the front door, then waited to be invited in. A polite pause would follow as she latched on to some excuse for a personal chat. "Find something of common interest to both of you," company literature advised. "You are a housewife, too, so you can talk in their language." A family photo, new drapes, or a nearby toddler usually did the trick.

Before guests arrived, Mary Kay would set up the card table that every American home seemed to have. Next she would unfurl a display cloth, with its Stanley logo, and spread it over the card table to lend the proceedings an official air. During the 1940s, she set up in front of the hearth because it was the room's focal point. During the 1950s, she set up in front of the television.

Then came products. Making small talk while looking as glamorous as possible in her dress and heels, Mary Kay would unpack her demonstration case: sales literature; "stick goods," meaning brushes; and sample sizes of "chemicals," as the company called its cleaning products. It would have been impossible to pack all the hundred or so brushes in the Stanley line, so she concentrated on the bestsellers: the radiator brush; the bowl brush; and the many variations—"Senior," "Professional," "Junior"—of the oval toothbrush and its rectangular, more masculine counterpart, the tufted toothbrush.

Salespeople were warned not to go overboard. The idea was to whet the audience's appetite by putting fifteen to twenty top sellers on the card table, then, once the party started, select six or seven items and talk about them for two or three minutes apiece.

As Mary Kay bantered and bustled, her hostess set up refreshments. Brochures glamorized parties by showing stylish women sipping bottles of Coca-Cola. But those cost money. So in the real world, and specifically in the environs of the Sixth Ward, the usual refreshments were tea and cookies or coffee and cake.

Finding the right hostess was half the battle. Since the hostess didn't get a penny for opening her home and handing out refreshments, you had to find someone who threw the kind of party that put guests in a generous mood. The hostess, in turn, had to trust that Mary Kay would make enough sales to give her a decent hostess gift—a dry mop and split duster set at the very least. That meant that the hostess was motivated to get as many prospects as possible, since her own gifts were calculated according to number of orders placed, percentage paid in cash, and bookings of future parties. Twelve to fifteen guests was ideal. Ten was workable. Under ten was more common than most dealers liked to admit.

In theory, every party was supposed to yield two more bookings so that—again, in theory—booking and selling and recruiting stretched to an infinity of opportunity. In reality, that was so rare that the company awarded the hostess an extra gift when the hoped-for two bookings happened. Should any booking try to renege, social pressure was usually enough to get things back on track: a gentle warning that the hostess would have to give back her gift. What a shame that would be.

"You also had to be thoughtful about the fact that you were talking to some women two or three times because these ladies were all friends," said a dealer, "because they would ask their friends to come again if they weren't getting enough people to the next party." Despite that, every dealer had stories about arriving for a party and finding nobody home. Or knocking on a front door and seeing the living room lights switch off.

"You are not selling brushes. You are not selling chemicals," Mr. Bev reminded dealers. "You are selling what they will do." Before, Mary Kay had been furthering family happiness with child psychology books and improving national nutrition with aluminum cookware. Now Mr. Bev told her: "You are selling health and sanitation."

Once the party got underway, Mary Kay would polish a piece of silver to demonstrate the rouge cloth. She would show how handily the split duster dealt with vexing venetian blinds. She would whip out the Furniture Cream and get to work on something nearby, all the while talking up the product's ease and efficiency. Early on, dealers learned not to demonstrate on anything too large or too dirty. One beginner, who had decided to show how well Furniture Cream worked on the family piano, was summoned back by a hostess hollering, "You can't walk away and leave me with half a polished piano!"

Women who had purchased products were encouraged to chime in and tell other ladies how well they worked. Many did. Then, after the recommended half hour of standing at the card table, it was time to pass out catalogs and order forms.

As part of its Golden Rule policy, Stanley officially discouraged a hard sell. So after she had scrubbed and polished, Mary Kay would find ways to give away prizes and get the ladies feeling obliged to buy. Booklets of Stanley riddles and puzzles might be distributed. Guests might play the S-T-A-N-L-E-Y game: writing the letters in a vertical column, then writing the name of a Stanley product that began with each of those letters. The winner was whoever named the most products within two minutes. Among women attending several parties a month, competition was fierce.

The prize might be a packet of rustproof sewing needles or a claw and pan lifter, something to prompt positive associations with Stanley. To encourage their liberal distribution, Stanley sometimes gave these away with a large prepaid order. More often, they were sold at a steep discount. Mary Kay had to lay out only three cents apiece for a vegetable brush, Keytainer, or percolator brush. A really impressive gift, like a bridge table cover, set her back a quarter.

Stanley's steady sellers were Window-Clean, Furniture Cream, and toothbrushes that sold three for a dollar. Almost everything was under $4. Most things were under $2. Mary Kay's commission ran around 45 percent, which meant she had to sell the equivalent of a mitten duster, waffle iron brush, child's toothbrush, and dish mop to earn her first dollar. To cover expenses, she had to sell three or four times as much. To make a modest profit, she had to sell ten or fifteen times as much. Hostess prizes and free gifts came out of her own pocket. So did product samples, transportation, and babysitting.

Then, after all that planning, the party might last an hour. The ladies had to get back to their responsibilities. Mary Kay positioned her parties as the highlight of any housewife's day, an antidote to the loneliness and drudgery. She talked up the fabulous amounts to be earned while chatting with friends for an hour—$20! $30! $40!—while accommodating the schedules of husbands and children. She left out the orders to be tallied and submitted to headquarters; the merchandise to be received, repacked, and delivered; and the moneys to be collected.

That last was never easy. Here again, peer pressure helped. A hostess's gift was payment in kind for product sold at her party, which meant that if Mrs. X didn't pay for her Furniture Cream, then Mrs. Y wouldn't get her rubber shampoo cape. With appropriate concern in her soft, girlish voice, Mary Kay was thus able to remind Mrs. X of the social consequences of reneging.

Selling Stanley wasn't just parties. Each Monday, Mary Kay was also expected to attend her unit manager's sales meeting. After the singing of "two appropriate songs," the meeting would tackle sales skills, such as how to make an appropriate opening comment or how to work Stanley's uplifting history into a sales pitch. The skill would be rehearsed through role-play until the meeting wound up with at least one more song: maybe a rollicking "We'll Be Leadin' All the Others," sung to the tune of "She'll Be Comin' 'Round the Mountain." The next week, another skill would be honed. And so on and so on. Through twenty-five topics covering every last possibility of staging parties, repeated in rotation for a total of fifty mandatory meetings each year.

Hostess prizes, games, cleaning a stranger's living room in your good clothes while other women sat and watched. Ironing board pads, Furniture Cream, toilet bowl brushes, and asking Tillie Bass to look after the kids. Coaxing customers into paying. Over and over again. Then again.

All through that year, she kept her eye on the prize. Long before visualization became a motivational cliché, Mary Kay cut out a picture of an alligator handbag and carried it around in her own cheap purse. Practicing "Tell somebody what you are going to do," she wrote weekly goals in soap on the bathroom mirror, adding soapy hash marks as she ticked off party after party.

In those days, winning any kind of Stanley contest took some doing. Women were signing up by the thousands. Before the end of the war, Stanley was one of few national companies to allow females in its sales force, its party plan had yet to be widely copied, and a woman could supposedly schedule selling around her homemaking. If a woman decided that she wasn't cut out for Stanley, she could return the demonstration case and get her money back, less the cost of any used chemicals and the rouge cloth, which could not be resold.

Because Stanley gave prizes for recruiting, its sales force grew as recruits gathered newer recruits. Most joined with something specific in mind: usually buying a refrigerator. Some never got that far. Some quit as soon as they did.

Of those who stuck with it, hundreds poured heart and soul into their Stanley careers. Around the time that Mary Kay made her trip to Dallas, a woman named Ruby Elmer was discharged from a six-day hospital stay only to discover that her husband was being shipped to Hawaii for the duration of the war, stranding her in Arkansas, where she didn't know a soul. With three kids to support and a hefty hospital bill, Elmer's assets totaled $10, a dozen laying hens, and a thirteen-year-old jalopy that couldn't make it up a hill. Out of desperation, she joined Stanley.

Her sales were dismal, but she plugged along until she was holding three parties a day, six days a week. In between, she practiced constantly, trying to dream up housecleaning tips for her dems. One week, she held 52 parties. Another week, she booked 112. At those parties, she came across other women in the same boat and recruited them to sell Stanley.

Underscoring the breadth of "the Stanley Opportunity," rallies showcased dealers like Elmer. Or, better still, those more dramatically handicapped. Like Mamie Jeffreys, a blind African American woman living in rural West Virginia. Jeffreys learned braille, joined Stanley, and, within three months, became the fourth-ranked saleswoman in her branch office.

There were so many like them. Like Mary Kay, who spent a year picturing that alligator bag on her arm and arrived at the next rally with a crown-compatible hairdo.

She had seized her chance. She had changed her life, as those *Acres of Diamonds* sermons and Dale Carnegie broadcasts had promised she could. She was Queen of Sales. Congratulated by bosses, applauded by peers. Exactly as she had pictured it.

Except that there was no alligator bag. Some area manager—some man—had gone and switched the prizes. "And wouldn't you know, they changed the prize and gave me something else. I don't even remember what it was—I just know it *wasn't* an alligator bag." After all that work, the letdown was enough to break your heart.

For the rest of her life, Mary Kay would tell the story of that alligator bag. She would repeat it so often that it became part of her company's foundation lore. In 1964, at that company's first sales convention, she would award pricey purses to top sellers. The next year, when business took off, she would upgrade to alligator. For herself, she would splurge on an alligator briefcase with her initials stamped in gold and make sure that every journalist, vendor, and consultant took notice.

She would include the story of the alligator bag in her first book, in speeches, and in scores of interviews. As the years went by, she would sound freshly frustrated every time she mentioned it.

She would never get over it.

Later the alligator bag story got all mixed up with another story, one where Stanley gave away a sales prize so outlandish that no woman would want it.

Mary Kay was giving an interview to *The Houston Post* in 1978, a time when recruitment was down, her company was about to report an abrupt drop in earnings, and Wall Street analysts were having themselves a high old time making fun of her pink Cadillacs. She mentioned none of that. Nor did the reporter ask. The story was scheduled for the women's pages.

Reading those pages, anyone would assume business was great. A banner headline crowed: THE DALLAS COSMETIC EMPRESS WHO KEEPS A 38,000-MEMBER SALES FORCE IN THE PINK. Mary Kay told the reporter that she attended St. Joseph's Catholic Church while growing up in the Sixth Ward and reminisced about her days as a Red Coat and debater.

A sidebar profiled "a beaming young African-American named Lois Burrell" with the lead "She was once a shy and retiring schoolteacher. Today she has diamonds, a pink Cadillac, access to furs—'everything a woman wants'—and she's done it all in her spare time." Playing off the schoolteacher reveling in newfound luxury, Mary Kay talked up her incentives, pointing out that direct-selling companies run by men had been distributing much sillier incentives to much less effect: "Once a branch manager won a flounder light—what you need with hip boots when you go gig fishing." In the *Post*, that gig light hadn't happened to her.

Pretty soon it had. "Once I worked terribly hard and you know what I got for a gift? A flounder light. Do you know what that is? It's a thing where you put on hip boots and go out and gig fish." Mary Kay would tell the story hundreds of times. The gig light was translated into Spanish and Russian and Mandarin. It was reported in *Fortune.* When the company celebrated its fortieth anniversary, the gig light was part of the foundation lore recorded and sold on a set of compact discs. When she died, it was in her obituaries.

Sometimes she added an extra "Would you believe it?" Sometimes a stage-whispered "Hmmm." Women would hear about alligator bags and gig lights and recall their own encounters with cavalier and clueless managers. Especially the ones who were men.

In public, Mary Kay never mentioned the name of the manager who switched the prizes. To the press, she was sweet as could be when she spoke of Mr. Bev. She might resent Stanley's failure to promote women, but if she resented salesmen like Homer Perkins, a contemporary who went on to become Stanley's president and then its chairman of the board, no one ever heard her say so.

In any case, Perkins didn't remember Mary Kay from her stint at Stanley. Decades later, the two would encounter each other at industry functions. By that time she'd long since quit Stanley, worked her way up someplace else, then quit there too, been divorced and widowed and divorced, then divorced and widowed again. While Perkins stuck it out at Stanley, stayed married to the same woman, had seven children.

In 1993, when he had become the elder statesman of Stanley and Mary Kay had become a mediagenic millionairess, her company planned a "This Is Your Life" segment for Seminar. Since everybody had listened to the stories of gig lights and alligator handbags hundreds of times, they asked Perkins to come down and surprise her. The idea was that the president of Stanley would step out from behind a curtain and present her with that long-overdue alligator bag.

Perkins went along with the gag. He flew to Dallas and checked into a hotel outside town. "On the appointed day, they put me in another room, closed the door. She listened to a tape of me retelling the story, didn't know my voice. Then I brought out the alligator handbag and presented it to her. I said, 'I'm here to settle this issue once and for all and make sure you get your alligator handbag.'"

He'd heard versions of the story mixing up alligator bags and gig lights and God knows what else. To him, the whole thing was a joke: "Mary Kay says we gave her an underwater fishing lamp. Why the hell? Where would I find an underwater fishing lamp to start with?"

At that point, though, details didn't matter. What mattered was how women identified with her disappointment. Alligator bags and mink coats and diamond rings proved that you were worth something to someone. Her audiences knew what it was like to have your heart set on something and not get it.

If, as Mary Kay got more and more famous, different newspapers printed different versions, that didn't matter either. The story had always been a teaching tool to show how sales incentives were supposed to work. Although as thirty, then forty, then fifty years passed, it seemed strange that someone as successful as Mary Kay could still get so worked up over an alligator bag.

But in the 1940s, newspaper interviews and speeches and stage presentations were still a long way off from life in the Sixth Ward.

The girl who had reveled in her status as a crack typist, extemporaneous speaker, and member of the Red Coats had traveled all over the state of Texas to compete in tournaments and march in parades. She once had a future so promising that she had hurried through high school and rushed to meet it. Now all she had to show for those big dreams were two babies by the age of eighteen. With a husband who looked like he would never amount to much.

At the Rice Institute, her friend Dorothy Zapp had gone from triumph to triumph: duchess of her junior class, duchess of the Huntsville Ball, a "vivacious blonde" whose comings and goings were chronicled in the *Post.* Dorothy got her degree and married her college sweetheart. While Mary Kay, just as smart and even more hardworking, was still in the same house in the same neighborhood. Having the same kind of marriage as her mother. Sending her own children to the same school down the same mud-sunk brick sidewalks.

Being the fastest typist to ever work in the office of Tabernacle Baptist hadn't gotten her anywhere. Selling those books hadn't lasted long. Peddling cookware was worse because her husband was involved. Stanley was turning out to be her best shot.

At Stanley, she had kept going long after anybody else would have quit. But even there, the people selling were mostly women and the people managing were mostly men. Men who didn't understand how an alligator bag could give you dignity in front of your customers. Stir up some envy. Show that you had changed your life.

She had staged parties and smiled until she was blue in the face. And still she couldn't get what should have been hers. Still a man had let her down. That manager in Dallas who switched the sales prizes.

Soon that manager would be her husband, a marriage she never mentioned.

CHAPTER SEVEN

"S-T-A-N-L-E-Y, Stanley All the Time"

As the country prepared for war, working mothers became a subject of national debate.

Leaving a child in the care of paid professionals was still known as "baby farming," a phrase linked to lurid, Progressive-era exposés showing skeletal tots chained to cribs while their mothers—who prostituted themselves, worked for wages, or worse—cavorted without a care in the world. The Children's Bureau, a federal agency founded in 1912 to combat child abuse, had yet to budge from the middle-class model of breadwinning father and stay-at-home mother as its standard for a "suitable home." In 1926, the year that Lula left Colby's Rooms for longer hours at Blanchard's Restaurant, a bureau bulletin proclaimed that pensions and public assistance would be preferable to working women and professional childminding. Not even the Depression shifted America's aversion to working mothers: In 1930, only 8 percent of mothers with children under the age of ten admitted to working outside the home; in 1940, it was 7.8 percent.

War wasn't going to get them out of the house either. The War Manpower Commission declared that "the first responsibility of women with young children, in war as in peace, is to give suitable care in their own homes to their children." In weekly radio broadcasts, Father Flanagan reminded stay-at-home mothers that theirs was both a full-time job and sacred duty. Respected as one of the country's foremost experts on childcare ever since Spencer Tracy played him in a movie, the celibate Catholic priest appeared at Senate hearings to inveigh against mothers working in war plants, invoking his constant refrain: "Let's keep the mother in the kitchen, where she belongs." Pundits predicted a generation of latchkey children who would come to no good end. Mary Kay, a latchkey child herself, heard that having a working mother was the worst possible fate, one that doomed offspring to a lifetime of unhappiness and ill-health.

But Mary Kay may have decided that didn't apply to her. While historians later hailed Rosie the Riveter and women's wartime entry into the workforce, it was easy to ignore women who had been working all along, like Lula, Aunt Birdie, Ida, and Mary Kay. Selling Stanley Home Products wasn't regarded as a real job anyway. Certainly not by the government. Female dealers who joined Stanley after 1939 didn't show up on statistical surveys and didn't count as being employed. They were independent contractors, willing to work without salary or benefits. Virtually none had a Social Security number.

Stanley didn't "count" as an employer either. During the lead-up to war, a federal bureaucrat visited company headquarters in Westfield, Massachusetts, to gather information for forthcoming gas rationing, only to discover that the company did not fit any of his assigned categories. The U.S. Commerce Department classified direct sales as "sales by manufacturers direct to consumers," leaving out Avon, Fuller Brush, Stanley, and about six thousand other firms selling door to door through independent contractors.

Or Mary Kay may not have had time to notice the naysaying. Each day, she got up at five, as she had learned from Lula. Housework came next, an opportunity to apply principles gleaned from her study of self-improvement books. If she had cleaned the kitchen in fifteen minutes the day before, she timed herself to see if she could do it in less. She allowed two minutes to make a bed, three minutes to iron a shirt. After that, she woke the kids, got them to school, and headed to one or two

Stanley parties. "I needed a method by which I could earn money and not be gone eight or nine hours a day. A Stanley party lasted approximately four hours, maybe five by the time you got there and got home again," she said, and in those four hours of setup, selling, and cleanup, Mary Kay claimed she made an "equivalent amount that you might make in those days on a full eight-hour job." Then again, what a woman earned for an eight-hour job wasn't much.

When the kids came home, she got dinner ready, fed them, left them with a babysitter, then drove off around seven so she could fit in another party. On a really good night, she might squeeze in two. The kids were asleep when she got home. A few hours later, she woke up and did it all over again.

With slight variations, this was her schedule for the next decade. Selling Stanley was a merry-go-round of weekly sales meetings, weekly specials, two-for-one deals, contests, deliveries, orders, invoices, and so much other paperwork that a woman barely had time to think. Her youngest child later described the selling she did during the 1940s as "a dog and pony show": "It was a deal and price and gimmick and 'This is special' and 'That's special' and . . . 'Let me show you how this cleans, honey. You've got a spot on your carpet somewhere. Let me show you how good this works.' . . . It would remind you of the old peddler's atmosphere of a guy in a wagon, and he comes into town and he opens up his doors, and he shows his wares. The only difference is that . . . it occurs in the home."

But Mary Kay was good at it, and determined to get better. Stanley had over a hundred products, and she knew them like the back of her hand. Reagan High's prizewinning declaimer could counter almost any objection, chat up the shiest stranger, pass along tips about dusting and polishing, win over the women who hadn't wanted to come to the party in the first place, and often recruit them as hostesses. Mary Kay could make scrubbing crusty pans sound like something noble.

Her own housekeeping was irreproachable. Her own appearance was flawless. Her eyebrows were nowhere near as high-flying as they had been during her days at Reagan, but they were penciled just as carefully. Her hair was darker than the mousy brown of high school but still styled to a fare-thee-well. She seemed never to not be wearing lipstick. As Mr. Bev recommended, she pored over each new self-improvement book. Reading up on sales strategies, she learned to tilt her head to the side to express interest and convey credibility. She smiled her half smile whether she felt like it or not. She practiced staring into a prospect's right eye because that was supposed to be better for closing a sale. True, it hurt her feelings when people said she seemed like a girl with too much on the ball to be peddling toilet bowl brushes. When that happened, she tried to take it as a compliment.

For those times, and for all the times when selling Stanley seemed more like a Sisyphean struggle than an unlimited opportunity, Mr. Bev had an employee motivation program at the ready. Repurposing a "company philosophy" that a later generation would have called a mission statement, Mr. Bev tweaked his 1932 "Seven-Year Plan" into a "Seven-Step Self-Improvement Program" that refined and reiterated what had worked so well at Fuller Brush.

As he had at Fuller, Mr. Bev preached an evangelical capitalism that all but ignored product information, minimized the mechanics of selling, and failed to mention monetary rewards or other quantifiable goals. Instead, Stanley's seven tenets sounded like a series of sermons: "A Program of Study," "A Program of Self-Analysis," "A Program of Personal Development," "A Program of Helpfulness," "A Program of Serving," "A Program of Personal Production," and "Becoming an Important Part of the Organization to Which You Belong," soon to be rephrased "Catching the Stanley Spirit."

Mr. Bev never stopped there. Each point was amplified by aphorisms from the heroes of his personal pantheon: men like John H. Patterson of the National Cash Register Company and salesman-turned-evangelist Dwight Lyman Moody. Once Mr. Bev got going on "A Program of Study," he could rarely resist citing Moody's motto: "I want you to be the kind of men who can go out and eat soup with a one-tine fork!" Then he would add: "You can go out and do it too, if you have to. If you can't get the best, get the next best. If you can't get that, get something else and do the best you can with it." It was rousing rhetoric, stronger stuff than Mr. Bev had used at Fuller Brush. And it worked: In the Depression decade between 1933 and 1943, Stanley sales went from $149,577 to $6,555,519.

Mary Kay probably needed the pep talks. Like her sister Daisy, she was effectively a single mother. Rogers was rarely home. Lula had remarried. At age fifty-six, Lula wed forty-five-year-old George William Murphy, whose first wife and three sons lived a ten-minute walk away on Decatur Street.

A Northerner, Mary Kay's stepfather was short, swarthy, and tattooed, a manual laborer with a seventh-grade education. During World War I, the army stationed him at Fort Sam Houston, where he met and married a local girl. After the war, he and his Texan bride headed to Houston at roughly the same time and for roughly the same reasons as the Wagners, gravitating to neighborhoods near the garages along Washington Avenue. There, Murphy found work as a vulcanizer, sweating through ten-hour days in the stink of burning rubber. When that marriage ended, Murphy stayed in the Sixth Ward, working in garages a few doors down from Wagner's Café, which at one point was registered as his legal residence. By October of 1941, when a marriage license made him Mary Kay's stepfather, he was working for a tire dealership just down the road.

Whatever the reasons that Mary Kay's mother married Murphy, none involved his money or good name. Lula referred to herself as the Widow Wagner, paid her bills that way, listed herself as Mrs. Lula Wagner when she got a telephone again, and kept up her 112-hour workweeks at the café. Having waited two years to have a clergyman convalidate her first marriage, she waited two years to have a clergyman bless her second. In any case, Murphy was not around much. Men generally weren't.

In women's magazines, male editors scapegoated working wives for America's increasing divorce rate. But in places like the Sixth Ward, women were just trying to get by without a man's wages. Across Kane Street, Mary Kay's friend Tillie Bass had lost her father while she was still a young girl. Raised by a single mother, Tillie grew up to marry a good man with a good job who died of a heart attack when he was thirty-one, stranding her with two sons. In Mary Kay's own family, Uncle Doc had moved back to live with his parents and work as a painter and paperhanger, leaving Aunt Birdie behind to clerk at the bakery and fend for herself for a few months. Lula was still serving up coffee at a café named after her dead first husband. Mary Kay kept right on typing, selling toilet brushes, and trying to find whatever work she could.

Then Rogers reappeared. In some versions of this story, Mary Kay had recently realized her dream of attending either Rice University or the University of Houston, wedging a premed curriculum into a schedule that included taking care of two young children, keeping house for six people, and selling Stanley full time, while getting by on three or four hours of sleep each night. Sometimes Mary Kay or a ghostwriter added details, like telling people that she attended classes with her wedding ring worn on a chain around her neck so that she would look like a bobby-soxer. The part about getting by on three or four hours of sleep each night was probably true.

Much later, as her company's public relations team offered the world a more sainted Mary Kay, she claimed that she'd intended to become a doctor, a profession all but closed to women in Depression-era Houston, as well as an unusual goal for a woman notorious for not liking math or science. In the 1981 autobiography, her ghostwriter added the fillip that Lula, married and delivered of her first child in her teens, had once been a nurse, "and she didn't want that for me." Later still, Mary Kay said that her mother talked her out of medical school, predicting that she would do more for humanity as a saleswoman. One version had university officials concurring: "It was because I had a greater aptitude for working with people, as the dean of my college finally told me." Today, neither alleged alma mater can find any version of Mary Kay's maiden or married names on enrollment lists. City directories listed her as a waitress at Wagner's Café.

Rogers, who had a 3-A draft classification as a married man with children, popped up around the same time that the army started drafting divorced men. Divorce would equal an automatic and almost immediate induction. For an able-bodied man living in Texas in 1942, being married was good. Having children was better. Having more children would be best of all.

The whole country was baby crazy.

After long years of a Depression that depressed the national fertility rate, Americans were reproducing left and right. By 1941, magazines were using the phrase *baby boom* to describe the results of the previous year's draft-inspired marriages. *Life* wrote of America "winning the baby war against Hitler." In 1943, U.S. fertility zoomed to 94.3 births per thousand—its highest since 1927.

People who could not have babies were buying them. Black markets sprang up. Where demand was high and supply scarce, like the Farm Belt, a healthy infant might fetch $2,000. Near large cities and military bases, oversupply brought the price down. Houston, a port city, sustained a going rate of $200 to $500. Harris County brought charges against a couple who bought a baby for $112, then resold it for $218. In another case, a Houston abortionist convinced an Alabama farm girl to trade her baby for two new dresses, priced at $1.98 and $2.98, then resold the baby for $350. When one Houston couple advertised their unborn child for sale, the first buyer to turn up made an offer for their fifteen-month-old daughter instead, whereupon the father used his $500 windfall for a $200 car down payment and lost half of the remainder in a dice game.

Surrounded by baby mania and surrendering to the attentions of her often-absent spouse, Mary Kay was soon pregnant again. That put paid to any big ideas about college, legal separation, or moving out of her mother's house. On April 15, 1943, at age twenty-four, she had her third and last child: Richard Raymond Rogers, named after two of her husband's brothers. Like his mother before him, the baby of the family would grow up watching his mother work long, hard hours, later recollecting his childhood and adolescence as "without a normal home life to speak of."

For years, three generations of Mary Kay's family and the occasional single boarder or married couple had been crammed into a studio apartment. Lula came home to sleep, change clothes, and head back to work. Everything else fell to Mary Kay: care of the baby, seeing two children off to school, laundry, cooking, cleaning, and helping out at the café. Unless she could move out of her mother's house, there would be no getting away from it.

With war declared, the forced intimacy didn't last much longer. Wife and children or no, Rogers was at last swept up by the draft. In public, Mary Kay would later say that her marriage was already unhappy when her husband went off to serve in World War II. In private, she made cracks about losing him to a redhead.

Decades later, she described holding the family together until her husband came home and demanded a divorce, knowing that many women in her audience had exactly that experience. In 1945, the year that Mr. and Mrs. Julius Ben Rogers dissolved their union, the U.S. divorce rate hit an all-time high, and it would go higher still in the first year of peace. The war's toll on homelife would become one of the complaints of her generation; something that happened to thousands and thousands of women who found themselves left behind.

But it didn't happen to her. Not quite that way. Rogers found another woman without leaving town.

That other woman seemed to have a lot in common with Mary Kay. Only ten months older, Leona Madelene Frieda was petite, pretty, Texan, and Baptist. She was born in the Hill Country of Burleson County to parents who came from German farm families that, like Mary Kay's, had recently left the land. Her father sometimes worked as a laborer. Her mother sometimes worked as a cook. Like the Rogerses and the Wagners, the Friedas moved around Southeast Texas before landing in Houston, where Leona's father eventually found work as a trolley driver. She graduated from high school, then, not long after, married Heinrich Friedrich "Henry" Schwettman Jr., a boy from back in Brenham, a little town in Washington County where her parents had lived for part of the 1920s. The young couple lived with the bride's family, then went out on their own when Schwettman got a job managing a gas station. At one point, Schwettman had his own station. It was not a success.

Yet the two women somehow ended up as different as night and day. It wasn't just that Leona was childless and never had to earn her living. She didn't have that drive to outwork the world bred into Mary Kay. She didn't ache for the trophies that made Mary Kay's heart beat faster. She had never been second-fastest typist in the city of Houston, had never won an American Legion medal. She didn't seem to care if she ever did.

Rogers finally left for the army in February of 1944, the date Mary Kay would cite as the start of their legal separation when she initiated their divorce the next year. Following custom, she was the one to file, citing cruelty and "tyrannical conduct." He did not contest. She did not request alimony. The divorce became final on August 13 of 1945. She paid court costs.

The war in Europe had ended; the war in Japan would be over soon. The financial bounty of the Servicemen's Dependents Allowance Act would be ending too. The mother of three began paying bills as "Miss Mary K. Rogers" and looking for more work. With soldiers headed home, wages for women were worse than ever. For men, the average annual wage was $2,079. For women, it was $980. Although what a woman got in Texas was whatever they cared to give her.

Within a week of the divorce, the former second-fastest typist in the city of Houston lined up secretarial work at Stanley and applied for a Social Security number. Finished with both his eleven-year marriage and his eighteen-month army career, Private First Class Rogers was ordered to pay $70 a month in child support—an impossible amount for a man whose prewar income topped out at $1,200 a year.

Within a year, Mary Kay would remarry. Rogers would not wait so long. He got a new marriage license the next day.

CHAPTER EIGHT

"Salesmen Are Not Born, but Made"

The next time, Mary Kay married her boss.

Clarence Blair Eckman was as unlike Julius Ben Rogers as a man could be. Not even his new bride would try to position this one as a tremendous catch. He was old enough to be her father and was, in fact, a grandfather with two married sons: one her age, another four years older. At five feet four inches, he wasn't much taller than Mary Kay. Except for a little potbelly, he was scrawny. He was bald. His ears stuck out like jug handles. He wore bifocals. He had diabetes.

He was no Hawaiian Strummer heartthrob, but C. B. Eckman had other virtues. Foremost among them: his status as area manager at Stanley Home Products, a firm that was really taking off with the party plan. Eckman not only had a salaried job, he had as good a job as you could get in direct selling—near the top tier of Stanley, as one of its area managers.

Blair, as his family called him, hadn't started with many advantages. No more, he reminded her, than Mary Kay. No more than most others. Born in Apollo, Pennsylvania, in 1891, Eckman was raised in the stretch of Armstrong County between Punxsutawney and Pittsburgh, where his people had lived for as long as it had been part of the United States: farmers who called themselves "hardy as pine knots." Eckman's father,

Harvey, was a day laborer, trying to support a wife and family when the local gas and oil booms were over and so was the smaller prosperity that had come with the Pennsylvania Canal.

Eckman never went to high school, but he did get himself to the big city. By 1914, he was in Pittsburgh's Hazelwood neighborhood, running William Bartrum's old store on Second Avenue as the "Eckman & Snyder" grocery in partnership with his wife's brother: two titans-to-be set up with an oleomargarine license, a horse-drawn wagon, and a marquee proclaiming HEADQUARTERS OF HOME-DRESSED THANKSGIVING TURKEYS, CHICKENS, DUCKS AND GEESE.

That soon changed. By 1917, Eckman was peddling groceries in the employ of the Jewel Tea Company, an interstate business that could practice economies of scale that a small grocer could not. Founded in Chicago in 1901, Jewel had started as a one-horse operation: one among hundreds of "tea wagons" selling door to door and getting customers to pay top dollar by goldbricking them with almost worthless premiums—maybe a flower-painted eggcup—for repeat orders.

But while most remained one-horse ventures, Jewel prospered by advancing truly covetable premiums. Reversing custom, a housewife with her eye on a pretty Haviland china teapot could get the teapot first. Then she would apply the credits of her Jewel orders until that teapot was earned. By that time, she was usually ready for the teacups to go with it. When Eckman joined, Jewel had just expanded, incorporated, and built the world's largest coffee-roasting plant. By 1917, Jewel ran nearly 1,700 routes and reached nearly $16 million in annual sales.

Working for Jewel was no picnic. Eckman was expected to report by 7:00 or 7:30 a.m. and to be knocking on doors by eight, when the week's forty-hour clock started. Eckman made upward of three dozen calls a day, visiting each house on the same time of the same day on biweekly rounds. At 5:00 p.m. he was off the clock and back at the office handing in that day's cash and loading his wagon for the next day. Saturdays, also off the clock, were full of collections and paperwork.

For all this, Eckman earned a tiny base pay and a 10 percent commission, remitted only after he proved that he could recite "The Jewel

Way," the company's 655-word manifesto, from memory. His wife, Lillian, and son, Leon, born in 1914, lived upriver in McKees Rocks, but Eckman never spent much time there.

Jewel was a calling. And not just for Eckman. Jewel salesmen were "industrial soldiers." Company literature showed salesmen rowing groceries to housewives during floods and braving blizzards on sleds borrowed from their children. Then World War I came, and the government commandeered its coffee-roasting plant and turned Jewel's industrial soldiers into the real thing. Jewel was forced to use women on some routes. Sales plummeted.

Yet Eckman prospered. After his second son, LeNaire, was born in 1918, Eckman began recruiting salesmen through newspaper ads that announced "Salesmen are not born, but made." Promoted and transferred to Hartford, Connecticut, the city that happened to house the headquarters of the Fuller Brush Company, Eckman soon switched from groceries to stick goods and got himself on a managerial track at Fuller Brush.

Not yet thirty, he already looked the successful sales executive: stout, balding, immaculately attired. A relative recalled, "All around him men would be in shirtsleeves. He'd stand there with his jacket on, his tie knotted, conservative and proper." Modeling prosperity was part of a sales manager's job, which meant that proprieties were observed. The family sent custom-engraved Christmas cards. They dressed for dinner each night. Promoted and transferred to Illinois, Eckman joined the Mount Joliet Masonic Lodge and was raised to Master Mason within months. His picture appeared in the *Chicago Tribune* to endorse a pricey mechanical pencil. His wife's doings at the Colony Club were reported in the society pages.

At Fuller Brush, director of sales Frank Stanley "Mr. Bev" Beveridge had created a culture that celebrated ordinary men who ascended through gumption and hard work, preferably with some two-hankie setbacks along the way. The more dramatic the rise, the more power it held as a recruitment tool. Founder Alfred C. Fuller loved to brag of his humble beginnings—all the better to egg on his sales force as they pursued their own prosperity. "My life is proof of the tremendous power available to everyone to vault above his own deficiencies," wrote the millionaire benefactor of orchestras and opera companies, who persisted in calling himself a "country bumpkin." Next best was boasting of his executives' unpromising origins: "There were no highly powered personalities at all, no geniuses in salesmanship or business management."

Under Mr. Bev's tutelage, Eckman became proficient in practices that would dominate direct selling for the rest of the century: recruiting through newspaper classifieds, calling salesmen "dealers" to reinforce the principle that every man worked for himself, and then convincing those dealers that the selling opportunity he offered was better than work with base pay or benefits.

At Fuller Brush—as it would be at Stanley and later at Mary Kay Cosmetics—dealers bought the product outright and resold it at a price set by the company. They also paid Fuller Brush for the privilege of obtaining sample kits and anted up three cents for each "free" Handy Brush that they were obligated to leave behind on sales calls. In return, dealers received not only the opportunity to make money but also the opportunity to serve a higher calling. Sales tips were embedded in morality tales illustrating the Fuller Brush Man's triumph over the forces of negativity, ignorance, and indifference. Homilies and inspirational messages were reprinted in *The Bristler* magazine and other company literature, sending forth salesmen with stirring words such as "Yours is the spirit that broke the prairies, settled the West, and carved a civilization out of the wilderness."

Eckman lapped it up. Learning every motivational maxim by heart, he bought a book about writing sermons and volunteered as a lay preacher. Because if patriotism didn't do the trick, Fuller Brush had no qualms about invoking the Almighty. Fuller's gloss on the gospel: "Christ said, 'To him that hath shall be given.' I would paraphrase that in its applications to us: For him who does much for others, much also will be done."

But earthly recognition was not lacking. Mr. Bev distributed praise and pins and prizes galore. In 1923, after a 25 percent price increase left Fuller Brush with unsold inventory, the company increased incentives. When that worked, incentives increased again. Then again. By the time Eckman was transferred to Chicago, Fuller Brush was famous for banquets, trips, and corsages for the dealers' wives. And those were just the inducements originating in the national office.

Added to all those were incentives dreamed up on the regional level, foremost among them monthly contests conceived by Albert "Fine and Dandy Al" Teetsel, who joined Fuller in 1923 and soon, as New York district manager, became Eckman's colleague. One month, Teetsel sponsored an essay contest on "my most difficult customer and how I won her over." Another month, he held a "Smile King Contest," with $100 going to the wife who snapped the photo of her husband setting off to sell with the sunniest grin.

Mr. Bev might preach positive mental attitude, but Teetsel went the boss one better. Teetsel pledged dealers to live by the motto "Positive Always," which he called the Silver Rule. His habit of answering the most perfunctory "How are you?" with a booming "Fine and dandy!" inspired formation of the "Fine and Dandy Club," which amounted to an excuse for Teetsel to treat top salesmen to yet more performance-based banquets and outings. Through the worst of the Depression, Teetsel's own income topped $50,000 a year, about $1.29 million in today's dollars, and he made sure that everybody knew it. Fine and Dandy Al wore a big diamond ring, had two gold front teeth, favored loud neckties, peeled $5 tips off a $500 roll, and smoked one fat cigar after another, an addiction shared with Eckman.

Teetsel could also take credit for the peppy lyrics that Mary Kay and thousands of other direct sellers would sing for decades to come. The version of "Tramp! Tramp! Tramp!" that she learned during the 1940s was word-for-word Teetsel:

If we only think we can, we can do a lot of things
That we used to think that we could never do

For Eckman, all was well at Fuller until the one-two punch of Mr. Bev's departure and the stock market crash. At the end of 1930, he left for Electrolux, a Swedish vacuum cleaner company that had just built its first U.S. factory.

In Europe, direct selling was no fit occupation for a man with any other option. *Sex in Chains,* a 1928 German film, portrayed peddling Electrolux as an act of desperation, resulting in the hero's financial ruin, prison, and a torrid affair with another male inmate. Whereas, in the Land of Opportunity, sales ranks swelled with the type of upstanding young men who sat down to sales meetings in steakhouses and, like Eckman, drove around in gleaming motorcars while puffing oversize cigars.

Slumps spelled good times for direct sales, and the Depression was a doozy, giving Eckman his pick of talent. At his new job, Eckman made use of Mr. Bev's motivational maxims. "He had several clichés that he used during Monday-morning sales meetings," recalled one employee. "He also loved to tell jokes and if he told a good joke and got a good

C. B. Eckman (*lower right*) at an Electrolux sales meeting.

response, he would use it over and over." In his unhurried, professorial way, he would drill recruits in sales patter. Taking a new man out in the field "to break him in," Eckman would coach the rookie on timing and delivery, demonstrating how to get a laugh out of prospects to soften them up. It also helped that Electrolux offered the best benefits in the business: no outlay, a 35 percent commission, and a pension plan. U.S. sales went from $980,447 in 1933 to $2 million in 1938.

Eckman's only problem was personal: When Electrolux transferred him to Peoria, his wife did not want to move. He went without her.

Scandal ensued. His wife divorced him, stayed in Chicago, took up with a younger man, then committed suicide. Through it all, Eckman did not miss a day of work, taking his son LeNaire to sales banquets instead of his wife. Dissatisfaction came only when war disrupted the supply chain between Europe and the U.S.

At the same time, Eckman couldn't help noticing that Stanley Home Products, the stick-goods company started by his former mentor, was coming on like gangbusters. So in 1942 Eckman switched to Stanley, where, as a known quantity, he became an exception to its policy of promoting from within. Next thing he knew, he was being transferred to Texas, the largest state in the union, and opening an office out by the country club. As an area manager, he was near the top of the Stanley hierarchy, bested only by a few regional managers and Mr. Bev himself. Rank-and-file dealers like Mary Kay reported to unit managers, who reported to branch managers. In Texas, those branch managers reported to Eckman.

Eckman earned more than four times what Mary Kay's first husband made and was part of a sales organization breaking through to the big time. Looking at him, Mary Kay decided she should be able to do it too.

There's no knowing when she first had her eye on him, or he on her. During the first half of 1945, as the war between the young Mr. and Mrs. Rogers wound down, Eckman was occupied elsewhere. As her boss's boss, he didn't have much contact with Mary Kay. Not at first. As she became more successful, they got to know each other. Especially after that incident with the alligator bag. While Eckman was sympathetic, nobody had actually promised her a purse. Sometimes Mary Kay just got these notions, these expectations.

Eckman's first marriage had ended a full decade before. His first wife had been fanciful, dreaming that her son Leon would earn first chair in the Chicago Symphony, claiming that LeNaire was named after a character in a racy French novel. In the divorce, most of the family, including his mother-in-law, took Eckman's side. A man had to work. Besides, his wife had been the one to break up the marriage, then go off with someone else. He had not.

Later, he had lady friends. In Peoria, he kept company with a younger woman, a single mother who worked in the building where Electrolux had its offices. After her, he had another lady friend who went with him to visit LeNaire and his bride, Evalyn, up in Delaware. The two couples took in some sights, made a trip to Longwood Gardens, and afterward the lady friend mailed LeNaire and Evalyn a batch of poems she'd written "oozing with love and babies." That was too much even for Eckman, a softie known to get all dewy-eyed over greeting cards and Christmas carols. No more was heard from her.

Not much later, Eckman was getting ready to marry Mary Kay. If she had less than a year between marriages, there was no shame in that. Secretaries married bosses all the time. Young mothers were supposed to find good providers. Eckman's own father, a widower, had taken a second wife almost two decades younger.

This marriage also would give Eckman the chance to play mentor, a role he relished. Believing that a little push from the right person could help, he would say, "It is very important what you know, but also very important *who* you know." At Electrolux, he had wangled a summer job for his son LeNaire and gotten LeNaire's best friend, Edward L. "Bud" Berthold, started in the service department with the idea that it might be a foot in the door to sales. "My father died when I was nine, so C.B. was like a second father," Berthold remembered. "C.B. was so good to me."

"C.B. was so good to me." Eckman with Bud Berthold.

A child of the Depression, Berthold held no illusions about the security of factory or office work. He'd watched his mother work the graveyard shift for $15 a week, only to be laid off and forced to beg for government relief. Eckman taught him that selling was a different sort of life, where your prospects were whatever you wanted to make of them. Leaving Electrolux for the U.S. Army Air Corps, Berthold piloted thirty-five missions and earned the Distinguished Flying Cross. Then, when the war was over, he went back to sales, the profession that C.B. had helped him learn.

True, Mary Kay would lose her Houston customers if she married Eckman. That couldn't be helped. The "Memorandum of Agreement" she had signed with Stanley stated that she could sell only in her assigned territory, a policy left over from the days when the company's door-to-door salesmen were allotted either ten thousand people or two thousand households—a policy that had not changed now that the sales force was mostly female and the selling was mostly party plan. If a Stanley dealer moved, as many did when husbands were transferred, she lost her customers. Infringement on anybody else's territory was grounds for dismissal. On the other hand, Mary Kay could expect her pick of territories. She would be married to the area manager.

And she would finally get out of the Sixth Ward. If she needed additional enticement to marry Eckman, she got it that July, when he found the perfect house. Built in 1929, 5206 Maple Springs Drive had the look of a storybook cottage, with gable windows, a wide chimney, and a steeply pitched roof. Its 2,250 square feet included three bedrooms, a big kitchen, a breakfast room, a dining room, and a small study. The master bedroom had its own balcony, with a spiral staircase that led down to a nice-size backyard edged with shade trees. At the back of the property was a freestanding mother-in-law cottage roughly the size of 2111 Kane Street.

The neighborhood, Oak Lawn Heights, was full of families in tidy Tudor-style houses on roomy lots. Mothers stayed home. Fathers went to work. Kids played in the backyard. There was a park on the next block. Maple Lawn Elementary, more modern than the Dow School, was only a few blocks away. Eckman explained how much the new place looked like Mr. Bev's own home up in Westfield, the very house that had been the model for the familiar, round company logo. From now on, it was going to be as if they lived inside that same charmed circle.

On July 19, 1946, having put down almost half the purchase price of $13,125 in cash, Eckman signed the deed for their new home. Two weeks later, the fifty-five-year-old sales manager and his twenty-eight-year-old secretary were married there, in a ceremony performed by the minister of Highland Park Presbyterian, the much-admired modern congregation that Eckman had joined when he moved to Dallas.

Seeing the bride and groom, no one would have guessed that it had been one hundred degrees all day. Both looked like they had stepped out of a bandbox. Both spoke their vows in voices that were strangely soft for such determined little people: Mary Kay's almost girlish, Eckman's gentle and deliberate. As they were pronounced man and wife, Eckman's brown eyes misted over. It was the rare wedding where the groom seemed more moved than the bride.

With that out of the way, Mr. and Mrs. Eckman went back to work. Eckman had always been conscientious to the point of compulsion. Leon, a toddler during his father's Jewel Tea days, complained that Eckman never had much time for family. "He [Eckman] spent most of his life at work," Leon's daughter remembered. Another grandchild referred to him as "a workaholic." "Never missed a day of work," said a friend from Peoria. That did not change in Dallas.

Responsible for the entire state of Texas, Eckman spent hour after hour behind the big wheel of his 1940 Chrysler Windsor, a car marketed toward "persons of short stature." Perched on its padded Airfoam upholstery and smoking his cigars, he was in perfect heaven.

Mary Kay had her own version of paradise, which involved living hundreds of miles from Wagner's Café, having a husband with a steady job, and owning a big house with a mother-in-law cottage that she could fill with babysitters. FREE RENTAL, she advertised that autumn. "Private room and bath, rear, in exchange for occasional housework and care of children."

Later, as she became legendary for her ability to recruit women into direct selling, Mary Kay allowed herself to be portrayed as forced to provide for her children, the implication being that she yearned to be a full-time wife and mother. The alternative would have been admitting that she was ambitious, competitive, and bored to tears by homemaking. In the Oak Lawn Heights of 1946, such things were not said.

For the time being, Mary Kay stuck to the Stanley storyline that the flexibility of party-plan selling allowed women to concentrate on their primary duties as wives and mothers. Most soon discovered that selling Stanley was not so easy. By that time, though, they were often using the same line to recruit somebody who was equally eager to get out of the house and equally unable to admit it.

Let someone else do the woman's work: "If a woman delegates some of those household tasks to a housekeeper, she has more time and energy for her family," Mary Kay would say years later, when she was encouraging her sales force to do the same. "This often makes it possible for her to come home after work and devote one or two hours of undivided attention to her children." And there was no denying that one or two hours was an improvement on what she had gotten from her own mother.

Nor did she let the argument rest with a simple defense of what another generation would call "quality time." Ever the resourceful declaimer, Mary Kay stretched logic to the point where it sounded as though mothers should be away from children. "I found that when I was away from my children for a few hours a day, I was a better mother than when I was there all day long. They seemed to appreciate me more and I was more patient with them." Selling was a great way to avoid what Mary Kay called "the screaming-meemies." From there, it was only a short jump to the conclusion: "Being a working mother helped me to remember my priorities: God first, family second, career third."

Somehow that always meant more time at work. "You do well at your work to provide comfort and security for your family," said Mary Kay. "Making God and family top priorities does not demean the role work plays in our lives. After all, where do we spend more of our waking hours than at work?"

That question was clearly rhetorical. In Dallas, as it had been in Houston and would be wherever she went, her workday was as long and hard as she could make it. She might not be doing Stanley secretarial work or staging Stanley parties that entire time, but she would be doing her best to give Stanley any available minute. She would open the door of her Magic Chef oven and put in the tuna casserole with the biscuits on top that Bubba liked. Then go back to Stanley. Potty train Richard. Go back to Stanley. There are no mentions of hobbies, crafts, collections. No long nights listening to the classical canon or racy French novels of the type that the first Mrs. Eckman enjoyed. Whatever else Mary Kay did, she went right back to Stanley.

Eckman was there, coaching her, telling his corny jokes. Neither son had made a career in sales, but this second wife represented a kind of legacy. He could give her the benefit of all those years at Jewel Tea and Fuller and Electrolux and make her understand why Stanley was the finest outfit of them all.

Because Eckman believed that it was. When LeNaire married his college sweetheart, the proud father pondered the matter of a wedding present and concluded that nothing could be better than the entire Stanley product line. "We ended up with over a hundred brushes," Le-Naire's wife remembered. "We had no idea what some of them did." Eckman believed he was bequeathing the essentials of a healthy and happy life, with the good luck of a guarantee that "Stanley products are made from quality materials under clean, sanitary and wholesome conditions by happy and contented people."

Eckman knew that Stanley took care of its own. Now that the war was over, Stanley feted its veterans and gave them jobs as close to their prewar work as possible. Salaried associates, who did not have the unlimited selling opportunity available to Stanley dealers, could partake of its profit-sharing plan.

Dealers like Mary Kay did not get salaries or profit sharing, but they were lavished with what Mr. Bev loved most: education. At the start of his own career, Mr. Bev had been the kind of earnest young man who studied The Power-Book Library, a multivolume series in which a former Methodist minister summarized "the philosophy and practice of personal power." On his quest for self-improvement, he had written away to the International Correspondence Schools of Scranton, the Mc-Wade System of Selling Goods by Mail in Rochester, the Emerson Institute of Efficiency in New York, and a slew of other advertisers in the back pages of magazines like *System: The Magazine of Business* and *Opportunity: The Magazine of Progress.*

Most lasting were the lessons of Arthur Frederick "Fred" Sheldon, the self-designated business scientist who came up with the Rotary Club motto "He Profits Most Who Serves Best." Sheldon taught that service was enlightened self-interest. Customers would gravitate toward a company that "best serves the world with its products." Good employees would gravitate toward a company that best served them.

When Mr. Bev's career finally took off, he gave credit to the Shel-

Lessons in the Fuller Correspondence Service were commissioned from Arthur Frederick Sheldon, author of *The Science of Business.*

Finally, and in conclusion, let us study the law of cause and effect as related to life as a whole, by what must needs be here a brief consideration of what we shall term the four G's, to which the mathematics of life finally resolves itself.

For the sake of convenience we shall designate the four G's as G1, G2, G3 and G4. Each is a triangle, and of equal dimensions, and ultimately, in the mathematics of life, these four triangles are equal.

In the consideration of these triangles we shall consider G4 first. Here it is:

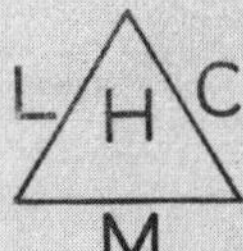

The above triangle represents the concept of Getting, or, Acquisition; and represents that which we all, as normal human beings wish to get, namely, reward or profit.

The letter H in the centre of the triangle stands for Happiness or Content, a thing that we are all seeking consciously or unconsciously.

The letter L on the left of the triangle represents

14

Love of Fellow man. If you prefer to do so, call that element, Respect of Others.

The letter C at the right of the triangle stands for Consciousness. If you prefer the term, call that Self-Respect.

The letter M at the base of the triangle represents Money, the medium of exchange, the symbol of material values.

The acquisition of Happiness or content, as we have seen in a previous chapter necessitates the spiritual and mental values of Love or Respect of those with whom one comes in contact, and consciousness or Self-Respect as well as material gain, represented by sufficient money to enable one to live, and not just exist, if Happiness is to be the result.

Let us look upon some of these things which added together make profit in the broad sense of that term, as the final effect in the mathematics of life.

But what is the cause of that effect? This brings us to triangle G3. Here it is:

15

In Sheldon's science, *H* stands for *Happiness* supported by *M* for *Money.*

don School's course in scientific salesmanship. And when those lessons landed him in Fuller's senior management, Mr. Bev commissioned Sheldon to write *Service and Man Building*, a series of pamphlets that initiated the Fuller Correspondence Service. Written in a style that capitalized *Confidence* and *Respect* and illustrated with diagrams proving Money provided the base for Happiness, Sheldon's dozen pocket-size primers redacted human interaction to a "chain of cause and effect." They were required reading for Eckman and the other ex-Fuller employees who now ran Stanley, and who would pass along their mindset to Mary Kay.

Self-improvement could never stop. "Study and practice! Practice and study!" Mr. Bev said time and again. Dale Carnegie's *How to Win Friends and Influence People* was at the top of his reading list, followed by Elmer Wheeler's *Tested Sentences That Sell*, the bestseller that gave the world "Don't sell the steak, sell the sizzle!" Mr. Bev also endorsed magazines such as *Personality*, *You*, and *Yourself*. He praised *Life* as "useful for a busy person. . . . The beauty of a magazine like that is that we can absorb it pretty fast because it's largely made up of pictures." Mary Kay would subscribe to another of his time-saving titles, *Reader's Digest*, for the rest of her life.

When money poured in during the 1940s, Mr. Bev earmarked yet more for education. Sheldon had died, but Mr. Bev came up with other ways to school associates. Now, besides sales manuals, lessons at weekly sales meetings, training classes, and product tips in *The Stanley Standard*, Mary Kay could practice the sales techniques devised by Elmer E. Nyberg, who became the company's director of education in 1945.

Known around Westfield as "the Professor," a nod to his former employment at NYU's School of Commerce, Nyberg focused on the psychology of sales. Moving beyond memorization, Nyberg began instructing dealers never to disagree and to build each presentation to a climax—then stop, leaving the suspense-filled customer eager to fill an awkward pause. Above all, Nyberg championed enthusiasm. When a customer spoke, the salesperson should "listen enthusiastically."

Practicing what he preached, Nyberg wrote thousands of peppy missives on his "From the Little Red School House" letterhead, which showed a boy in short pants and a girl in pigtails skipping toward a school where Old Glory waved. "Extra Effort Still Wins," said a typical letter. "When you read the biographies of successful men and women, you find without much exception that they rose above others because they were willing to work longer and harder than the average person."

By those criteria, Mary Kay couldn't help but be successful. For her, and the thousands of women signing up to sell Stanley, working "longer and harder than the average person" was nothing new. What made Stanley different was its recognition of their labor. All those tiaras, trophies, and titles. All that education. For those, they were willing to sell their hearts out. From 1939, the last year before its full integration of women, until 1945, the year before Mary Kay's marriage to Eckman, companywide retail jumped from under $1 million to over $13 million. In that last year, a war year, sales were up 143 percent. Everyone expected 1946 to hit $15 million. Or more.

With so many new dealers to supervise and so many parties to stage, Mr. and Mrs. Eckman spent evenings together only if they happened to be attending one of Stanley's rites of recognition. Eckman would put on a boiled shirt with detachable collar and shirtfront, settle a butterfly bow tie beneath its collar points, then slip on the jacket of his peak-lapel tuxedo. Mary Kay would select a stylish dress; do her hair, her lipstick, her jewelry; and put a lacy handkerchief in her pocketbook. Then the two would spend an evening singing Stanley songs, applauding achievements, and listening to success stories.

Mr. Bev said she was getting the equivalent of a bachelor's degree; her major was "People." Everyone from Stanley's director of education to the husband sitting next to her reminded Mary Kay how lucky she was to have such an opportunity. After so many years on Kane Street, she could hardly imagine anything better.

Dallas was packed with prospects. Golf courses were now neighborhoods. Farm towns were now suburbs. Boosters had taken to calling it "Dynamic Dallas."

When Mary Kay got to town, Dallas was still riding a reputation earned during the Texas Centennial Exposition. While she was stuck in Houston with one baby in diapers and another on the way, Dallas had turned into the most exciting place on earth. Through that summer and fall of 1936, well over six million visitors descended on a state fair site remade as a $25 million "Magic City" of Art Moderne buildings featuring the latest in air cooling. The president of the United States visited. Gene Autry made a movie. Next door, Fort Worth staged a rival Frontier Centennial, hiring Broadway showman Billy Rose to come up with attractions like "Sally Rand's Nude Ranch," where topless white women wearing well-placed six-shooters could be observed in zoo-like enclosures.

"The mood of the Centennial was still going strong into the next decade. The mayor had declared an end to the Depression of the 1930s and everything was on go," said Ebby Halliday, who arrived in Dallas in 1938 as a Dust Bowl refugee named Vera Lucille Koch and made herself into a real estate mogul during the city's postwar population boom. "There was an incredible can-do spirit . . . a sense that anything was possible."

From 1940 until August of 1946, the month that Mary Kay moved there, the population of Dallas increased by 50 percent. At the start of that year, planned construction included four hotels, a million-dollar Merchandise Mart, several shopping centers, and a long list of office buildings and factories. Having nearly doubled its sales during the 1940s, Neiman Marcus announced a $1 million annex, then a new store in Highland Park.

Everything was on the upswing. That year's state fair, the first since the war, would be bigger and better than ever. A. Harris & Co., a department store that had been around since 1887, found itself needing an addition. Sears, Roebuck & Co. and J.C. Penney were building stores. There seemed to be no end to the money to be made from all the people moving in. As Mr. and Mrs. Eckman well knew, all those newcomers would be setting up house and attending Stanley parties so they could meet their neighbors.

And Mary Kay was not just pushing old-fashioned stick goods and chemicals anymore. Besides the "Big Three"—Furniture Cream, E-Z Cleaner, Window-Clean—Stanley's line now included products like Lengyel Dusting Powder, Ivar After-Shave Lotion, and perm sets. Products that practically required the dealer to have a stylish appearance.

Mary Kay herself had never looked better. She wore her light-brown hair waved and brushing her shoulders. Eckman's teasing about the awful hat she had worn to her first Dallas rally was easier to take now that she had new hats nestled in pretty round boxes on the shelves upstairs. She was particularly proud of a showy number with ostrich feathers that fluttered over her forehead. People said it looked like something Ginger Rogers would wear.

Customers considered her a smart dresser, a role model, a lady who never looked mussed or wilted even in the drenching Dallas humidity. Nice as could be too. Never forgot to write thank-you notes or mail a card at Christmastime.

She had work, a husband with a steady job, and a nice-size house in an up-and-coming city. Until March, when Eckman collapsed.

Eckman did not believe in giving in to diabetes. Didn't hold with fancy diets. Wouldn't give up cigars. Stuck to a schedule that would have laid low many a younger man.

But the strain was hard to miss. His rings were loose. Suits drooped off his shoulders. By May 14, two days after her twenty-ninth birthday, things were bad enough for Eckman to make out a will. Handwritten, with a couple of hasty spelling mistakes, his simple "To Whom It May Concern" letter was just long enough to specify that Mary Kay would have the Maple Springs house, its furnishings, and his stock in Stanley. Eckman's other bequests were $1,250 to each son and $500 to his sister Maida back in Pennsylvania. Leon should get the Masonic ring with the diamond. LeNaire should have his other ring, the one with a ruby and a diamond.

He wrote that letter just in time. At 7:40 a.m. on June 1, a Sunday of skies stormy enough to augur Armageddon, Eckman had a heart attack in room 262 of Baylor Hospital. He died instantly. As planned, his body was removed to Crane–Shelton–Longley, one of the new funeral homes out on Ross Avenue. The funny little man with the smelly cigars was gone. Mary Kay's second marriage was over in less than a year.

CHAPTER NINE

The God of Abundance

Mary Kay wasted no time filing the will.

The next morning, she was at the county courthouse registering Eckman's last testament with the help of Nathaniel Jacks, a well-connected member of the Dallas bar. Eckman's brief letter had not named an executor, so his widow came prepared with a drafted application for letters of administration and probate, ready to take over the job of executrix herself. At that point, there was no reason to believe that there would be any problems over the division of assets. LeNaire, at least, had been glad that his father had remarried, but Leon was moodier and might be trouble. You never could tell.

In their petition, Mary Kay and her lawyer listed Eckman's assets: $4,905 equity in the Maple Springs homestead, another $3,000 worth of furnishings, $2,000 in bonds, $1,000 for his car, and another $2,000 in his bank account. There was no mention of his stock in Stanley Home Products. Or why the home equity was $1,000 less than the cash Eckman had put down on the house the year before. The application stressed Eckman's debt to the bank without mentioning that it was the mortgage on her house, as well as unknown debts to "other persons," making it sound logical that principal legatee Mary Kay should also settle those debts as administratrix. No mention was made of life insurance. None passed to his sons.

Funeral arrangements were next. The death was expected, so family now gathered in Dallas: Leon and his wife, Lucylle, from Los Angeles; LeNaire, traveling by himself from Wilmington; Eckman's former mother-in-law, Mary "Grandma Danny" Snyder, coming from Colorado. Other family planned to convene in Eckman's hometown of Apollo, Pennsylvania, where his body would be buried.

Mary Kay moved down her checklist. Newspapers called. Names, spellings, photographs supplied. Paid notices ran on Tuesday, giving the time of the funeral the next day, the address of the church, and the list of survivors: Mary Kay, sons Leon and LeNaire, two brothers and two sisters back in Pennsylvania, a sister in Los Angeles. No mention was made of Mary Kay's children.

The death also rated a short obituary in Dallas dailies. That same Tuesday, *The Dallas Morning News* repeated the information in the paid notice and included a cartoonish close-up of a grinning Eckman, giving his age as fifty-five, not the actual fifty-six, and padding his résumé by calling him a Master Mason, which he had not been since the middle of the Depression, when his membership, like so many others, lapsed for nonpayment of dues.

On Wednesday morning, the sheriff's office posted Mary Kay's application for probate of will and letters testamentary at the Dallas County Courthouse, setting the hearing for June 16, less than two weeks later. Since both of Eckman's sons were in Dallas when the writ was made public, everything was on the up and up.

That afternoon at two o'clock, the funeral was held at Highland Park Presbyterian with both blood relations and Eckman's "Stanley family" in attendance, the muggy Dallas day made more pleasant by the sanctuary's air-conditioning and stained-glass windows. The presiding reverend was another draw. Instead of the local minister, Mary Kay had booked Harry Sarles, a former army chaplain who served as assistant minister at City Temple Presbyterian downtown. Sarles had made a name for himself as a motivational speaker: a Protestant pastor who founded

Leadership Institutes, roused Rotary Clubs, and addressed synagogues. He was the ideal choice for a salesman's memorial.

It was a good turnout for a weekday afternoon. There were Scripture readings and teary eyes and plenty of good words about Stanley Home Products. Eckman would have been in his element.

After the service, the family made the fifteen-minute drive back to the house, where the widow acted as hostess and posed for snapshots. By then, the temperature had hit the mid-nineties. As ever, Mary Kay's appearance was immaculate: her brown hair curled and topped by a toque, her black dress worn with high-heeled black sandals. Maybe she was not wearing that year's New Look, but in Dallas, where locals had formed a "Little Below the Knee" club to protest the longer, leg-concealing skirts proposed by Christian Dior, no one thought much of the latest Paris fashions. To the rumpled, somewhat dazed in-laws gathered at the house, Mary Kay looked like a movie star that day.

Fulfilling wifely duties to the letter, the Widow Eckman then made the trip north, accompanying the body to Armstrong County, where

After the funeral (*left to right*): Leon and Lucylle Eckman, Mary Kay, LeNaire Eckman, Mary "Grandma" Snyder.

Eckman's siblings and LeNaire's wife, Evalyn, joined his sons for the interment. At the second service, as at the first, the family commented favorably on Mary Kay's smart style. "Nice as could be," they declared, a little in awe of her. Decades later, Evalyn, who was the same age as Mary Kay, recalled her stepmother-in-law wearing a light-blue dress with a wide belt. Evalyn also remembered that, by the end of the day, Mary Kay's pretty dress was covered in the coal dust that seemed to get into everything in that part of Pennsylvania.

Back in Dallas, Mary Kay got ready for the June 16 hearing. Since the will was holographic, she and her attorney came to court with two expert witnesses: Stanley stalwarts able to swear to the authenticity of Eckman's handwriting and signature. Everything went as expected. The application was unopposed; the ruling was made in Mary Kay's favor. She took the oath of administration and went to a guarantor to post the $10,000 bond. Appraisers were appointed, then the slog of settling the estate got underway. Inventory and appraisal were completed in August, taxes paid in October, attorney's fees paid in February, a final accounting filed in March. Still, it would take almost a year after his death—May of 1948—until Eckman's estate was discharged and his Stanley stocks were safely in her name.

For all its glories, there was no security in direct sales. No salary. No stipend. No sabbatical or sick leave. Stop selling and you would end up right back where you started. Or worse.

In the year after Eckman's death, Mary Kay was left with three children to support in a house that she could not afford. Not if she was selling part time, as Stanley assumed women were. Not on the $70 in monthly child support that she was supposed to be getting from Rogers. A good chunk of the estate's cash had gone to Eckman's three bequests. Lawyer's fees had taken some of the rest.

Bills kept coming. The kids grew out of clothes. They needed things for school. Modest as Mary Kay's $48-a-month mortgage might be, it seemed like a lot to someone who had never paid rent. All those big words about betting on yourself and investing in the future translated to being stuck with more cans of Quick Lustre and Rug Shampoo than you could use in a lifetime. With no cash coming in.

In 1947, a top Stanley dealer cleared about $1,500 a year: less than half the average annual salary for a man, but good money for a woman. There was no chance that Mary Kay, a secretary, would move into the boss's job, no matter how smart she was. Not when there were men ahead of her. Eckman's replacement, John Brittingham, was soon installed in the office at 86½ Highland Park Shopping Village, where he would build on Eckman's foundation and be promoted to regional manager, Stanley's highest rank.

Mary Kay was just another dealer now. There would be as many Stanley celebrations as ever—the territory was booming—but she would have to earn her invitation to each one. There would be no more of Eckman's corny jokes, no more of his tips and tricks, no special status.

Mary Kay must have met a lot of people during her first year in Dallas. Later, she never mentioned any. When she spoke about this time in her life, she talked only about selling. Stanley was reaching eighteen million people a year, about one in every eight people in the United States, and growing faster than ever. A valued member of the "Stanley family," Mary Kay was part of that glory. As long as she kept singing the praises of its toilet bowl brushes and E-Z Cleaner. Until she could not.

The way she usually told the story, her sickness started like a flu. She ached all over. Then she hurt so much that she could barely move. Weeks passed. Nothing improved. Getting out of bed took effort. Doctors diagnosed rheumatoid arthritis. In other versions, it was simply "rheumatism." Years afterward, when she was reframing her life story into object lessons for her sales force, she wrote that specialists at Scott and White Memorial Hospital "told me it was progressing so rapidly that within a matter of months I would be a hopeless cripple."

In Dallas, there was no one to take care of her. In Houston, there was no one either. By 1947, the Sixth Ward was a run-down neighborhood of recent immigrants and absentee landlords. Lula had rented out 2111 Kane Street and moved to rooms above Wagner's Café, where she took in boarders. Rogers, who would stay married to Leona until the day he died, had found himself a sales job and moved to the other side of town.

Then there was the problem of supporting herself. No matter how fast she typed, she couldn't feed three kids and pay her mortgage on a secretary's salary. Selling had been the only work where effort and outcome seemed to have any connection. But taking so much as a month off would mean starting over. Stanley had over fifteen thousand dealers. More were signing up every day. Any one of them would have been happy to have her territory.

Direct selling taught you to take responsibility. The message was pounded into you at every sales meeting and every rally, spelled out on every bit of paper that came your way. You were your own boss. You decided your own earnings. You controlled how far you went. You and you alone.

At Stanley, where a "Program of Self-Analysis" was point number two in the Seven-Point Plan, Mary Kay heard a message of self-determination that seemed to encompass every aspect of existence. "What's the matter with me? There's always something. . . . What's holding me back?" Mr. Bev adjured dealers to ask themselves. "Lack of going out there and trying over and over again?"

From there, he was always good for a quote from Ralph Waldo Emerson's "Self-Reliance," a stanza of inspirational poetry, or a paraphrase of one of Winston Churchill's wartime orations. Then he might segue into a reading of the Johnny Mercer song "Ac-Cent-Tchu-Ate the Positive," uttering its snappy lyrics in a voice slow and sonorous enough for Shakespeare.

You've got to accentuate the positive.
Eliminate the negative.

To that Mr. Bev might add, "We do not urge you to do better than other people, but to do better than you yourself have done." There could be no letting up, no slowing down, no pessimism, no depression.

Every author on the Stanley reading list reinforced that message: Dale Carnegie, who framed the biographies of men like Abraham Lincoln and Ulysses Grant as lifelong struggles against illness and adversity; Norman Vincent Peale, who determined, "People get sick largely because they cannot control and discipline their minds."

Maybe she wasn't trying hard enough.

Mary Kay knuckled down. Latched on to the affirmative. Smiled her way through more Stanley parties. Ignored doctors who told her to rest. In a chapter of her autobiography called "Put On a Happy Face," she would write, "I realized that in order to be successful, I had to leave my personal problems at home."

When there weren't enough parties on her calendar, she knocked on doors, "prospecting." She would put on lipstick, heels, sometimes that fur piece that she was so proud of, then, appearing as prosperous as possible, pick a promising street. "In Texas in those days people were more than happy to open the door for you," a Stanley dealer remembered. "You would show them a brochure, explain the advantages of throwing a party, be invited in for an iced tea."

Most of the time, iced tea was all you got. If it was a bad day, Mary Kay might knock on dozens of doors before she found anyone willing to listen. If it was a good day, she would be turned down nine times out of ten. Eventually, though, someone always agreed to a party. If you smiled like you didn't have a care in the world. If you talked enough. If you knocked on enough doors.

Three decades later, telling her story to an audience raised on pop psychology, Mary Kay diagnosed herself as suffering from self-pity. She was running her own company by then, trying to show women how to take control of their lives. "One by one, my problems seemed to go away," she would write. "But if I had allowed myself to be depressed, I wouldn't have done a good job selling, and my problems would have been compounded."

At the end of the 1940s, Mary Kay saw her recovery as proof that good things were bound to happen if she believed in herself. Just like Dale Carnegie promised in books and broadcasts. Just like Mr. Bev always said. She felt better, she made more money, and, by the summer of 1948, she had inherited Eckman's Stanley stock.

The next summer, things got even better. On June 7, 1949, Stanley Home Products had its long-expected public offering, which sold out within two hours. Eckman had done his job well, delivering so much territory that, by the time of the stock offer, Texas led the entire company. The next month, the company opened a Dallas distribution center to serve customers in Texas, Louisiana, Arkansas, and part of Oklahoma, plus its plentiful but unofficial south-of-the-border sales. Mary Kay's territory was a gold mine.

If she was not a rich widow, she was more comfortable than most. In her early thirties, she looked like a woman with money in the bank and property in her name. Her figure had gotten fuller, but with the help of a girdle, she got herself into dresses that made her the model of a prosperous matron. She drew brows that were more conventional than the high-flying pencil lines of her teenage years. She wore her brown hair shorter, more tightly curled. She owned hats and that fur piece. She had grown into the straight nose and strong bones inherited from her mother and grandmother. She was a handsome woman.

To hear her tell it, neither doubt nor depression ever crossed her mind again. Come what may, she stayed on schedule: up at five, housework, wake the kids, get them to school, then Stanley. When the kids came home, she got dinner ready, fed them, scared up a babysitter for Richard if his sister wasn't around, then drove off to Stanley parties. Later she said she carted the kids to Galveston for two weeks every summer. Even though Galveston was nearly three hundred miles from Dallas. Even though, with her fair complexion, Mary Kay didn't much favor the sun or the Gulf.

And she certainly didn't like wasting time on vacations.

Stanley trips were a different story.

Once a year, she was treated like a queen. Joining other dealers from her home branch, she would make her way to company headquarters for the three and a half days allocated to the Texas Area during Stanley's summerlong rotation of sales rallies.

Most dealers paid their way to Westfield. Mary Kay got there courtesy of the company, her reward for having won yet another sales contest. After the long, long bus ride from Texas, she, and the other women with whom she might be sharing a room, checked in at the huge Hotel Kimball in Springfield, with its mahogany floors and marble lobby and history of hosting headline makers and Hollywood stars. She wouldn't have missed this for the world.

At the Kimball, the women barely had time to unpack their evening gowns before being whisked onto buses for the ten-mile trip to Stanley Park. On the way, they sang Stanley songs. Once arrived, they sang some more. Passing the park's wishing well, they tossed in pennies to make their dreams come true. Assembling in an open-air pavilion backed by the blue-tinted Berkshire Mountains, they recited the Stanley Prayer and sang the Stanley Prayer Song.

To Westfield locals, Stanley Park was a pretty spot for company picnics, school ceremonies, or Fourth of July with the family. To the Stanley faithful, it was a sacred place: Mecca, Jerusalem, and the Garden of Eden rolled into one. Dealers compared it with the Holy Land and referred to their annual visits as Pilgrimages with a capital *P.*

Legend credits the genesis of Stanley Park to a miserably muggy evening in 1943 when, unable to sit in the company's unair-conditioned office a minute longer, executives adjourned to a glade purchased for a factory site. Conducting business there proved to be so much more pleasant that, when darkness fell, the men circled their cars and wrapped things up with the help of their headlights. Seeing the Good Lord's hand in that success, Mr. Bev forgot about the factory and earmarked the acreage for the creation of Stanley Park.

Mr. Bev dedicating another plaque in Stanley Park, accompanied by a boy backpacking his portable amplifier.

Mr. Bev had started selling as a means to an end, and that never-achieved end had been a college degree in horticulture. Nothing was too good or too grandiose for Stanley Park. After stocking the park with memorials and plaques, Mr. Bev added themed gardens, themed outbuildings, and, by decade's end, a ninety-eight-foot gold-domed carillon tower dedicated to world peace. Trying to keep the boss's mind on business, national sales manager Albert F. "Reggie" Regensburger whipped up his sales units until they were vying to endow amenities. But the more they gave, the more Mr. Bev behaved like a man reunited with the love of his youth.

Stanley Park stood as irrefutable proof that "the Stanley way of doing business" was more than a gimmick to sell brushes. Bequeathed to the public in 1949 and endowed in perpetuity by the Frank Stanley

Beveridge Foundation, the park would grow from thirty-eight acres to about three hundred, with the company retaining ownership only of the pavilion area to ensure continuance of its Pilgrimages.

Because no other company had anything like that park. A pilgrim had only to lay eyes on the park to understand the scope of Mr. Bev's ambition that Stanley Home Products could save the world. From its beginning, Stanley had conducted sales rallies like old-time camp meetings. From 1944, those rallies had the classic camp meeting setting too. Religious references were everywhere. Wearing a boutonniere cut from his own garden, Mr. Bev stood at a pulpit and told pilgrims:

> You are here for a period of refiring—refiring your determination to go out and have outstanding sales as Stanley dealers. . . . As we go about our work, we must expect to meet with some reverses from time to time. It is our duty to overcome these. It is our duty not to pay too much attention to these. It is our duty to think of the grove in Stanley Park.

To free the pilgrims' minds for finer things, the company took care of practical matters. Women whose lives were a sunup-to-sundown slog of housework, cooking, and childminding had no worries once they got to Westfield. All they had to do was get dressed and show up. Sitting in the pavilion with her unit, Mary Kay was welcomed by E. J. "Ted" Samuel, the director of public relations, and C. C. "Mr. Mac" McPherson, the executive sales manager. During those three and a half days, nothing was too good for her.

Piling into buses after being greeted by top brass, the pilgrims sang their way to Easthampton. Welcomed by a huge hand-lettered sign on the side of the Stanley factory, they pulled up to the main entrance, known as the "Door of Opportunity." Touring the plant in groups of twenty-five, they peered at the laboratory and gawked at its five thousand feet of conveyor belts, saw a dispensary that cared for workers who felt out of sorts, and learned that Stanley served its workers free coffee and doughnuts each morning. They heard that Stanley was considered such a fine place to work that over five thousand locals were on the waiting list for its nine hundred jobs.

Then they peeked inside Mr. Bev's office and read the motivating mottoes on his walls. If they knew where to look, they could also see that Mr. Bev's upholstered wing chair had built-in speakers so the hard-of-hearing Mr. Bev could lean back and look thoughtful while he listened to sound amplified by microphones hidden on the sides of his desk. As they left, Mary Kay and her fellow pilgrims broke into song again, serenading the tour guides, elevator operator, and loading dock crew with company songs.

In the afternoon, they sang their way back to Stanley Park, gathering in the pavilion to applaud each other and savor high praise of the Texas Area's achievements. Then came the procession to the Enchanted Oak. Heeled and hatted as if she were headed to a ladies' luncheon, Mary Kay picked her way down dirt paths that wound past the fountain, the statue of Saint Francis, and the boulder with a brass plaque of Joyce Kilmer's "Trees" poem.

Joining hands, the pilgrims formed a ring around the old oak, which had been considered beyond redemption until Mr. Bev commissioned tree surgeons to cut away its decay and patch its trunk with cement. In between songs—"In the Garden," "Just a Song at Twilight," "Give Me That Good Old Stanley Spirit"—Mr. Bev began his ritual retelling of how the now-mighty oak had been slated for the axe. Told them again how he had never given up hope. Described how he had ordered its scars tarred over, two thirds of its trunk reinforced with concrete. How faith and determination had brought about the flourishing specimen that stood before them. Then Mr. Bev promised that a wish made in this sacred grove would come true "if you go home and work at it." Mulling that, Mary Kay and the other dealers made their way back to the buses as, right behind them, a local boy followed at a discreet distance, clearing the paths of fallen leaves and footprints to make everything perfect for the pilgrims' next day.

As they would be at Mary Kay's own Seminars, the second and third days of Pilgrimages were given over to pep talks and pointers. Mr. Mac would reappear to remind them that everything was up to them: "A dealer can make a good living if he works. If you don't work, the Lord help you, because nobody else will be able to!"

Speaking with the authority of a man who had written plays performed on big-city stages, Elmer "the Professor" Nyberg passed along professional tips on hooking an audience, along with admonitions that they had heard hundreds of times before. "People do respond to gentility," he reminded. "Never argue."

Toward the end of those days, Reggie himself would appear, stage-lit by the slanting afternoon sun like a movie star in a follow spot. Dazzling them with the possibilities of direct selling. Riveting them with hour after hour of inspirational anecdotes. Reeling off axioms like "Work will win when wishing won't." Sitting in the pavilion, Mary Kay wrote down every word. Including the ones she had heard so many times before.

In the evenings, she heard more speeches and watched talent shows, fashion shows, skits featuring burly men dressed up as housewives, and spoofs, like the one put on by the sales unit that sang "Mañana" while clicking castanets made of Swirl Mixers. There was always a chance to hobnob with managers, because, as Reggie reminded them, there were no snooty "swivel chair artists" among Stanley executives. In the local bowling league, vice presidents played on the same team as guys from the loading dock.

The last night was Awards Night, time for announcements of prizes and achievements. Branch managers read their reports in ascending order as the Texas Area held its breath in suspense. Individual accomplishments won group cheers. That could be you up there.

Seven years of service earned a dealer a ten-karat-gold Stanley lapel pin set with a tiny diamond, accompanied by a corsage of flowers from Mr. Bev's garden. Setting a sales record might earn a $25 savings bond. Winning a sales contest could be worth as much as a set of luggage. Mary Kay would hear her name, shake Mr. Bev's hand, relish the recognition.

"We want every one of you to grow mentally, spiritually, physically, and volitionally," Mr. Bev reminded the pilgrims. "When we come to Westfield, we get a new vision of our business. It is like being on a mountaintop. But we cannot remain on the mountaintop. No growth, no development, is possible without the ceaseless toil of the valley."

Too soon, the Pilgrimage would wind up with a stirring sing-along of "God Bless America." Then it was time for the buses, the hotel, the trip home to Texas, and the long year until the next Pilgrimage.

Mary Kay returned ready to better her best. Reminded that Stanley was not about peddling toilet bowl brushes and E-Z Cleaner but about improving yourself and serving your fellow man. Fired up from hearing Reggie and Mr. Bev, she left Massachusetts determined to win whatever contest came her way.

One year, when her branch held a contest to see who could get the most recruits in a week, Mary Kay handed off her parties and the income that came with them, signing up seventeen recruits. For that, she got a tiara, a sash, and the title of "Miss Dallas."

She could not have been prouder. She knew other women would feel the same: "I was convinced that I wasn't the only competitive woman around. I believed other women would work hard for recognition, the way I did, even when sometimes they wouldn't work that hard for money."

Soon she met a perfect example.

It was a dark and stormy night.

In January of 1949, through freezing rain so severe that the next morning's paper reported over fifty fender benders, Mary Kay set out to stage a Stanley party.

Nights like this were the reason that Reggie stuffed his sales force full of inspirational verses. Every Pilgrimage, every song at every weekly meeting, and every bit of company literature conditioned dealers to see adversity as a test of character. By this point in her Stanley career, Mary Kay would have heard Berton Braley's "Opportunity" hundreds of times:

With doubt and dismay you are smitten
You think there's no chance for you, son?
Why, the best books haven't been written
The best race hasn't been run.

"You never knew what [a party] might bring," one Stanley dealer remembered. "You just kept going. This could be the one that changed your life." The next party might lead to that downline of bookings and sales and recruitment that landed you on easy street.

For Mary Kay, this would be the one, although the night would get worse before it got better.

Making it to the address safely, she inched her way up icy steps to discover a starter apartment with a tiny bedroom and a single sad room that functioned as kitchen, living room, and dining room. Besides its half-size refrigerator and narrow stove, Mary Kay's demonstration area was crammed with the newlywed hostess's sofa, table, and two chairs, plus a couple of folding chairs borrowed for the evening. "It was a bitterly cold night, when the streets were sheeted with ice and the radio was warning people not to leave their homes—but I had a Stanley party scheduled," Mary Kay recalled. "I was conscientious, and if I had a party booked, I went. So I did."

As Mary Kay later told the story, there was one guest, a Sunday school teacher who had come only because she knew how badly the young hostess wanted the free hostess gift. The treacherous drive had been a total waste. No use even doing the demonstration.

The Sunday school teacher told a different story. She remembered three guests that evening. She also remembered that Mary Kay went through a full dem as if she were in a stately home surrounded by a large audience, all the while reminding them how important it was for a wife to keep a clean home for her family.

In either case, when all present sat down to cake and coffee, Mary Kay and the Sunday school teacher found they had an uncanny amount in common. Both had been bright little girls loaded with responsibilities beyond their years. Both had weak fathers, absent mothers. Both had graduated from high school early and gone straight into bad marriages followed by teenage pregnancies, divorce, and stints as single mothers. Both arrived in Dallas as adults. Both liked music and nice clothes. Both were go-getters. Smart as whips. Able to talk the legs off a chair.

The Sunday school teacher, Mary C. Crowley, later recalled, "The two of us just clicked. We agreed about God's being a God of Abundance who wanted us to have lots of good things, both material and spiritual."

For all the fervor of her belief, the God of Abundance had not made Himself much manifest in Crowley's life before her move to Dallas. Born in Slater, Missouri, in 1915, Mary Elizabeth Weaver came from another family that had fallen on hard times long before the Depression. When she was eighteen months old, her mother died of pneumonia three months after giving birth to her brother, and Crowley was sent to live with maternal grandparents on a farm in Sweet Springs, Missouri.

She would not meet her father again until she was six and a half years old. By that time, Lennox Grove Weaver had married a woman wicked enough to be a stepmother out of the Brothers Grimm. While her father was often absent teaching accounting and Latin in remote parts of Washington state, the little girl took over all the shopping, cooking, cleaning, and household management. When she turned thirteen, a court ruled her stepmother unfit and allowed the girl to return to her adored grandparents, who were then managing a farm in Arkansas.

Like Mary Kay, she was clever and hardworking enough to condense her schooling by a year. Unlike Mary Kay, she was also able to skip another year. After graduation, she married high school sweetheart Joe Carter and had her first child the following year. Hers was a bad marriage, made more difficult by the Depression and living with in-laws in small-town Sherman, Texas. Like Mary Kay, she soon found herself pregnant with a second child. She then concluded, "If Don and Ruthie were to have the bare essentials, it would be up to me to provide them. My husband could not shoulder responsibility."

She could. With two babies at home, she baked bread and sewed—charging twenty-five cents for a cotton dress—to eke out her income. When her daughter turned one, old enough to be left with someone else all day, she marched into a local emporium and offered to work for free so that they would see how good she was. In short order, she was on salary, winning the store's weekly $1 sales prize, bringing home $8 a week, and looking to move on.

Next, she got herself a $100 Rotary Club scholarship loan to study accounting in Dallas, working full time at an insurance agency there during the day, taking courses at Southern Methodist University at night to become a certified public accountant, and taking the bus seventy-five miles back to Sherman each weekend to see her children and work another job at Montgomery Ward. By 1939, she was able to move the children to Dallas, find herself a nice little house about the size of the ones in the Sixth Ward, and hire an African American housekeeper named Minerva to do the woman's work. On weekends, she taught Sunday school downtown at First Baptist, where she devoutly tithed a tenth of her tiny income.

By the time she met Mary Kay, the God of Abundance had delivered a new husband in the form of former army captain David M. Crowley Jr., a war hero who had won a Bronze Star during the Battle of the Bulge. A strapping six-footer who was three years her junior, Crowley met his future wife when she worked at the insurance company. He then wrote to her every day of the four years that World War II kept them apart. Wedding in 1948 after a seven-year courtship, Crowley would enjoy a second marriage as different from her first as day from night.

Not that happiness slowed her down. A paragon of Southern Baptist womanhood, Crowley taught Sunday school, sang in the church choir, kept her house spick-and-span, overproduced, overachieved, and overdelivered in every way she could. She became notorious for concocting recipes like the lime Jell-O filled with cream cheese, crushed pineapple, whipped cream, pecans, and marshmallows that her family referred to as "Mary's Green Goop." She also kept her eight-to-five job as an accountant at Purse & Company, a family-run furniture manufacturer where, when she finished her other work, she could pop into its showroom to dispense decorating advice and do some selling.

Because CPA or not, Crowley was born to sell. In an industry where aw-shucks admissions of shyness seemed obligatory—Alfred C. Fuller told the world of his timidity, Mr. Bev bragged of his bashfulness—Crowley reveled in speaking to strangers. Putting them on to a good thing was doing God's work. Only her reluctance to leave a steady paycheck kept her from going into sales full time.

Crowley remembered her CPA salary as $100 a week. Mary Kay remembered it as $66. Either way, it was almost what a man might earn. Both agreed that before the cake crumbs were cleared that first night, Mary Kay was doing her best to recruit Crowley: boasting of the money she made, claiming that flexible hours allowed her to be home when her children finished school, reminding Crowley of time saved commuting. Working every angle.

Crowley resisted, but not for long. When Mary Kay drove to Crowley's home to drop off the Stanley order, she tried again. This time, she found Crowley more receptive. "The idea of selling to other women in their homes really appealed to me," Crowley later wrote. "As for sharing God's love, what better way than to be invited into homes where people didn't know Him? Why, I could even help women with their home-decorating, too."

The God of Abundance blessed them both. The Sunday school teacher was a natural with Stanley, just as she had been with everything else. She grasped the tax benefits of an at-home business right away. Trained in cost analysis, she realized the benefit of ordering in bulk and drafted Don and Ruthie into divvying up orders. Before long, she had an assembly line on her screened porch. Within months, she'd quit accountancy to sell Stanley full time.

This was followed by the discovery that she had been misled. "I really wasn't always at home when the kids arrived from school. Being a full-time salesperson means putting in a full-time workweek." But like many a recruit before and after, Crowley could find ways to work around that. Balancing books had been fine, but direct selling was a higher calling with higher earnings. The God of Abundance had sent Mary Kay into her life.

His blessings soon devolved on Mary Kay too. As one of about 1,200 unit leaders, she watched her unit ascend Stanley's ladder of success on the strength of Crowley's many, many sales. Crowley was a one-woman whirlwind, a force of nature put on this earth to prove that if you believed in yourself, you could make anything happen. Crowley never seemed to doubt.

"Everyone wants to be like someone. Mary Kay wanted to be like Mary Crowley," a sales director at Mary Kay's company would say after years of observing their complicated relationship.

Only three years older, Crowley became Mary Kay's friend, her confidante, her star performer. They were Mary C. and Mary K. The two were like sisters. Soon they would be sisters-in-law.

In the meantime, Mary Kay got married to somebody else.

CHAPTER TEN

"A House Is Not a Home"

"A house is not a home unless you make it that way," Mary Kay told prospects as she tilted her head and smiled.

Back at Maple Springs Drive, much of the homemaking was delegated to Lenola Carter, the African American woman who lived with her husband, Taft, a grocery store porter, in the cottage in Mary Kay's backyard. Thanks to Carter's help with the kids and housework, plus speed honed during years of challenging herself to make a bed in two minutes flat, Mary Kay could whip through domestic chores in record time. That gave her more hours to devote to Stanley Home Products.

By 1950, the city directory and telephone book no longer listed her as the widow of Clarence B. Eckman. She now went by "Mary K. Eckman." When census takers came, she informed them that she was a supervisor for a chemical products company and had a workweek of forty-five hours, a total that sounded laughably low to anyone who knew her. Raising three children while maintaining an irreproachable home and impeccable appearance, Mary Kay saw herself as proof that a woman could excel at a career without shirking her domestic duties or forfeiting her femininity.

Without surrendering her Stanley career, she set out to complete the picture of perfect postwar womanhood. On June 9, 1950, another humid Friday, Mary Kay married Alfred "Al" Lewis Miller, who had married Mrs. Lila Rose Garrett the previous July and divorced her by February. Mary Kay's other weddings had been Baptist and Presbyterian. Miller's most recent had been Methodist. This time, they used a Congregational minister.

Then Miller moved in. Closer to Mary Kay's age than her last husband, Miller had nothing that could be called a career. The year before, he had been employed at the Inspiration Room, the in-store art gallery at Sanger's, a department store where the ladies of Oak Lawn Heights shopped on "Thrift Thursdays" or took the kids to see Santa. By the time he married Mary Kay, Miller was selling art at Joseph Sartor Galleries, where the well-to-do came to buy pictures when they decorated their homes. Sartor sold the kind of art that Mary Kay loved. She thought about doing some painting herself someday and, four decades later, would dabble in acrylics. In 1950, she just didn't have the time.

That summer, Mary Kay, who had not stayed in touch with Eckman's sons, shipped them his remaining furniture and mementos. This would be her last contact with the family, who never associated the founder of Mary Kay Cosmetics with her ten months as their stepmother.

Stanley had overtaken Fuller Brush.

In 1950, when sales figures for the previous year were tabulated, Stanley sales were $35 million to its forerunner's $32.25 million. When *Time* magazine ran an article called "The Brush Man" in January of 1950, there could be no doubt that the headline referred to Mr. Bev and not his former boss.

Time opened that story at a Stanley party in Springfield, Massachusetts, quoting the corny jokes of dealer Mrs. Mabel Hayden (Stanley combs "never go to the dentist because their teeth stay in") and calculating that, during a forty five minute party, Hayden showed fifty items, took $43 in orders, and earned a $14 commission.

The article made it sound like easy money. No mention was made of sales meetings, orders, deliveries, or collections. A reader couldn't help but make mental comparisons to waitressing, tending a cash register, or working in a typing pool. In any of those, a woman would be lucky to earn $30 for a fifty-hour week.

Paid publicity could not have made a better case for selling Stanley, but there was plenty of that too. After years of advertising in the likes of *American Legion Magazine*, Stanley's marketing department began sending slicks to big-circulation periodicals *Ladies' Home Journal*, *Good Housekeeping*, and *Life*. Using a format meant to mimic magazine features, most advertorials had a comic strip or photograph to illustrate the ease of holding a Stanley party. When a hostess was shown, she was often a middle-aged white woman who looked like she did not need the money. "Charming Mrs. Albert W. Stender [described as "wife of the owner of New Jersey's fine hotels"] says: 'I like being a Stanley Hostess.'"

The following January, *Coronet*, a magazine with a bigger circulation than *Time*, ran "The Stanley Way of Making Money," which told of a young couple who earned so much as Stanley dealers that the husband was able to quit his job as an aviation engineer. Then the story segued into Stanley's "It's never too late" philosophy, compared Mr. Bev with a Horatio Alger hero, and set forth soaring sales and recruitment figures: "In 1949, the company's 17,000 dealers, many of them women working only part-time, collected an estimated $66,000,000." It was all there for anyone to read.

Mary Kay could not stop now. With Stanley, there was always an event to attend, always a contest to enter. Trophies, titles, and crowns to be won. When he acquired a ranch in Florida, Mr. Bev added visits there as a reward for sales achievements. And always there were Pilgrimages to be made. Selling Stanley may not have been as easy as the magazines made it sound, but its promise was limitless. Mr. Bev said so himself.

In 1951, Mr. Bev commissioned an internal survey of Stanley dealers, showing that the majority were female (93.7 percent), were married

(94.6 percent), and had children under the age of eighteen (75.7 percent). Their preferred reading was *Life*, *Good Housekeeping*, and *Ladies' Home Journal*, followed by *Reader's Digest.* They appreciated the "treatment and cooperation which the company gives to them" and praised its hostess gifts. Hidden among those numbers were the differences between Mary Kay and most Stanley dealers. Few considered Stanley a full-time job (34.2 percent) and few had spent more than five years with the company (14.6 percent). Most had worked a year or less. Most made under $2,000. What they considered a stopgap was what Mary Kay called a career.

With Miller, whatever his faults, Mary Kay had again found a husband who did not expect her to stay at home. He was a salesman, a bit of a sweet talker, but he had no objection to a wife who worked. Miller was all in favor of her making good money; no sooner had he married Mary Kay than he was able to convince the courts to dismiss a debt and sequestration case against him. Like Rogers, Miller would go from one job to the next without ever landing in anything that could be called a life's work. The year after their marriage, he would be a manufacturer's rep. He would move on from that too. Mary Kay was left to make her visits to Lula or Grandma Hastings without him.

And Mrs. Mary Kathlyn Wagner Rogers Eckman Miller was not about to let her new husband or anybody else take time away from her pursuit of sales awards. She was outstaging Stanley parties every chance she got: passing out leaflets showing how Stanley products made a housewife's role easier, distributing pamphlets with public service messages that extolled that role.

Company literature missed no opportunity to convey the symbolism of a spotless home. *A Guide to Homemaking*, the twenty-eight-page paean to domesticity that Stanley published at its own expense and donated to the Girl Scouts, was full of fine words. "Everything we do, and the kind of people we grow up to be, is influenced by the spirit of our homes." Showing them what they had to look forward to, the authors included a chapter titled "Look Pretty, Please!" advising Scouts to attire themselves in cotton dresses and aprons with deep pockets. "You'll find it more fun if you dress to do housecleaning, too."

Mary Kay bustled through her own house in a blur of cleaning and straightening and cooking, checked off every duty on her list, then got out again. She was almost never home. She didn't need to be. By the early 1950s, only Richard, the baby of the family, lived with her. Bubba now called himself Ben Jr. and had moved back to Houston to live with Ben Sr. Marylyn had moved back to Houston to live with Lula, who still worked the same hours she had worked when Mary Kay was in high school.

Like her mother, Marylyn would enroll at John H. Reagan Senior High School and rush into marriage. On March 8, 1952, sixteen-year-old Marylyn swore to a justice of the peace that she was nineteen, left high school, and eloped with twenty-year-old Korean War vet Vernon Schumacher. On November 17, she became a teenage mother, like her mother, grandmothers, and great-grandmothers before her. Like her daughters and granddaughters after.

At thirty-four, Mary Kay was considered middle-aged. She was a grandmother who had been divorced and widowed and, it was now becoming clear, would soon be divorced again. Like her father and first two husbands, Miller was often away from home. Then seemed to vanish entirely.

In the leafy, picture-perfect precinct of Oak Lawn Heights, that didn't give her much to brag about. Chatting up prospects at parties, she kept mum about her marital history, another habit learned from Lula, who identified herself as the Widow Wagner, listed herself as "Mrs. Wagner" in the phone book, kept working at a café named after a long-dead first husband, and otherwise behaved as if her marriage to Murphy had never happened.

In business, however, Mary Kay was a unit manager at a company that staged ten thousand parties a day—soon it would be twelve thousand—and stood at the top of America's $1 billion direct-selling industry. Its advertisements in *Life* and *Good Housekeeping* set just the right tone for recruiting housewives without antagonizing husbands. Some used the slogan "Stanley Offers Opportunity for Women" along with a portrait of the very proper-looking Miss O'Brien, "Stanley's Executive Vice President, Treasurer, and General Manager."

A dozen years after Stanley adopted the party plan, most unit managers were women, while all salaried executives were men. It was the same everywhere else. "Help Wanted, Male" ads for sales executives offered "guaranteed salary" jobs with retirement, insurance, and vacation. "Help Wanted, Female" ads read "Housewives everywhere: Earn cash in your spare time," and specified whether the applicant must be "young," "attractive," or something else: "Waitresses over 200 pounds, apply at Bomber Ton of Fun." Executive roles were too time-consuming, too demanding, too much of a conflict with women's primary responsibilities as wives and mothers.

Miss O'Brien was the exception. Mr. Bev had rewarded her with

Miss O'Brien and Mr. Bev presenting a sales trophy.

the titles of executive vice president, general manager, and treasurer in recognition of early service juggling invoices, forestalling suppliers, and superintending a start-up in an unheated barn. In 1951, he gave her the title of president. Because Miss O'Brien had never married, her promotion did not violate the company mandate that wifely duties and motherhood come before career. Miss O'Brien herself said, "There is no getting away from the fact that a woman who is determined to make a successful career must have a one-track mind." Nobody contradicted her.

Wife and mother though she may have been, Mary Kay considered her own promotion long overdue. Like thousands of women once so grateful to walk through Stanley's "Door of Opportunity," she now wanted more than uplifting rhetoric and an annual Pilgrimage. Hard-won trophies were losing their luster. "The handles fell off sometimes after you had them for a year or two," she said. "You got them for selling $1,000 wholesale or $2,000 worth of mops and brooms in a single calendar month. That was a lot of selling to get that stupid little cup."

Mary Kay would later say that Stanley offered her three chances to become a branch manager. From her descriptions, it was not hard to guess why the jobs were open. The first was in Canada, which she remembered as limiting the amount of money she could take out of the country. The second was in West Virginia, a state she remembered as "absolutely poverty-stricken." The third was on the West Coast near Portland. Each involved a move. Each meant ceding her Dallas territory to someone else and starting at the bottom. She passed.

In the meantime, thanks to the unstoppable Mary C. Crowley, Mary Kay's unit ranked third in the country. The two women were coworkers and—when they weren't selling, attending rallies, making Pilgrimages, cooking, cleaning, attending church, or catering to kids and husbands—friends. Crowley, who would later write, "The best way to insure mental health is to marry well," also taught a weekly Sunday school class for young marrieds. Soon, Crowley was trying to convince her friend that marriage to Miller had been ill considered. She didn't have to argue very hard.

The next year, Stanley's slogan was "Forward Again! '53 Is the Year for Me!"

That January, Mary Kay put words into action by filing for divorce. Miller failed to respond. The divorce became final on March 30, 1953. She did not bother to ask for alimony. He did not bother to show up in court.

Like husband two, husband three was edited out of her life story. She was going to stay focused on the positive. Napoleon Hill's *Think and Grow Rich* and *The Laws of Success*, two of her favorite books, convinced Mary Kay that positive emotions carried people toward material wealth. It seemed inarguable that if she just worked harder and spent more time selling Stanley, then she would be richer and more successful.

Now that Mary Kay was free, Crowley sold Mary Kay on the idea of marrying her little brother, Charles "Charlie" William Weaver. Crowley thought the marriage would be good for both of them.

Weaver was not an easy sell. Only sixteen months younger than Crowley, he had none of his big sister's ambition. The two had not been raised together. Growing up, Weaver had been moved from house to house, then worked maintenance jobs. In 1949, he'd married a Missouri girl, who was already out of the picture. People described him as "a little Napoleonic kind of guy": short, bossy, occasionally foul-tempered. Despite repeated help from his go-getting sister, he had never settled into a career. That meant he was less likely to object to a wife who worked. With Crowley's encouragement, Mary Kay stopped giving in to her doubts about Weaver. She practiced positive thinking.

In the summer of 1954, she let her Oak Lawn Heights house for a top-dollar rent of $135 a month and followed Weaver to St. Louis, a city where her husband had a bad marital history and she had no family or friends. Stanley's strict policy about sales territories meant that she was also sacrificing her customers, recruits, status as a unit manager, and independent income. And for what? Weaver seemed to go from job to job without caring what he did.

Mary Kay's two older children were left to their lives in Houston, where Marylyn was soon pregnant again. Taking Richard with them, the Weavers moved into a two-bedroom ranch house in Kirkwood, about twenty minutes from downtown St. Louis. There, over nine months that included a miserable Missouri winter, Mary Kay sampled life as a suburban homemaker. Later she summed up the experience as "St. Louis was just not for me."

Another divorce seemed imminent. Then Weaver's wife and sister sold him on a compromise.

Back in Dallas, Crowley had inherited Mary Kay's mantle as unit manager. Within weeks, she was chafing at Stanley's management and, in particular, its policy of assigned territories. Crowley knew things would be better if she was allowed to do them her way.

She was not alone. Lots of Stanley managers were feeling their oats. Star dealers like Brownie Wise, who would use Stanley's party plan to turn Tupperware into a cultural phenomenon, were defecting in droves. The stop-at-nothing spirit that had made them so good at selling Stanley was now contributing to their dissatisfaction with a company they considered hidebound and hierarchical.

Crowley was in the middle of another disagreement with her supervisor at Stanley when she discovered that her recruits were being lured away by a start-up called World Gift, a direct-sales company that a young navy veteran named Edwin Richard "Dick" Kelly ran out of his apartment.

Kelly claimed he got the idea for the company the night that his wife came home from a Stanley party with a mop she didn't need. Kelly said he'd sent her off to the party with the warning "Don't buy nothing." But when his adored Mary Ellen came home with a mop and said, "Let me tell you the story of this mop," a light bulb went off. Kelly remembered taping a carton of cigarettes to each calf and hiding them under sailor's bell-bottoms while he treasure hunted Tokyo streets for the war souvenirs that were now in the back of his closet. "I began to think of a woman who would buy a mop because of an interesting story," he wrote later. "Why wouldn't a woman buy a beautiful handmade item for the wall or shelf that also had an interesting story?" Party-plan selling had possibilities.

He'd tried almost everything else. After surviving service that included the worst of Iwo Jima, Okinawa, and Guam, Kelly had returned to the States in 1946 and gone to Southern Methodist University to major in psychology, until "our professor took us out to a mental institution and I saw these poor people drooling and I thought 'I can't help them, I can't do this.'" He left without finishing his degree. He then racked up stints as lifeguard, wire service reporter, radio announcer, and station manager. Within another year or two, he'd added Ford salesman, East Texas manager for Light Crust Flour, and convenience store manager. None was a good fit. By 1953, he was selling life insurance and didn't like that any better, especially after watching a coworker named Aaron Spelling take off for Hollywood to pursue dreams of a screenwriting career. Kelly himself had recently received a call from God while taking a nap. On the evening that his wife came home with the mop, he had been thinking about becoming a minister.

His idea for a direct-selling company could get him flying around the world to have more adventures while he searched out more souvenirs. His hook would be stories. Housewives were going to love hearing about ancient traditions and good-luck rituals and foreign craftsmanship.

Crowley later claimed that Kelly came to her asking her to be his sales manager. "He knew how to import merchandise but he didn't know anything about training women to sell on the party plan."

Kelly disagreed, claiming Crowley called, "complaining that I was stealing away her salespeople. . . . Then she became intrigued."

It would not be their last difference of opinion. Either way, Crowley quit Stanley without a backward glance. With this new venture, she would have a chance to show everyone how selling should be done. She began by recruiting her sister-in-law.

Mr. and Mrs. Charles W. Weaver headed home to Houston.

CHAPTER ELEVEN

Storyteller

Houston was a place where hard work might put things right. Weaver would have his own gas station. Mary Kay would open territory for World Gift.

They had a promising start. "The city where seventeen railroads meet the sea" was now a city of superhighways, and Weaver's Shell Station had a prime location on Telephone Road, next to the new Gulf Freeway. That part of town was packed with moms in Country Squires and dads in Bel Airs who needed windshields cleaned, tires checked, and tanks topped off with Super Shell.

Surely the Weavers could not fail to prosper there. During the decade Mary Kay had been away, developers had been turning truck farms into subdivisions at the rate of twenty thousand lots a year. Most of that expansion was in South Houston, a dozen miles and a world away from the run-down Sixth Ward. There, in a subdivision called Freeway Manor, the Weavers signed a twenty-year, $8,950 mortgage for a one-thousand-square-foot ranch house with three bedrooms, a bathroom, a powder room, and an attached garage. Like thousands all around it.

Not that Mary Kay was there much. She was out selling every chance she got. World Gift specialized in conversation starters that let housewives add a personal touch to their assembly-line houses: ceramic figurines, cuckoo clocks, camel bells, and items like the hand-painted plate from Holland that showed a Dutch boy whose pants changed color when it was going to rain. On the back of the plate, Dick Kelly glued a piece of paper explaining that the Dutch boy "will not only enrich your home with its bright colors but will lead your thought back into history." With the grandiloquence of a Leon Uris or James Michener, he wrote of windmills as "the mightiest weapon against the sea," then gave the rundown on how the folk of Volendam came to wear such baggy pants. Kelly even spelled *blue* as *bleu* to make his prose more Continental. He never missed a trick.

His sales manager didn't miss many either. When a fresh shipment of knickknacks arrived from Holland, Mary C. Crowley sent displayers to the Dallas Merchandise Mart dressed as Dutch maids, winged bonnets atop their bouffant hairdos. Crowley wanted her displayers to feel daring, to get their minds off what she called "the terrible three Ds—diapers, dishes, and debts." A displayer for World Gift remembered, "Tupperware might have been functional, but it didn't have the same appeal, didn't make you feel the same way."

And World Gift wasn't just some snooty European outfit. If your decor was Early American, then World Gift could sell you brass plaques of quaint colonial scenes. If your taste ran to the exotic, you could buy silver-plated goblets from India. Or something else so special that you couldn't help but want to start a collection. Something the kids could give you on Mother's Day. Plus practical items. On a buying trip to Germany, Kelly discovered a small stainless-steel spoon with its bowl turned at a forty-five-degree angle to make it easier for infants to handle. Back in Dallas, it became the "German Educational Baby Spoon." He also offered the latest in lazy Susans, fake flowers, and artificial Christmas trees. "I'm the guy you can blame for making artificial Christmas trees so popular," said Kelly.

Kelly once told a reporter that, after being inspired to try party-plan selling, he sold six seabags of war souvenirs to members of a Fort

Worth bridge club while regaling them with tales of his travels. According to him, that was all it took for him to quit a salaried job, move his wife and two sons into a duplex apartment, and sell the family house and car. The part about upending his family was true.

The foundation story was not. Before putting together a product line, Kelly recruited twenty or thirty saleswomen. Most were experienced Stanley dealers like Crowley. From them, he learned about Stanley's incentives, hostess gifts, and mandatory Monday meetings. Merchandise came from Dallas-based importers and wholesalers like United China and Ardinger. More than one bank turned him down for start-up money. Office space was whatever corner of a bedroom or porch could be spared. Inventory was shelved in the garage that came with his duplex.

It wasn't until he had a falling-out with Ardinger that Kelly wangled a ticket on KLM, the Dutch airline promoting a "fly now, pay later" plan that gave him four months to pay back a round-the-world ticket. "World Gift was nothing but a post office box," he said. "Everywhere I went they would do a story about me because that was part of my agreement to publicize KLM. I would land in Hong Kong and they would do a story about this Texan guy going around the world looking for merchandise. As you can imagine, I was inundated with offers of merchandise." By the end of 1953, he'd done $15,000 in business and hired Crowley, who brought her sister-in-law on board the next year.

Together they came up with a different way to talk about direct selling. Hostess parties became "gift shows" because, according to Mary Kay, "party had come to mean to the average person, 'one of those things that I have to go to and be bored to tears and buy something on top of it.'" Dealers were "displayers," which elevated their role to a kind of guidance. Likewise, the annual sales rally became "Seminar," which sounded like a symposium for self-improvement. And just as stick goods had been replaced by exotic gewgaws, the drudge work of Stanley dems would be replaced by stories that educated and entertained.

To no one's surprise, Mary Kay turned out to be a natural-born storyteller. Noticing that her gift shows had double the sales of anybody else's, Kelly made a trip to Houston to watch her work, accompanying her to an afternoon show because, she explained, her husband fussed less when she was home in time to get his dinner.

That afternoon, the hostess was the wife of a Rice University professor and the gift show was in a big house in a nice neighborhood. Before the show's start, Mary Kay asked her twenty-six-year-old boss not to introduce himself, saying that she'd prefer to tell the ladies he came to help her set up. Soon after, he learned why. Her first story was about him.

"I represent a company called World Gift, out of Dallas, whose president and founder was a prisoner of war of the Japanese."

"OOH!" said the fourteen women in attendance.

It wasn't true, but it worked. After that, she was off and running. While Kelly watched, she held up a wood-fiber flower churned out by a Rhode Island factory and announced: "Ladies, this beautiful rose is handmade in a small town in Germany by elderly women who are blind!"

"OOH!" said the ladies.

Mary Kay booked six more shows that night. Afterward, Kelly complimented the performance and asked Mary Kay where she got her stories. According to him, she answered: "I just made them up, where did you get yours?"

Kelly asked her to stick to company-sanctioned stories. When she did, she sold as much as ever. After so many years of pitching Furniture Cream and E-Z Cleaner as the secrets to a happy home, she knew what women wanted to hear.

Dreams of alligator handbags and Cadillac cars were coming true at last.

By the end of her first year, Mary Kay's territory accounted for 53 percent of World Gift's business. Mary Kay herself was making $1,000 a month and had recruited almost two hundred displayers. Her hair was now as blond as any beauty queen's, made all the more dramatic by the dark clothes she wore to downplay a few extra pounds. With her Roman nose and impeccable grooming, she looked a bit like Isobel Elsom, a British actress cast in parts that called for regal bearing. Maybe her customers couldn't name the actress, but they just knew that Mary Kay reminded them of someone refined.

Now, when she won a sales contest, she wasn't just headed to Stanley Park for another rally 'round the Enchanted Oak. Seeing how Tupperware had taken off after it started giving away mink coats, television sets, and glamorous junkets, other direct sellers were making changes. Recruitment rhetoric might still be full of fine talk about self-realization and service to fellow man. But if that didn't get 'em, the prizes did.

Early on, when World Gift could not afford it, Crowley insisted that Kelly send her to Cuba as a sales prize. Soon after, she had her displayers striving to win similar trips. Mary Kay found herself on junkets to Mexico, where she and Weaver would dine, dance, and whoop it up alongside Kelly and, increasingly, her many thankful and well-remunerated recruits.

On those trips, Kelly began to notice how Weaver enjoyed playing lord and master. It wasn't just that Weaver complained when Mary Kay had a nighttime gift show and wasn't around to put his supper on the table. He made fishing trips to the Gulf and told everyone that he did it to get away from her. Then he complained because she did not go with him. He let her visit Grandma Hastings on her own, then behaved as if she had abandoned him. He was a smoker. He liked his beer and got nasty when he had too much of it. He belittled her. He bullied Richard.

Her other children tried to avoid him. Like her mother, Marylyn, who now lived in Fairway Manor, had two babies by the time she turned twenty and discovered that teenage marriage had not been a good idea. Like his father, Ben married when he was nineteen and became a father the next year.

To make Mary Kay's homelife easier, Weaver went on the World Gift payroll as Houston office manager. The timing and location of Weaver's Shell station had been ideal: During the 1950s, the number of cars in Houston more than doubled. Gulf Freeway was bumper-to-bumper during rush hour, and in 1956, seventy-acre Gulfgate Shopping City, talked up as Texas's answer to the Piazza San Marco in Venice and Rockefeller Center in New York, opened less than a mile away. People came from far and wide to visit "the largest shopping center in the South" and had to fuel up for the trip home. For all that, Weaver's business had not been the expected success.

They soon made a new—even better—start.

A marriage might dissolve in disappointment. Direct selling was different. You got back what you put in. Selling rewarded you in proportion to your effort and enthusiasm. Mr. Bev always told her that. Now she was telling her own recruits.

During her second year with World Gift, direct selling was paying off in ways she could not have imagined during her days demonstrating radiator brushes. There were still slammed doors and deadbeat accounts, but there were also fancier parties in more affluent homes, where she could put World Gift's *Treasures of the Earth* LP on the stereo to create an atmosphere while she spun stories about "the Bells of Bengal" or "the Hakata Dolls." Mary Kay was selling enough combo bell-and-candle holders, cherub-shaped wall pockets, and nine-and-a-half-inch replicas of the *Venus de Milo* to buy herself a dream house straight from the pages of a glossy magazine, complete with a Cadillac in its carport. Potential recruits were bound to understand what it meant to live in a house like that. The place would practically pay for itself.

This time she wouldn't be stuck in the kind of generic box that Weaver could afford. Her new house would be a "Home for All America," a craze that started with a 1954 issue of *Better Homes & Gardens* that defined the ideal American dwelling as a 1,400-square-foot single-story house with two bathrooms, three bedrooms, a combo living/dining room, and a semiopen kitchen. For years after that issue, "Home for All America" was shorthand for the latest in modern living. While Mary Kay endured exile in Missouri, the Houston Home Builders Association had given away a $25,000 "Home for All America" model house built in a swank subdivision called Glenbrook Valley. That year's Mrs. America had come to Houston to open the event.

When Mary Kay got back to town, it did not take her long to decide that Glenbrook Valley was where she wanted to be. For direct selling, this "most highly restricted development" presented a promised land of prospects: 1,400 affluent, house-proud homemakers with time freed by the latest in labor-saving dishwashers and ovens. Without selling the Fairway Manor bungalow, Mary Kay paid $22,900 for a "Lowe's All Electric Home" in 1956 and moved to Glenbrook Valley the next year. Marylyn would remarry and move into the "Texas Colonial" three doors away.

And on that street lined with show houses, no house was more time-saving and efficient than Mary Kay's. Its laundry room was within sight of the cooking area so a wife could fix her casserole and still know when to put the clothes in the dryer. A built-in Talk-a-Radio allowed the family to communicate without having to be in the same room at the same time. Bathrooms boasted both heat lamp and sunlamp, should the porcelain-skinned Mary Kay feel an urge to tan.

For her, its selling point was the kitchen, which had a dishwasher, oven with double rotisserie, center-island griddle, and NuTone—a gizmo that could blend drinks, juice fruit, and sharpen knives. Best of all, while her chickens roasted and her dishes washed themselves, Mary Kay could sit in the kitchen alcove touted as "a compact miniature office where the housewife may conveniently handle correspondence, payment of bills, and make phone calls."

She would make good use of that alcove. True, she was probably working too hard: Her left eyelid had started to twitch when she was overtired. But she couldn't stop now. Direct selling had put her inside the "Home for All America" that was every woman's dream.

Now that she had her dream house, Mary Kay was never there.

During her second year at World Gift, Kelly made her area

manager, a job that she resigned as soon as she realized that her new salary would never equal her old commissions. Then Kelly, whose "internationally famous" company had yet to breach the borders of Texas, invented the position of national training director for her. With that, Mary Kay finally had the kind of salary and title that C. B. Eckman had enjoyed. The barnstorming began.

Mary Kay took the company into forty-three of the forty-eight states. She would fly to a new city, run a classified ad like the classified ads that Eckman had used, then check into a hotel and wait for someone to show up. Sometimes she stayed with local displayers. Sometimes she split a hotel room with a female manager.

A prospect might make an appointment and never appear. A prospect might appear and be the wrong kind of person. Regardless, Mary Kay would fly to the next spot to repeat the routine, routing herself through Houston less and less often. The new house was only six blocks from the airport, so it was easy to get a ride if Weaver forgot to pick her up again. When she was not able to avoid Houston, she filled her time with gift shows and meetings for recruits.

At those meetings, she shared what she had learned while peddling lazy Susans and *Venus de Milo* statuettes. She knew that, Crowley excepted, good salespeople were rarely good with numbers. She had seen what happened when women who had never been allowed to handle money got their first checks. She'd watch them buy a refrigerator or make a mortgage payment, too excited to remember that they still had to pay the company for the products. Higher sales volume meant higher accounts receivable, so the very women she wanted to keep, the real go-getters, were in the greatest danger. Mary Kay wasn't too clear on the ins and outs of accounts receivable herself, but she knew what would happen if a displayer got into debt and wasn't able to pay. Husbands hit the roof. Tears were shed. Promising careers were nipped in the bud. She'd watched it happen time and again.

Coverture was both custom and law in Texas. Husbands held veto power over wifely employment, contracts, and financial affairs; courts had been known to absolve debts on the grounds that a wife was no more accountable than a child. In 1957, a complex amendment to state law allowed married women age twenty-one and older limited power to enter contracts over separate property, provided that they claimed their rights with the county clerk before they signed a contract. Few women knew about the law. Fewer understood it. Nothing changed for Mary Kay's displayers. Husbands remained wary of wives' "pin money projects." No man wanted to be saddled with debt and stuck with a truckload of ceramic figurines, cuckoo clocks, and camel bells. Females were known to be gullible. That Weaver woman might be taking advantage.

"You can do it!" Mary Kay told displayers as she also passed along life lessons like how to keep a spouse from commandeering earnings for beer money, where to find a bank willing to open a separate account in a lady's name, and how to cope with an "old bear" of a husband. She explained that, for independent contractors, money spent on rent and the family car could be tax deductions. She advised having an onion ready to toss into a pot of boiling water so when a husband walked through the door, the displayer could sing out, "Dinner will be ready soon," to make him think she'd been slaving in the kitchen all day.

That lasted until Kelly heard her spiel about separate bank accounts and shushed her. There were already enough divorced women in direct selling.

World Gift was now one of about three thousand direct-selling companies. Mary Kay was one of at least 1.5 million Americans in direct sales.

No one knew how many were women, but everyone agreed there were more each day. Party-plan selling was almost exclusively female. Forward-thinking publications like *Charm*, "the Magazine for Women Who Work," ran articles that touted selling opportunities. So did conservative publications like *Woman's Home Companion*, which headlined a Tupperware feature HELP YOURSELF TO HAPPINESS. As America's birth rate climbed and its small towns and suburbs filled with stay-at-home moms, those moms signed up to sell by the tens of thousands—faster than their mothers, aunts, and grandmothers had signed up before the war. By 1953, Stanley's advertising in *Life* claimed, "These Hostess Parties are the most popular of all within-the-home shopping parties. More than 12,000 take place each day." But that was only one company.

At least sixty companies now used some variation of Stanley's party plan, including J. R. Watkins, which had been in the direct-selling business since 1868; Avon, which had started as the California Perfume Company in 1886; and Fuller Brush, Mr. Bev's erstwhile employer. Commissioning a survey of its competition, Stanley found that both its dealers and its core customers regularly attended parties for House of Stuart, Club Aluminum, Avon, and Fuller Brush.

But Stanley still outsold the rest. When *Fortune* published its first Fortune 500 list in 1955, Stanley debuted at number 448. By the next year, when it made the list again, it had an estimated twenty thousand dealers and had grossed nearly $58 million on $105 million retail. But as Fuller begat Stanley, so Stanley now begat another generation. Of these, the best known became Tupperware, a department store vendor that did not start direct-sales distribution until the late 1940s, when a few enterprising Stanley dealers started selling it as a sideline.

Foremost among them was Brownie Wise. Born in Buford, Georgia, in 1913, Brownie Mae Humphrey Wise was a divorced single mother who, in late 1945, who called herself a widow and was working as a secretary when a Stanley dealer came knocking. After listening to his spiel, she decided she could do better. By February of 1946, she had quit her job, exchanging security and routine for an open-ended selling opportunity and the culture of constant striving that came with it.

Wise came to Stanley with a habit of self-reliance, a desperation to prove herself, and an upbringing that featured a working mother, an absent father, and an erratic education. Like Mary Kay and Crowley, Wise went through a misguided marriage to an unambitious man and a divorce that did not yield reliable alimony or child support. Like them, she committed her heart and soul to Stanley. Like them, she was soon promoted to unit leader, only to discover that Stanley offered nowhere to go from there.

On a Stanley Pilgrimage, Wise was told that native ability and superhuman determination could overcome her bad start and spotty schooling. Hearing that enthusiasm was the key to success, she decided to show Stanley how enthusiastic she could be. During routine orientation as unit leader, she demonstrated super-duper enthusiasm by taking down every word in perfect secretarial shorthand and—lest a single slogan be lost—creating her own sheets of carbon by covering the back of each notebook page with scribbled pencil. Copying lists like "How to Get Best Results from Your People," she made so many annotations and additions that she ended up with her own version. For her Detroit-area unit, she wrote and mimeographed a long, chatty newsletter called *The Go-Getter* and dreamed up slogans like "Be Wise! Stanley-ize!" Like Fine and Dandy Al Teetsel before her, she pursued every possible prize, title, and contest for herself, then invested in incentives like corsages and lipsticks to spur her unit to greater glories.

Frustrated when Stanley's selling opportunity was not as open-ended as she had been led to believe, Wise took up with Tupperware in 1949. Soon after, she resigned from Stanley to devote herself to burping bowls. Within a year, she was off to open Tupperware territory, moving from Michigan to Florida as if she were following a star. Not even Tupperware's mercurial management and messy distribution could dissuade her. Instead, Wise took it upon herself to convince eccentric inventor Earl Silas Tupper to sell exclusively through the party plan. By the spring of 1951, she was vice president in charge of sales.

At Tupperware, Wise gave direct selling the pep and pizzazz it had never had with old Fair and Square Beveridge. Mr. Bev invited dealers to rural Massachusetts; Wise invited them to sunny Florida. Stanley pilgrims tossed pennies into an old-time wishing well to make dreams come true; Tupperware dealers put their hopes in Tupperware containers, then watched them disappear down a twentieth-century version. Mr. Bev awarded an occasional car; by the end of 1952, Wise had handed out keys to seven Cadillacs. And she was just warming up. Other direct sellers had used extravagant incentives as attention-getters and recruitment tools. Wise would outdo them all.

Brownie Wise conducting a Tupperware party.

Earl Silas Tupper presenting Brownie Wise with a pink Cadillac.

In 1953, New York public relations firm Ruder & Finn began pitching stories about Wise and the "mere women" who sold Tupperware. A *Life* photo essay documented the company's first Jubilee in 1954, showing "633 salesgirls and managers . . . 90 percent of them women" shoveling for $48,500 of prizes that included buried mink stoles, gold watches, and the keys to a 1954 Ford. Captions explained that medics were on standby due to dealers' tendency to faint from excitement. In March of 1955, *Coronet* published Ludwig Bemelmans's tale of joining Wise and six prizewinning dealers on a tour of Paris, where they stayed at the Ritz and sipped Cokes and iced tea at Maxim's. In 1956, *Life* went back to Jubilee for "A Wealth of Wishes," yet missed documenting the Wish Fairy, who wafted through "Treasurama" bestowing toasters and televisions with waves of her wand.

Converts by the hundred presented themselves for baptism at Poly Pond, the man-made lake at Tupperware's thousand-acre headquarters. As Tupperware parties turned into a cultural phenomenon, the product became so popular that, at the New England factory, workers were suspected of smuggling bowls in their bras. Wise tooled around Kissimmee, Florida, in a pink Cadillac courtesy of her employer. She took up residence in a lakeside villa worthy of a movie star.

On April 17, 1954, she became the first woman on the cover of *Business Week*, with the cover line "If we build the people, they'll build the business." Inside, the magazine ran a portrait of her with a bowl on her head. Dozens of similar stories followed. As Mary Kay later would, Wise used reporters' condescension and lack of curiosity to her advantage. Although her formal education had ended around the eighth grade, most profiles gave Wise a year or two of college. Despite the fact that her ex-husband had a tendency to show up at Kissimmee headquarters unannounced and roaring drunk, newsmen described Wise as a widow. And because it was taken for granted that no one got into direct selling without some kind of sob story, *Cosmopolitan*'s profile of the "Sunshine Cinderella" misinformed the world that Wise started selling because her son was sickly.

Soon Tupperware ascended to the number two spot in direct selling, right behind Stanley. Wise wrote a book, *Best Wishes*, promising "success in sixty seconds," with a foreword by former direct seller Norman Vincent Peale, whose own *The Power of Positive Thinking* had just spent 186 weeks on the bestseller list. But by the time Wise's book was published in 1957, Wise was on the outs with Tupper, who hated having anyone think that a woman was responsible for Tupperware's success. In January of 1958, the cranky Yankee inventor fired Wise without warning, burying hundreds of copies of her book behind headquarters. That September, he sold Tupperware to the Rexall drugstore chain for an estimated $16 million in cash and stock options. He also divorced his wife, renounced his citizenship, and moved to a private island in Central America.

While all that was happening, Stanley had been going through shake-ups of its own. Mr. Bev had died on December 4, 1956, at age seventy-seven. As planned, his role as head of the company passed to Miss O'Brien, his longtime second-in-command. With a woman in charge, dealers deserted by the score. Calling his new boss "a jumped-up secretary," Regensburger, the head of sales, quit. Stanley dropped off the Fortune 500.

Undaunted, Miss O'Brien planned snazzier prizes—including an all-expenses-paid, first-class week in Paris.

A week so luxurious and gay,
That's Continental in every way.
Something you will always remember
A trip to Paris in September.

On the evening of December 11, 1957, Miss O'Brien headed into a New England blizzard to personally conduct Stanley's twenty millionth party.

Crowley knew she could do better.

Picking a fight with Kelly, she told him that she disagreed with his commission structure. Adding to her indignation, she was shocked—

shocked!—to discover alcoholic beverages being consumed at a company event. It was nothing but her Christian duty to share her concerns about Kelly's alcohol consumption with World Gift's suppliers and salespeople. Getting wind of her plan, Kelly had Crowley's personal effects delivered to her home along with the message not to bother coming to work.

Within ten days, Crowley got even by signing a slew of World Gift's best displayers to an exclusive three-year contract. Then, as now, many direct sellers worked more than one line. Mary Kay, for example, had been selling a line of locally made skin care for years. By contrast, Crowley's recruits committed to a single company. Their fortunes would rise or fall with hers.

Next, Crowley secured a line of credit with Ardinger, one of World Gift's original suppliers. They, in turn, referred her to other wholesalers, while her attorney, a fellow First Baptist congregant named Ralph Baker, drove to Austin and walked her paperwork through the state bureaucracy. On the morning of December 5, 1957, Crowley met Baker in his office, where the lawyer led all present in a prayer asking God to guide the new company. She then signed her articles of incorporation in front of her husband, her mother-in-law, and a handful of investors, later writing: "I was pleased to know that each person there was an active Christian."

Like dozens of others, the new company stuck to the Stanley formula of praise, prizes, and recognition. Crowley stuck to Stanley's schedule too, right down to the mandatory Monday meetings. Other appropriations were specific to World Gift, like referring to salesladies as "displayers" and calling the annual convention "Seminar." In no time at all, Home Interiors and Gifts was up and running with a line of fruit-shaped kitchen canisters, frog-shaped candleholders, and the Lord's Prayer written out on a wall plaque. Let World Gift keep all that foreign stuff.

Crowley decided that she didn't need tales of ancient traditions and good-luck rituals and foreign craftsmanship. She had something better. "Home Interiors and Gifts was a way in which God could use me, Mary

C. Crowley, to help other women see themselves as He sees them!" The new company's first commandment: "We believe in the dignity and importance of women."

Far from the first to preach female empowerment, Crowley made it sound like she was. In direct sales, women were expected to be grateful for the selling opportunity. Women were customers. Sometimes they were dealers. Men were executives. At Avon, for example, the sales force remained female and the management male. The industry had exceptions—Wise at Tupperware, Crowley at World Gift, O'Brien at Stanley—but men made most decisions. "Women had to wait their turn," a Stanley veteran explained. "Many of the men [executives] had been with the company since Mr. Beveridge started it in the 1930s."

Crowley did not want to wait. She did not want to put up with assigned territories or ceilings on commissions. Her displayers were welcome to work as hard as they wanted and earn as much as they could. If a displayer recruited someone who built her own unit, she would get a share of those sales. As displayers became more experienced and built bigger units, they would rise through the ranks. No salaried male manager would lord it over them. Women would manage other women. Crowley was bursting with other ideas too, like "room concepts" so customers would never have to wonder what went with what. Crowley would tell them.

Thereafter, little love was lost between the pious Kelly, a Sunday school teacher, a Scoutmaster, and an elder of the Presbyterian Church, and the pious Crowley, a Sunday school teacher, choir member, and future director of the Billy Graham Evangelical Association.

Each would forever regard the other as the devil's minion.

Mary Kay stayed put.

She saw no reason to leave World Gift, where she was now a salaried, stock-owning executive. She knew that she had none of Crowley's skill at balancing books. Certainly no accounting degree. No taste for the battles that Crowley fought with such gusto.

Private Richard R. Rogers, Allen Academy, 1959.

She stayed married to Crowley's brother too, although things had gotten so bad that she headed back to Dallas, where she and Richard temporarily moved in with Kelly and his family. She was on the road three weeks out of four anyway. At Kelly's suggestion, she took fifteen-year-old Richard, who was becoming quite a handful, out of Hartman Junior High and enrolled him at the all-boys Allen Academy, a military school that was Kelly's own alma mater. At Allen Academy, two hours from Houston and three hours from Dallas, Richard would get an education alongside the scions of Texas's moneyed movers and shakers.

To help Marylyn, Mary Kay recruited her to World Gift. Lula, now in her seventies, remained in residence over Wagner's Café, looking after boarders when she wasn't downstairs working.

Meanwhile, Crowley had a happy marriage and was the adored head of her own company. Soon that same sister-in-law would be a Dallas-based millionaire known for charity work, founding a company that operated on the Golden Rule, and preaching the empowerment of women. Soon that sister-in-law—the very one whom Mary Kay recruited to direct selling—would be spouting the slogan "Think mink!" and awarding Cadillacs to her top sellers.

CHAPTER TWELVE

"A Golden Door Marked 'Men Only' "

But Mary Kay was not doing too badly. Kelly let her talk him into starting a line of beauty products.

Jewel Tea had one. So did Stanley Home Products. Fuller Brush offered "seven bewitching shades of face powder" through its Débutante line, which sold through either the party plan or the "Fullerette," a female counterpart to the Fuller Brush Man who paid $9.50 for her sample kit and anted up two cents for each mini lipstick she was required to leave behind on sales calls. Dozens of smaller companies, like Linda Lee Cosmetics and Beauty Creators, bought beauty products from jobbers, slapped on labels, then sold the products through hostess parties. Out in California, Jan and Frank Day were making a go of Jafra, the party-plan cosmetics company they'd started in 1956 after Jan's stints with Stanley and Beauty Creators. Brownie Wise went from Tupperware to Cinderella International, which sold Magic Wand cosmetics on the party plan. Everybody seemed to be trying it.

Avon made the beauty business look easy. Between 1950 and 1960, Avon sales went from $31.2 million to $168 million, more than twice the sales of Stanley. An incessant "Ding Dong, Avon Calling" campaign from Dreher Advertising depicted the gloved-and-hatted antithesis of

Avon advertising, 1955.

the down-and-outers who had knocked on doors during the Depression. Outfitted in her elegant tailleur, the Avon Lady conferred exclusivity and affluence on the broad, low-end line. Avon stock split, then split again.

World Gift's entry into that market, "World of Beauty," was based on formulas that Mary Kay encountered while selling Stanley in Dallas in 1952. Like most World Gift products, these came with a catchy backstory: An old coot who lived up a holler in the Ozarks noticed that decades of curing deer hides had kept his hands soft and wrinkle-free, prompting him to get into the beauty business. After his death in 1935, a daughter, who had married and moved to Texas, sold the skin care as a sideline to her hairdressing and cosmetology. Mary Kay convinced Kelly to pay $1,200 for a copy of the hide tanner's formulas from the daughter, who'd been brewing them in her bathtub. Kelly then had a few batches run up by a local jobber.

With World Gift now bringing in about $4.5 million retail a year, Kelly began touting his company as "the country's largest direct seller of gifts." He rarely stopped there. Marketing to Cold War consciousness, he extolled World Gift as a weapon in America's battle against communism, propaganda that the U.S. Information Service translated into twenty-seven languages and broadcast on the Voice of America. He also styled himself the "modern Marco Polo," and when *Around the World in 80 Days* became a box-office hit, he spun his annual round-the-world buying trip as a real-life version of the Technicolor adventure. Newspapers fell for it every time.

By November of 1959, thirty-three-year-old Kelly and his company had outgrown the modest digs on Sovereign Row and moved to the sixth location in seven years: a purpose-built headquarters/warehouse

World Gift owner Dick Kelly.

on Regal Row. In a full page of *The Dallas Morning News* that bore no bylines and read like something that Kelly had written himself, displayers testified to the delights of making money with World Gift. One said, "All my life I have wanted a Cadillac and this year I achieved this goal with World Gift sales only." Take that, Home Interiors.

Along with publicity photos and paragraphs of puffery, the paper ran profiles of World Gift's management: five men and Mrs. Mary K. Weaver, who, as director of training and education, went at the bottom of the page below the warehouse manager. In her two-paragraph bio, Dale Carnegie courses and aborted attempts at college became "educated at the University of Houston and several schools of management." Accompanying numbers reported "over 7,000 gift shows, with an outstanding average of approximately $100 per show," which would have yielded commissions of over $125,000 a year, well more than Kelly made himself. But its ending rang true: "Her ability to impart her profitable experience to others has endeared Mrs. Weaver to hundreds of women."

Soon Mary Kay would realize that her future did not lie in selling German Educational Baby Spoons or handmade-in-Greece replicas of the *Venus de Milo.*

Crowley's example was there to remind her.

When Crowley was not in the choir singing the praises of her God of Abundance, she was testifying to His glories with her diamond-decked hand on her mink-covered Bible. "Think mink!" she enjoined adherents, who already numbered in the hundreds. "Think the best! Attempt great things." That's what God wanted.

By the end of 1958, Crowley seemed to be one of the anointed. Home Interiors had been profitable practically from day one, paying a small stock dividend at the end of its first year and distributing modest bonuses to its staff. When two banks turned her down for a $6,000 expansion loan, Crowley, unable to fathom why a banker would not fund expansion based on untallied accounts receivable, read the refusal as sex discrimination. She turned that into a recruitment tool. From then on, she preached: "Any female who feels she is being discriminated against in her work should quit her job and find employment with someone who doesn't practice discrimination." Like Home Interiors.

Nothing stopped Crowley. Not even cancer. Diagnosed with cervical cancer in 1957, a time when cancer was not to be mentioned in public and reproductive organs were not to be mentioned anywhere, Crowley attacked the disease without embarrassment. God was on her side: "Had not God begun a wonderful, mighty work in Home Interiors and Gifts only the year before? Wasn't I really needed to bring the dreams to fruition?"

There could be no question of resting. Nor allowing anyone to care for her. Pursuing the most aggressive treatment, she asked her oncologist for then-experimental radium implants. Goading herself with repetitions of "Don't stop at the first tired" and "If it is to be, it is up to me," she dressed cheerfully (memoirs mention a bright-pink dress with a polka-dot scarf) and headed to Baylor Hospital for her radium and cobalt, refusing to consider the possibility that she might not recover. Negotiating with her doctor, she won two hours a day to run Home Interiors. Her son, Don Carter, and a devoted support staff handled everything else.

When her cure came, it was one more proof that God had blessed her venture. In no time at all, she was back to singing in the choir, teaching young marrieds in her Sunday school classes, concocting recipes to rival Mary's Green Goop, chairing the local chapter of the American Cancer Society, and accomplishing more in her eighty-hour week than any ten people would have attempted in a month. As recruitment burgeoned, she went right on awarding mink checkbook covers and mink pencil caps to her displayers as if nothing had ever happened.

In 1960, Mary Kay made another fresh start. In the midst of her frantic training and traveling for World Gift, she found time to divorce Weaver on grounds of cruelty. He did not contest.

The official separation began in January. Most of the settlement was complete by March. Mary Kay paid him $2,000 and kept the Fairway Manor and Glenbrook Valley houses. She also kept her Cadillac and Chevy, while he got the 1955 Ford pickup, the 1958 Karmann Ghia, and Rags the dog. When the divorce became final the week before her forty-second birthday, Mary Kay commenced calling herself "Miss Weaver," just as she had rechristened herself "Miss Rogers" and "Mary K. Eckman." She now had only herself to support on an annual salary that she said was $25,000 (about $280,000 today).

Her life was in Dallas now. Ben and Marylyn had their own families. Richard was safely through high school and was about to be the first in the family to attend college. At Kelly's suggestion, Mary Kay invested in two new townhouses on Northwest Parkway, then moved into one and rented the other. When she wasn't on the road, she presided at World Gift events in the Peacock Terrace Room of the Baker Hotel, where she distributed silver punch cups—"which were practical and usable"—considering them an improvement on the trophies she'd won from Stanley. A Dallas newspaper noted that when a housewife joined World Gift in hopes of earning enough money for a car, Mary Kay presented her with a jeweled key ring, as if car keys might materialize any minute.

As workweeks went from sixty hours to seventy hours and beyond, the eyelid twitch grew worse. She declared herself too busy to pay it attention. Not even her sister Daisy's death in 1960, from non-Hodgkin's lymphoma, inspired a doctor's visit. As the tic spread, Mary Kay took to wearing sunglasses during nighttime gift shows and training sessions. Frustrated that her tic had not responded to the mind-body programming in *Psycho-Cybernetics*, the bestseller written by plastic surgeon-turned-self-help author Maxwell Maltz, she kept up her positive self-talk and channeled her unconscious mind while the left side of her face twisted into a grimace and twitched several times a minute. Except for the recommendation to relax, she followed his system to the letter.

In 1962, after years of being nagged by customers and coerced by coworkers, Mary Kay agreed to see a doctor, who sent her straight from his office to the hospital, where, after hours of tests, she was diagnosed with a progressive neuromuscular disease called hemifacial spasm. Warning that her case could lead to loss of sight, smell, and speech, the Dallas doctor referred her to W. James Gardner Jr., a neurosurgeon at the Cleveland Clinic.

Piggybacking brain surgery onto a recruiting trip, Mary Kay headed north. Determined not to waste workdays, she checked into the hospital at the start of the 1962 Labor Day weekend. In her purse were four airline tickets for the prospecting trips she planned to continue as soon as the weekend was over.

Positive self-talk and channeling her unconscious mind did not help this time either. Mary Kay's operation lasted eight hours and kept her in the hospital for two months. While Cleveland-area displayers filled her room with flowers and behaved like a loving family, she lay in bed, practiced her new smile, and plotted to get out. In an interview given nineteen years later, she was still complaining about the waste of the plane tickets.

Earlier than her doctor would have liked, Mary Kay bought herself a wig and went back to work. From then on, she was rarely without a wig, grateful for the salon trips and styling time they saved, especially now that she had a scar on her forehead. Following the model of Miss O'Brien at Stanley, Mary Kay was now a successful female executive who drove a Cadillac and toted a toy poodle everywhere. She owned two residences in Houston and two in Dallas. She attended Seminars and sales celebrations. When her recruits won trips to Honolulu, Mexico City, or Nassau, Mary Kay was often there too, dancing, celebrating their success, having a fine time right beside them.

Then she met George Arthur Hallenbeck.

A salesman on his second marriage, Hallenbeck had been around. Unlike Weaver, he was neither a smoker nor a drinker. A snappy dresser, he was medium height, slim, and had the faded brown hair of a

George Arthur Hallenbeck at Coe College in 1936.

middle-aged man who had once been a fair-haired boy. Born in Chicago in 1914, he called himself an alumnus of Coe College, which he attended for three years but never managed to graduate. He worked in an office supply store in Iowa City, then a department store in Cedar Rapids, where his fifty-eight-hour workweek brought $37.50 before taxes. During the war, he served in Europe as a first lieutenant and won a Bronze Star and a Purple Heart. After the war, he went back to the department store. After that, he sold trousseau linens on the party plan. A divorcé, he did not stay in contact with his two sons in Iowa.

Hallenbeck was forever on the verge of a big score. In the mid-1950s, Hallenbeck's All Sports, a Denver-based scheme to clean and repair sports uniforms, seemed a surefire winner. But his backer dropped out and the business went bust in less than two years. Lee Bower and his wife, Wanda, who both worked without salaries on Hallenbeck's business, recalled that they "also invested a couple of thousand of our own money." They lost every penny.

Hallenbeck's luck proved better in California, where he went to work for Nutri-Bio, a line of vitamin products sold through a he-man, hard-sell network headed by motivational speaker John Earl Shoaff, who had joined the company in 1957 after quitting Abundavita, another line of vitamin products sold through a he-man, hard-sell network headed by yet another motivational speaker.

Known for a "Laws of Success" lecture that would ultimately bring bigger payoffs than pitching supplements, Shoaff sold self-actualization in ways that would later inspire an industry's worth of self-help coaches. For Shoaff, the universe operated according to a set of invariable, inarguable laws that ranged from the law of gravity to the "law of abundance." Like a latter-day Newton, Shoaff set out to demonstrate that negativity attracted further negativity. Abundance attracted further abundance.

The bigger the dream, the better. "Make no small plans, for they have no magic to stir men's blood!" Shoaff would intone, leaving listeners with the impression that he was invoking Shakespeare. But if he realized that he was paraphrasing the Beaux-Arts architect Daniel Burnham, he also realized that Burnham's name would mean nothing to his audience. Like Mr. Bev and many a motivator before and since, Shoaff soft-pedaled attributions and anything else that might distract from his message.

Tramping door to door was not for him. Nor would he cajole housewives into hostess parties. Big bucks came from "network marketing," his preferred term for multilevel marketing, a variant of direct selling in which the selling was far from direct. As practiced in the mid-twentieth century, multilevel marketing usually involved distributors who then sold the product to someone else, involving multiple levels of markups. As practiced by Shoaff, convincing someone to buy into the organization was just as important—or more important—than convincing a customer to buy the product. You bought your starter kit or franchise or distributorship, then made money when you convinced someone else to do the same. That continued like a chain letter until everyone was wealthy beyond their wildest dreams.

To Shoaff, multilevel marketing proved that abundance attracted abundance. Nutri-Bio bigwigs pulled up to Beverly Hills headquarters in Cadillacs and Lincolns, spent Christmases in Hawaii, and were photographed in Las Vegas nightclubs with beaming blond wives wrapped in mink stoles. A dropout, Shoaff assured other men who hadn't graduated from high school that they could make $50,000 after a year. He was careful to add that millionaire status would take at least four years, which was the time it had taken him to go from department store pants presser to Beverly Hills fat cat. Hallenbeck grasped the concept immediately. Putting principle into practice, he gave his address as Beverly Hills while he still ate, slept, changed clothes, and collected mail at a modest bungalow in the valley.

Other dealers had tried to open Dallas territory for Nutri-Bio. None demonstrated Hallenbeck's mastery of the law of abundance. Moving to Dallas not long after Mary Kay's divorce came through, Hallenbeck and his pretty, dark-haired second wife, Anne, took up residence in a splashy Spanish-style villa out on Country Club Circle, in much the same way that C. B. Eckman had modeled upper-middle-class prosperity when he moved to Dallas twenty years before.

Similarities with Stanley ended there. Nutri-Bio was not for housewives trying to earn money for a new refrigerator. Hallenbeck represented multilevel marketing at its most grandiose. Scorning the kind of cost-saving travel done by Mary Kay, Hallenbeck designated himself "national field coordinator" and flew around the Southwest conducting "distributor seminars." At a time when recruitment at Stanley and Tupperware was down, Nutri-Bio sometimes claimed 50,000 or 70,000 dealers. Sometimes it was 115,000.

Modernizing the snake oil pitch with "better nutrition through biochemistry," Nutri-Bio claimed to fix anything from "busy schedules" to "digestive problems." In large-circulation magazines like *Life* and *Look*, full-page ads pitched Nutri-Bio as nutrition insurance "to help each member of your family to be more alert, calmer, more pleasant and to enjoy a greater zest for life." Touted by TV star Robert Cummings, who was also the spokesman for Winston cigarettes, Nutri-Bio spread like wildfire.

Then, just as fast, the company began appearing in newspapers and magazines for different reasons. Nutri-Bio's claims to treat and prevent everything from lack of normal intelligence to heart trouble were characterized as "misleading" by government agencies. More misleading claims were found in rereadings of Cummings's 1960 book, *Stay Young and Vital.* By then, Winston had another spokesman, *The Bob Cummings Show* was in reruns, and the Food and Drug Administration was seizing product left and right.

Hallenbeck was out of work again. Kelly recalled him coming to World Gift looking for a job.

He found one, but not working for Kelly. Less than a year after surgery fixed her face, forty-five-year-old Mary Kay and forty-eight-year-old Hallenbeck decided to marry. She was going to have her own Bronze Star–winning, war hero husband. Just like Crowley.

On May 5, Hallenbeck placed a cryptic ad in *The Dallas Morning News* requesting "a particular type of man: One who will take an interest in my business. He must be 25–50, preferably married, with direct-sales experience. He must be full time, aggressive, and prepared to start immediately." In a strategy worthy of Shoaff, Hallenbeck acted as if he were already world-famous and simply signed the ad with his own name. No mention was made of product. Only potential compensation of "$1,448 per month and up." He got no takers. Next he tried Mary Kay.

According to later legend spinning, World Gift asked Mary Kay to train a young man who would be promoted over her at twice her salary. The magnitude of the injustice may have been exaggerated—twice her $25,000 salary sounds like more than Kelly would have paid anyone—but the rest sounded right. Her love of recognition would have made her yearn for the title of sales manager, the position once held by Crowley. Later, Mary Kay admitted that she never asked for the job, expecting that her hard work would be rewarded.

It was not. Instead, the title went to a new hire who had little experience with party-plan selling and none with a female sales force. Mary Kay was supposed to show him the ropes. Kelly claimed he considered Mary Kay for the job, then decided against it, "since her health was not the best." She was too good at what she was doing.

Being passed over for promotion was not the real problem. Kelly was planning something that Mary Kay found far more upsetting: switching from an old, Stanley-style model of independent dealers to a modern, Nutri-Bio–style franchise system. He was going to sell territories and save himself administrative headaches while keeping the round-the-world sourcing adventures that had always been his favorite part of the business. Displayers and managers would not be running their own shows anymore.

Mary Kay was delegated to break the bad news. In Kelly's mind, franchises would net a neat profit with less work. In Mary Kay's mind, it was betrayal, pure and simple. Decades later, he would appear in her book *Mary Kay on People Management* as the unnamed and blundering owner of a company where she once worked; each of his management missteps followed by her own neat pointers on how matters might have been handled better.

Things came to a head that spring. Egged on by Hallenbeck and excited by the mink-coated success of Crowley, Mary Kay quit World Gift at two o'clock in the afternoon on Monday, May 13, 1963. Having invested $500 in executive stock options that she was obliged to offer back to Kelly, she walked out of his office with either a check for $18,000, a check for much less, or no money at all—depending on who was telling the story. Kelly tended to exaggerate the payout. Mary Kay tended to omit it.

One detail was always consistent: Mary Kay admitted that, after she quit, she "went home and did the same thing that most other women would have done, I cried all night." Sometimes she confessed to regretting her move and wanting her job back. Sometimes she left out that part.

In one retelling, Mary Kay sometimes said that an outside efficiency expert informed the company that she wielded too much power, whereupon World Gift offered her a supervisory position over the entire United States, "but I would have had to move every six months. I turned it down and resigned." In a 1970s version, she said, "I found that no matter how well I did my job, no matter how smart I was, I still always seemed to reach a golden door marked 'Men Only.'"

In the 1980s, as the term *glass ceiling* came into currency, Mary Kay reframed the story. She said she was devastated by her lack of promotion, decided upon abrupt retirement, and planned to write a book that solved problems faced by women in business. In what a later generation would call therapeutic journaling, Mary Kay sat at her kitchen table every morning, writing on a legal pad. She wrote down what was wrong with direct selling, what was right, and what she could do better. She kept that up for two weeks.

She did not mention that all of this happened within a month of Home Interiors announcing its first million-dollar year. Nor did she mention any payoff from Kelly. Or that her new beau was a direct-sales executive who was out of work.

Less than a month after leaving World Gift, Mary Kay announced that she would start her own company.

Now all she had to do was find a product.

For a while, she considered a scheme to lease large floral arrangements to offices and industrial venues. She also considered plastic plants. Then she thought of something better.

Unrepentant after the flameout of Nutri-Bio, Shoaff was now in the beauty business with a line called Ovation Cosmetics, which he planned to sell through multilevel marketing. Hallenbeck convinced Mary Kay that they should do the same.

Their product line would be another iteration of the skin care sold by World Gift, itself an iteration of the skin care developed by John Wesley Heath, the hide tanner from Big Fork, Arkansas, who experimented on himself and reputedly died at age seventy-three with nary a wrinkle nor an enlarged pore. A decade before, Mary Kay discovered the products when Heath's daughter, a beautician named Ova Spoonemore Standridge, was a hostess for one of her Stanley parties. When the women gathered in the kitchen for the inevitable coffee and cookies, Mary Kay saw Standridge passing out little jars of skin care to the friends who had attended the party. She decided to try it too.

By that time, Standridge had spent years trying to turn her father's hide-tanning receipts into cosmetics. In those days, the stuff stank and came in makeshift jars with handmade labels. That night, the shoebox that Standridge handed to Mary Kay included night cream inside an old Cloverine Salve tin and skin freshener inside a salvaged pharmacy bottle that still had its prescription label. Instructions were scribbled in pencil on a sheet of notebook paper. Mary Kay swore by the products and began selling them as a sideline.

Standridge had never been much of a businesswoman, though. More than once, she had to take out newspaper ads announcing that she was not legally responsible for commitments that others had made in the name of BeautiControl. Nor of HairControl, a potion brewed in the back room of her beauty shop, which came complete with case histories proving it could make hair grow back on bald spots.

Standridge died in 1961, but her own daughter, a multiply married and divorced cosmetologist named Dathene Dark, was still very much around. Dark, who had inherited the family business acumen along with the family formulas, was so broke by 1963 that she couldn't afford to brew up a batch of BeautiControl unless a customer fronted money for ingredients. As a single mother trying to support herself, five children, and a compulsive shopping habit, Dark took Mary Kay's $500 for the formulas and did not ask questions.

Mary Kay took the formulas to Elwood Goodier, the jobber over in Oak Cliff who already manufactured them for World Gift. Goodier camouflaged the stink of Heath's brew in a slightly different way and packaged the results in nice white jars with labels edged in gold. Mary Kay then found a storefront in the perfect spot: Exchange Park was Dallas's up-to-the-minute mix of office space, retail, and recreation. Hundreds of women worked in its office towers every day. Hundreds more visited its air-conditioned restaurants, stores, and thirty-two-lane Mickey Mantle Bowling Center. She would be inundated with customers.

Beauty by Mary Kay was set to open in September. Hallenbeck envisioned a franchising business that would outearn anything John Earl Shoaff ever dreamed up. Big things were bound to happen.

He and Mary Kay married in July.

One month later, on August 13, Hallenbeck headed out for his pre-breakfast jog along Northwest Parkway. Even that early in the morning, the Dallas heat and humidity were brutal. Temperatures had hovered around one hundred degrees for the last two weeks. The weatherman said they were in for the hottest day of the year.

But Hallenbeck had grown up in Iowa, where he had been something of a hometown hero on the track, and it got pretty hot during those summers too. Back in Cedar Rapids, he had been elected Health King, the healthiest boy in his junior high school, praised for perfect posture and not having a single filling in his teeth. He had played competitive badminton. He prided himself on staying fit.

After his run, he sat down to breakfast and began telling Mary Kay how he planned to handle that afternoon's meeting with their accountant. Yet again, he was nattering on about financial matters that baffled and bored her. Better to let him talk. Until her new husband had a heart attack mid-monologue. He died while they sat at the breakfast table.

Later, after the temperature had dropped to ninety-nine, Mary Kay had her own talk with the accountant. The news was not good. Hallenbeck had so many irons in the fire, including a deal with S&H Green Stamps, that Mary Kay couldn't keep them straight. She had no idea how to manage sourcing, inventory, or contracts. For years, she had called herself "the gal that could make a sale, but never could add up a ticket." No one who knew her disagreed.

She knew nothing about franchising. Once again, she found herself widowed less than a year after her wedding. The marriage to Hallenbeck, and maybe his last divorce, did not bear much legal scrutiny. She was unemployed. Going to another company, if she could find one willing to take a grandmother in her forties, would mean starting at the bottom. No sales company was going to hire a woman as a manager.

She decided to ditch the new venture.

CHAPTER THIRTEEN

Friday the Thirteenth

Thirteen would be her lucky number.

Thirteen years later, she would become the first woman to chair a company on the New York Stock Exchange. She would own a factory with thirteen in its address. Eventually, she would preside over a Fortune 500 company from a headquarters building with thirteen floors and thirteen elevators. China would become her thirteenth international subsidiary. After 2013, it would become that company's largest market.

In 1963, none of that had happened yet. When Hallenbeck died on August 13, the number looked nothing but unlucky. Mary Kay had a day or two to bury her bridegroom and decide what to do about the start-up. Her life savings were lost to leases, labels, and packaging. Nothing had resale value. Her lawyer and her accountant advised her to cut the losses. Forget the business.

That would be the official story, the one that would win her the Horatio Alger Award for "triumph over adversity," make her the only woman in *Forbes Greatest Business Stories of All Time*, and get her invited to the Smithsonian Institution to lecture on American entrepreneurship . That story would be cited in Harvard Business School case studies and land her in the Wharton School's "Top Twenty-Five Business

People of Our Times." Like a favorite fairy tale, the business press would come back to it time and again, so that, even after her death, she was still being accorded titles like "Greatest Female Entrepreneur in American History." Forever after, she would be the feisty little businesswoman who defied the naysayers.

That story also left out a lot. On the day of Hallenbeck's heart attack, Mary Kay knew next to nothing about the company he planned to build with her name and her money. During their month as man and wife, she had sidestepped marital strife by not asking too many questions. Now she found herself fronting the kind of selling scheme she had always hated: where all the money flowed toward a fat-cat franchise owner and not the women who were doing the selling.

Savings from all those years of talking up toilet brushes and *Venus de Milo* statuettes had vanished into a tangle of contracts and leases. Bills that she thought were paid came boomeranging back. She had given up her office, title, and $25,000 salary for nothing. Dick Kelly said he felt sorry for her. Said he would take her back.

Ignorance compounded embarrassment. Mary Kay did not know enough about Hallenbeck to supply the coroner's office with his parents' names for the death certificate. He did not have a will. Creditors were coming out of the woodwork. When she opened her bills, she saw that the fur coat he had given her as a wedding present had been charged to her own account. An ex-wife appeared to argue that the marriage to Mary Kay was not valid.

Filling out paperwork, she listed Hallenbeck as president of his own food products company. In death notices, she omitted mention of profession. Using the funeral home that had served for Eckman, she buried Hallenbeck at Hillcrest, near his jogging route. The gravestone listed his military rank and decorations. No mention was made of wives or children. Two weeks later, she had herself appointed temporary administrator and started settling the estate. Paperwork and litigation would drag on for over a year while offers in compromise flew back and forth.

Mary Kay began referring to herself as a widow and listing herself "Mary K. Weaver" in the telephone book. That was the name she used when she signed her articles of incorporation. That was the name she used when Beauty by Mary Kay opened a month later, on Friday the 13th.

Within a day of Hallenbeck's death, Mary Kay resigned herself to returning to World Gift with "my tail between my legs." Then her sons arrived for the funeral.

Each came with his own "You can do it!" Ben told her, "I think you could do anything in this world that you wanted to," and handed over his savings passbook. All $4,500 was hers if she needed it. "That's the day I forgave him for all the problems he had ever caused," said Mary Kay, who made no secret of the fact that Ben was not her favorite child. When Ben also offered to come and work for her, she admitted thinking, "Heaven forbid."

Richard, who was not the sort to get sentimental over the loss of his latest stepfather, was already coming up with ways to turn the situation to his advantage. He told her, "If you could be successful working for somebody else, we know you can do even better working for yourself."

Afterward, it was hard to be certain who talked whom into what. Within a day or two, Mary Kay decided to continue with her company. Richard would fill in for Hallenbeck. "Richard became my business partner, mostly because Richard would work for $250 a month, which was all I could afford to pay, and there were just not many people standing in line for that job." His mother gave him the title of general manager. "I saw Richard as being able to pick up boxes I couldn't and fill orders and things of that sort."

Both had watched an even more unlikely mother-and-son partnership succeed. Mary C. Crowley's son had been a hell-raising hot-rodder who dropped out of Crozier Tech High School before they could flunk him out. But a stint in the air force, long hours at Home Interiors, and a mother's prayers—"Dear God, let Don do great things. Just let them be legal"—had turned Don Carter into a God-fearing Baptist businessman who helped his mother build a million-dollar company.

Mary Kay must have prayed things would work out as well with her own prodigal. After leaving the all-male, military rigor of Allen Academy in the middle of his senior year to sample the co-ed attractions and undemanding curriculum of Hillcrest High in Dallas, Richard had graduated with too many incompletes to get into Southern Methodist University, where he wanted to go to college. Enrolling at North Texas State, he left during his second semester to sign up for the U.S. Marine Corps Reserve and go off to boot camp in California. From there, he headed back to North Texas State, where he took two marketing courses and some data processing before leaving again. By the summer of 1963, he was back in Houston.

Richard was enough like his mother to talk his way into a job at IBM, an outfit where Crowley's son had also spent time. Waiting for his IBM job to start, he took a salesman's job at Prudential Life Insurance. By June, on the strength of the $480 a month Prudential had been paying him, twenty-year-old Richard married sixteen-year-old Linda Ann Provenzano. By August, when he arrived for his stepfather's funeral, the IBM job still had not started. Later, Richard recalled his mother offering $350 a month to come work for her. She recalled offering $250.

In either case, the money was moot. At boarding school, when other boys boasted of fathers who were army generals or CEOs, Richard boasted of a mother who, as he told those stuck-up rich kids, was the best in the world at what she did. Now, trading in his sweet little Corvette for a clunker and banking the $1,200 difference, Richard stepped out of the running for the IBM job, quit Prudential, turned a deaf ear to the in-laws who told him he was ruining their daughter's life, and moved his teenage bride to Dallas. Untold riches could not fail to follow.

Sitting at her kitchen table, Mary Kay and Richard rehashed the ideas that had been belittled by her bosses and her bridegroom. To her mind, it stood to reason that a company would make money if its salespeople were happy and making money. That was why she was against franchises. True, a new company could get rich quick by franchising. But Mary Kay was certain her way was better. That meant taking time to build a sales force. To Richard, that meant they were going to need a secondary source of revenue.

She knew just the thing: wigs, like the ones she always wore. They would sell Fashion Tress, a brand that pledged instant, albeit pricey, transformation. Made of human hair and retailing between $100 and $300, Fashion Tress wigs were advertised in *Vogue* and *Harper's Bazaar* with taglines like "Be the woman you want to be . . . in 60 seconds!" Mary Kay, who wanted to hide her gray hair and the small scar on her forehead, was never without one.

Wigs would be a way to get customers through the door and convince recruits that real money could be made. In Dallas, where the city motto "Think Big" was taken literally in matters of hairstyle, every woman would want a wig. And since she was getting them wholesale, Mary Kay could use them as sales incentives. With that settled, Mary Kay flew off to Fashion Tress headquarters in Miami Beach for a week of wig school.

If she needed reassurance that a quirky, family-run beauty business could beat the odds, she was in the right place. Fashion Tress was owned by Rowland Schaefer, a serial entrepreneur who'd started selling magazine subscriptions door to door at age eleven, after his father abandoned the family. During the Depression, Schaefer had dropped out of high school to sell vacuum cleaners door to door before trying his luck at prospecting for gold and, when that didn't work out, prospecting for oil. Other surefire moneymakers included a three-hundred-tee driving range and a miniature golf course. Years later, after he'd hit it big with a vending machine business and was looking to move on, his wife, Sylvia, came home with a wig and informed him that he should get into the wig business. Schaefer said he knew nothing about wigs. Supposedly she countered with "What did you know about your other businesses before you started them?"

Together, the Schaefers started Fashion Tress in 1961. In less than two years, the company was traded over the counter and known as the country's largest importer of wigs and hairpieces, with a generous advertising schedule that guaranteed editorial coverage in glossies like *Vogue*, *Harper's Bazaar*, *Mademoiselle*, *Glamour*, and *Ebony*. Just before Mary Kay and Richard came calling, Schaefer had given an interview to *Vogue* about the "Do's and Don'ts of Wig-Owning," in which the magazine cited him as an authority who estimated that the U.S. wig market would soon be worth $100 million.

Surely any company serving such a market could not fail to prosper. Proceeding as if her marriage to Hallenbeck had never happened, forty-five-year-old Mary Kay signed her articles of incorporation as Mary Kay Weaver on Monday, August 26, with two well-connected Dallas lawyers as her incorporators. By Friday, state filings and registrations were finished. Twenty-year-old Richard, whose chief qualification was confidence, would be her second-in-command.

Neither knew how to run a business.

Hallenbeck probably pictured himself as head of a lucrative racket like Nutri-Bio. Mary Kay did not.

Based on recipes that had been around for thirty years without producing much profit for anyone, Beauty by Mary Kay planned to launch with nine products, five of them in its core skin care regimen. They would not come cheap.

Mary Kay priced her regimen at $15.95: Cleansing Creme for $2, Magic Masque for $4, Skin Freshener for $3.50, Super Nite Cream for $4.95, and Day Radiance, a foundation available in light, medium, or dark, for $1.50. In today's dollars, that would be a layout of about $175. In 1963 dollars, that made her skin care far more expensive than other direct-sales brands. Avon's bestselling masque cost $1.25, less than a third of Mary Kay's. Other direct sellers' were even cheaper. So were drugstore brands.

Her prices put her on par with department store brands like Elizabeth Arden, Helena Rubinstein, and Revlon. Her jars looked like they belonged in Neiman Marcus. Creams that used to come in Cloverine Salve tins and salvaged pharmacy bottles were packaged in weighty white glass with gold lids and gold labels—except for the Skin Freshener, which came in clear glass so women could see it looked like liquid gold.

She planned to sell products individually, although that would soon change. Like many a beauty brand before and after, Mary Kay would tell customers that her products worked best in synergy. In her words, breaking up the Basic Set was "like giving you my recipe for chocolate cake but leaving out an important ingredient. It's just not going to be my cake." Soon the jars would be pale pink and packaged as a set. Fresh from her makeover, a customer either bought the boxed regimen for $15.95—$24 if she wanted the glamour products too—or went back to looking like she did before the beauty show. Take it or leave it.

For now, individual sales would be fine. Any sale would be fine. Consultants were to be equipped with a "Beauty Showcase," a $4.95 blue vinyl case from Woolworth's that Mary Kay described as looking like "something your grade schooler would pack for a sleepover." Inside were product samples plus a couple of mimeographed pages that constituted the training manual. Stanley Home Products had charged her $30 for a starter showcase and let her work off the cost. Mary Kay would charge $25 for hers and stipulate full payment up front. She wanted her consultants committed.

Her sales channel would be another iteration of the party plan. There would be no door-to-door selling. No standing on a porch and smiling while some stranger slammed a door in your face. Her beauty shows would combine the demonstrations she had used at Stanley with the self-improvement spin she had used at World Gift. The hostess would invite five or so friends to her house for a free facial followed by a chance to try on a wig; Mary Kay would then educate them about health and beauty. Skin care, after all, dictated regular use and repeat purchase, as well as having wholesome associations with hygiene. That made it a perfect product.

She was not the first to think so. In the 1880s, Chicago socialite Harriet Hubbard Ayer escaped an abusive marriage and made a fortune pitching skin cream. At the turn of the century, Chaya Rubinstein, a Polish immigrant to Australia, started with skin care and went on to become Helena Rubinstein, the richest self-made woman in the world. Canadian nursing school dropout Florence Nightingale Graham did much the same after renaming herself Elizabeth Arden in 1910. As did

Josephine Esther Mentzer from Corona, Queens, who turned herself into Estée Lauder in the 1940s. The idea, then and now, was that a satisfied customer for skin care would repeat the purchase and become a customer for makeup and other ancillaries. "Everybody has skin," said Mary Kay.

Ideally, beauty shows would be conducted at the dining room table. A kitchen table would do. Every home had one of those. Most tables seated six, so that became the ideal number of guests. While products were passed around and women stuck their fingers into the little jars, the consultant would stay on her feet, moving around the room to instruct and advise. Everyone at the table had to participate. Mary Kay had staged enough parties to know that women who sat back and watched were not women who bought.

The plan was for each woman to wash her face, experience the Magic Masque, moisturize, then apply makeup and marvel at her transformation. Each place was set with a paper place mat and a flimsy tray to hold dabs of product. After each show, a consultant was supposed to sterilize the tray by swiping it with rubbing alcohol and putting it in a 140-degree oven for sixty seconds until its surface was slightly melted. Turn the oven too high and that was the end of the tray. Jar lids did in a pinch.

In Texas, most municipalities required a cosmetology license for facials or makeup application, so Mary Kay warned consultants never to touch a customer's skin. Using a lemons-to-lemonade approach that went legal compliance one better, she declared that everyone else did makeovers the wrong way. Women, she said, did not like to take off their makeup in department stores in front of strangers. Women could not always reproduce the results of a professional. Women wanted more time for consultations. She later wrote: "When a woman applies the makeup herself with a trained Consultant instructing her, she learns how to do it correctly. She can then repeat what she did that day."

Each makeover commenced with cleanser. An emollient that liquefied at body temperature, Cleansing Creme was massaged into the face with fingertips, then removed with a damp cloth. Magic Masque, the

Beauty by Mary Kay's Lip and Eye Palette, flagship of the line's "glamour cosmetics."

product that allowed Mary Kay to bill the beauty show as a "free facial," came next. An oatmeal-based powder, the masque was mixed with water until it had the consistency of plaster of Paris. If the client hoped for a little bleaching to get rid of freckles or age spots, it was mixed with lemon juice or buttermilk. Either way, it solidified within minutes. Once it was on, the client couldn't do much more than mumble and nod without cracking the crust. That's when the consultant launched her spiel. Then the masque was washed off and the client was encouraged to touch her face and feel the dewy freshness of her complexion.

After that, it was time for the Skin Freshener, a liquid that tingled as it dried. Next was Super Nite Cream, the hero product. That's where the hide tanner story came in. Made with ammoniated mercury, a chemical exfoliant, it left complexions pink-cheeked in much the same way that alpha hydroxy acids would when they debuted three decades later. In 1963, there wasn't much like it. Because it caused redness and rashes on sensitive skin, Mary Kay cautioned clients to test Super Nite Cream on their arms first. Later she would reformulate; later still, the Food and Drug Administration would ban the ingredient. For the present, she lavished Super Nite Cream on her own skin and touted it as the final step in every Beauty by Mary Kay facial. Again, the client touched her face and found her skin softer.

Liquid foundation came next. No powder followed. Since more stock-keeping units (SKUs) meant more investment in inventory, her product line was pared to the minimum. Color cosmetics were the finishing touch. Palettes were the rage in department stores, so Mary Kay offered a single palette with five lip colors on one side and five eye shadows on the other. The packaging was pale pink Cycolac, which Mary Kay commended as the same sturdy material "your phone was made out of."

The saleswoman who once tied a bow around a broom and pitched it as "the perfect gift for your mother-in-law" now informed women that a lip color should be applied with a brush: "It's a known fact that continuous stretching of the lip tissues with a lipstick tube causes fine lines around the mouth, permitting the lipstick to bleed into them." She also pointed out that those five shades of lip color would convert to at least fifty-three shades by mixing, "so it doesn't matter what fashion turns to this season, she can mix the exact shade of lip color to go with whatever clothes she might be wearing." She said the same thing about the eye shadows.

Her cream rouge was a basic red that was "really a million shades in one" because "in a matter of seconds it changes to match your skin tone," which echoed the change-on-contact claim pioneered by Tangee, a beauty brand that debuted in the 1920s and had its heyday in the 1940s. By 1963, the idea that makeup changed color to match your body chemistry was so out of fashion that it sounded new. No such claims were made for units of mascara and eyebrow pencil.

Wigs would come last. Customers would be dying to try them on. This guaranteed that everybody would sit through the beauty show.

Beauty by Mary Kay opened for business on Friday, the 13th of September, because that was the day her lease started.

At 9:00 a.m., Mary Kay and Richard unlocked the front door of their five-hundred-square-foot storefront. As if to offer a glimpse of glamorous goings-on, its front window was draped with a diaphanous pink curtain, sewn by Mary Kay herself, that was drawn to one side and gathered by a silky pink cord. Inventory rested resplendent on a $9.95 steel rack from Sears. Her office was a back room crammed with secondhand filing cabinets, curlers, hair dryers, and Styrofoam heads wearing wigs in various stages of styling. Out front, all was flawless.

To promote the opening, she splurged on a display ad in *The Dallas Morning News.* Its tagline, "No Woman Need Ever Look 40," echoed language that companies like Helena Rubinstein and Elizabeth Arden used for the "hormone creams" that dominated high-end skin care. Underneath, she announced that $100 Fashion Tress wigs would be marked down to $69.50 and that René of Paris would be on hand to personally style—for free!—any wig purchased on opening day. Mary Kay was also giving away free cosmetics. Free champagne too. Anything to get people through the door.

It was not an auspicious beginning. Businessmen came by to ogle the wig model and guzzle champagne but showed no interest in wigs or beauty products. No one sent flowers. The only good-luck gift was a spindly ivy plant with six leaves, which she nicknamed Oscar. In the issue of *Vogue* that hit newsstands that day, Fashion Tress ran a strange ad that showed a woman with tears streaming down her face. It was hard not to see that as an portent.

In the days that followed, the storefront remained empty for hours on end. Mary Kay had counted on foot traffic; at least five hundred women worked in the high-rises facing the parking lot. Too late, she discovered that those women were allowed only thirty minutes for lunch, and all of them took it at the same time. After work, they raced home to family obligations. Her single stroke of luck was her spot near the coffee shop. Women had to walk past her storefront to get there.

Like most beauty brands, Mary Kay counted on a makeover to put her products across. So she found herself condensing her hour-long transformation into fifteen minutes and aiming an electric fan at the secretaries so the Magic Masque would dry in time for them to get back to work. When sales were not forthcoming, she tried to get them to go to a beauty show.

But she did no better with beauty shows. At her first, sales totaled $2. She had been confident that customers who sampled her products would beg for more. When they did not, she was too flustered to ask for orders. She forgot to pass out order cards. As soon as the ordeal was over, she burst into tears.

Recruitment stalled too. By opening week, she had signed eight women as consultants. Most were friends or friends of friends. None expected the venture to last. The first was thirty-two-year-old Dalene Brewer, forever after famous as "Mary Kay Consultant Number One." Brewer had worked for Hallenbeck during his Nutri-Bio days and joined with the idea that she was going to help out his widow. A cowgirl who could ride and rope with the best of them, Brewer had no interest in cosmetics, but "at the time, there just weren't many really good opportunities for women in sales."

In October, despite her resolution to avoid classifieds, Mary Kay began running the kind of help-wanted ads that had lured salespeople to Fuller Brush, Stanley Home Products, and World Gift. Wigs were the attention-getter. FASHION WIGS ran in large type, followed by "Mary Kay Cosmetics" in smaller type. "Sell by wearing—socially or on the job." It didn't help.

Nothing helped. Mary Kay was working harder than she had ever worked selling salve, books, cookware, brushes, knickknacks, or anything else. Waking at five each morning, she got to Exchange Park early in case anyone wanted to stop in before work. Nobody did. She stayed late in case anyone had an hour to kill after work. Nobody did. She had been sure her own sales would get things off the ground. That was not happening.

Richard matched her sixteen- and eighteen-hour workdays. Cosmetics came in when none had gone out. With no place left for inventory in the wig-crammed back room, Richard rented basement storage. They had gone through Ben's $4,500, deposited in the company account just in time to write a $3,815 check to the Goodier factory. By the first week of November, Mary Kay had sold her futuristic, electric version of the "Home for All America" in Glenbrook Valley. Then things got worse.

On November 22, President John F. Kennedy was shot in Dallas. Two days later, shooter Lee Harvey Oswald was gunned down at Dallas Police Headquarters. Dallas became known as the "City of Hate." News commentators reminded the rest of the country how, only weeks before, the good people of Dallas had struck and spat at Adlai Stevenson, the former presidential candidate. Pundits with longer memories recollected the city's long association with the Ku Klux Klan and its 1920s reputation as "Hate Capital of Dixie." Columnists came up with new definitions for "the Big D"; *Despondency, Defeat,* and *Despair* were among the most popular. Everyone's business was affected. Even Crowley had displayers resign.

Nobody was in the mood for Magic Masque or $300 wigs. Mary Kay, who had no orders and no recruits, called together her little band of consultants each Monday and passed along what she'd learned during decades of direct selling. She talked up the profit potential of recruiting. None of them saw the point.

Visiting Houston for Thanksgiving, Mary Kay rounded out the roster by handing her daughter the Beauty Showcase that no one else seemed to want and saying, "Here, do something with this." She kept up the classifieds that she had been running in the "Help Wanted, Female" section of the paper. Finally, in December, she switched tactics, now promising "Win a Free Wig" and "Earn $500 between now and Christmas."

Her advertising was starting to sound desperate. On December 8, a display ad in *The Dallas Morning News* announced a grand-prize drawing on December 15 with a free $125 Fashion Tress wig as grand prize. One hundred consolation prizes would also be given away; all the newspaper reader had to do was fill out the entry blank with a name and address and have it postmarked by the 11th. *FREE* was the largest word in the ad, followed by *HURRY!*

Beauty products were the consolation prize.

CHAPTER FOURTEEN

"Praise Forward to Success"

Within months, Mary Kay's company was profitable.

Wigs were the draw. "We kept the wigs in the car, because if you brought them out they created so much excitement that you could never get through the facial," Mary Kay said. "So we . . . insisted that they had to get their makeup on and perfect before they could try on the wigs." Wigs made the money. "Really we hadn't gotten into the cosmetics business yet."

Women were wig crazy. Wigs were not yet sold in Dallas department stores—not even Neiman Marcus—so Mary Kay had a chance to corner the market. While she and Richard sold $300 wigs from the shopping center storefront with home-sewn curtains and shelves from Sears, her beauty consultants would be taking orders during beauty shows.

Each consultant was equipped with hair swatches from Champagne Beige to Cleopatra Black, plus a sample wig or two for customers to try on. Each time the consultant sold a wig or passed along a referral, that consultant would earn a 30 percent commission, a sideline with the potential to yield $100 or more per month.

Wigs would also be incentives for recruits. If she ever got any. Fashion Tress, advertised in *Harper's Bazaar* and *Vogue*, should attract just the kind of women she wanted as customers and consultants. Until then, wigs were a way to keep the lights on while she built the blockbuster direct-selling business that was bound to follow.

At first, it worked like a charm. For $67.50, Mary Kay and Richard could buy a top-of-the-line wig from Fashion Tress that they could turn around and sell for $300 or more. Overcoming the problem that most women did not have $100 to $300 to spend on a wig, Richard followed the example of used-car dealers and offered Presto Charge, a financing plan from Preston State Bank, so aspiring wig wearers could purchase on the installment plan. In October, the company's first full month in business, Beauty by Mary Kay sold $5,000 in wigs, with a cost of goods that ran about $800 plus another $1,000 or so in styling expenses. Richard plowed those profits back into the company.

But the wig business also came with problems Richard couldn't solve. Once bought, a wig usually had to be styled and shaped, which meant that a hairdresser had to be hired. High-end hairdressers were often French, almost exclusively male, and unaccustomed to being contradicted by clients. Madame might wish her wig to look a certain way. Monsieur, however, had his artistic integrity and wielded his scissors accordingly. Whereupon Madame might yell, "I ain't payin' for this!," and storm out. After which Richard would fire Monsieur. Then have to hire a replacement with similar training and temperament.

Just as often, a husband would nix his wife's new look. Then the returned wig would be restyled and displayed on a Styrofoam head at Exchange Park, where, sooner or later, someone would like the look of it. At that point, whoever was minding the store would launch a pitch along the lines of "Boy, have I got a deal for you!" and unload it at a reduced price.

As 1963 drew to a close, Fashion Tress was the only part of the company turning a profit. Even so, Richard hated dealing with the hairdressers' egos. He hated those returns. He hated the wig business.

With an eye to winning a free wig and a little Christmas cash, a twenty-nine-year-old legal secretary named Jackie Brown answered one of the ads that Mary Kay had been running in *The Dallas Morning News.*

Up until then, Brown had been dogged by the same bad luck that sent so many countrypeople to cities like Houston and Dallas. Brown was raised in a small town in the Ozarks. Her father died when she was three days old. Her mother supported ten children by working as laundress, maid, or whatever else was available to a good Christian woman with an eighth-grade education. Brown married her childhood sweetheart, who died soon after she put him through college, leaving her with a toddler to support and her own dreams of college crushed. Remarried and living in Dallas, she held down a full-time job to support her daughter because her second husband would not. At night, she tried to take college courses. When she met Mary Kay, it was one year to the day after a miscarriage. She had never sold anything except the Cloverine Salve she peddled as a kid. She did not win a pony either. Working as a secretary at a white-shoe law firm, she was earning $500 a month. It wasn't enough for her.

Brown looked at Mary Kay and decided, "She was glossy. She radiated money and abundance. She was exactly what I wanted to be." Mary Kay looked at Brown and saw potential. She praised her. Hearing that Brown had talked a coworker into driving her to Exchange Park during a snowstorm, Mary Kay called her a natural saleswoman. The next thing Brown knew, she was getting a makeover.

First came skin care. As cleansing commenced, Mary Kay told the story of the hide tanner. Brown, who hailed from Arkansas herself, was enthralled. As Brown sat immobilized by the Magic Masque, Mary Kay explained how the beauty shows worked. With the same pitch that she had been using since her days at Stanley Home Products, Mary Kay told Brown that each beauty show should yield at least two bookings for further shows. After each stage of the facial, Mary Kay asked Brown to touch her skin and feel how much softer it had become. Brown was awed. When it was time for glamour, Brown chose the shades of foundation, eye makeup, lipstick, and brow pencil that Mary Kay was wearing.

Then came the coup de grâce. "Would you like to try on a wig?"

Eager to see herself as Mary Kay, Brown reached for a wig that was platinum blond. One look in the mirror was all it took for her to sign up on the spot. She did not even call her husband for permission to write the $25 check.

Within a week, Brown was selling the line to other legal secretaries. Her first beauty show lasted five hours and sold $70 in beauty products. That brought her a profit of $28, more than she earned in a full day at the law firm. When those same women ordered wigs, she earned hundreds more, bringing her total for that first show to more than a full week's combined wages for her and her engineer husband. That same week, she scored a high-ticket private sale to a single mother who needed a wig to wear to bed for her part-time job as a call girl. Brown sold her a hand-tied, $300 platinum blond wig just like the one Mary Kay wore.

Brown's makeover continued. She wore false lashes like Mary Kay. She borrowed a Fashion Tress wig until she could earn her own. Proud of her wig sales, she could not understand why Mary Kay and Richard were not as excited. She called Mary Kay almost every day to report her results, although her mentor always brought the conversation around to recruiting and skin care.

At the same time, Mary Kay was using the same methods on Dalene Brewer. Until she met Mary Kay, Brewer had never worn makeup. A ranch-bred rodeo queen raised on a two-thousand-acre spread in Texas Hill Country, Marjorie Dalene Boren Brewer had majored in speech and music at Texas Christian University, married while she was in college, then taught dyslexic children. She had a policeman husband, was raising two daughters, and sang with the Fort Worth Opera in her spare time. Selling for Mary Kay brought back her girlhood glory as a champion barrel racer. "I remember how proud I was when I finally came in with a $400 week," she later wrote. "Mary Kay told me how well I had done, and then she added, 'And next week, Dalene, you'll do even better!' Well, I went out there and broke my neck so I wouldn't let her down, and I did do better the next week."

Word got back to Brown, who was already jealous of Brewer's friendship with Mary Kay and status as consultant number one. "Everybody wants to be like somebody," said Brown, an olive-skinned brunette who began wearing extra-light foundation, blue eyeliner, and blond wigs to look more like her pale-skinned, blue-eyed, blond boss. "Mary Kay wanted to be like Mary Crowley. I wanted to be like Mary Kay."

One day, Brown would be a business rival facing Mary Kay across a Dallas courtroom. In the meantime, sales soared off the charts.

Three days before Christmas, Mary Kay combined the company's holiday party with a sales meeting.

In 1931, Mr. Bev's first "Stanley Meeting" had been seven people getting together to celebrate Christmas over a seventy-five-cent turkey dinner. Nobody got a bonus because the company couldn't afford one. Their present was an Extra-Stiff Clothes Brush. Mary Kay was going to do better.

Dalene Brewer arrived early to help Mary Kay cook for the party and found the boss in house slippers and wrapper, wig parked on a kitchen doorknob. Brewer helped out, went home, changed clothes, and returned to a town house neat as a pin. Food was ready. Christmas presents were ready for every single invitee. Mary Kay was made-up, wigged, and petting her poodle like a lady of leisure.

At the end of 1963, Beauty by Mary Kay was on target to clear about $17,500, but almost every penny had come from wig sales. That night, Richard got the party started by bringing out a blackboard and drawing diagrams to illustrate how recruiting could multiply earnings. He reminded the small sales force that anyone who became a sales director could earn up to an additional 12 percent on recruits. Eyes lit up. They were finally getting it.

When it was Mary Kay's turn to speak, she announced that the consultant with the highest cosmetics sales for December would win an elegant prize. Taking Brown aside, Mary Kay informed her that she was in contention for the elegant prize. She also said that if Brown did not win, then Brewer probably would.

Brown was determined to beat Brewer. Later she would write, "As a legal secretary, there was no opportunity to excel. At Mary Kay, there was." Heading home to Arkansas for the holidays, Brown took her demo case and, on the day after Christmas, got her first recruit: a high school classmate aiming to buy a pickup truck for her husband and a diamond ring for herself. The minute she got back to Texas, Brown staged a beauty show in her own home. Telling her guests about the Beauty by Mary Kay selling opportunity, she found four interested in getting in on the ground floor.

When it came time for the January sales meeting, Brown walked in to see a box wrapped in shiny pink paper tied up with a white bow. The elegant prize. Watching Brewer try to hide her disappointment, Brown heard Mary Kay announce her as the winner. While the other women clapped and cheered, she unwrapped her shiny pink package to find a leaded crystal dish on a silver pedestal. "Such praise had never fallen on me," she later wrote. "The praise was the prize; it filled a void inside of me I hadn't even known was there. If that was true for me, then I knew it must be true for countless others."

For the rest of that sales meeting, Mary Kay focused on booking beauty shows: how to use the right words, how to persist until a hostess said yes. Then Mary Kay went around the room asking each consultant how many beauty shows she had scheduled for the coming week. Brewer had the most. Mary Kay predicted great things from her and piled on the praise. Then Mary Kay announced the next month's sales contest and said anyone with a $500 wholesale cosmetics order would win a Fashion Tress wig.

That February, Mary Kay targeted the well-heeled readership of *The Park Cities News* and the *Texas Jewish Post* with ads proclaiming "No Woman Need Ever Look 40." Trying a "Bring this ad with you" gambit to get customers to Exchange Park, she again marked $100 Fashion Tress wigs down to $69.50. No mention was made of selling opportunities. That was saved for the recruitment ads she ran in *The Dallas Morning News'* "Help Wanted, Female" section.

Mary Kay was sure that her business was about to break through. She just had to be more confident, work a little harder, hold on a little longer. She sold her house in Freeway Manor. Through March, she advertised "Hold Fabulous Wig and Beauty Shows." Then the ads became unnecessary.

As Brown and Brewer battled it out, recruits multiplied. Some were housewives. Some were secretaries or schoolteachers. Most had been cheerleaders, homecoming queens, straight-A students, young girls with big dreams. Mary Kay knew what they wanted to hear.

She applauded and complimented and congratulated, following each bit of praise with an assurance that they could do even better. She said she believed in them. Told them to believe in themselves. She suggested that recruits take out a loan, even if they didn't need the money, then pay the loan promptly so they could establish credit in their own names. As she had done at Stanley and World Gift, she passed along her tried-and-true tactics. When a consultant encountered a woman who resisted hosting a beauty show, Mary Kay told recruits to look that woman in the eye and say, "I'm sorry, I think you would have been wonderful," then walk away. When consultants tried to recruit, Mary Kay urged them to "reverse sell" and figure out what a woman hoped to get from joining the company.

Borrowing a motto from Crowley, Mary Kay told her sales force to make "God first, family second, career third." Despite a lifetime of evidence to the contrary, she continued to push the idea that direct selling was a flexible part-time job perfect for the woman who wanted to be there when her kids got home from school. That was no more true than it had been before, but no one argued the point. Her selling opportunity seemed closer than anything else.

Husbands could hardly object. Unlike at most direct-selling companies, it was impossible for a woman to go into debt with Mary Kay. Harking back to her years at Stanley and World Gift, when she lost so many stellar sellers because they built up accounts receivable faster than they could pay them off, Mary Kay eliminated accounts receivable. With that decision, she also eliminated the stress of unbalanced bank accounts, past-due notices from the parent company, chastened consultants, and outraged spouses.

Using the system that Crowley used at Home Interiors, consultants bought products outright. Only cashier's checks or money orders were accepted. Planning for the sure-to-come day when Beauty by Mary Kay would have thousands of consultants and multiple layers of management, Richard designed a system where beauty products went straight from Exchange Park into the hands of the consultant, who put them in the hands of her customer. There were no distributorships, no intermediaries, no markups.

There was no ringing of doorbells either, none of the "prospecting" or house-to-house selling that went on at Avon or Stanley or Fuller Brush. None of that undignified "foot in the door" pushiness of trying to go where you were not wanted. Like Crowley's company, Beauty by Mary Kay had dress and comportment codes. Hose, white gloves, and a girdle were required on company business. Smoking, chewing gum, and the wearing of pants were not permitted. Retail or secretarial employment would have asked the same.

Lest couples fret that a high-earning wife would upset the balance of their marriage, Mary Kay schooled consultants to say that husbands provided necessities while wives provided niceties. She herself could not have been less threatening. A widowed grandmother who did not cuss or smoke or drink, Mary Kay could never be accused of being one of those man-hating she-males. She was a churchgoing Baptist who never raised her voice. She never seemed to disagree with anyone, never to object outright. No one was better groomed. No one was a better housekeeper. She could cook up a storm too. "When I met her, I was so relieved she was so feminine," an early hire recalled. "In those days there just weren't that many women in business, especially feminine women."

Mary Kay was never without her false lashes and platinum wig. Like a signal of self-determination, her eyebrows were penciled higher with each passing week. When she click-clacked around Exchange Park in her high heels, poodle in her arms, there was no mistaking her. Long before she gave away her first pink Cadillac, she had made herself into a brand.

On April 1, Brown and Brewer started the process that would make them the company's first sales directors. During this director-in-qualification period, their respective units were required to purchase $4,000 retail each month for three consecutive months. Wig sales would not count toward the total. If either woman made it, she would have the title of sales director, which would make her an executive. She would also get overrides on everyone in her unit, which meant commissions on sales that other women made. If both women became sales directors, Mary Kay promised to split any unaffiliated consultants between the two teams, which would broaden their earnings bases still more. Both women began booking and recruiting with a vengeance.

Now that the company had enough orders and recruits to make it worthwhile, Richard computerized as much of the back office as he could. Then he promoted himself to vice president. Richard and his mother were still working until two or three o'clock most mornings, so as orders multiplied, brother Ben was asked to join them. Richard hated filling orders and rearranging shelves almost as much as he hated the wig business. His mother and brother considered Ben ideal for inventory work, especially since he was willing to do it for $250 a month. Besides, the company had outgrown its space in Exchange Park. Beauty by Mary Kay would be moving soon.

Ben, who had a wife, two children, and a mortgage on his home in Houston, had been earning $750 a month servicing oil and gas wells for Lyons Co. His in-laws told him that he would be ruining their daughter's life if he ran off to Dallas. He went anyway. Big sister Marylyn stayed in Houston, where, on May 29, she gave birth to a fourth daughter.

Already earning three times more with Beauty by Mary Kay than she earned at the law firm, Jackie Brown quit secretarial work that June. Brown could now afford shortcuts—hiring a maid instead of doing her own cleaning, buying clothes at Neiman Marcus instead of sewing them, wearing a wig instead of setting her hair—that let her devote twelve or more hours a day to building her Mary Kay business. The more money she made, the more recruits she got. The more recruits she got, the more money she made. By July 1, Brown and Brewer had qualified as sales directors, a milestone that Mary Kay celebrated with an engraved crystal bowl for each, a small ceremony, and so much praise that Brown again found herself on the verge of tears.

"Praise forward to success. . . . Pretend that everyone you meet has a sign on their back that says 'make me feel important.'" The more successful Mary Kay became, the more profound those Dale Carnegie–inspired slogans of hers began to sound. Mary Kay cited her company's momentum as proof that women were desperate for recognition: "Nobody has applauded these women since they graduated from high school."

Before the summer was over, Beauty by Mary Kay moved to a one-story headquarters/warehouse at 1220 Majesty Drive, which featured proper offices, a kitchenette, and a conference room big enough for sales meetings. Cocksure, Richard predicted that the company would outgrow its new headquarters in five years.

Mary Kay no longer had to hold training sessions in her town house. Gone were the days when an order sent Richard racing into the thirty-six hundred feet of Exchange Park's tunnel system, where he would jog half a block, head to the basement while peeling off his coat and tie, then jog another hundred yards to the storage locker to grab products before reversing the route as he quick-changed back from sweaty stock boy to suited vice president.

While brother Ben presided over five thousand square feet of warehouse space, Richard now had an office as nice as Dick Kelly's office at World Gift. Instead of a closet-size back room furnished with bunged-up filing cabinets and Styrofoam wig stands, his mother now had herself an office with an executive desk set, a curlicued candle-holder on the wall, and her named spelled out on a brass plaque. Her lucky Hotei statue shared space with pretty porcelain figurines. Oscar the ivy plant flourished. Monet the poodle came to work with her each day, and if he tended to mark his territory too much for everyone's liking, well, it was considered his to mark.

Few thought her luck would last. Mary Kay had never run much of anything. Neither had that smart-aleck son of hers. As the company spread beyond Dallas–Fort Worth, she was putting women in charge who had never held any kind of job at all. The place was like a sorority.

To keep it that way, she started *Beauty News and Views*. Every week, she typed up product tips and sales strategies, added slogans and sketches, ran the results through the mimeograph machine, and mailed them off. When a consultant booked more than the usual number of parties or had even the smallest sales success, Mary Kay praised her by name and printed the particulars. When a consultant came up with a good idea, Mary Kay named her, praised her, and printed the idea. Women were soon vying to see their names in the newsletter.

Plenty of Stanley units had newsletters too, but most did not print sales totals next to each name. Mary Kay made sure that Brown could see how much Brewer was earning, down to the penny. So could everyone else. "In that culture, you weren't supposed to talk about how much you made," said an early recruit. "We were continually exposed." If seeing someone else's earnings brought out a woman's competitive spirit, so much the better.

Beauty by Mary Kay would end its first full year with $198,514 in sales. Over 90 percent of those sales had been made since January; fewer and fewer came from Fashion Tress. To celebrate, Mary Kay planned a sales convention for the company's September 13 anniversary. She decorated the new cinder block warehouse with gauzy pink curtains, pink crepe paper streamers, pink balloons, and upside-down pink paper parasols. Borrowing the name Seminar from World Gift, she borrowed some of its pep songs too. Then she hired the same people to play them. To the tune of the old Sunday school round "I've Got That Joy, Joy, Joy, Joy Down in My Heart," consultants belted out "I've Got That Mary Kay Enthusiasm," the same way the same tune had been reworded by other direct sellers.

That morning and afternoon were full of motivational speeches, beguiling charts of commissions and potential earnings, and pretend beauty shows so consultants could practice selling. Consultants were encouraged to bring potential recruits, who were easy to spot as the only women not in wigs. Brown and Brewer gave motivational speeches. Mary Kay's accountant explained the tax advantages of being an independent contractor. Husbands were included so that men would be more tolerant of wives' work. Bumper stickers reading ASK ME ABOUT MARY KAY were distributed to everyone in attendance. Bursting with pride, Mary Kay introduced twenty-one-year-old Richard, who, in his crisp business suit, looked like a teenager interviewing for his first job. Richard produced charts explaining commissions, a compensation system so complicated that no one else understood it. Husbands wrote him off as a greenhorn. Wives were riveted.

After adjourning so consultants could hurry home and change into evening gowns, Seminar wound up with an awards banquet. Mary Kay catered the event herself, reheating chicken in the turkey roaster she used for family Thanksgivings and dishing out "the good stuff," her cornbread-jalapeño dressing, to go with it. Earlier that week, having realized that her paper plates would not stand up to much slicing, Mary Kay had cooked and boned a hundred chickens. She made a carrot Jell-O salad too. She had thought of everything.

Of the 318 women signed as consultants, almost 200 showed up to eat chicken and the good stuff off soggy paper plates. Ellen Notley, a consultant from Tyler, Texas, brought a "Happy First Anniversary" sheet cake from home. A consultant's daughter sang operatic arias. Then everyone cheered while Mary Kay made a speech and awarded $300 Fashion Tress wigs to the ten top performers and a black-and-white television to the woman with the highest sales. When the Jell-O salad melted in the September heat, that became part of Seminar legend.

That night, every woman got a charm for her charm bracelet. No one went home empty-handed. "She stood up and praised EVERYONE!" a consultant remembered. "She praised people until you were ready to fall off your chair. That filled a need. No one was doing that for these women."

As soon as it was over, Mary Kay slipped off her heels, changed out of her gown, and started cleanup.

The next week, the company got a write-up in the fat Sunday edition of *The Dallas Morning News.*

Beneath the headline OLD MAN HAD YOUTH'S SKIN, readers of Dallas's largest-circulation newspaper saw a beaming and bewigged Mrs. Mary Kay Weaver posed with a soaring sales chart and two smiling sons: twenty-one-year-old Richard, looking like butter wouldn't melt in his mouth, and twenty-eight-year-old Ben, in eyeglasses that made him look a college man.

Leading with the tale of the tanner "who died at 73 without a wrinkle," reporter Rosalie McGinnis played up the products' Arkansas origins. Another single mother who'd come to the big city searching for work to support her children, McGinnis hailed from Arkansas herself. So did her editor. Misidentifying Mary Kay as the hide tanner's daughter, she did not press for details like names or hometowns. Quoting Richard, she printed his pitch for the wigs made by "Fashion Tress of Germany and France," along with his inference that competitors' wigs might have hair that fell out or be made of "yak and whatnot." Sounding like his mother in her World Gift heyday, Richard spun a tale of wigs made from human hair "taken from nuns and others" who had to "eat certain foods to be in perfect physical condition to sell hair." It was that kind of story.

Reporting that the business was launched in October of the previous year for $15,000, McGinnis quoted Richard as saying the company was about to close its first year with a quarter million dollars in sales. He expected the next year to bring $1 million.

He got in a recruiting plug too. After explaining that recruits made money on other recruits and unit leaders got additional commission, he allayed the fears of any husbands who happened to be reading by saying that consultants were not allowed to go into debt to the company.

Press like that beat paid advertising any day. McGinnis introduced the world to a glamorous grandmother who had founded a thriving company on $15,000 during the worst year in Dallas history. Succeeding publicity would be more of the same.

CHAPTER FIFTEEN

That Mary Kay Enthusiasm

As time went on, the start-up story became simpler and easier to remember.

There's no way of knowing what figures Mary Kay gave *The Dallas Morning News*. Or what she based them on. Or whether the reporter got it right. Convinced it was counterproductive to correct the press, Mary Kay based her publicity policy on Dale Carnegie's first fundamental for handling people: "If you want to gather honey, don't kick over the beehive." Later, a company manual would spell this out as "Don't complain if your story isn't printed or if it is rewritten. If the printed story contains an inaccuracy, don't call it to the editor's attention or ask him to print a correction unless it is of *major* importance. (A misspelled or incorrect name is not major.)"

In subsequent stories, the initial investment would be $5,000, not $15,000. That lower figure put her squarely in the tradition of Stanley Home Products, which Mr. Bev had started in a run-down tobacco barn for a few thousand dollars and built into a Fortune 500 company. It was also lower than Mary C. Crowley's $6,000 stake for Home Interiors.

Truth be told, at the end of 1964, there was probably no one who knew how much money had been poured into Beauty by Mary Kay. Between settling Hallenbeck's estate and funding her start-up, Mary

Kay had been liquidating assets left and right. In November of 1963, her Lowe's All Electric Home in Glenbrook Valley sold for $17,400. Four months later, she sold the house in Freeway Manor for equity. At one point, the company's bank balance was down to $250.

But it never went into the red. The naysayers and know-it-alls had been wrong. For the rest of her life, Mary Kay would relish the retelling: how, after Hallenbeck's death, a male lawyer and male accountant did everything they could to scare her off. Everyone seemed to have a cautionary tale.

Look what happened to Brownie Wise. Like Mary Kay, Wise came up through the ranks. Years of pushing brooms for Stanley and burping bowls for Tupperware had given her plenty of ideas for improving direct sales. Her bosses did not want to hear them. After Tupper fired her in 1958, she struck out with one business after another. Recruited to be president of Cinderella International, a beauty and home products company, Wise was pressured to resign after her first year. A stint with Viviane Woodard Cosmetics went nowhere. As did the launch of a line called Carissa in 1963. The men couldn't understand why Wise got so worked up. Or spent so much money on prizes. And they had the last word.

That was not the case with Mary Kay. Year after year, she would tell her start-up story to women who knew what it was to be shushed. She would build pauses into her narration, hesitating just enough to let listeners think back to how they felt the last time it happened to them. World-famous and wealthy beyond her wildest dreams, she would stand at the podium with her diamonds flashing in the follow spot. She would stop just short of smiling. She would let out the slightest sigh. Thousands of women would shake their heads at the foolishness of the men who had doubted her.

As the company grew, differences started to show.

Mary Kay's claim that her consultants would make more money turned out to be true. Her products were roughly twice the price of competitors'. In theory, they should have made twice the profit; in practice, they made more. After Mary Kay decided that the skin care set could not be split up, customers had to shell out for the entire $15.95 set. To make the same profit, the Avon Lady might sell a dozen different products and still come up short, since Avon gave representatives only 20 to 40 percent of the retail price. Tupperware officially gave 35 percent but took out 10 percent to pay for party prizes.

Mary Kay gave 40 to 50 percent. Her beauty shows were also more efficient than the "Ding Dong, Avon Calling" ringing of individual doorbells. A Mary Kay consultant could work up to six prospects at once, enticing them with the promise of a free facial, a makeover, and the chance to try on a wig. Each skin care class had a format; each evening had a natural progression. The best part came at the end.

Mary Kay also had fewer stock-keeping units (SKUs) than Avon, World Gift, Tupperware, Stanley, Fuller Brush, or almost anybody else in direct selling. So far, her biggest addition had been the Mr. K line, which repackaged the products in dark colors, renaming Cleansing Creme as Cleanser and Super Nite Cream as Moisture Balm. When other direct sellers counted SKUs in the high hundreds, Mary Kay rarely had more than two or three dozen, which cut down on sales training for her and inventory management for Richard.

Other direct sellers made it impossible to deliver instant gratification. Mary Kay made it easy. She pushed consultants to prebuy products so they could complete orders on the spot. By telling every consultant to arrive at every beauty show with no fewer than six skin care sets, Mary Kay eliminated buyer's remorse along with an awkward collection and delivery process. In her plan, while customers sat around the table complimenting one another's newly soft and rosy complexions, the consultant had only to go out to the car and get enough skin care sets from the trunk. No more skulking back a week later to plead for payment. No more going through the sales pitch all over again. That time could be put to better use booking beauty shows.

Other direct sellers rewarded big orders with discounts or prizes. At Beauty by Mary Kay, those discounts could be so deep and those prizes so desirable that women got carried away. A $400 order, for example, might earn an extra $65 in free products, which then brought the consultant close to qualifying for a monthly sales award with a beguiling prize like a purse or bracelet.

Even in the early days, that led to inventory worries. How could a woman be sure she wasn't going to be stuck with all those skin care sets in the trunk of her car? Getting started at Mary Kay's company was already a pricier proposition than laying out $25 for the vinyl consultant's showcase. There were no accounts receivable and none of the pay-as-you-go policy that had gotten young Mrs. Rogers started at Stanley. Recruits were supposed to buy plenty of inventory before booking their first party, which could push start-up costs to $200 or more. Mary Kay would always push for more, saying, "You can't sell from an empty wagon." By her logic, a bigger buy-in gave consultants more incentive to clinch a sale.

With some, it did. With many, it did not. Emotions ran high. Recruits would quit, and when they did, Mary Kay would always try to talk them into giving it another go. Some would try again. Others would accuse Mary Kay of coercing them into spending money on products they couldn't sell. The problem of managing inventories against expectations would persist long after 1970, when the company joined the Direct Selling Association, and would continue long after that trade association's Code of Ethics mandated that member companies take back unsold products. Despite a written guarantee that consultants could get 90 percent of their money back as long as the products were under a year old, undamaged, and not part of a prize, many women never attempted returns. Some became embittered, enraged, or embarrassed. Some still hoped to give it another go. Nobody wanted to admit she had gotten carried away.

Speaking to a promising young woman, Mary Kay used syntax and vocabulary that a corporate hiring manager might use with a promising young man. There was no talk of pin money. She spoke of "your career" and "managing your business." She made it clear that there would be no male manager lording it over her, because there would be no male managers. A manager would be another woman who had started the same way. Someone she could imagine herself becoming.

Mary Kay also prescribed the methods of management. "Even if she falls on her face . . . we tell her how beautifully she fell and make suggestions as to how she could do even better. We never criticize. Always praise, praise, praise," said Mary Kay.

Differences emerged in recruiting policies too. Most direct-selling companies gave a recruiting bonus. Usually the company paid an override—a percentage of the recruit's sales—to the person responsible for signing the recruit. Because override money came from company coffers, it was rarely more than 1 or 2 percent. Depending on the company, that percentage dropped off after anywhere from a month to a year. To Mary Kay's mind, that wasn't much incentive.

Mary Kay paid higher bonuses and paid them in perpetuity. A recruiter was motivated to find herself a real go-getter because her own income rose with the go-getter's sales. Mary Kay reasoned that a recruiter would move heaven and earth to make a new consultant successful because she would be doing herself good at the same time. When the new consultant saw her recruiter rake in override money, she would be inspired to repeat the pattern. On and on it would go, as women pushed other women up the ladder.

In line with the Sheldon motto "He Profits Most Who Serves Best," Mary Kay encouraged consultants to take over beauty shows when another consultant was sick or had a family emergency. Likewise, she instituted an adoptee program, which meant that directors fostered recruits who were not part of their own downline. If a consultant was recruited in Texas, she remained part of that Texas unit no matter what. If she moved, she became an adoptee of the director in her new hometown while, back in Texas, the original director was still getting a percentage of her sales. The director doing the adopting got nothing for her troubles. But if one of her own recruits moved, another director would do the same for her. According to Mary Kay, it would all even out in the end.

Mary Kay refused to assign sales territories, encouraging reps to recruit anyone from anywhere. Sometimes that inclusiveness was framed as a tenet of her religious beliefs. Sometimes it was framed as a reaction against assigned territories at Stanley. Either way, it was something the big direct-selling companies were not doing.

When Avon wanted to boost profits, it could reduce a representative's territory and add more representatives—a strategy that usually capped individual earnings. Mary Kay took the opposite approach, insisting that territories were inefficient and damaging to women. She had watched too many Stanley saleswomen lose income when their husbands were transferred. During her own short-lived move to St. Louis, she had lost customers, commissions, and prestige. As a result, Stanley had lost her.

A Mary Kay consultant knew that she had only to get off a plane, train, or automobile—on her honeymoon, her vacation, or her Thanksgiving with the in-laws—and recruit the right person to initiate a downline that could keep her in mink stoles and diamond cocktail rings for the rest of her days.

The women coming to the company were not the women who joined Stanley in hopes of making money for a new refrigerator. Mary Kay recruited women with other dreams. She treated them as though they were burning with ambition. Many found that they were.

Schoolteachers were a gold mine. They had short workdays, long summer vacations, and contacts aplenty; no mother was going to turn down an invitation from her child's teacher. The beauty show, formatted as a class in skin care, was a natural for them. Teachers also needed the money. "As a teacher with a master's degree and five years of experience, I was not even making five thousand a year in the Dallas public schools," wrote a woman recruited in the 1960s.

"You got married. You had your two kids. You had the kids bathed and supper on the table when your husband came home at six o'clock, and maybe he let you work as long as nothing interfered with that," a 1965 recruit explained. "Women had no opportunities then," Jackie

Brown recalled. "I got ambitious women who weren't being paid what they were worth: teachers, secretaries, smart women."

Some of those women had never been paid for work. One of them, Ouida Caldwell, went into headquarters to buy skin care and came out as a recruit. "I went down there, and as soon as I got in the building, I was given an application," she said, recalling the commotion when she went to the bank to borrow her $250 start-up cost without bringing her husband to cosign the loan. Caldwell would spend the next fifty years selling Mary Kay, twenty-five of them as a director. She would win awards and drive pink Cadillacs and hear the same thing from Mary Kay each time: "She [Mary Kay] would go and put her arm around me and say, 'Ouida, you can do a little better, you can do a little bit more.'"

Women in the prosperous precincts of Highland Park, women with the kind of lives that other housewives dreamed about, were joining too. That July, Jackie Brown recruited a Highland Park housewife who signed up after her husband, a retired Texas Industries executive, fussed at her for buying a $1.98 ivy plant. Later, Helen McVoy said she had gone to her first beauty show for the free facial, because "when you're broke you need a facial," and then signed up to sell so she could buy an ivy plant whenever she wanted.

Recruits could relate to that story, even if McVoy was far from broke. After a comfortable upbringing, she had traveled the world with her first husband, an agricultural envoy to Saudi Arabia (often upgraded to ambassador if Mary Kay was telling the story). When McVoy started with Mary Kay, she and her second husband had one child in a pricey private school and another in college. Her calendar was full of golf, bridge, and dinner parties. Already in her forties, she had never earned her own money or held a job, except for an awful six-month secretarial stint. "I did it [Mary Kay] mostly as a lark. It sounded like fun, selling two or three hours a week," she said. "I always felt inferior because I was just a housewife and hadn't finished college. My husband Alex was a graduate of the Harvard Business School."

McVoy thought it was great fun to come back from a beauty show, dump her loot on the dining room table, and have her Harvard MBA husband help her count it. Running into Mary Kay at headquarters one day, McVoy made a flippant comment about becoming a director. There and then, Mary Kay looked her in the eye and said, "You will be just great. You'll go straight to the top," then launched into thirty minutes of one-on-one coaching. McVoy said, "I guess that propelled me because I didn't want her to be wrong in her esteem of me."

Seven months later, McVoy was a director. Within a year, she had earned $17,000 (over $175,000 today); her Mighty Macs were one of the Top Ten units in the company. She and her husband invested in oil wells and a fishing-worm farm, while McVoy flew all over the United States setting records for recruiting.

Confidence was contagious. At company headquarters on Majesty Drive, women flounced in and out, showing off finery and fancy cars. Products flew off warehouse shelves. Meeting rooms were booked solid. Catching the fever, Barbara Acker, who had been Mary Kay's secretary since the days at Exchange Park, quit to become a consultant.

That July, the company began phasing out Fashion Tress. Mary Kay wasn't about to give up wearing wigs—they saved her too much time—but Richard convinced her that the business no longer needed them. Stocking them was expensive and ate up warehouse space. Richard predicted problems as the company expanded; it would be impossible to include a wig salon and styling service in every town with a new Mary Kay consultant. Furthermore, as inexpensive Korean imports flooded the market, the category was losing cachet. Mary Kay still worried. Consultants doing a steady sideline in wig sales threatened to quit, then did.

The next month, sales went up $20,000.

By the close of the company's second year, directors were living the high life.

Conspicuous consumption lured recruits like honey caught flies. Mary Kay, who went to her first Stanley convention with two dresses to her name, knew the power of nice clothes. She also knew that nobody else was telling those wives and mothers to do something for themselves. Mary Kay told them to get a new dress; the dress would pay for itself by lifting their morale and impressing their customers. She also told them to get a housekeeper. She had one herself. "Don't waste dollar time on penny jobs," said Mary Kay.

In September, when it came time for the second Seminar, the company had 857 consultants. Sales topped $800,000. It might not have been the $1 million Richard predicted, but it was more than quadruple first-year earnings. The turkey roaster, goopy Jell-O, and gussied-up warehouse belonged to an already distant past. Themed as "Faces of Fortune," the second Seminar was exponentially more elaborate than the first, a sign of soon-to-come days when Seminar would take over Dallas for weeks on end.

That year, Mary Kay launched the company's Career Apparel program with an ensemble exclusive to directors: a long-sleeved black wool suit with matching cowgirl hat. Notwithstanding a spell of sticky, ninety-five-degree weather, she wore the getup herself. So did her directors, who happily paid for the privilege. As intended, Career Apparel became a status symbol that spurred some consultants to the next stage of their Mary Kay careers. Every year after, Mary Kay would come up with costumes that, whatever else they might be, were not imitations of men's business suits. "I remember having a godawful mauve dress with a tie," one director said. "I was so proud that I had the right to wear it." Some women would be so proud of their Career Apparel that they would ask to be buried in it.

Setting another precedent, Mary Kay charged for Seminar participation, reckoning consultants would have a greater stake in the proceedings if they spent their own money to attend. That fee, though, did not begin to cover her costs. A two-day affair at the Adolphus Hotel, the second Seminar started on Friday morning and wound up the next night with an awards banquet in the Grand Ballroom, among the grandest of all ballrooms in Texas. No detail was overlooked. Mary Kay booked rooms at the Adolphus for her directors so they could work late and start early the next morning. On Awards Night, waiters in white dinner jackets served consultants in sparkling gowns and towering wigs. Outshining them all, Mary Kay floated through the room in her own sparkling gown, bestowing alligator bags on top saleswomen and piling on so much praise that the pricey purses seemed beside the point.

Mary Kay, who never gave out one prize when she could give out two, declared Brown and Brewer tied for top sales unit. Each received an engraved silver ice bucket, a mink stole, and a standing ovation. As thirty-year-old Brown, so heavily pregnant that she could not see her own feet, came forward to accept her award, Mary Kay treated her like a beauty queen, filling her arms with long-stemmed roses and draping an Autumn Haze mink stole over her shoulders. Hundreds of consultants clapped and cheered. Following Mary Kay's lead, Brown gave a speech heaping praise on the women in her unit.

That night, Brown went to bed with the closet door open so she could spend every waking minute gazing at her new mink stole. Having built her unit and opened territory throughout her high-risk, Rh-negative pregnancy, she was not about to stop now. Brown worked until it was time to check into the hospital. Then, safely delivered, she said prayers of thanks and attended a baby shower at company headquarters, where Mary Kay herself presented a sterling silver baby cup and spoon.

Those first nights, Brown lullabied her baby girl to sleep with "I've Got That Mary Kay Enthusiasm," the song that she had sung to her in the womb. Then she hired a nanny and went back to work.

Later, both Crowley and Dick Kelly would take credit for another difference between the first and second Seminars: the presence of a stocky sixty-year-old salesman named Mel Ash.

Kelly claimed that Mary Kay met her new beau in the World Gift office when Ash was job hunting, which was the same story he told about Hallenbeck. In Crowley's version, Ash was also job hunting but paused to ask, "Are there any more at home like you?," causing Crowley to set him up with the woman who had divorced her brother. Both versions may be equally true. After they married, Mr. and Mrs. Ash told the press that they were set up on a blind date and were smitten as soon as they laid eyes on each other. On subsequent dates, Ash often accompanied Mary Kay to social events staged by her directors. That made him a keeper.

On Awards Night, a tuxedo-clad Ash pitched woo like the hero of a romance novel. With practiced moves, he waltzed her around the Adolphus ballroom. A chatty charmer in a town of tight-lipped cowboys, Ash was, like Mary Kay, a keen student of *How to Win Friends and Influence People.* That night, he evidenced mastery of Dale Carnegie's advice to be "hearty in your approbation and lavish in your praise." He declared Mary Kay a vision. Mary Kay ate it up.

Not long after, Ash popped the question and presented her with a suitably showy engagement ring. Baptist bride and Jewish groom planned a Presbyterian ceremony and set the date for December 6. A giddy Mary Kay published the banns in *Beauty News and Views*, inviting any and all consultants to attend. Directors were drafted as bridesmaids. Dresses were bought. As a wedding present, directors chipped in to give the bride and groom a set of expensive luggage for the honeymoon. Two days before the big event, the happy couple was feted at a formal dinner.

The next afternoon, the groom-to-be did a bunk. Ash disappeared for days, then weeks. Plenty of time for Mary Kay to change her mind. She did not.

The run of bad luck continued when, the night after Christmas, a man came to the door of Mary Kay's town house asking to see the rental next door. Producing a gun, he pushed his way inside, put on a Halloween mask, and let in two more masked gunmen. They bound and gagged Mary Kay, ransacked her duplex, and made off with a $9,000 haul that included two watches, three fur coats, cash, and several rings. After an hour of struggle, she was able to work her hands free and call the police. MASKED GUNMEN TIE UP AND ROB WOMAN EXECUTIVE made the front page of the next day's paper.

Rumors flew. One insisted that Ash had dispatched thieves to retrieve his ring, although, as it turned out, the ring was at the jeweler's being sized. Shaken, Mary Kay vowed never to be alone in the house again.

Less than two weeks later, Ash reappeared and became her next husband.

CHAPTER SIXTEEN

Thursday-Night Hallmark Cards

Mel had always been a salesman.

The oldest son of immigrants Louis and Saydee Eschwege, Melville Jerome Eschwege was born in a German Jewish neighborhood on the Upper East Side of New York and raised in Reading, Pennsylvania. His father worked in stores and offices. When times were good, his mother had a girl to help with housework. Mel made his bar mitzvah, finished high school, did a stint at the Citizens' Military Training Camp in Maryland, then went back to Pennsylvania to live with his parents until he turned twenty-one and married a nice Jewish girl from a good family.

Mel was raised with middle-class mores. Gentlemen pulled out chairs for ladies. Husbands opened doors and stepped aside. Wives hosted bridge parties. Married couples attended dinner dances. Families vacationed in Bermuda without having won a sales contest.

Never the kind of peddler who went door to door, Mel worked as a drummer for medical suppliers, started a business called Ash Medical Supply, and spent time selling televisions. He was repping giftware when he met Mary Kay. His first wife had died in 1933, less than two years after the birth of their only child. A 1936 marriage lasted until 1941, when Mel appeared on tax delinquency rolls and that wife sued him, complaining that she had invested $2,000 in his business yet he refused to support her. In 1945, he was back in Pennsylvania living with his parents, when he was indicted on charges of selling a mislabeled and adulterated drug in Washington, D.C. His next marriage produced two more children before the divorce. The one after that lasted barely two years. Sometimes he went by the alias Melville Jerome. By the time he moved to Texas in 1965, he had been anglicizing his surname for years and had lived in New York, New Jersey, Pennsylvania, Florida, Georgia, and California.

Women liked him, but not for his physical charms. Over a dozen years older than his latest bride, Mel was five feet eight inches tall, portly, bald, and needed Coke-bottle glasses. Like most of Mary Kay's husbands, he smoked. Like Hallenbeck, he was not close to his children. When his daughter Judith married in 1959, Ash did not attend the wedding.

She returned the favor by not attending his. The sales directors, whom Mary Kay called her daughters, did not attend either. As it turned out, almost no one did. Forgoing the big wedding they had once planned, bride and groom opted for a small ceremony on Thursday, January 6, 1966. Mel shaved a few years off his age for the marriage certificate, which had been preceded by a prenuptial agreement probably intended to forestall objections from Mary Kay's children. Although details were never discussed, Mary Kay found a way to sweeten the pot: After Mel's death, probate showed that he had drawn a modest salary from the company, had once held company stock worth upward of $240,000, and had substantial investments held jointly with his wife. Then there was Mary Kay's "competitive nature." In one of his less gallant moods, Ash was heard to say, "Mary Kay always gets her man."

With their honeymoon delayed by the demands of the company now known simply as "Mary Kay," the couple spent their wedding night at the Adolphus Hotel, where Mary Kay attended a sales meeting from 6:30 to 11:00 p.m. and had a two-day sales conference starting the next morning. Later, after their honeymoon trip to Europe, Mary Kay reminisced about dining at an open-air restaurant in Rome and selling skin care to a stranger at the next table. Later still, when that stranger became a repeat customer, Mary Kay put the honeymoon story in her autobiography.

After moving into Mary Kay's duplex on Northwest Parkway, Mel began to behave as though he were retired. Mary Kay, however, soon had the two of them on a schedule that harked back to her travels for World Gift: crisscrossing the country while, back in Dallas, secretary Anna Arnold minded Monet the poodle. "In those early days, travel was very informal," an employee recalled. "A director would call from Phoenix and she [Mary Kay] would have herself on a plane. She and Mel would be flying all over the place because she was so anxious to help those people."

"Mel was the sweetest man. He would say, 'You are my daughters,'" a consultant remembered. Sometimes he would write his own notes of encouragement or congratulation. Consultants adored him because he could flatter and flirt without being disloyal to Mary Kay. The subject of previous wives and children never seemed to come up.

Despite telling reporters that he was "the chairman of the chairman of the board," Mel proved nowhere near as bossy as previous husbands. Unlike them, he accompanied her on family calls, including visits to Lula, who had finally been forced to give up her 112-hour workweeks and move to a nursing home on the edge of Houston. Buttering up the old lady, he would thank her "for having such a gorgeous, wonderful daughter." Back in Dallas, in the middle of his not-very-full days, Mel frequently phoned Mary Kay at the office to tell her that he loved her. Or so Mary Kay said.

If even half of what she told the world was true, Mel was a motivational genius himself. According to Mary Kay, every Thursday for the rest of their lives together, he gave her a Hallmark card and a gift to celebrate the day they married. Usually the gift was something like Ms. Bear, a stuffed bear that said things like "I love you. You are terrific. You can do anything" when you pulled its string. Mary Kay liked that one so much that she had an Executive Bear made for directors; it wore a pink dress and said, "You're wonderful. You're headed for the top."

Mel was allowed to call her "Mary," a privilege accorded no one else. On business trips, he made her take time for sightseeing, although, as her assistant said, "she was really happier when it was work-connected." Back home in Dallas, the two took ballroom dancing classes to keep their skills sharp. Mel liked musicals, so they went to Dallas-area dinner theaters. Mary Kay liked Tex-Mex, so they went to El Fenix, where, on Wednesday nights, Mary Kay could get a dollar off the cheese enchilada special—tortilla soup, two enchiladas, refried beans, and rice—and wash it down with a big glass of iced tea. In contrition, the two would go on and off Weight Watchers and other diets, breakfasting on recipes like an apple microwaved in diet cola.

Gone were the slimming dark dresses. As if she had been dying to wear them all her life, Mary Kay now wore ensembles like a leopard-fur coat tossed over a winter white suit with leopard-fur cuffs. She behaved differently too. Because Ash wanted her home by "a decent hour," her staff would announce, "It's time," and pack her up. Monet, the poodle, would emerge from the warehouse, where he napped most of the day. Leaving her office no later than six forty to allow for delays on the drive, she made sure she was home by seven so that Mel wouldn't fret. While she was en route, her housekeeper would set the table, make a salad, and take one of Mary Kay's prepared meals from refrigerator to oven. Once in a while, Mary Kay would be caught short and resort to a TV dinner. She claimed that, since she put it on a plate, Mel never knew the difference.

After supper, they sat in the den in front of what Mary Kay called "the idiot box." At least Mel did. Mary Kay would force herself, television's "waste of time" made bearable by sitting next to Mel and signing the dozens of business letters, contracts, and personal notes that she brought home each evening. She loved telling the world how, when they sat together after all that signing was done, Mel massaged her feet. She bragged that he helped her fold the papers and put them in envelopes. Most nights, they were in bed by ten thirty. Most mornings, she was up at five so she could get in two and a half hours of work before Mel woke up at seven thirty and she made him breakfast. Her assistant explained,

"She had one of those dictating machines and she would sort of whisper into it so she wouldn't wake him."

Behaving as if being Mrs. Mel Ash were a real feather in her cap, Mary Kay told anyone who would listen about Mel's sales acumen and successful career. As the marriage went on, descriptions of their partnership became ever more romantic and ever less plausible. Despite no apparent source of income, Mel was the "man of the house," who paid for everything and lavished her with jewelry—a pink sapphire ring set with diamonds, a diamond bracelet—to make up for what was lost in the robbery. Before they met, he had been a brokenhearted widower, although sometimes he was a lonely bachelor. Always, he was a man whose life changed when he found Mary Kay.

Both knew what they wanted from the marriage.

According to Mary Kay, both dreamed of an ultramod house. Producing pictures torn from the August 5, 1966, issue of *Life* magazine that showed a house shaped like a flying saucer, Mary Kay consulted Frank L. Meier, the twenty-eight-year-old architect designing her corporate headquarters. With Meier moonlighting from his commercial partnership, he and his client began meeting on Sundays. As they sat at Mary Kay's kitchen table, the woman Dick Kelly described as "still holding on to the first nickel she ever made" announced that she was pulling out all the stops to commission a forty-two-hundred-square-foot house that was completely round. The duplex on Northwest Parkway was nice enough, but its decor was too feminine for a man like her Mel. With this house, she was going to have things just the way she wanted. She insisted, for example, that Meier drive out to White Rock Lake to see a house finished with white marble rubble. She wanted that same effect for hers.

So that's what she got. "She put tremendous trust in me. She treated me like a son," said Meier, who already worked long hours in his architectural partnership and now spent his nights and weekends drawing up Mary Kay's plans in his garage. Describing her as "overall, a dream client," he recalled one habit she couldn't shake: "We would shop together for the house or her office. I'd line up things at the Market Center for her to look at. We'd walk in places and look at furniture or artwork or whatever, and we'd walk out—so many, *many* times we'd walk out—and she'd say, 'Those are the worst salespeople ever! I could spend fifteen or thirty minutes with them and make them into a heck of a salesperson!'"

In the summer of 1968, Mary Kay paid $21,000 for a lakeside lot in Windsor Park, an up-and-coming neighborhood next to Preston Hollow, then chose a female contractor, Beverly Harris, for the complicated construction project. When Mel showed up to put in his two cents, Mary Kay would take Meier aside, pat the architect's arm, and say, "Listen to him. Make him feel like he's a big part of this." The crew would then defer to Mel's opinion. After he left, things had a way of proceeding as originally planned. "Sometimes he'd have ideas, and I'd bounce 'em off of her, and if she didn't like the idea she'd go talk to him," Meier recalled, "but it all worked out." Construction finished on time and on budget.

The resulting Round House was the talk of the town. In the spring of 1969, after Mr. and Mrs. Ash moved in, both Dallas dailies devoted long, loving stories to its avant-garde architecture, lakeside landscaping, and rounded pool. Descriptions conjured a decor equal parts *Jetsons* futuristic and Texas Baroque: the gold vinyl kitchen with its newfangled Tappan microwave copied from the "Kitchen of the Future" display at the Texas State Fair, the cleverly disguised office space, the sixteen telephone jacks hidden throughout the house, and the lemon-yellow Kodel shag carpet that felt like such heaven when a woman kicked off her high heels and wiggled her toes in it. At its heart, the Round House had an air-conditioned solarium with gold-capped columns ringing the *Venus de Milo*, Mary Kay's own full-size version of the nine-and-a-half-inch statuettes she had sold for so many years.

With its open prospects and lack of conventional walls, her living room proved ideal for hosting her directors in qualification. Each month, Mary Kay would ask women on the verge of becoming directors to come to Dallas at their own expense, because "if a woman comes here and she has paid her own expense, she is going to absorb all she can." Many had never been away from home, never gone anywhere alone, never stayed in a hotel. To the husbands left at home, Mary Kay sent thank-you notes expressing her appreciation for all the men had to do when their wives were gone.

In Dallas, freed of housework, cooking, and childminding, directors in qualification (DIQs) found their every waking minute accounted for. Classes could last until ten or eleven at night. When not taking notes or role-playing, they might sing inspirational songs like "Climb Every Mountain." Candles were lit. Vows made. The conversion experience, though, was the visit to the Round House.

Two by two, DIQs descended from the bus to a Hollywood-perfect exterior with flawless landscaping, an impression that Mary Kay had been known to help along by sneaking out after dark and adding artificial flowers when no one was looking. At the front door, Mr. and Mrs. Ash stood in welcome. Here, in the flesh, was the successful businessman they had heard so much about, who built his wife this dream house and showered her with jewelry. Delighted to play host, Mel would say how much he enjoyed being surrounded by beautiful women, profess his undying adoration of Mary Kay, and tell them about the first time he laid eyes on her: when she answered her front door in a black dress and backlighting made it seem as though there were a halo around her. DIQs loved that one.

Floating through the group in her hostess gown, Mary Kay served hot spiced tea and warm-from-the-oven cookies that her housekeeper baked from homemade dough that Mary Kay mixed and froze ahead of time. Sitting in her huge open-plan living room, Mary Kay talked about the company's limitless vistas while the DIQs looked out at a Windsor Park landscape where every last wire, pipe, and utility had been buried so deep that the scenery looked like something out of a fairy tale. Standing in front of her floor-to-ceiling fireplace, Mary Kay smiled and posed until every single DIQ had a souvenir snapshot.

Then came the best part. The group split, with Mel and Mary Kay each leading a tour of the house. DIQs could peer into the den, its shelves lined with *Reader's Digest Condensed Books*, and see the couch where Mary Kay sat in front of the television and did paperwork while Mel rubbed her feet. Nothing was off-limits. Not kitchen drawers, where DIQs found everything perfectly aligned. Not closets, where DIQs saw clothes in color-coded order with coordinating purses above and matching heels below.

DIQs would ooh and aah, biding time until the highlight of the tour: Mary Kay's personal bathroom, a paradise of pink moiré vinyl wallpaper, swagged window treatments, classical statuary, white shag carpet, and twenty-four-karat-gold-plated faucets shaped like the swans swimming on the lake outside. Beneath a rainbow-crystal chandelier sat the legendary sunken bathtub, said to be so big that it took twenty minutes to fill. One by one, fully clad DIQs would climb into the empty tub as a rite of initiation. Superstition held that unless you had your photo taken in the tub, your directorship would not last. Month after month, year after year, DIQs would lower themselves in, smile for the camera, and emerge as true believers.

By the time she commissioned the Round House, Mary Kay could afford all the Kodel shag and moiré vinyl she wanted. So could Richard, who bought a house in the same neighborhood and hired Meier to remodel it.

After the company's second year, people were paying attention. Richard's crazy sales projections and Mary Kay's relentless sloganeering had been backed by double-digit growth. Plenty of direct sellers and Dale Carnegie devotees had parroted "Maintain a positive outlook" and "Make the other person feel important." Mary C. Crowley may or may not have been the first to say "God first, family second, career third." But that Mary Kay Ash was making money as fast as any of them. Faster than most.

And she was still getting started. In January of 1966, she rolled out her "Cinderella gifts." She would announce an absurdly extravagant prize, spell out the preposterous production quota required to win, and then get consultants stirred up with the same "You can do it!" that her mother had used on her.

Cinderella gifts were never what a practical, hardworking housewife needed. That was their point. There would be no *Queen for a Day* prizes of Hamilton Beach food converters, Hoover floor polishers, or West Bend griddles. "I decided that where women are concerned you should give them things they would not normally go out and buy for themselves, like a pink Cadillac, a mink coat, a diamond ring—the things that we wait around for that guy on the white horse who never shows up to bring us," said Mary Kay. Her gifts were for the young girls with big dreams. "She [the consultant] would usually wait for the man in her life to give it to her. If she went to buy it for herself, it would weigh very badly against the hamburger that could be bought with the same money, and she would probably wind up not buying it or buying a very inexpensive one for herself."

Her first company-wide initiative was the "Golden Goblet Club." At a time when top producers were bringing in wholesale orders of $150 a week, Mary Kay announced that she would sanctify each monthly wholesale order of $1,000 with a chalice-shaped, twenty-two-karat-gold-electroplated goblet, much like the gold-plated hollowware she had been buying for herself. Comparisons were made to quests for the Holy Grail. Richard thought the whole thing was hokey: No woman would work that much harder to get a $6 electroplated cup that she could buy herself. Mary Kay thought otherwise. That year, she gave away thirty-five golden goblets.

With all the pomp of the American Legion School Award ceremony that capped her Dow School career, Mary Kay conferred goblets on a stage decked with six-foot-tall, glitter-covered goblet cutouts, then provided a publicity photo and press release to the consultant's hometown paper. Winners got a big beribboned orchid corsage that matched the one Mary Kay wore when she made the presentation. Husbands got a carnation boutonniere that matched the one Mel wore as he stood by her side.

Before long, Mary Kay had ribbons that spelled out whether the consultant was winning her second or third or tenth golden goblet. Women wore golden goblets on golden chains. Gold-plated trays were added for women who had won a dozen goblets, gold-plated pitchers for women who had won twenty. One woman won sixty-five goblets. People ran out of places to put them. During the nine years that the company kept the Golden Goblet Club going, Mary Kay sometimes gave out over nine hundred goblets a month, switching suppliers several times to keep up with demand.

There was no stopping her. As if righting a lifetime's worth of wrongs, Mary Kay announced yet more sales contests, dreamed up yet more prizes. Following her launch of the Golden Goblet Club, she announced that anyone with a $500 wholesale during her birthday month would win a beautiful handbag. Newly married to her Mel, in the planning stage of her dream house, and the adored head of her own company, Mary Kay seemed as thrilled by the announcement as any of her salespeople—looking for all the world like she was back at that Stanley rally receiving her dreamed-of alligator bag.

Jackie Brown still longed to be like Mary Kay.

During the last two and a half years, she had become a speaker so poised that Mary Kay nicknamed her "the Girl with the Golden Words." She made her first plane trip flying to the West Coast to open territory. Thanks to staging all those beauty shows, she had become a practiced driver who proceeded to buy herself a used Cadillac that looked like the one Mary Kay drove. And when she totaled it driving home from a beauty show late one night, she was making enough money to buy herself a new one. Now earning over ten times her secretarial salary, Brown owned a dozen Fashion Tress wigs. She had moved to a bigger house, which held closets full of clothes from Neiman Marcus. When she wanted to recruit someone, she showed them her commission checks. After that, they couldn't wait to sign up.

It wasn't enough for her. Brown decided that Mary Kay and Richard were reneging on a plan to establish a third tier of commissions, then threw "a colossal fit over the deception." She said she was upset that Mary Kay may have "stolen people" by luring consultants from World Gift or Home Interiors. And when she heard gossip that Mary Kay had been married nine or ten times, she did not bother to ask if it was true. Instead, she conferred with Marjorie Slaten, the former first-grade teacher who was her star recruit, then the two of them decided to go out on their own.

Brown and Slaten tracked down Dathene Dark, the tanner's granddaughter, and convinced her that Mary Kay was trying to steal her birthright. The *Dallas Morning News* story was quoted. The Bible story of Jacob and Esau was cited. The two volunteered to rectify the situation by going into business with Dark and paying a generous salary to the perpetually cash-strapped mother of five, who had not been able to pay the fees needed to keep the original BeautiControl corporation active. In March, after Slaten's husband confirmed that the name BeautiControl was still available, plans were made to reincorporate. On the q.t., a partnership agreement was drawn up. Brown and Slaten each pledged $10,000 of their Mary Kay earnings. Suppliers were contacted. Most were suppliers who also dealt with Mary Kay.

Word got back to Mary Kay and Richard. Put on the spot, Brown acknowledged the impulse, denied the rumors, and hurried to rent office space. Once that was settled, Brown and Slaten decided to confront the boss. The showdown was set for April 15, 1966.

At ten that Friday morning, Brown and Slaten marched into Mary Kay's office dressed in their ladylike best, which meant suits with matching hats. Wigs were conspicuous by their absence. In a memoir published decades later, Brown claimed that Mary Kay's wig was askew and that she made a snide comment about Brown's and Slaten's hats. That's when the gloves came off.

Brown informed Mary Kay and Richard that she and Slaten were quitting to start their own company. Twisting the knife, she told Mary Kay that she was going back to the tanner's formulas and relaunching BeautiControl. She and Slaten would be going into business with the tanner's granddaughter, the very woman who had sold Mary Kay a copy of the formulas in 1963. They planned to sell a virtually identical line with the same backstory in the same sales territory. That very night, the two women were convening meetings of their sales units during which they planned to publicly resign from Mary Kay Cosmetics, then tell everyone present about the new BeautiControl, its generous and many-tiered commission structure, and the fabulous selling opportunities that awaited. According to Brown, Mary Kay replied, "Jackie, even with Jesus, there was Judas."

Brown would be doing what both Crowley and Mary Kay had done after leaving World Gift. What Brownie Wise and dozens of others had done after leaving Stanley. What Mr. Bev had done after he left Fuller Brush. What Alfred C. Fuller had done after he left Somerville Brush and Mop. Mary Kay had spent a lifetime watching direct-sales companies improve upon predecessors: a march of progress that invariably involved shanghaiing suppliers, consultants, and customers.

Afraid she would lose everything, Mary Kay soon sued Jackie Brown.

Brown sued her right back.

CHAPTER SEVENTEEN

"Next Year, You'll Do Even Better"

The next day was Saturday. Brown and Slaten went to work anyway.

A month later, Mary Kay's lawyer filed an injunction in the 162nd District Court against Brown, Slaten, their husbands, the tanner's granddaughter, and everyone else involved in the rebirth of BeautiControl. A week later, BeautiControl opened for business as planned. By that time, Brown and Slaten had their own lawyer and were filing a countersuit against Mary Kay.

Mary Kay said that the defendants appropriated her products, incentives, and ideas. Brown and Slaten said they did nothing of the sort. True, they used formulas from the same tanner. Yes, their recruiting and commissions were structured much the same way. But BeautiControl planned to pay the extra override that they claimed Mary Kay had once promised. Other similarities were purely coincidental. Brown may have given out a mink stole, but so what? Did Mary Kay have a monopoly on mink?

Brown preferred to point out differences. BeautiControl used wiglets instead of wigs as sales incentives. BeautiControl called its men's line Ol' Tanner instead of Mr. K. BeautiControl called its hostess party a clinic instead of a beauty show. BeautiControl's Diamond Deb Club offered a genuine gold ring to any consultant with a $1,000 wholesale, not the electroplated golden goblet she would have gotten from Mary Kay. BeautiControl even had its own songs, with lyrics courtesy of Anna Arnold, who was now selling BeautiControl after quitting her job as Mary Kay's secretary and poodle minder.

It was the birth of a blood feud. On one side, a generation that had never known a selling opportunity without mink stoles and remunerative downlines. On the other side, a generation that had prevailed through flounder lights and fixed territories. Each felt betrayed by the other.

Beginning in the summer of 1966, plaintiffs and defendants appeared before Judge Dee Brown Walker, where, as Brown later wrote, "the atmosphere in the courtroom was so cold we could have killed hogs." Time after time, the judge issued temporary injunctions. Time after time, he reprimanded both sides for ignoring them. All kinds of people came to watch, including Dick Kelly, who was still selling his own version of the tanner's formulas at World Gift.

Mary Kay gave her first deposition in the summer of 1966, but the case ground on for years, a *Jarndyce v. Jarndyce* entangling most of the city's Baptist establishment. Although Mary Kay attended another church, Mary C. Crowley and other prominent Baptists—up to and including former Fuller Brush Man Reverend Billy Graham—were congregants at First Baptist, whose pastor, Reverend W. A. Criswell, held sway over the entire Southern Baptist Convention. Brown's husband, a codefendant, was a deacon there. Ralph D. Baker, Mary Kay's lawyer, was head deacon. And so it went. As the court case commenced, it seemed that half of First Baptist's huge congregation refused to speak to the other half. Sunday school classes split. Brunch dates were canceled. Accusations of sabotage and skullduggery flew.

In March of the suits' second year, Arkansas-born BeautiControl representative Ramona Jean Rochelle, nerves further frayed by the selling opportunity that was supposed to change her life, shot herself in the chest with a .22-caliber revolver, leaving four daughters age seven through twelve. Women wept at the thought of those motherless girls. Each faction pointed a finger at the other. The court cases continued.

Mary Kay's remaining directors vied to show their loyalty. Sales meetings were lovefests. Everyone was on a first-name basis. Hugs replaced handshakes. Air kisses flew. Monthly directors' meetings doubled as potlucks with Mary Kay's own Gypsy Round-a-Layer Cake given pride of place. Recipes were swapped for specialties like Mary Kay Delight, a fruit-and-coconut concoction dreamed up by Dottie Huse of Irving, Texas. Selling and recruiting strategies were shared. Doretha Dingler, a regular at those meetings, remembered, "Mary Kay always said, 'If you have an idea and I have an idea, we each have one. If we share, we each have two.'"

When compliments were given, consultants were schooled to respond with thanks only. No word of denial or self-denigration was to be added. No "aw, shucks" allowed. "Mary Kay taught us to toot our own horn. The first thirty minutes were devoted to crowing. We were just sittin' there, just braggin'," said Dingler, who would go on to drive thirty-three pink Cadillacs, earn over $10 million, and retire as Number One Worldwide. "Mary Kay always said one negative thought could poison 80 percent of the brain." Every meeting had a little pot in the center of the table; if a director said something negative, she had to put a quarter in the pot.

Mary Kay taught directors to weave setbacks like divorce, illness, and death into a narrative called an "I-story." In a good I-story, obstacles were overcome, hard work paid off, and women demonstrated control over their lives. When a consultant had a bad week, a director could counter with an I-story. Dingler recalled Mary Kay saying, "Only tell them your success story, and next week they'll do better."

When directors gave her framed photos of themselves for Christmas, Mary Kay used the portraits to create a hall of fame at company headquarters. Places of honor were based on production figures. Forty years later, a business rival would say, "Mary Kay may not have had a successful personal life, but what she could do was connect with her sales force. She knew how to love her women."

Eventually, in 1969, the court battles ended in a draw. Neither company was supposed to poach personnel from the other. Both had. Both continued. The judge ruled that BeautiControl was allowed to use J. W. Heath's name and image as the inheritance of Heath's granddaughter, who remained on the BeautiControl payroll. Mary Kay was allowed to use the hide tanner story but no family names or photos.

As it turned out, nobody cared about family names or photos. Within a year, Mary Kay was running a slick four-color ad called "Beauty and the Beasts," which began: "Some years ago there lived a hide tanner who spent his days changing the coarse hides of the beasts into soft, supple pieces of leather."

Mary Kay did not win her court case because she had not been able to prove that her business suffered. During the first year of the trial, net sales doubled. By the time the trial wound up, Mary Kay would be a millionaire heading a publicly traded company. Nothing seemed to stop her. Early in the proceedings, Brown made sure that a lawyer read the long list of Mary Kay's married names into court records, sure that the world would be astounded to learn of Mary Kay's many husbands. The world took no notice. Recruits were happy with whatever Mary Kay chose to tell them.

So were reporters. Mary Kay made for great copy. She would reminisce about cooking potato soup for her invalid father, then recite the recipe. She would pose for as many pictures as it took. In private, she might complain when reporters asked her age ("They would never ask a man"). In public, she would turn it into a little joke ("A woman who will tell you that will tell you anything"). Never did she correct errors of omission or assumption. Whatever the story said, she sent a thank-you note.

Hearing her rags-to-riches story, a new wave of recruits came to the company: women who had lived hard lives, whose success selling beauty products seemed improbable at best. Mary Kay stared them in the right eye and told them, "You can do it!"

In 1967, sixty-three-year-old Mary McDowell of Odessa, Texas, a preacher's widow who looked like a real-life Ma Kettle, joined the company while recovering from a stroke. The local recruiter, who had been trying to sign someone else, was not happy to have her. Not that it mattered to McDowell, who was a barn burner from the start. At the end of her first month, McDowell had an orchid corsage pinned to her bosom and was marching up Mary Kay's red carpet to get the first of an eventual forty-six golden goblets. Not long after, a second husband died and her adult son pressured her to retire. To spite him, McDowell decided to become a director.

When she got her first $2,000 monthly commission check, she mailed a photocopy to her son. She did the same for her first $3,000, $4,000, and $6,000 checks. Every time her name was in *Applause!*, the company's in-house magazine, McDowell clipped the story and sent it to her son. When she spoke to local schoolchildren on Career Day, she took along a photocopy of Helen McVoy's $40,000 commission check. McDowell had spent the Depression in coal country, trying to support a child and invalid husband by working in an overalls factory that paid $4.27 every two weeks. Compared with that, being turned down for nine out of ten beauty-show bookings seemed too good to be true.

When a would-be hostess hemmed and hawed about scheduling a beauty show, McDowell followed Mary Kay's advice to behave as if that hostess would be missing out on an especially wonderful hostess gift. Obeying company dictum to keep plenty of product on hand, McDowell devoted an entire room in her pink home to inventory. To entice more women into free facials, she got telephone books from surrounding towns and mailed postcards by the hundreds. She put ads in the local paper. She hired a secretary and booked a cleaning lady. She read Mary Kay's favorite authors until she could respond to almost any situation with a quote from Napoleon Hill, Maxwell Maltz, or Norman Vincent Peale. Like Mary Kay, she thought nothing of hopping on a plane to help a recruit with extra training and encouragement. Sometimes she took along one or more of the company's dozen Super 8 training films

(*An Invitation for Someone Special, A Successful Close*) and the projector she purchased to play them. She invented songs, including a ditty that began: "*The McDowell unit is the way / To reach the top in Mary Kay.*"

To recruit, McDowell would say, "You can teach school twenty-five years and when you retire you will probably be making very little more than the day you started." She would buttonhole waitresses in restaurants, salesgirls in dress shops, fellow passengers on planes. Then she would clinch the deal by looking a recruit in the right eye and, imitating Mary Kay, declare, "I think you would be wonderful." When she was crowned company-wide Queen of Recruiting, the Seminar audience gave her a ten-minute standing ovation.

The next year, she would be enthroned as Queen of Personal Sales for the third time and take center stage at Seminar with another sparkly crown perched on her cake-frosting curls. The year after that, she published an autobiography called *Never Too Late.* In its preface, she contrasted her memory of heading to church not knowing "where my next meal was coming from" with the satisfaction of driving to church in a $15,300 Cadillac wearing a $5,000 mink coat and a $7,800 diamond pin, knowing she owned a $100,000 home furnished with "$64,000 worth of antiques, $34,000 worth of silver and $3,000 worth of hand-painted china, all paid for with Mary Kay money."

The company also benefited from a change in Texas law that made it harder for husbands to stymie a direct-sales career. Up until January 1, 1968, a wife was not supposed to write a check, accept a job, or make decisions about her property without permission from her lord and master. That changed when Louise Raggio, a former assistant district attorney appalled by women's lack of rights in family court, drafted the Marital Property Act. Herself a married mother of three, Raggio had been the only woman in her law school class at Southern Methodist University and knew her way around the boys in the state bar. Her act passed partly because the Texas legislature had recently reviewed a bill proposing equal rights for women, a notion so radical that the

Marital Property Act seemed mild by comparison. From then on, coverture remained custom. But it was no longer law.

The Seminar stage filled with women who hadn't graduated from high school, Mexican immigrants who did not speak English, weather-beaten farmwives who had never been paid a penny for their work. In Mary Kay's company, they found themselves wearing tiaras and pageant sashes and parading in evening gowns while hundreds clapped and cheered. Crowned and congratulated by Mary Kay, one Arkansas farmwife summoned her husband to the stage, asked him for a match, and proceeded to torch the farm mortgage she had been carrying in her purse.

In a time and place when few acknowledged the grind of housekeeping or other "women's work"—and the few who did treated it as an act of altruism—the company seemed to offer glittering fourteen-karat-gold-plated proof that drudgery was no one's natural lot. "We've found that housewives who are getting into the job market for the first time thrive on the praise we give them," Mary Kay later wrote. "No housewife has anyone in her family exclaim, 'Oh, what a beautiful, clean floor!' 'What nice, clean diapers! Aren't they white and fluffy!'"

Mary Kay kept the praise and personal recognition coming too. If a consultant's sales fell, she was apt to get a personal note with "You can do it!" encouragement. If a consultant's sales rose, she would get a note of praise suggesting that she would make a terrific director. Every consultant got a signed birthday card, a practice that would continue as the consultant count went from hundreds to thousands. Sounding as if she spoke from personal experience, Mary Kay said, "Sometimes the only birthday card she gets is from me. We become very important to her."

Pink slips were warm, personal, and pink. If sixty days passed without a minimum wholesale order of $100, the consultant received a cartoon of a sad-looking computer saying, "Can It Be True?" with notice of looming termination, usually two weeks hence. Included was the cheery reminder that the minimum could be met with a mere $1.66 a day. Should malady or misfortune render the consultant temporarily unable to sell, she was urged to share the extenuating circumstances.

As the consultant count grew, Mary Kay organized, standardized, and planned. Her girls were going to get their "railroad track to run on." She briefed consultants on "kitchen coaching" to get the hostess on board before a beauty show began. She gave them a flip chart as a script. She made sure that each page of that chart told consultants what to say and when to say it. "These words have worked. Get in front of a mirror and memorize them," consultants heard. "Don't change the words. It's a magic formula that works."

She didn't stop there. Mary Kay advised each unit to hold its weekly meeting at 10:00 a.m. on Monday and end no later than noon. The meeting should start with two rousing "Tunes for Toppers" company songs (five minutes), followed by an Early Bird Drawing based on summary sheets (suggested cost of gift: fifty cents), introduction of guests (five minutes), roll call (five minutes), and short crowing session (five minutes). All this was spelled out in her *Director's Manual*, which had grown to over one hundred copyrighted pages punctuated by emphatic capitalizations and exclamation points, soon to be joined by LPs that covered simulated beauty shows, booking, recruiting, and company songs. As consultants arrived, unit leaders were supposed to be playing the record, which offered familiar tunes with fresh lyrics. Its version of "The Battle Hymn of the Republic" began:

Mine eyes have seen the glory of the big commission check

Its rewrite of "The Caissons Go Rolling Along":

Sell it far, sell it wide, show them how to tan a hide!
Watch the money keep rolling on in!

To the country-and-western tune "This Ole House," consultants sang:

Ain't time to clean the closets, or to patch up any holes
For the gravy train's a waitin', goin' out to make my goal!

Lots of companies recommended reading. Mary Kay recommended not only what to read but how to read it. She suggested taking a book like Frank Bettger's *How I Raised Myself from Failure to Success in Selling,* reading it into a tape recorder, then listening to the tapes while getting dressed, doing housework, and driving. Encouraging consultants to advertise on community bulletin boards, Mary Kay offered templates that began, "Are you tired of staying home? I was!" All the consultant had to do was copy the template and press a thumbtack into the cork.

Because Mary Kay wanted each unit to have its own contests, she included suggestions for those too: "The 10 Shows a Week Club," "The Over $500 a Week Club," "The 4 Percent Recruiting Club." Each unit leader was supplied with the address of a wholesaler for trophies and ribbons. Each unit was structured so that every consultant had a title. Over and above treasurer, reporter, and hospitality chairman, a unit might have a Unit Song Leader, Social Chairman, and Name Tag Chairman. The secretary who took roll call was supposed to announce, "Miss one Sales Meeting, you're sick; two, you're dying; three, you're DEAD!" The Bumper Sticker Chairman checked the parking lot to ensure that every car sported a sticker promoting the company. The Think Positive Chairman collected fines for negative comments. The Sunshine Chairman used fines from that Negative Comment Kitty to send birthday or get-well cards to unit members. As the manual explained, "If you can satisfy this craving for a 'feeling of importance' you will hold people in the palm of your hand."

Following a tradition established at the first Seminar, every consultant got a gold-plated charm bracelet at the end of her first year, which arrived with a card signed by Mary Kay. That was followed by another charm and another card every year after. On the fifth year, charms would have a tiny diamond, something that had taken seven years to earn at Stanley. Anyone who became a director got a birthday present and a Christmas present. One year, that present was a sonic jewelry cleaner to keep her Mary Kay diamonds sparkling. Spectacular sales feats, such as coming in number one in the company for that month, merited no less than a telegram signed "Lovingly, Mary Kay."

Keeping track of all this fell to forty-three-year-old Erma Thomson, hired in August of 1966 as Mary Kay's secretary and the company's tenth employee. Within minutes of meeting Mary Kay, an embarrassed Thomson confessed to being a divorced single mother and learned "that wasn't of any interest of her, because she had done the same thing." From then on, they were fast friends. "We thought everybody else was a kid.

"Nobody was hanging over my shoulder telling me what to do, so I had to invent what all I needed to do." Night after night, Thomson found herself taking home paperwork like her new boss. When it was time for Seminar, she moved into a downtown hotel for the duration, right alongside Mary Kay. That way, neither woman had to interrupt work long enough to drive home for showers, meals, or fresh clothes.

Seminar was already as much of an extravaganza as Mary Kay could afford to make it. By the third Seminar, her keynote speaker was one of Mr. Bev's favorites: Elmer "Don't Sell the Steak, Sell the Sizzle" Wheeler, author of the 1930s bestseller *Tested Sentences That Sell.* The next year, she distributed diamond rings and hired Vaughn Monroe to sing 1940s hits like "Dance, Ballerina, Dance" and "Mule Train." Each year, Mary Kay introduced Awards Night by asking, "Are you ready for the most exciting night of your life?" Each time, the affirmative roar was deafening. Everyone knew what came next. For hours on end, Mary Kay would crown and congratulate, conferring Cinderella gifts on as many women as possible. Each category had its queen. Each queen had her court. Every one of them would get a hug from Mary Kay, who would lean in and whisper, "Next year, you'll do even better."

She would never give away one prize if she could give away ten. Or twenty. Or thirty. At minimum, Mary Kay recognized the top ten salespeople in categories like sales or recruiting. More often, it was the top twenty. As the company grew, Mary Kay built in multiple plateaus, setting ludicrously high goals for each level, challenging consultants to meet them and, when they did, moving the goals higher.

In direct selling, where yearly personnel turnover of 300 or 400 percent was industry standard, Mary Kay claimed the highest retention rate in the business.

In 1964, when the company moved to a dolled-up warehouse ten times the size of its original storefront, Richard boasted that it would outgrow the space in five years. He was wrong.

On September 13, 1967, the fourth anniversary of its opening-day fiasco, Beauty by Mary Kay moved to 8900 Carpenter Freeway. Lest any driver miss its eye-catching architecture, which featured an undulating facade designed by Frank Meier, Mary Kay had the twenty-two-thousand-square-foot building painted pink and mounted her logo on its front. On that busy stretch of the Dallas Highway Loop, more people were asking about Mary Kay every day.

Success came with its own problems. The biggest was the supply chain. In the beauty industry, few firms owned the factories where their products were made. In 1967, Mary Kay Inc. was essentially a reseller that bought almost everything from Goodier, a jobber in Oak Cliff that had been its supplier from the start. Goodier had guided the novices through sourcing, formulation, and staying on the right side of FDA regulations for four years. It had invented a machine with no purpose other than filling the little pans of lip color in Mary Kay's Lip and Eye Palette. Mary Kay and Richard felt loyalty was owed.

Now, even with extra shifts and weekend work, Goodier was reaching capacity. Owners Elwood Goodier Sr. and Elwood Goodier Jr. were bending over backward to accommodate the account that was now 95 percent of their business. They had neither funds nor financing for a bigger factory.

The company needed a new supply chain or a new way to work with Goodier. Either was likely to be pricey. Up until now, Richard had paid cash for everything. No bank would have lent money to Mary Kay, a woman, or Richard, a twentysomething college dropout working for his mother. This time, though, getting past the production bottleneck was going to take more cash than he had on hand.

Maybe it was time to reconsider franchising. A consortium had already offered Richard and Mary Kay $100,000 for an exclusive franchise in Birmingham, Alabama. Direct-sales franchises were cash machines. Most had a pyramid structure that made it possible to profit even if you sold little or no product. All you had to do was sell franchises that would push you further up the pyramid. That's how franchisers like Nutri-Bio produced the income for John Earl Shoaff's Beverly Hills high life and, when that imploded, the schemes that followed. In the late 1960s, the hottest company in direct sales was a beauty franchiser that called itself Koscot Interplanetary, a contraction of "Kosmetics for the Communities of Tomorrow." Everything about Koscot made Mary Kay's company seem small-time. Koscot's pitch was more high-pressure, its origin story more melodramatic, its success more sensational.

Koscot had been dreamed up by an eighth-grade dropout named Glenn Turner, child of a South Carolina sharecropper father and an unwed mother who had contracted scarlet fever during her pregnancy. Born with a harelip, Turner grew up in a rural South still recovering from the Depression. He peddled sewing machines door to door. After that, he got involved with Holiday Magic, a cosmetics franchise built on multilevel marketing. That inspired him to start his own show. His miracle ingredient would be mink oil, which had gained fame as a cosmetics component in the late 1950s after a New Jersey mink rancher claimed that his hands became softer after tanning mink hides. That gave Turner his story.

From its start, Koscot sold more motivation than mink oil. Using the logic that it took him just as long to sell a $5,000 distributorship as a $2 lipstick, Turner did not bother to manufacture, stock, or sell cosmetics during his venture's first eight months. He was making too much money selling dreams. Anybody who bought a distributorship could sell more distributorships. If, for example, a franchisee succeeded in selling a $5,000 franchise to somebody else, he—and it was almost always a man—got a $2,650 commission. With a little luck and a lot of pressure, the new franchisee would then do the same. One distributor could sell twenty distributorships, each of those could sell twenty more, and Koscot would continue like a chain letter. Thus the sharecropper's son became a millionaire.

Turner did nothing in a small way. "Mr. Enthusiasm" favored outfits like a bright-red suit with a lapel pin that rendered Old Glory in rhinestones. He wore a bad toupee. His high-heeled cowboy boots were made from unborn calf. Cartwheeling twin dwarfs were his constant companions. At Koscot rallies, acrobats turned handsprings up and down auditorium aisles while pretty girls pinned hundred-dollar bills to the lapels of recruits.

After the first year, when he added "Dare to Be Great" motivational franchises, Turner's businesses would be in forty states and Canada, and Turner would be on his way to addressing the Harvard Business School and racking up an eventual $300 million (over $2 billion today). When *Life* magazine, then in its high-circulation heyday, ran a long feature story about him, Turner bragged that he had been on its cover. He had not. That issue's cover story was the rock opera *Jesus Christ Superstar.* Missing the irony, journalists printed his claim as fact.

To Mary Kay and Richard, Turner was a huckster taking direct sales back to the days of snake oil and sideshows. At the end of 1967, his nationwide notoriety was working to their detriment, since few appreciated the distinctions between Turner's "anyone can be a millionaire" style of multilevel marketing and Mary Kay's "You can do it!" style of direct-sales recruiting. Potential recruits, and the husbands of potential recruits, were wary of ending up at the bottom of a Koscot-type pyramid. No, franchising would not do.

Richard got ready to go public instead. In January of 1968, Mary Kay formally named herself chairman of the board and promoted twenty-four-year-old Richard to president. Ben, still running the warehouse, became vice president of merchandising. Announcements in the press noted that the company had started in 1963 with a ten-woman sales force and ended 1967 with three thousand women doing $5 million retail.

Mary Kay with twenty-four-year-old Richard in January of 1968.

Preparing for an initial public offering, Mary Kay hit the hustings. Excerpts from a speech to her thirteen hundred Seminar attendees appeared in *The Dallas Morning News* as an unbylined news item. In her new chairman-of-the-board persona, Mary Kay made optimistic pronouncements about the future earnings of women and told the newspaper that, the year before, one of Mary Kay's directors had made over $40,000 (over $378,000 today); ten had earned over $25,000 (about $236,000). The newspaper then contrasted Mary Kay Inc. with the rest of the world: "By way of comparison, the highest average salary listed for any single female profession by the Bureau of Labor Statistics . . . is $5,720 annually for executive secretaries in the public utilities field." Less than 1 percent of working women earned over $10,000 a year.

Despite her impatience with business boosters and her disaffection for hobnobbing, Mary Kay made the rounds of civic organizations—Rotary Club and Lions Club included—with a presentation called "The Fountain of Youth." She wrote checks and lent her name to co-op ads that reminded the citizens of Dallas to attend church more often and to be kinder to their fellow man. Richard lined up Rauscher, Pierce & Co., investment bankers with a Dallas pedigree, to underwrite the IPO. Just before Easter, Richard registered 195,000 common shares with the Securities and Exchange Commission with 165,000 shares outstanding. For luck, the announcement hit the papers on April 13.

With the IPO underway, Richard got a middle-of-the-night phone call from a man in Melbourne who wanted to open Australia for Mary Kay. Since the company was not in all fifty states yet, overseas expansion was too early by years. Anyway, Canada would make more sense.

Longing to say no and go back to sleep, Richard realized that the man on the phone had spent two years working for the Success Motivation Institute, which sold Dale Carnegie–style self-improvement courses. During that time, he had worked with dozens of directors. His wife had hosted a beauty show. He knew the company, understood its recruiting, and had a copy of its training manual. There was nothing to stop him from starting a copycat. Trying to avoid another BeautiControl, Richard stayed on the phone. Setting an indefinite future date for a possible merger, Richard encouraged the Australian to find a local cosmetics jobber and set up a company. Then they would see.

Less than five years after its disastrous debut, Mary Kay's company was ready to take on the world.

On August 8, 1968, eighty-three-year-old Lula died of a heart arrhythmia.

After a lifetime of rising before dawn to start her sixteen-hour workdays, Lula's sole asset was the Kane Street house, now valued at $5,500, much less than the mortgage payments she had struggled to make. Through her late seventies, she had lived above Wagner's Café, taking in boarders while she rented out her house. Describing Lula's belated retirement, Mary Kay made it sound like her mother's health problems were caused by enforced leisure.

On regular visits to the Autumn Leaves home on the edge of

Houston, Mary Kay brought her beauty showcase so she could give her mother a facial, do her mother's makeup and hair, then help her into a nice dress. When her mother's roommate asked for a facial, Mary Kay did that too.

Mary Kay also met with Houston consultants when she came to town. At one such meeting, Mary Kay sold them on the idea of staging beauty shows at the nursing home as a gesture of goodwill. Daughter Marylyn was dispatched to do the first, securing a $156 order after Lula corralled six fellow residents into attending. Retelling the story in her autobiography, Mary Kay recalled: "After that, a Mary Kay Consultant went back each week and gave a beauty show." Afterward, Mary Kay sometimes said her mother died at age eighty-seven, sometimes at age eighty-four. What never varied was the claim that Lula died with a lovely complexion.

In the middle of the IPO that would make her a millionaire, Mary Kay headed to Houston, accompanied by Mel. The funeral was held on Friday, then Lula was buried at Resthaven near Mary Kay's father. Obituaries made no mention of Lula's marriage to Murphy, who was long gone.

On Monday morning, Mary Kay was up before dawn to start her workweek.

CHAPTER EIGHTEEN

A Pink Cadillac

On August 29, 1968, Mary Kay's not-quite-five-year-old company went public.

The stock offering did what it was supposed to do: It brought in cash and established market value. Shares opened near $12, went to $30, and settled around $25. Richard sold 30,000 unissued company shares, netting $333,000 for reinvestment and expansion. Mary Kay, who had been earning less than some of her directors, sold a chunk of her 585,750 shares and netted $1,831,500 for herself. Richard and Ben retained 119,625 shares each. When the day was done, 76 percent of the company remained under family control. The next morning, *The Dallas Morning News* headlined its story $1.8 MILLION, MARY KAY COLLECTS ON STOCK. *The Fort Worth Star-Telegram* ran a photo of grinning investment bankers handing oversize checks to a stiff-looking Richard and a beaming Mary Kay.

Neither took time to celebrate. On September 13, one year after moving into the headquarters on Carpenter Freeway, Richard bought a $1.3 million parcel of land for the bigger, better headquarters he planned to put on Stemmons Freeway. A few weeks later, he was able to announce that, for the first nine months of 1968, the company had year-over year increases of 79 percent in sales and 105 percent in earnings. He attributed those increases to geographic expansion. Then he announced that, from here on out, expansion would go farther and faster. Stock prices rose.

With everything going according to plan, Richard could now secure the supply chain. Having established the stock's market value, he initiated the deal that had inspired the IPO: acquiring Goodier through a secondary offering of 150,000 shares to be split equally between Elwood Sr. and Elwood Jr. As the three men had agreed, Elwood Sr. was welcome to continue an independent operation as a perfumer and chemist while Elwood Jr. ran the factory. By the time the contract was approved by the boards of both companies and signed in December, the market price of Mary Kay Inc. shares made the deal worth $7.5 million. Goodier would henceforth be known as Cosmetic Creations. Supplier became subsidiary.

With Cosmetic Creations signed, sealed, and delivered, Richard bought eleven acres on Regal Row, down the road from the onetime World Gift headquarters. Just before Christmas, while his former partners at Fashion Tress filed for Chapter 11, Richard announced that he was building "the most modern cosmetics manufacturing plant in the Southwest" on the $750,000 site. Construction was underway by March. A young man in a hurry, Richard went to Republic National Bank and arranged for $2 million in interim financing to get his factory finished by September. His next round of horse-trading had him proposing to pay that off via a convoluted subordinated debenture deal with Allstate Insurance.

The new 108,000-square-foot factory would cost close to $3 million and have more capacity than the company could possibly use. That was part of the plan too. Richard hired a salesman and had a private-label business up and running within a year of the factory's completion, producing bubble bath, body lotion, and cologne for Neiman Marcus while retaining ownership of the formulas. That factory—painted pink—helped to fund Richard's next projects, a nationwide network of distribution centers. He planned the first for Los Angeles, despite the fact that the Western territory had only three hundred consultants and only eighty of them were in California. He was sure there would be more.

In an industry served mostly by jobbers, this was seen as pure hubris. If business ever slowed, the factory and distribution centers would be write-offs, salable only as teardowns. But business did not slow. Control of the supply chain became another coup. Before the first distribution center was finished, Richard was planning more. Mary Kay believed that women were impulse buyers and therefore time between buying and delivery should be minimal. She wanted none of the waiting that had so exasperated her when she sold for Stanley and World Gift—waits still standard at Avon, Tupperware, and other direct sellers.

Within a decade, the company would have distribution centers near Dallas, Los Angeles, Atlanta, Chicago, and Toronto, plus a New Jersey location halfway between Philadelphia and New York. Each would have meeting rooms big enough to conduct trainings. Each would be decorated with directors' portraits so the recruits could see the payoff of those trainings.

Mary Kay milked the expansion for all it was worth. "Each time we'd try and outdo what they'd done before," said Frank Meier, the architect responsible for company headquarters, the Round House, Richard's house, and now the distribution centers. To break ground for a twenty-five-thousand-square-foot distribution center outside Atlanta, the company found a dainty bulldozer, painted it pink, named it Daisy the Dozer, put a cartoon face with long eyelashes on its grille, then made sure that the reigning Miss Georgia was on hand so the stunt made the papers.

Months later, when that center was finished, Mary Kay herself was on hand for a "Mary Kay Blossoms in the South"–themed ribbon cutting, which featured consultants in antebellum attire arrayed around the building while a helicopter scattered fifty thousand rose petals from on high. Until, in a photo op that the local press would never forget, the helicopter hovered so low that its backwash whooshed the consultants' hoopskirts over their heads.

Two years later, when the company had outgrown that center, Mary Kay went back to Georgia, looped the pink reins of a pink plow around her waist, yoked the pink plow to a pink Cadillac, sat a director in a pink suit behind the wheel, and broke ground for a bigger facility. This time, consultants in contemporary, slim-fitting skirts spelled out "Mary Kay" in a Reagan Red Coat–style formation, while another helicopter hovered—higher—overhead to capture the aerial view.

By then the company was in all fifty states and maintained a fleet of pink Peterbilt trucks that crisscrossed the country like eighteen-wheel billboards. It also had its first foreign subsidiary. Less than a year after going public, the company had completed acquisition of Rachel York, the Australian direct seller founded with Mary Kay's marketing model and product names. In private, Mary Kay griped that they paid $1.5 million to acquire a company that they could have had for free. Then she got on a plane to tell Australia about the Mary Kay selling opportunity. Papers there ran headlines like TANNING HER HIDE MADE MILLIONS above stories describing Mel as her second husband.

From the company's first day, Mary Kay had praised Richard as "a computer genius." Knowing nothing about computers herself, she had, to use one of her own phrases, "praised [him] forward to success." When the North Texas chapter of a trade association named twenty-six-year-old Richard as its Marketing Man of the Year, his mother behaved as if he had won the Nobel Prize in Economics. When the stock offering was successful, she praised Richard as a financial genius and handed him her newly minted millions to invest. Once again, he did not disappoint. Richard put Mary Kay's money in oil wells, where it multiplied as miraculously as loaves and fishes.

Mother and son worked in sync. She motivated. He managed. She was the booster, the boss who baked cookies, the dreamer. He was the hatchet man, the number cruncher, the moneyman. Like his mother, Richard could charm the birds out of the trees. Unlike his mother, he rarely bothered. He preferred press that described him as an ex–Marine sergeant and reveled in his reputation as a tough guy. While Mary Kay consoled consultants who came to her with personal problems, her son was said to respond to bleeding-heart stories with "Please don't bleed on the carpet."

Richard had become a father when he was twenty-one and his wife was eighteen. His second child arrived in 1969 during the round-robin of financing, factory construction, and structuring the earn-out acquisition of Rachel York in Australia. Now, as his much-wed mother settled into marriage with Mel, Richard's own marriage was faring less well. "He was datin' all the girls," recalled Meier. Richard would divorce in 1972, remarry in 1974, then divorce and remarry again.

He was not the only one. Ben would divorce and remarry too. Marylyn would have three husbands. One of her five daughters would continue the family's tradition of teenage marriage and make Mary Kay a great-grandmother at the age of fifty-three.

Mary Kay, however, remained giddy as a newlywed. In 1969, she celebrated her dream house, dream company, and dream bank balance by commissioning a portrait of herself from Jack Wittrup, a painter with a sideline doing pinup girls. The three-quarter-length pose showed

Mary Kay in the living room of the Round House, 1975.

Mary Kay gowned in impasto lace, her head cocked to the side, her mouth closed in her half smile, her figure a bit slimmer than it may have been in real life. Officially a present for Mel, it would hang above the fireplace in the living room of the Round House, where the portrait of a successful businesswoman in a happy marriage provided a perfect background for posing with DIQs.

Her second husband taught her the importance of modeling prosperity. Her fourth husband's sister built a business around the slogan "Think mink!" Her fifth husband told her that abundance attracted abundance. Now she was going to show them all. She was going to get her A+.

When she started making money with World Gift, Mary Kay bought herself a Cadillac. That big, shiny car made her look prosperous to customers and potential recruits. It got her noticed. Hence, in 1967, with company sales and income more than double what they had been the year before, Mary Kay headed to Frank Kent's Cadillac dealership in Fort Worth to celebrate with a Cinderella gift to herself. Ordering a 1968 DeVille, Mary Kay asked for a custom paint job in the same shade as her packaging, a pale pink identical to the "Mountain Laurel Blush" that General Motors retired in the 1950s.

The salesman advised her to stick with something more practical. When she did not, he predicted that she would be back for a paint job. Instead, driving her new Cadillac for the first time, she discovered the perks of driving a pink car nearly nineteen feet long: "As I approached each intersection, everyone noticed my car, and many people waved me through. They smiled and nodded approvingly; some gave me a thumbs-up and motioned me to go ahead of them."

More perks soon manifested. Throughout their '50s girlhoods, Mary Kay's directors had seen the great and famous pilot pink Cadillacs, yet somehow had grown up to find themselves sitting behind the wheels of wood-paneled station wagons. They took one look at Mary Kay's pink Cadillac and wanted one too, then started recruiting like crazy so they could afford it.

The parking lot at pink headquarters filled with so many pink Cadillacs that women could be seen checking license plates to figure out which one was theirs. Some added heart-shaped opera windows for help. At the driveway entrance, Mary Kay put up a RESERVED FOR PINK CADILLACS sign. "Our small office was on the way to the Dallas–Fort Worth Airport and everybody started noticing that sign," Erma Thomson remembered. "That got more advertising than she had on anything else." It did not take long for Mary Kay to decide that pink Cadillacs should be sales incentives.

In direct sales, that was not without precedent. In 1952, when he was still grateful to Brownie Wise for making him a millionaire, inventor Earl Tupper gave her a pink Cadillac as a sign of appreciation. Throughout the 1950s, both Stanley and Tupperware had awarded the occasional Cadillac to top sellers, albeit always in a tasteful color suitable for a family car. More recently, multilevel marketer Holiday Magic had grabbed publicity for awarding a Rolls-Royce as grand prize in a 1966 sales contest, with a Lincoln Continental going to the runner-up.

Mary Kay had a better idea. She would give away Cadillacs as unlike family cars as possible. Consultants would drive them on leases while the company retained ownership. Never to be run-down, repainted, or resold, the cars would double as shining pink advertisements for her selling opportunity. Reminding Richard of their golden-goblet bonanza, Mary Kay urged her financial-genius son to run his numbers. By the 1969 Seminar, five women had qualified. On Awards Night, Mary Kay stood onstage conferring car keys while a humongous pink Cadillac revolved on the dais behind her. When she read out the name of Lovie Quinn, a divorced mother of five who lived in Houston without a car, Quinn ran past Mary Kay to plant a kiss on the hood of her new six-passenger, 375-horsepower beauty, smacking it with such gusto that the dais came to a dead stop.

Women went all out to win pink Cadillacs. Mary Kay awarded ten in 1970, twenty in 1971. Over at BeautiControl, they gave away a gold Cadillac. In 1973, after Richard hit on an algorithm that opened the award to the entire company, Mary Kay gave away fifty-two sets of keys. As consultants chanted, "Little pink jars mean big pink cars," the number continued to climb. One year, Mary Kay awarded so many car keys that, when the pink presentation basket was carried onstage at Seminar, its bottom gave way under the weight.

To women who had been unlucky for most of their lives, Mary Kay offered a dream that had nothing to do with rescue by a knight in shining armor, strokes of good fortune, or accidents of birth. There was no surprise or serendipity to winning a pink Cadillac, no Tupperware-style "Wish Fairy" who wafted through Seminar bestowing benefaction with a wave of her wand. Getting those car keys took dogged persistence and absurd amounts of work, things most women already understood. If a consultant failed to meet monthly production quotas, her new car could vanish as fast as Cinderella's pumpkin coach. Women understood that too.

Mary Kay, though, did everything in her power to keep a consultant in a pink Cadillac. So did the consultant's director, whose own income was tied to sales. Again and again, consultants heard "You're in business for yourself, but not by yourself." Pregnant women won pink Cadillacs, women in wheelchairs won them, women barely out of a hospital bed.

For consultants not quite at Cadillac status, Mary Kay added pink Buick Regals with bumper stickers that read WHEN I GROW UP, I'M GOING TO BE A CADILLAC. Each year, her Career Car program became ever more elaborate. As the company expanded internationally, prizes would be tailored to territories—a pink Mercedes in Germany, a pink Toyota in Taiwan—until the whole world seemed to be making fun of Mary Kay's pink cars. Her response would be a tilt of the head, a half smile, and a sweet-voiced "Well, what color car did your company give you?"

Diamond bumblebee pins came next. Mary Kay said she based the idea on a Thursday present from Mel, who gave her a jewel-studded pin and called her his queen bee. Offering bumblebees in three sizes, with carat weight calibrated to sales, Mary Kay proclaimed the bumblebee a perfect symbol for women who had flown to the top: "Aerodynamics have proven that the bumblebee cannot fly. The body is too heavy and

The diamond bumblebee: "a wonderful symbol of women who come into our organization and don't know that they can fly."

the wings are too weak. But the bumblebee doesn't know it. He goes right on flying. . . . I thought this was a wonderful symbol of women who come into our organization and don't know that they can fly."

Consultants were soon wearing swarms of bees to company events. Emulating Mary Kay's own way of wearing jewelry, bees flew from lapels to shoulders, from front to back, then began alighting on sleeve heads and upper arms. At Seminar, women would be covered with bees and assorted awards, sometimes with horse show–style ribbons fluttering from shoulders, sleeves, and skirts. Consultants could size each other up in an instant. Golden goblet giveaways now ran to thousands of goblets a year. Minks grew in size and splendor from stoles to jackets to coats to opera-length floor sweepers—absent pink mink, which Mary Kay considered tacky.

Other glitzy, girly awards debuted as fast as she could dream them up. Instead of appliances, consultants won shopping sprees at Neiman Marcus and dream vacations as unlike family outings as Mary Kay could make them. Sales rose. Cinderella gifts multiplied. Sales rose again. Mary

Kay explained: "If we awarded a cash bonus, a woman would probably use it to pay her utility bills, make a house payment, or replace her washing machine. Once she spends the money, she doesn't think about it again. But every time she sees that diamond ring on her finger, she remembers her well-deserved moment of glory."

Mary Kay kept right on telling consultants to hire a housekeeper. She told them that it was a waste of time to be scrubbing toilets when they could be selling skin care. No consultant contradicted her. When Marabel Morgan's *The Total Woman* taught that good Christian wives were supposed to be ironing love into their husbands' shirt collars, Mary Kay told those good Christian wives that their husbands would never notice the difference. She was still encouraging them to buy a new dress when their self-confidence was low, still saying it would pay off in the long run.

It had already paid off for her. Routinely identified as "the millionairess founder of Mary Kay Cosmetics," Mary Kay was a symbol of high living. Her home and household habits had been featured in both Dallas dailies, hundreds had toured the Round House, and you could set your watch by Mel, who got into his Lincoln and drove to the Merrill Lynch office at the same time every morning.

All of that also made her an easy target. Thus, one midweek morning in August of 1974, when Mel had driven off to read newspapers at Merrill Lynch and the maid had not yet arrived, Mary Kay opened her door expecting a repairman for the sprinkler system. Instead she found a man with a toolbox who pulled a gun, forced her to reveal where she kept her jewelry, bound her wrists, taped her ankles, and stuffed cotton in her mouth. When Mary Kay managed to get one leg loose, he came back, knocked her down, then dragged her into the dining room. After he left, Mary Kay spent an hour crawling to the bedroom, where she was able to activate a silent alarm.

Less than nine years before, when thieves had gotten away with $9,000 in loot, the robbery made the front pages of Dallas papers. This time, the stolen jewels were valued at over $53,000 and wire services sent the story nationwide.

She was going to show that "the Mary Kay way" was better. Better than Stanley. Better than World Gift. Better than any franchise.

In late middle age, Mary Kay behaved as if she were still trying to prove something to Mr. Bev. She would outdo "the Great Encourager" with more praise, more personal notes, more tours of her home. She would give away diamonds and minks instead of gimcrack trophies. She would structure her company so that no woman ever lost her overrides when a husband's job took the family to a new town. She would take Mr. Bev's "better your best" philosophy and reinterpret it in ways that yielded diamond-studded cocktail rings and big shiny cars. Most of all, she was going to give the really ambitious ones a way to keep moving ahead. Stanley had lost Brownie Wise and Mary C. Crowley and who knows how many others because they felt stymied. She was not going to make that mistake.

As the company grew, she added echelon after echelon, so that there was always some higher step, some more desirable and more prestigious status that was almost within reach. Recruits gung ho on their new careers could aspire to become Red Jackets, which meant they were entitled to wear a red blazer signifying that they had recruited three others to the fold. "Really, three recruits is nothing, but that's not why she did it," Doretha Dingler explained. "A red jacket gave them status. It taught them how to dress, how to look professional. Got them thinking they were on their way." Five recruits made the consultant a Team Leader. Eight made her a Future Director. Ten earned DIQ status and the right to pay for a weeklong trip to Dallas, where she could visit the Round House, share spiced tea and cookies with Mary Kay and Mel, and have her picture taken in the empty tub.

Toward the top of the ladder, Mary Kay had invented the title of Senior Sales Director (SSD) to signify a director who recruited five women who also became directors. In 1971, with directors now numbering in the hundreds, Mary Kay devised the rank of National Sales Director (NSD) for Helen McVoy and Dalene Brewer (now remarried and known as Dalene White), which signified that they had recruited and mentored a minimum of ten "offspring" directors. McVoy was closing on $100,000 a year (over $810,000 in today's money). White was not far behind. And no sooner had Mary Kay made the announcement than half a dozen other women announced that they were going to be NSDs too.

She couldn't stop there. She had brooded over missed opportunities for too long. Promotions at Stanley and World Gift had always seemed so subjective, so closed to women, so bound to an old boys' network. To Mary Kay, those were the only possible explanations for their failure to promote her. Her next totem, the Ladder of Success pin, was meant to symbolize the company's policy of spelling out what it took to advance to the next level. A consultant earned the right to wear the pin when she was designated a Star Consultant, a status that signified she was consistently selling products. After that, itty-bitty diamonds, sapphires, or rubies were added to the rungs of the gold-plated ladder to signal how much she had sold in that calendar quarter.

To get consultants climbing, Mary Kay made sure they understood the rewards for reaching that next rung. And the one above. And the one above that. As the company grew, Mary Kay continued to add rung after rung, title after title. Entering the company, a woman could go from Beauty Consultant to Star Consultant to Golden Girl. Arcane to outsiders, titles were well understood within the company. Seeing *Future* before a title meant a consultant was almost at the next rung. *Executive* meant she had helped a defined number of other women achieve a certain status. *Elite Executive* signified that she had helped a greater number. At each level, a woman's success depended upon the success of the women who followed. If they slacked off or quit, her own status was in jeopardy.

So was her income. Commission structure was common knowledge. From the start, Mary Kay printed individual earnings in her newsletters. If a woman wanted to earn more, she knew how much she had to sell or recruit. By the early 1970s, each director got a monthly computer printout showing what her unit had ordered. If her unit's monthly total was under $1,000, she earned nothing. If her unit sold between $1,000 and $2,000, she got a 9 percent override; $2,000 to $4,000 earned 10 percent; $4,000 to $6,000 earned 11 percent; and anything over $6,000 earned 12 percent.

If the day came when her unit sales fell below the minimum for two consecutive months, then she was a director no more, the company equivalent of a sergeant being busted to private. Regaining rank required a DIQ do-over, including another three-month qualification period and another training trip to Dallas.

That happened more often than anyone cared to admit. The year might start with 400 directors; another 300 might qualify. But because so many dropped out, the total might increase by only 150. Husbands griped. Kids had to get to games and practices. In-laws needed looking after. By the mid-1970s, Richard had an algorithm predicting how many directors the company would have at the end of the fiscal year. Overall, about 80 percent of the sales force left each year. Compared with Tupperware's 100 percent turnover, Avon's 150 percent, and other direct sellers' 300 or 400 percent, that gave Mary Kay one of the best retention rates in the business.

The same policies, commissions, and rewards applied to everyone. Unusual for a U.S. beauty company in the 1970s, much less one south of the Mason–Dixon line, Mary Kay fielded a sales force that was about 20 percent African American and 10 percent Latina. Mary Kay, great-granddaughter of a Confederate infantryman, hugged and kissed and crowned and congratulated them all.

Skin care had little to do with skin color. Makeup was a different story, but the company was still selling Lip and Eye Palettes, and those looked pretty much the same on everybody. A few more shades of Day Radiance and Shadow Erase took care of the rest. Hence women of color went from customer to consultant to director, with pastors' wives proving a particular blessing. Well educated, well spoken, and well groomed, they were naturals at explaining Mary Kay's own golden rule: "God first, family second, career third." And there weren't many other ways for a preacher's wife to make money. Not real money.

Pillars of the African American community, these were women who knew how to motivate. Among them: civil rights leader Juanita Abernathy, architect of the Montgomery bus boycott and wife of Reverend Dr. Ralph Abernathy. Trained by Mary Kay herself, Abernathy became a consultant after the assassination of Dr. Martin Luther King Jr. and spent two decades as a senior sales director, reaching the number two recruitment spot for the entire company while traveling the world on peace missions, dodging rubber bullets in Northern Ireland, and driving one pink Cadillac after another.

Formidable as she was, Abernathy would be outrecruited by another pastor's wife, one who had the kind of backstory that was direct-sales gold. At age eleven, Arkansas sharecropper's daughter Ruell Jackson Cone was chopping cotton for ten hours a day. Getting herself off the farm and through college, she married a man pursuing his PhD in theology, only to find herself trying to support him and their three children on the pittance she earned by directing a church choir and giving piano lessons, all while living in a house with no curtains and almost no furniture. The family slept in two trundle beds. Cone said that she signed up to sell Mary Kay in 1971 because she was hoping to clear $50 a month for a furniture layaway.

In short order, she was decked in diamonds, driving a pink Cadillac, and standing onstage in floor-length mink. By 1976, she stood shoulder to shoulder with McVoy and White as an NSD. She posed alongside Mary Kay for newspaper features, company promotions, and advertorials in *Black Enterprise*. After acquiring all the curtains and furniture she could ever need, Cone would buy a Mercedes-Benz for her husband and put all three children through college and medical school. Twenty years later, she would still be with the company when *The Wall Street Journal* reported: "Black women have sold their way up the Mary Kay hierarchy and now hold 10 percent of the company's lucrative sales director slots."

The Latina contingent would take longer. Spanish-speaking DIQs had been regulars at the Round House beginning in the late 1960s, when Mary Kay would hand them a cup of spiced tea, Mel would pass the Wham Bam! cookies, an interpreter would ensure that no aphorism or anecdote was lost, and everybody would take her turn climbing into Mary Kay's tub. Among them were dozens like Etelvina Hernandez, who had been a beauty queen in her native Mexico before she found herself as a mother of six living in Houston without being able to speak English or drive a car. After joining the company in 1971, Hernandez became a senior sales director and was enthroned as National Queen of Personal Sales three times. "I just put the basket [of cosmetics] by the door in the morning," she said, "and I don't go to bed until I sell it."

These new directors adored Mary Kay. But there were now hundreds of them. Too many for the sorority-style potlucks that had been such fun. Instead, directors shared pointers in *Idea Exchange*, another weekly newsletter. The *Directors' Manual*, which had started as a couple of smudgy mimeographed sheets, was now 170 professionally printed, single-spaced, indexed pages. According to Richard's algorithm, the number of directors was going to double in the next five years.

So Mary Kay formalized the directors' confab as a Leadership Conference and added it to her DIQ sessions, Jamborees, Seminars, ground breakings, ribbon cuttings, press tours, and prize trips. She scheduled more celebrations at the Round House. She dropped in on

Mary Kay at her custom-made round desk in 1975.

more regional events so directors could get to know her. She couldn't let them down.

During the recession of 1974, women flocked to Mary Kay.

Over its eleven years, the company had averaged annual increases of 30 percent. That year, the consultant count was almost twenty-nine thousand. Net sales went from $22 million to over $30.2 million. Richard's gamble with the distribution centers had already paid off.

Not everyone had been so lucky. In 1972, the same year that thirty-two states initiated legal action against Koscot, an unabashed Glenn Turner prophesied that he would one day be president. The next year, a judge consolidated over a thousand lawsuits into a class-action suit seeking $1 billion, setting off a chain of calamities that included two weeks in the slammer and loss of most of Turner's Cadillacs and the private planes with his face painted ten feet high on the tails. The castle he had been building would never be completed. Turner and his family decamped to its boathouse, a crenellated white tower with a weird resemblance to the Round House.

Holiday Magic went bust too. Founded in 1964 by Turner's onetime teacher William Penn Patrick, the cosmetics company with the fruit-based ingredient story and multilevel marketing structure brought in so much cash that Patrick claimed he spent more than $1 million—newspapers estimated it was probably a third of that—campaigning as Ronald Reagan's ultraconservative opponent in the primary for governor of California. Undeterred when he got less than 3 percent of the vote, Patrick charged Reagan with rigging polls, put a pin in his own plan to be elected president in 1972, and founded the Leadership Dynamics Institute, which mandated that aspiring Holiday Magic managers participate in $1,000 weekend encounters that could include being stuffed into a coffin or strung up on a cross. "I don't think those things are damaging," Patrick explained. "A little painful, but a man learns from his pain."

At the start of the 1970s, Patrick was being investigated by the Federal Trade Commission, the U.S. Postal Service, and several state governments. He was also being sued by Avon and brought up on an array of charges by survivors of Leadership Dynamics, Mind Dynamics, and Sales Dynamics. In 1972, a pilot in a vintage warplane from Patrick's private museum crashed into an ice cream parlor, killing twelve children and ten adults. The year after, Patrick died piloting a stunt plane that crashed after failing to maintain sufficient height after takeoff. Two weeks later, the Securities and Exchange Commission brought charges against Holiday Magic for bilking distributors of $250 million.

Losing a battle begun in 1932, when the FTC first accused it of duping and coercing children, Wilson Chemical sold Cloverine Salve to a company that did not use direct-sales distribution. Jan and Frank Day sold their direct-sales beauty company, Jafra, to Gillette. Fuller Brush sales had been falling for years when the company asked women to sell more than toiletries, a move reported in headlines like A GOOD MAN IS HARD TO FIND—SO THEY HIRE WOMEN. Two years later, Fuller Brush was sold to Consolidated Foods.

Diversification ruled the day. Beauty businesses were a prime target. Led by executives with no expertise in the category, multinational corporations went on a buying binge. British American Tobacco scooped up Germaine Monteil. Pfizer, flush from its most profitable year of vaccines and antibiotics, bought Coty. In 1971, Eli Lilly used earnings from Darvon, an opioid that was later banned, to acquire Elizabeth Arden, while Squibb Beech-Nut acquired Charles of the Ritz and Lanvin. Two years after, Norton Simon bought Max Factor, and Colgate-Palmolive turned Helena Rubinstein into its wholly owned subsidiary. Most would go through at least one more round of being bought and traded before folding or fading away.

While Richard kept the company narrow and deep, Avon diversified in ways both lucrative (costume jewelry) and less so (hair salons and greeting cards), signs of the soon-to-come day when Avon would overpay to acquire Tiffany & Co., the Fifth Avenue jeweler. Still the kind of Wall Street darling that made its stock a mainstay of college funds and retirement accounts, Avon weathered sex-discrimination suits and recalls of contaminated products, giving the men in charge little motivation to change its boys'-club management or to trim its ponderous product line. By 1974, Avon was saddled with an inventory of over eight hundred SKUs, to Mary Kay's three dozen or so. As its sales continued to trend slightly up, Avon's earnings began to trend slightly down.

Viviane Woodard Cosmetics, now a neglected subsidiary of General Foods, vowed to trim its line of over eight hundred SKUs by half, but its days of snappy taglines and trendsetting promotions during Brownie Wise's stint as CEO were long over.

Wise herself had vanished. In 1967, she had taken a final crack at direct selling, hired by another businessman convinced he could make a killing in the beauty business. A Midwestern contractor with no cosmetics experience, he vetoed Wise's every suggestion before firing her in 1969. Afterward, the first woman on the cover of *Business Week* would become a semirecluse living in Kissimmee, Florida, scene of her Tupperware triumphs, where she spent the next decades dabbling in pottery and spiritualism.

CHAPTER NINETEEN

Horatio Alger Stories

Mary Kay was succeeding where so many others had not.

When other companies copied her business model, it never seemed to work as well for them. Never able to equal Mary Kay's sales, BeautiControl was acquired by Tri-Chem, a direct-sales company that sold crafts like liquid embroidery kits and iron-on transfers. Out in California, one of Mary Kay's Cadillac-winning, diamond-ringed Top Ten directors took over a beauty company called Penegen, started a Goblet Club, gave away Oldsmobiles, and ran ads with the tagline "First Mary Kay, Now Penegen!" For a while, she made money too, but not as much as Mary Kay.

During its second decade, Mary Kay Inc. would grow another 670 percent. After securing every U.S. state and territory and consolidating its Australian operation, the company was getting ready to launch in Canada and South America as consultants dreamed of million-dollar downlines and world domination. In 1975, with annual net sales nearing $35 million, the company doubled the footprint of the factory that had seemed so oversize a year or two before. At 240,000 square feet, Cosmetic Creations was revved and ready in anticipation of Richard's next goal, the company's first $100 million year.

In 1976, a 28 percent spurt in sales astounded analysts. Mary Kay

Mary Kay and "fur person" in back of the Round House, 1975.

was not surprised. "We had a price increase, and we told our consultants it was coming three weeks in advance. They bought everything we had, emptied the shelves." Sales were up $9 million in a single month. "Women love bargains," said Mary Kay.

A few months later, Mary Kay became the first woman to chair a company on the New York Stock Exchange. Her company became the youngest firm listed. "New York Stock Exchange Welcomes a Lady" said an ad trumpeting the company's August 27 listing alongside the blue-chip likes of AT&T, IBM, and Exxon. Underneath a photo of the MKY ticker symbol, the ad noted compound annual growth of 34 percent and an average annual return of 25 percent over the last five years, predictive of the stock's future as a Wall Street darling on par with Avon. Richard proclaimed his biggest problem to be managing so many spikes in profitability. Stock certificates were pink.

Much as all that impressed investors, recruits counted for more with Mary Kay. Their turn to be awed came when Dalene White's lifetime earnings put her on track to become the first "Mary Kay million-

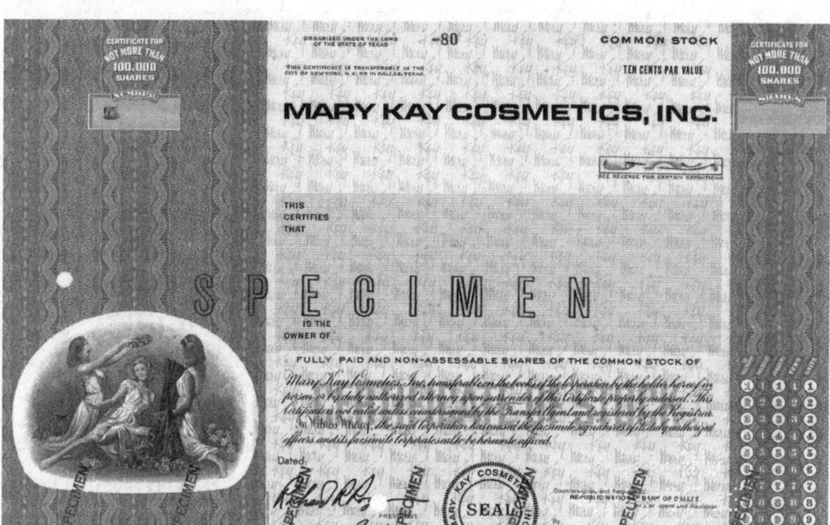

Specimen stock certificate for Mary Kay Cosmetics Inc.

aire." As ever, Helen McVoy was closing fast, outearning White that year with a total of $118,000, which allowed McVoy and her Harvard MBA husband to divest themselves of their fishing-worm farm and put the money in resort real estate. It was only a matter of time until McVoy pulled even with White. And until other NSDs caught up with her.

The sketchy Australian operation was doing better too. "Australia is about where we were in the 1920s as far as cosmetics are concerned," Mary Kay explained. "They've only been using deodorants for about fifteen years. The men in Australia still don't, and when you get off the plane, the odor knocks you out!" Australia was like 1920s America in other ways too. Finding a culture more resistant to women in the workforce than the one she had left behind, Mary Kay gushed over Mel, regaled Australians with tales of the hide tanner's skin care sorcery, and dazzled housewives with dreams of diamond jewelry and pink Cadillacs.

Returning from Down Under, she routed herself through towns where she was greeted by contingents of consultants belting out "I've Got That Mary Kay Enthusiasm." In between, she squeezed in speaking engagements like the "Positive Mental Attitude Rally," which charged arena-size audiences $10 a ticket to "discover the secrets of success from America's experts," a list that included broadcaster Paul Harvey, evangelist Robert Schuller, motivational speaker Zig Ziglar, plus Mary Kay, as the woman on the bill.

Cash up front, low overhead, and a pared-to-the-bone product line—survival strategies left over from early days at the Exchange Bank Mall—continued in company culture. SKUs increased, but never by much. Nothing was allowed to cannibalize the skin care, which remained close to 50 percent of the business. Hair products were added. Another fragrance appeared, named after Richard's new wife. When the company expanded its makeup line to include fall and spring color stories, they were "limited edition." When holiday gift sets appeared, they were limited edition too. Told that she could use direct mail and make an extra $25 million a year reaching women not served by her consultants, Mary Kay vetoed the idea. Her girls might think she was trying to take away prospective customers.

By the next year, the company had moved to a bigger, flashier building out on Stemmons Freeway, its fourth headquarters. Another Frank Meier design, the new headquarters was nearly 110,000 square feet and eight stories in gleaming gold from top to bottom. Richard crowed that he had paid for the $7 million project in cash, "down to the last paper clip." Five times the size of its precursor on Carpenter Freeway, this headquarters also featured rounded corners. "I did a lot of round-cornered offices, and it softens everything in the office," Meier remembered. "Mary Kay said, 'That way nobody can get cornered!' She had a turn of phrase."

Interiors were as sleek as Meier could make them, the public spaces filled with trees and hydroponically grown greenery in high '70s style. Richard, his lean years behind him, filled out his three-piece suits all the way to their vest buttons and wore a mustache big enough to balance his baldness. Up-and-coming executives followed his lead with their own wide-lapel wear and facial hair, assisted by slim young women with shag haircuts and midi skirts. Neither dress nor decor was what

Mary C. Crowley, *detail*, 1979.

outsiders expected. "She was against doin' pink in the office. She said, 'Pink and red incite women, and I don't want them incited,'" Meier recalled, "so it was a lot of whites."

Pink was banned from her personal office too, in favor of beige, which Mary Kay categorized as calming. Furnishings conformed to an idea of elegance that encompassed an enormous U-shaped sectional upholstered in velvet, a crystal chandelier, faux Queen Anne chairs, a faux Regency desk, and, on its perch suspended from the ceiling, the big-as-life brass peacock that she and Mel had picked up on a jaunt to Mexico.

Meier remembered: "When we were doing her office, she said, 'Now go look at Mary Crowley's office,' over at Home Interiors, who had been her sister-in-law, and of course she [Crowley] sells a lot of stuff like [hesitating] plastic stuff, and it was all hangin' on her walls. And the interiors guy and I walked out of there and he said, 'I've spent thirty-five years tryin' to get rid of clients like that.' And of course Mary Kay thought it was great. I don't think she had been exposed to that many really nice things."

Crowley remained her reference.

Divorcing Crowley's brother had not changed that. Nor had the expansion of Mary Kay Inc., which had overtaken Home Interiors and Gifts in territory, if not revenue.

Honors seemed all the sweeter when shared with Crowley. In 1975, Crowley was the first woman inducted into the Direct Selling Association's Hall of Fame; the next year, Mary Kay was the second. After that, she and Crowley became the first women invited to join the Dallas Citizens Council, the boosters and boss men publicly described as the city's "most influential civic body" and privately called the city's puppet masters.

Then came the finest honor of all, one that surpassed even that long-ago American Legion School Award.

In the late 1940s, the Children's Aid Society discovered that its young clients preferred comic books to the stolid prose of Horatio Alger. Only 8 percent had ever heard of the author of *Struggling Upward*, *Strive and Succeed*, and *Luck and Pluck*. Almost none had made it through one of his books. Taking action to dispel "the mounting belief among our nation's youth that the American Dream was no longer attainable," celebrity author and former aluminum pan peddler Norman Vincent Peale partnered with publisher Kenneth Beebe to start the Horatio Alger Association.

In 1947 and each year after, the association conferred its Horatio Alger Award on outstanding Americans whose "triumph over adversity" echoed Alger's fictions. Beebe awarded himself one of the first. Peale got his in 1953, mere months into *The Power of Positive Thinking*'s three-and-a-half-year stretch on the bestseller list. Most years, awards were divided among household names—Bob Hope, Harlan "Colonel" Sanders, Ronald Reagan—and business bigwigs. Sometimes women got them too.

In 1978, Mary C. and Mary Kay were the women on that year's list. The dozen male honorees included Hank Aaron, who'd grown up poor and African American in the segregated South before making it to the major leagues, and Wallace Rasmussen, who'd started as an ice-hauling grunt at Beatrice Foods before becoming chairman of its board. Using the ceremony as a scholarship fundraiser, that year's awards would be presented at a black-tie gala in the Grand Ballroom of the Waldorf Astoria in New York.

When the big night came, the ex-sisters-in-law arrived at the Waldorf looking like Rose-Red and Snow-White: Crowley with brunette bouffant and high-necked brown gown next to Mary Kay in platinum wig and pink fairy-godmother gown. The two listened as Peale limned their lives as Grimms' tales, speaking of Crowley's "cruel stepmother" and the "crippling illness" of Mary Kay's father. Both introductions mentioned Stanley Home Products. Neither mentioned World Gift.

In her acceptance, Mary Kay cocked her head to the side, smiled her half smile, and told the black-tie audience how little boys were brought up hearing "You can do it!" but little girls were not. She told her joke about God creating man and saying, "'That's pretty good, but I think I can do better,' so He created woman." Giving no credit to Ralph Waldo Emerson, she quoted, "Do not go where the path may lead, go instead where there is no path and leave a trail." Then she worked in a "You can do it!" before winding up with "May God bless you very richly."

Richly was revealing. Mary Kay and Crowley believed that they were being rewarded for their long-professed faith in the gospel of prosperity. Both believed that the more they gave, the more they would receive. To make her point, Crowley wore a necklace with two shovels, one tiny and one a little larger, telling people that the more she gave out with her tiny shovel, the more God put in with His larger one.

Known to shovel hard, Crowley tithed 10 percent of her $1.6 million salary. She funded a $2.5 million annex for her church. She sat on the boards of the American Cancer Society, the Salvation Army, the Red Cross, and the Billy Graham Evangelical Association. "Sometimes we would be praying over where we would get the funds," recalled Cliff Barrows, Graham's music and program director. "She would take out her mink checkbook and write a check and slip it across the table and say, 'Now let's get on with it.'" She acted as if it were nothing to write a $100,000 check to keep a women's college from closing. She hired the handicapped until they comprised 20 percent of her salaried employees. She bought a dude ranch and turned it over to a home for troubled youth. She started a Christmas tradition of taking hundreds of employees grocery shopping—eventually the count would top 750—and picking up the tab. That went over so well that she added sprees for back-to-school.

And that was just the PR stuff. Almost everybody in Dallas had a story about Crowley's private philanthropy. Like the time she took a poor kid down to the shoe store for new sneakers. Or how she supported gospel singer Ethel Waters, who had fallen on hard times. Or how she paid the college tuition of her cleaning lady's son.

There was no keeping up with Crowley. So Mary Kay honored the God of Abundance in her own way. She designed a pin that featured two gold-plated shovels dangling from the company logo. And as her company grew, she did more shoveling herself: notably at Northway Baptist, where blue-eyed Dr. Billy Weber was pastor.

Charismatic and ambitious, Weber was the kind of pastor whose flock grew so fast that church buildings always seemed to be bursting at the seams. Thus, in the spring of 1978, Mary Kay found herself raising funds for a new education center. Slated to address Sunday worshippers, she overslept. Unprepared, trying to avoid eye contact with Mel, she stood at the pulpit and announced to the assembled that she would match whatever they put in the plate. No pledges. Contributions would have to be cash or check because, Mary Kay reminded them, she did not believe in accounts receivable. Weber said he would call later with the total. She hoped for at least $1,000. When she heard nothing that night, she assumed that her fundraising had failed.

The call came the next morning. It had taken time to count, but her pitch had brought in $107,748. Weber gave her a chance to back out. Mary Kay blurted that she would honor the agreement, then hung up. She had no idea where to get the money. Her $100,000-a-year salary covered living expenses and left her with limited liquidity; everything was tied up in stock or investments. She dreaded telling Richard.

The phone rang again. It was Richard, calling to tell her that two oil wells had come in. Both were gushers. In the first month alone, her share would be roughly what she owed the Baptist church for the building fund.

Mary Kay saw that as a sign. She began autographing dollar bills with "Matthew 25:14–30" next to her signature, a reference to the parable of the talents, which told of one servant who buried his talent in the ground to save it and another who put his money to work and multiplied it, causing their lord to reward the industrious servant, "for unto every one that hath shall be given, and he shall have abundance."

Directors would send packets of dollar bills to be autographed and then use the bills as incentives, spurring consultants to sell and increasing company profits. In the meantime, the story of Mary Kay's building fund beneficence made the front page of *The Dallas Morning News*, where a reporter rounded up the donation to $110,000. Local press called her "the Pink Angel." Many were the blessings of her God of Abundance.

In the mid-1970s, a survey by Louis Harris and Associates showed how much direct selling had changed. And how much it had stayed the same.

Harris's poll estimated two million sellers were generating about $6 billion retail, a much smaller percentage of the population than had sold during the Depression. Moreover, most direct selling was no longer door to door. As a not-unrelated result, an estimated 80 percent of direct sellers were female, an inversion of prewar percentages.

One ratio had not changed: The lower the remuneration, the higher the number of women. Salespeople earning less than $100 a week were almost all female. And they were still hearing that direct selling was a great way to earn money without neglecting their primary responsibilities as wives and mothers.

That was what they were hearing from Mary Kay, who had nixed the white gloves and girdles but still insisted consultants wear skirts, pantyhose, and heels. She continued to wear them herself. She also continued to defer to her husband in public. Refusing to endorse or condemn the Equal Rights Amendment, she parried questions about politics with "Women are intelligent enough to make their own decisions." Stockholders adored her for that.

So did most of the media. Mary Kay became a mainstay of man-bites-dog stories about women who were successful in business. Profiling her, *Reader's Digest* wrote, "Nothing . . . liberates as fast as financial independence." *Business Week* put her in its "100 Top Corporate Women" with the narrative that she "found the male refusal to give a female a chance too forbidding."

Mary Kay not only said a woman's brain was as good as a man's but she said it with the same wording every time. She told interviewers that she wanted women to be "unequal" because she wanted them to be admired, a statement so retrogressive that no one noticed her sharp left turn into advocating equal pay for equal work.

She became fond of declaring that her company was founded on the same day that Congress passed the Equal Pay Act of 1963. She neglected to mention that the EPA did not actually pass until September 16 and that she probably didn't know what it was for years afterward. She also enjoyed calling attention to the statistic that, in 1963, women were earning about fifty cents on the dollar compared with men. "A female brain is worth more than fifty cents on the dollar," she would say time and again. Nitpickers might have argued that, in 1963, the national average was as high as fifty-five cents or fifty-eight cents. But everyone knew those were best-case scenarios. Women in Texas made less, as did other Southerners, women in rural areas, African Americans, Latinas, and immigrants—all groups well represented in her consultant count.

As the 1970s progressed, sitcoms like *Julia*, *Alice*, and *One Day at a Time* made heroines of single mothers who worked outside the home. Magazines like *Working Woman* and *Working Mother* appeared next to *Woman's Day* and *Family Circle* at supermarket checkouts. Yet the gender pay gap was as wide as it had been in 1963. Maybe wider. Some statistics showed women earning a penny or so less per dollar.

By then Mary Kay and her consultants were positioning her line as a way for women to support one another. Buy a skin care starter kit and strike a blow for gender equality. Rediscovering what African American entrepreneurs like Annie Turnbo Malone and Madam C. J. Walker had learned before she was born and what Crowley rediscovered in the late 1950s, Mary Kay saw that women who wouldn't fight for their own rights would fight for someone else's. Sisterhood was powerful, another reason to pursue the Mary Kay selling opportunity.

The more she said it, the more it became so. Playing up her equal-pay-for-equal-work credo, Mary Kay tapped into the emotions of every woman who had ever been patronized or underpaid. There proved to be plenty.

Now the only place big enough to hold Seminar was the sprawling Dallas Convention Center, which would soon expand to accommodate its best client.

Each year, Seminar made headlines for its Ziegfeld Follies–style staging and Mary Kay's over-the-top entrances. People couldn't wait to see what crazy thing those Mary Kay ladies were going to do this year. Self-taught special-events maestro Ron Trammell, who came to the company after stints as a semipro baseball player, ambulance driver, and short-order cook, was charged with making each Seminar more razzle-dazzle than the last. Hydraulic stairs were built so that the ascension of the NSDs would be more breathtaking. Vegas floor shows were studied. Broadway set designers were hired.

Mary Kay arrived onstage inside a Brobdingnagian box of skin care, alighted from a hot air balloon, ascended from a trap door, descended in a glass elevator, sat sidesaddle on a whirling carousel, burst out of a birthday cake, and rode onstage in a horse-drawn carriage as thousands belted all four verses of "I've Got That Mary Kay Enthusiasm" with all the gestures. Women patted feathered Farrah Fawcett hairstyles to show

"I've got that Mary Kay enthusiasm up in my head," smote their chests for "deep in my heart," bowed from the waist for the "down in my feet," flung their arms wide to demonstrate "I've got that Mary Kay enthusiasm all over me, ALL OVER ME TO STAY!"

Then, in 1978, Seminar made a different kind of headline when, days before its start, the murder of an NSD, Beverly Sue "Sue Z." Vickers, inspired a sensational, citywide manhunt.

As she did every year, Mary Kay had dreamed up new Career Apparel for Seminar, stipulating not only what consultants should wear but also how they should wear it. A mere director could not be seen to wear the same shade of blouse as a senior director, whose status surpassed hers. Befitting their rank at the top of the company, NSDs were assigned outfits all their own, which, that year, were in an odd purple that made it almost impossible to find the matching accessories favored by Mary Kay.

No one wanted to disappoint Mary Kay, though—least of all her seventeen NSDs. Tipped off to a store that stocked the right shade, Vickers had driven to a Dallas suburb and scored her matching shoes. Odd purple heels in hand, she was in the parking lot when she was abducted, robbed, raped, and murdered. A day later, her body was found behind a Baptist church. The perpetrators were caught because one sent his girlfriend back to the store to exchange the odd purple shoes.

Hearing of the murder, consultants burst into tears. The whole company knew Sue, who headed up the Vickeroos, "the company cheerleaders." Mary Kay had nicknamed her "Miss Enthusiasm" and invented the Miss Mary Kay Image Award to recognize Vickers for an outlook so positive that even Mary Kay admitted she had never seen anything like it.

Vickers had started as a single mother trying to support herself and her daughter on a $400-a-month secretarial salary. Less than a year after joining Mary Kay, she was a Top Ten consultant driving a pink Cadillac. By the time of her death, she had over five thousand "offspring," many of whom adopted *Z* as a middle initial in her honor, claiming it stood for *Zoozoom.* Vickers wore a gold whistle around her neck and blew it if anybody said anything negative. She kept a Christmas tree in her living room year-round. Once, she had swung on a star to deliver a speech. Another time, she dressed as the Statue of Liberty.

Such was Vickers's belief in the power of positive thinking that when she wanted to move to a luxury subdivision called Mount Olympus, she wrote her wish in glitter and positioned it where a light would shine on it every minute of every day. Once she attained Mount Olympus, she then bought a mansion in Mesquite, Texas, where she had planned a reception for fifteen hundred consultants during Seminar.

Instead, the show went on without her. Seminar, which now cost upward of $1 million to produce, proceeded as planned. On the grounds of the new golden headquarters, Mary Kay planted a Christmas tree in memoriam. She renamed Vickers's award the "Go Give Award" and made it an annual prize. "Her senseless death was a great loss to me, as well as everyone else who knew her," Mary Kay later wrote, "but we put on our happy faces, dedicated the Seminar to Sue, and went on as scheduled. I'm sure that's the way Sue would have wanted it."

Fed up with all that Mary Kay enthusiasm, *Texas Monthly* magazine dispatched a freethinking young feminist to dig up some dirt.

The resulting story, "The Hot Pink Empire of Mary Kay Ash," started as an exposé treating consultants as quasi–cult members, then turned into a big pink valentine, replete with the information that Mary Kay was able to buy her first house in Dallas due to her stellar Stanley sales record, and that—Stanley and Tupperware forgotten—Mary Kay's company "developed the home demonstration concept." After a few pages of that, the reporter wound up on a personal note, confessing that she bought Mary Kay's entire line.

Mary Kay had a similar effect on tough guy Morley Safer when he interviewed her for a segment on *60 Minutes*, television's top-rated show. Safer started by saying that Mary Kay's "instinct for doing business and making money is as finely tuned as a jungle cat going for the kill" and called his report "The Pink Panther."

Pink Cadillacs and mink, 1979.

Richard and Mary Kay at Seminar, 1979.

Naming the segment after a farce was probably not a coincidence. CBS filmed women singing "I've Got That Mary Kay Enthusiasm" with the full complement of gestures, then interviewed a group of consultants who, for reasons unexplained on camera, wore two-foot-tall pink rabbit ears and had cotton tails stuck to the backs of their skirts. Several of the bunny-eared belted out "M-A-K-I-N-G M-O-N-E-Y" to the theme of "The Mickey Mouse Club," finishing with a triumphant "Now's the time to say goodbye to all our POV-ER-TY."

Preparations did not go smoothly. Readying the Round House for CBS, Mary Kay inspected the premises until she found a scratch on the baseboard in her living room. Calling for a can of yellow paint, she took out her Retractable Lip and Eye Brush to do a touch-up. Mel got out the vacuum cleaner and helped until he knocked over the can and paint flooded the carpet. Mary Kay then dispatched him to the hardware store for a gallon of turpentine, which she poured into the carpet, causing a stench that required multiple cans of air freshener. Before the stench could dissipate or the carpet could dry, the CBS crew showed up just as the ice maker went on the fritz and flooded the kitchen. From there, CBS followed her to Toronto, where a freak Canadian heat wave and broken air-conditioning combined to leave Mary Kay and two thousand consultants red-faced and drenched in sweat.

No one would have guessed from the final edit. When the ten-minute segment aired on October 28, 1979, television audiences saw Mary Kay demonstrate her own unhurried upgrade of Mr. Bev's custom of reading song lyrics. Interspersed with organ music and a soprano singing a cappella, she intoned the lyrics of "Welcome to Our World" as a conversion narrative: "I'll be waiting here, with my arms unfurled." When Safer tried to bait her during the sit-down interview, the soft voice remained uninflected, the penciled eyebrows immobile. When Safer asked if she wasn't "using God" to sell cosmetics, the charter member of Debate Club cocked her head to the side and responded, "I sincerely hope not. I hope He's using me instead."

Like so many before, Safer surrendered in the end. The report wrapped with Mary Kay crowning NSD Shirley Hutton on the Seminar stage. As Mary Kay draped a beauty queen's sash over Hutton's new full-length mink coat and filled Hutton's arms with long-stemmed pink roses, Safer's voice-over concluded: "If women, when they are girls, have fantasies of dizzying lives—thinking diamonds clothed in mink—they quickly lose them to the mortgage and the children and the rest. But Mary Kay Ash, with a touch of marketing genius, proves it can all come true for anyone in middle life. There's a rich pink world out there and all ya gotta do is sell." When the market opened on Monday morning, company stock went up a full point on the NYSE.

And that yielded yet more recruits. Told that she was going blind, Marilyn Kogut used her remaining vision to practice doing her hair and makeup without looking in a mirror. By the time she was completely sightless, she was able to apply eyeliner by refrigerating it, then calibrating the cold and pressure on her lids. According to the version of the story in Mary Kay's autobiography, the blind and bankrupt Kogut heard the *60 Minutes* segment and decided Mary Kay was the answer to her prayers. Skipping a mortgage payment to pay for her starter kit, Kogut labeled everything in braille and rehearsed like a madwoman. Her first beauty show yielded $110 in sales, two bookings for more shows, and two recruits.

That year and the next, recruitment doubled.

Mary Kay's name was everywhere.

Making the most of *60 Minutes*, she crisscrossed the country doing more interviews, telling one reporter that CBS had only given her three days' notice of the segment's broadcast date, after which she had immediately put "the Mary Kay grapevine" into action and garnered the show a 47 percent audience share. "I told CBS that if they had given us three more days they would have had 100 percent of the audience," said Mary Kay.

Business pages reported that her stock was soaring, that her consultants made $50,000 a year. Local television presented her factory's solar heating with an announcement that it was the "largest solar complex in the Southwest that didn't use a dime of the taxpayers' money." Sports pages headlined THE MARY KAY CLASSIC when her company took over sponsorship of a women's professional golf tournament, moved it to the Bent Tree Country Club, upped the winner's purse to $130,000, and turned it into the flashiest fixture on the LPGA tour.

Then in May of 1980, Mel was diagnosed with lung cancer and given weeks to live. The doctor's office blurted the bad news over the phone. "She couldn't believe how cruel it was," Erma Thomson remembered, "so cruel to tell someone they had cancer over the phone and they were about to die. That's one reason for the cancer research that came later."

It was smoking again. C. B. Eckman's death had been hastened by his fatal fondness for cigars. J. Ben Rogers had died from lung cancer three years before, leaving Leona with a Chevy worth $250 and bonds worth $4,000. Ex-husband Charlie Weaver had already had his larynx removed and was dying of emphysema.

Even so, Mel's prognosis was a shock. All her life, Mary Kay had refrained from nagging her spouses—one of Dale Carnegie's rules for success—making an exception only to fuss at Mel about his cigarettes. A few years before, he'd gone to a fancy clinic and quit.

Mary Kay stayed home the seven weeks between Mel's diagnosis and his death. Putting off paperwork or phone calls until he had fallen asleep, not sleeping herself. Bags of work were messengered between headquarters and the Round House. Television appearances and radio interviews stopped. Chauffeured by Dalene White, Mary Kay accompanied Mel to treatments.

Within days of diagnosis, Mel added a six-page codicil reflecting increases in his income and investments in the decade since the seventeen-page will written in 1969. Bequests to his son and daughter, Richard and Laurie Iselin, increased from $10,000 to $25,000 apiece. A bequest to First Presbyterian was rerouted to Northway Baptist, and a bequest was added for Prestonwood Baptist. Daughter Judy Einsidler and her three sons would still get generous percentages of his estate, while trusts were set up for Mary Kay's three children. Mel's shares of community property, like the Round House, still reverted to Mary Kay, as did their twenty-five jointly held oil leases, their joint savings account, and a jointly held $325,000 certificate of deposit. Richard and Republic National Bank remained as coexecutors.

At the beginning of June, Mel added another codicil, naming company executive Monty Barber as executor. Aside from joint holdings with Mary Kay, his main assets were the $40,000 in his Merrill Lynch investment account, assorted small savings accounts, bonds, and a few insurance policies. Of the 20,000 shares of Mary Kay Inc. common stock that he had owned in 1969, only 705 remained, worth roughly $27,000.

Mary Kay refused to leave Mel's side. Months earlier, she had committed to speaking at the annual convention of the General Federation of Women's Clubs, which had given her top billing over Nobel Prize–winning economist Milton Friedman. She sent Dalene White instead.

On July 3, Mel developed secondary pneumonia and was transferred from Presbyterian Hospital to the Wadley Institute. Four days later, he died of respiratory arrest and Mary Kay went back to work.

CHAPTER TWENTY

"Reach Out and Touch"

Mel was pronounced dead at 2:15 p.m. on Monday, July 7.

His funeral was at Northway Baptist the next day, his pallbearers divided between company executives and husbands of NSDs. Interment at Sparkman–Hillcrest, which already held Hallenbeck and would soon hold Weaver, followed. Then Mary Kay was on a plane to the "Reach Out and Touch" Jamboree in St. Louis; sixty-eight hundred consultants had paid to see her, see her they would.

Thanks to deployment of the company's eighty-person special events staff, "Reach Out and Touch" went off without a hitch. As two organs played and consultants rushed the stage, Richard steered his mother to the spotlight. Addressing an audience who followed her life like the storyline of a favorite soap opera, she told them: "Mel kept saying, 'Mary, darling, I want you to go to Jamboree.' I said, 'No, not until you're better.' Now, he's better. He's with his Heavenly Father. He savored your letters. Your cards. Your flowers. I thank you from the bottom of a very grateful heart. I love you." Some consultants sobbed.

For three days, Mary Kay told the sort of inspirational stories that she had heard on Stanley Pilgrimages. Consultants sang "I've Got That Mary Kay Enthusiasm." Women won car keys. The Christy Minstrels entertained. Light shows played. Until, finally, proceedings wound up with a candlelight ceremony that seemed straight from an old-time camp meeting. In the hushed and darkened hall, directors lit candles to represent company values like courage and kindness; then Richard carried the last candle to his mother, who told her audience, "Remember, in Mary Kay, you never walk alone."

Mary Kay herself never walked alone, not during that trip. Condolences came nonstop. "Sometimes I feel like an octopus with eight legs and somebody on each leg," she told the *St. Louis Post-Dispatch* reporter who was also shadowing her. In an absurd-to-poignant progression becoming common in media coverage of Mary Kay, the resulting *Post-Dispatch* feature printed every silly verse of "I've Got That Mary Kay Enthusiasm" and photographed a grown woman shaking cheerleader pom-poms. Then came the quotes from consultants: "I used to be a secretary at McDonnell Douglas. Mr. Douglas didn't know I was alive, much less when my birthday was," said the winner of keys to a pink Buick. And always there were the believe-it-or-not business statistics: 83,520 consultants, 1,749 directors averaging $20,000 a year, 17 NSDs averaging $100,000 a year, sales up 70 percent during double-digit inflation.

From St. Louis, Mary Kay flew to Los Angeles for an annual "Gathering of the Greats" organized by the American Academy of Achievement. One week after Mel's funeral, she was at Disneyland, where the next "Reach Out and Touch" was being staged for twenty-four hundred consultants who had come from as far away as Guam. Then back to Dallas, where a new class of DIQs hit town. Since the highlight of these trips had always been the visit to the Round House, Mary Kay could hardly deny them. This time, though, there would be no singing of "We love you, Mel! Oh yes, we do!" as DIQs covered Mel's cheeks with kisses and made jokes about leaving lipstick marks on Mary Kay's husband. There would be no one to hold Gigi, the poodle who succeeded Monet, while DIQs cooed over the pink polish on Gigi's toenails. Nevertheless, Mary Kay served spiced tea and warm-from-the-oven Wham Bam! cookies. Then she packed her bags for a "Reach Out and

Touch" at the Fairmont Hotel in Philadelphia, where 4,500 women, some traveling from Puerto Rico and the Virgin Islands, were coming to see her. One newspaper called her A QUEEN BEE IN CONSTANT FLIGHT.

As the 1980s got underway, the zeitgeist seemed to be ever more in tune with Mary Kay Cosmetics. *Dallas*, beginning its reign as America's top-rated TV series, functioned like free advertising. Fiscal 1979 had ended with nearly fifty-eight thousand consultants. Fiscal 1980 could come close to one hundred thousand with sales up 83 percent. Citing statistics that sounded too specific to be made up, its public relations department announced Mary Kay Inc. as "the eighth fastest growing [company] in the world."

Once Jamborees wrapped, Mary Kay put cancer research at the top of her list of charities and added a second THANK YOU FOR NOT SMOKING sign to her office. With Mel gone, there was no one who could tempt her to take Fridays off. No one to force her to sightsee. No reason to interrupt work for a spin around the dance floor. Anyone who tried to distract her did not get far. When Richard invited her to watch a Cowboys game from his private box, Mary Kay brought a book. Asked if she might marry again, Mary Kay said it was too hard to find a man whose ego wasn't threatened by her success. When her time came, she planned to have her ashes placed beside Mel's. But before that happened, there was so much to do.

Six early risings, so said Mary Kay, netted her the equivalent of a nine-day week. She intended to fill every minute. As the sheer number of consultants made it more impossible, Mary Kay became more focused on a personal touch. Mail addressed to her had to be answered within twenty-four hours of receipt, even if the letters were asking for money or advice. In a single day, she might read and sign hundreds of responses drafted by her staff. "The letters I get are so personal," she said. "Maybe I am their mother. Maybe they don't have anybody else to talk to."

Every day, in the rounded script she had used since high school, she also wrote a dozen or so condolence and get-well notes. In them, not every sentence ended in an exclamation point, although most did.

Entire sentences might be printed in capitals punctuated by triple exclamation points. Her complimentary closure might be "Bless you!" or "Love you!"

Every consultant still got a birthday card from Mary Kay. Directors also got a birthday gift, Christmas card, and Christmas gift. For the hundreds of thank-you and birthday mailings that went out each day, Mary Kay designed cards printed with a facsimile of her handwriting and messages like "Precious things are very few, that's why there must be just *one* of *you*." Anything was a pretext for personal communication. A consultant who exceeded $1,500 wholesale for the first time got a letter of congratulations from Mary Kay. As did anybody who did anything extraordinary. Unless they got a telegram or a telephone call.

As the workload grew, Erma Thomson put a paperweight engraved I CAN DO IT on the boss's desk. Now signing about one hundred thousand cards and letters a year, Mary Kay kept seven secretaries busy—later there would be ten full-timers—in addition to Thomson and Jennifer Cook, a second personal assistant who had been full time since 1974. There were more unit newsletters to read, more area newsletters to read, more directors to advise, more awards to give out, more employee orientations to attend, more names to memorize. Factory and headquarters staff doubled between 1980 and 1983. With its golden headquarters bursting at the seams, the company leased eighty-three thousand square feet of space in a silvery office building on the other side of the freeway. That filled almost immediately.

Speaking to recruits, Mary Kay would act as if she already knew the answer to whatever question she was asking, nodding her head up and down until a yes came from the recruit. Should a consultant confess ambitions of becoming a director, Mary Kay reserved a place in DIQ training on the spot, looked the consultant in the right eye, told her that she was going to be wonderful, and said that she couldn't wait to show her around the Round House. If a woman called to say she was giving up her business—due to disease, divorce, death, or an equivalent circumstance—Mary Kay would tell her what she would have wanted to hear herself: that the consultant could and would be back to work in no time.

Unable to meet every potential consultant, Mary Kay rolled out a recruiting film called *All Your Tomorrows* that showed her strolling the grounds of the Round House with her poodle, counseling DIQs in her living room, then standing at a podium doing her unhurried reading of "The Impossible Dream": "And the world will be better by far. . . ." By the time the final cut was ready, she was prepping a follow-up called *Capture the Vision.*

And there was family life to fit in. A new round of grandchildren from her children's second marriages, great-grandchildren from their first. All those engagements and marriages and pregnancies and now a few funerals too. When her sister Dealia died in September, Mary Kay attended the services, then went back to work. Shortly after, she announced that *The DIQ Cookie Book* was in the works. This was no time to slow down.

In October, the flag of Argentina joined the flags of Australia, Canada, and the U.S. in front of headquarters. In November, Mary Kay fit in a quick tour of Canada and was back in Dallas in time to host fifty-three of her nearest and dearest for Thanksgiving, cooking up her jalapeño-cornbread dressing ("the good stuff") for the grown-ups and no-jalapeño dressing ("tenderfoot") for the kids.

As the first holidays without Mel approached, Mary Kay was in no mood to put up the kind of elaborate Christmas tree she had always had. Then she reminded herself that four hundred DIQs, the largest class in company history, would be visiting.

Up went the tree.

The new year was more of the same. Much more.

Prompted by the profile on *60 Minutes*, Harvard Business School published its first case study on the company. Furthering what was fast becoming the Mary Kay legend, the study cited biographical data from sources like a 1979 profile in *Positive Living* magazine. Hallenbeck was "her second husband." Fashion Tress was forgotten. Instead, a case writer concluded: "From the start, the problem was managing rapid growth, rather than achieving profitability." Misunderstanding the case study method, intentionally or not, her PR department crowed that the company was "studied at Harvard Business School."

Seminar had gotten so big that the Dallas Convention Center could no longer hold all the consultants who wanted to come. So in 1981, Seminar split into identical editions called Diamond and Emerald, doubling Mary Kay's audience to 16,500 and giving her twice as many chances to distribute Cinderella gifts. Themed "Dreams Come True," that year's Seminar cost $2.5 million and featured a turreted castle and a laser light show that spewed rainbows. Thanks to well-placed video screens, there was not a bad seat in the house. When a woman was onstage, every sequin on her evening gown and every last diamond on her cocktail ring could be seen from the top row.

"Dreams Come True" got underway at 8:00 a.m., but because Mary Kay consultants were the kind of women who showed up early, organizers had company songs playing as soon as the doors opened. A countdown clock commenced ten minutes before Mary Kay was due onstage, ensuring that she entered to a standing ovation of clapping, stomping, singing women. Motivation and recognition ran nonstop, culminating in Awards Night, when Mary Kay crowned and congratulated for five hours straight. Then did it all again for the second edition of Seminar, which started as soon as the first one was over.

Company stock was now going for $66 a share. Sales per consultant had gone from $1,233 to $1,750 in less than four years. *Forbes* took notice in "The Flight of the Bumblebee," a gushing profile of "profits powerhouse Mary Kay Cosmetics" full of gee-whiz statistics: sales that went from $54 million in 1978 to $167 million in 1980, net income that went from $5 million in 1978 to $15 million in 1980.

By the time that saw print, the company had outgrown both golden headquarters and silvery rental. Planning a $100 million corporate campus, Richard acquired 176 acres of prime Dallas real estate. Not long after, in a story published on the company's September 13 anniversary, Mary Kay made the magazine's first annual Forbes 400, soon to be nicknamed its "rich list."

All that was fine for the stockholders, but Mary Kay knew what set consultants dreaming. As she always told her girls, "Look successful and you will be successful." Makeup became more pronounced. Eyebrows flew higher. She let the NSDs talk her into retiring the pink fairy-godmother gown that she had worn to the Horatio Alger Awards and at least five Seminars ("Why not? I only wear it once a year!"). From now on, it would share the closet with Victor Costa couture.

Next came a sitting with Francesco Scavullo, the celebrity photographer famed for his Studio 54 frolics and cleavage-centric *Cosmopolitan* covers. Shooting in Scavullo's four-story carriage house on Manhattan's Upper East Side, stylist Sean Byrnes decked Mary Kay in diamonds, feathers, and furs sufficient to convey her status as the first woman to chair a company on the New York Stock Exchange; makeup artist Evan Richardson went to work with the tool kit he had used on Elizabeth Taylor; and Scavullo flattered her with the soft, bounced light that made him so beloved by women of a certain age.

Scavullo charged her $12,000, but she got her money's worth. Retouched and wrinkle-free, his Mary Kay had the half smile of a movie star Mona Lisa. Soon Scavullo silk screens hung in the Round House and company headquarters, a Scavullo portrait was on stock certificates, and a Scavullo photo was on the cover of that October's *Saturday Evening Post.* Inside, the magazine ran the same photo again to kick off an eight-page feature on "The Beautiful Make-Up of Mary Kay," which reported Lula's ownership and sale of the Hot Well Hotel, the potato soup recipe, a high school graduation at age eighteen, Mary Kay's ambitions for a medical career, and the Stanley convention cheese-and-crackers story. On the seventh page, in a caption underneath another Scavullo, was the teaser for her forthcoming autobiography.

That was the real news. While Mary C. Crowley had rolled out one personal history after another—*Women Who Win*, *Moments with Mary*, *Think Mink!* (later retitled *You Can Too*)—Mary Kay had spent years meeting with ghostwriters and trying to get her life story on paper. Convinced that only a woman could understand her story, Mary Kay had insisted on meeting only with women. Nobody clicked.

Then she met Bob Shook. Already successful enough to turn down clients he didn't like, Robert L. Shook was known for business books and the quick-read biographies he called "Shook books." By the time he met Mary Kay, he was making a specialty of salesmanship, with titles like *The Complete Professional Salesman*, *Total Commitment,* and *The Ten Greatest Salespersons.* Later he would make a subspecialty of direct sales, writing *The Shaklee Story*, about the Iowa chiropractor turned multilevel marketer, and ghostwriting *Longaberger: An American Success Story* for the Ohio maker of collectible baskets. Those were just the kinds of books Mary Kay liked.

She liked the way Shook did business too. Shook gave subjects final approval over manuscripts, reasoning that they would be more invested in the success of the finished product, more likely to promote the book, and more inclined to place big orders. He asked for nothing up front. "When they ask me, 'How do I pay you?' I tell them that we go fifty-fifty."

That's what he told Mary Kay. Saying, "This book is your legacy," Shook requested two days of interviews to produce three sample chapters. He prepared by steeping himself in Mary Kay's press, presentations, and speeches until he could quote her back to herself. It worked this time too. "He thinks like I do," said Mary Kay, who pronounced him the "perfect writer for it" and sent him home with a big box of skin care. Five weeks later, Shook returned to Dallas with three finished chapters and a face full of pimples. "Bob has been using the Mr. K line," she announced in a meeting. "Yes," said Shook, "I've finally got back my teenaged complexion."

The two would keep up the quips for years. On Saturday mornings, she and Shook might spend an hour on the phone catching up, even when they weren't working on her life story or the two books that came after. When Shook came to town, working sessions sometimes took place over dinners at the Mansion on Turtle Creek, with banter that Shook described as "flirtatious, although you have to take into account that she was my mother's age and a very religious woman."

When he was done, the autobiography read as if Mary Kay were in her living room having a heart-to-heart with her DIQs. Familiar anecdotes (cooking potato soup for her father, packing cheese and crackers for the Stanley convention) alternated with favorite aphorisms ("I believe you can have anything in this world you want—if you want it badly enough and you're willing to pay the price"). Using a strategy he often used with moguls, Shook structured the book as a Horatio Alger story, "because that way readers don't begrudge the success."

The book opened with a "You Can Do It!" chapter. After moving through her life story ("A Competitive Spirit," "Put On a Happy Face," "My Dream Company") came chapters on time management ("The way to use your twenty-four hours is not scrubbing floors and washing dirty dishes and ironing clothes all day") and getting husbands on board ("If he resents your career and constantly puts obstacles in your way, it's almost impossible to succeed in a sales job or, for that matter, any other job"). One chapter gathered I-stories from company stars. Single mother Nancy Tietjen wrote: "With no college education and no secretarial skills, the best-paying job I could find was packing shotgun shells on an assembly line. I worked the graveyard shift, from nine-thirty each night until seven the next morning." Then Tietjen discovered the Mary Kay selling opportunity and with it came eight pink Cadillacs, a new house complete with tennis court and swimming pool, a luxury vacation in Asia, and 1980 earnings of $187,121.

Debuting when the company looked likely to end 1981 about 40 or 50 percent over its record-setting 1980, *Mary Kay: The Success Story of America's Most Dynamic Businesswoman* sold through a third printing before it had been out a month. Shook, who soon had reason to describe himself as "the richest ghostwriter in the history of America," sat back to reap his rewards as Mary Kay started her fifteen-city book tour. "If we sell a million copies, imagine what that will do to recruiting," said Richard.

Mary Kay did her best. She lined up newspapers, magazines, and radio. She spoke to civic groups. She autographed for hours on end. Major newspapers ran display ads with the tagline "'You've gone pretty far for a woman,' They should never have told me that." She packed her platinum wig and pink Ultrasuede suit and booked herself on national, syndicated, and local television, happy to appear on less-prestigious middle-of-the-day shows when stay-at-home moms would be watching. She went on *The Today Show*, *The 700 Club*, *PM Magazine*, and *People Are Talking*. She did dozens of segments like *Today in Montana*, where the Great Falls correspondent told sixty-three-year-old Mary Kay that she looked like seventy-nine-year-old Barbara Cartland, the romance novelist infamous for garish makeup and fright-wig hair. Mary Kay smiled politely and changed the subject. Over and over again, she was asked if pink was her favorite color. Over and over again, she answered, "Not really," and segued into an explanation of marketing strategy. Each night, she wrote thank-you notes to everyone she had met that day.

A week might have thirty interviews. A day might last eleven hours or more. On one of those days, the schedule was so tight that Mary Kay and her entourage did not eat breakfast until four o'clock in the afternoon. "At the end of the day, we'd get videos to watch in the hotel suite," Thomson remembered. "We'd be in the living room and I'd look over and right away she [Mary Kay] was asleep. I'd say, 'Well, at least she's relaxing.'"

Mid-tour, Mary Kay came down with a case of shingles that felt like "a chest full of broken bones." Hugs were impossible. "Even clothes were agony. Her back was so painful that she couldn't stand to have straps or a bra across her back," Thomson said. "Her daughter-in-law finally found her something that was loose but looked all right in public." The pain and blistering put Mary Kay in the Wadley Institute, in the same hospital complex where Mel had died.

Not that it stopped her. Scheduled to appear on the top-rated *Phil Donahue Show*, Mary Kay checked herself out of the hospital for fifteen hours so she could fly to Chicago for the taping. Wearing the same fox-trimmed black suit shown on her book's cover, Mary Kay spent an on-camera hour bantering with Donahue and motivational speaker Zig Ziglar and fielding call-ins and questions from a studio audience seeded with her directors. She worked in a mention of a recent stock split, told the world that the company had done $400 million retail for the first three quarters of 1981, and said the top twenty-five women in her com-

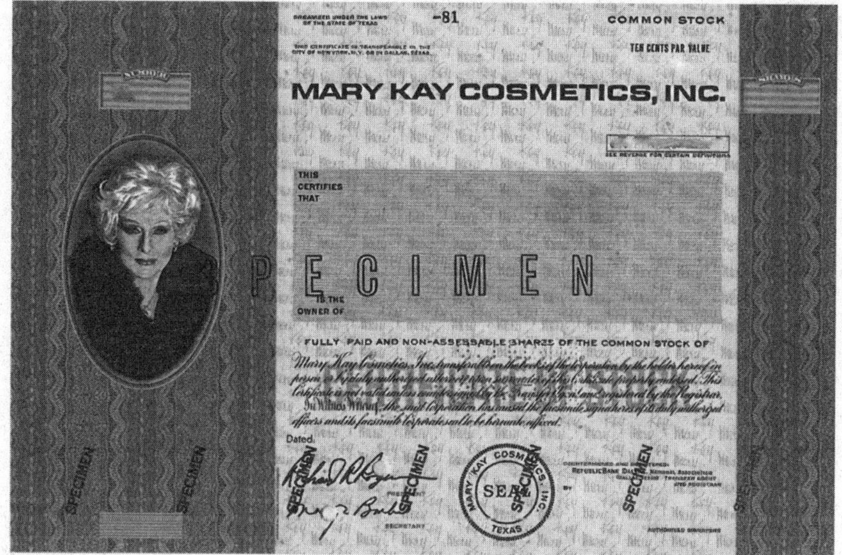
-81

COMMON STOCK

TEN CENTS PAR VALUE

MARY KAY COSMETICS, INC.

THIS CERTIFIES THAT

SPECIMEN

IS THE OWNER OF

FULLY PAID AND NON-ASSESSABLE SHARES OF THE COMMON STOCK OF

Dated:

PRESIDENT

SECRETARY

MARY KAY COSMETICS, INC. SEAL TEXAS

AUTHORIZED SIGNATURE

The company's updated stock certificate, which became a collectible.

pany averaged $144,000 a year. "The cosmetic industry in America today is about $9 billion, and we only have 2 percent of it. That means 98 percent are using the wrong stuff," said Mary Kay.

Then she flew home, checked back into Wadley, had paperwork brought to her in her hospital room, and wrote thank-you notes to Donahue and his crew.

Seminar was another story.

Under doctors' orders, Mary Kay was forbidden to try the tricks that made her look like she was appearing onstage in a puff of smoke or levitating eleven feet above the ground. No Ferris wheels, merry-go-rounds, or bursting out of birthday cakes either. She was not supposed to appear at Seminar at all.

That year, Richard presented awards while a bedridden Mary Kay congratulated via closed-circuit TV. Knowing that some consultants had never stayed in a hotel, flown on a plane, or been away from home, Mary Kay had her production team prearrange every possible detail.

Shuttles, breakfasts, and luncheons ran like clockwork. Convention center men's rooms were converted to ladies' rooms for the duration.

Both editions of that "Light Up Your Life" Seminar—Emerald first, Diamond second—sold out long before the company announced prizes or entertainment. When they did, judicious rounding up allowed the company to claim its first $10 million Seminar. Without going into details of car leases or volume discounts, Mary Kay's PR machine announced that 1,462 pink cars worth $8.5 million were given out, thirty-two opera-length white minks among a fifty-two-mink total worth $350,000, 578 emerald- and diamond-studded pieces of jewelry worth $600,000, and twenty Hawaiian vacations worth another $102,000. Staging and entertainment cost at least $1.5 million, as newspapers nationwide dutifully reported. Glen Campbell, having a come-to-Jesus moment after his stormy affair with twenty-two-years-younger Tanya Tucker and his ensuing months as a cocaine-bingeing tabloid mainstay, headlined Seminar. The only person on earth those consultants wanted to see more may have been Mary Kay herself.

She couldn't deny them. Declaring, "I can't have 16,000 women thinking I'm dying," Mary Kay made surprise appearances at both editions. Later, back on bed rest at the Round House, she gave a two-and-a-half-hour telephone interview, which paid off with a profile syndicated from Boston to Honolulu. "You miss the excitement of the crowd, the feedback, the love and energy," Mary Kay told the reporter. "It is a fabulous experience to have so many people loving me out there."

Eager to escape enforced time off, Mary Kay promised doctors that she would limit travel to one week a month. Or maybe ten days. Tops.

Consultant count had tripled in the two and a half years since the *60 Minutes* broadcast. Retail had quadrupled. After a rebroadcast in 1982, recruiting spiked again. Stock went up with it.

Giving thanks to the God of Abundance, Mary Kay and Richard pledged the first million dollars toward the latest building project at Prestonwood Baptist, the new home base of Pastor Billy Weber. Begun as a mission outreach of Northway Baptist, Prestonwood was now the fastest-growing church in the Southern Baptist Convention. In 1979, Prestonwood issued $900,000 in mortgage bonds advertised with the earthly enticement "earn up to 10.75 percent" and was soon blessed by a multimillion-dollar worship center universally acknowledged as the biggest and flashiest in Dallas, where congregants packed pews for productions that could include live animals, light shows, and indoor fireworks.

Mary Kay loved showing it off. Ebby Halliday remembered Mary Kay inviting her to a Christmas pageant so theatrical that, in the middle of one hymn, Mary Kay leaned over and whispered, "If that doesn't light your fire, your wood is wet." Now, with Mary Kay heading up the building fund for a 157,000-square-foot Christian Learning Center, Prestonwood raised $10 million in pledges within a day or two.

Richard had his own projects. After watching Don Carter bring an NBA franchise to Dallas, Richard made a run at buying the Dallas Cowboys. By the time that fell through, he was on his way to founding Million Air, a system of franchised bases for private jets. His first "aviation oasis," at Addison Airport outside Dallas, had a pool table, exercise equipment, a clubroom-cum-bar, a tanning room, and a Mercedes-Benz limo to ferry highfliers to and fro.

As the twentieth year began, the Harvard Business School published a second case study on the company. Mary Kay had almost 200,000 consultants and 5,000 directors. In celebration, employees commissioned a double portrait of Mary Kay and Richard from Robert Oliver Skemp, a painter whose recent commissions had included a full-length Jesus Christ. Later a *New York Times* reporter would point out that she was one of the few female CEOs to have her portrait painted. "Let's face it, there aren't that many women CEOs to begin with," said Mary Kay.

At the end of the first fiscal quarter, the company announced a two-for-one stock split and cash dividend. Her promise to limit travel forgotten, Mary Kay jetted hither and yon, booking press along the way. Over breakfast with *The Palm Beach Post*, she announced that, by the end of the decade, Mary Kay Cosmetics Inc. would double its revenues to

$1 billion and be the world's largest skin care company. She made it sound inevitable.

Kudos continued. Southern Methodist University saluted her as "Entrepreneur of the Year." *Ladies' Home Journal*, one of those magazines she never had time to read, hailed her as one of the "100 Most Important Women in America." The Napoleon Hill Foundation, named for the author of her favorite book, *Think and Grow Rich*, gave her a gold medal, its first for a woman. Accepting, Mary Kay stayed on message: "We tell our beauty consultants that any woman can do anything in this world she wants to—if she wants it badly enough."

Planning the company's twentieth anniversary, Mary Kay, a woman who prided herself on finishing Christmas shopping by the preceding January, outdid herself. She commissioned a commemorative plate from Wedgwood that replaced its traditional blue jasperware with pink and showed a Southern belle stretching toward something just out of reach. On the back, she put a copy of "On Silver Wings," the anonymous verse that she first heard in Australia in the 1970s:

I have a premonition that soars on silver wings.
It is a dream of your accomplishments of many wondrous things.
I do not know beneath which sky, or where you'll challenge fate.
I only know it will be high. I only know it will be GREAT!

Beneath, she added, "You are great! Love, Mary Kay."

That wasn't all. Next came *The Mary Kay Guide to Beauty: Discovering Your Special Look*. In its foreword, Mary Kay equated self-care with self-empowerment: "The first step is the hardest: making a commitment to yourself, *for* yourself." That was followed by photos of white, brown, and Black models next to self-care scenarios featuring competent women with families and jobs. A Book-of-the-Month Club selection, the $19.95 hardcover would be on *The New York Times*' bestseller list for eleven weeks.

Three years after adding a second Seminar, Mary Kay needed a third. Thus Ruby joined Diamond and Emerald, and twenty-three thousand women paid $80 each, plus transportation, food, and lodging, to come to Dallas. More keys to more pink cars were presented than ever before. Company wholesale ran over $300 million.

But the rest of the economy was booming too. In a strong job market, direct sellers had a better chance of landing traditional work with traditional benefits. Or deciding that they no longer needed the money. When third-quarter results came in, profits were off 29 percent from the year before. Based on past performance—that third quarter was always a stinker—profits were likely to rebound. Analysts sounded their alarms anyway.

Mary Kay worried what those alarms would do to recruitment. Calling their mindset "quarteritis," she declared that America would do better to imitate Japan, where companies reported financials only once a year. Stockholders were getting on her nerves too. One advised her to forswear pink Cadillacs for a tasteful gray. Mary Kay sent a thank-you note.

In the press, the marketing genius who could once do no wrong could now do no right. A front-page analysis in *The Wall Street Journal* reported that company stock had plunged 65 percent in six months, then compared company recruiting to seventeenth- and eighteenth-century press gangs. Stanley Home Products forgotten, *Journal* staff wrote, "Their salespeople either go door to door with their products or hold 'parties' in the homes of prospective customers—a sales approach pioneered by Mary Kay and Tupperware and known as the 'party plan.'" Cited as an industry expert, Crowley's son, Don Carter, declared: "The days of milk and honey are gone. We don't look to have the profits we had in the past ever again."

Elsewhere, analysts opined that direct selling could not last. Not when so many opportunities were available to working women, who were now averaging almost sixty-four cents on the dollar compared with men. Recruiting, which always fell when the economy rose, played into analysts' predictions. Stock fell to under $13 a share. Mary Kay's own net worth, by best guesses about $200 million at the start of 1983, was about $50 million by the start of 1984. Million-dollar donations came to a halt.

Mary Kay in February of 1984.

Strategies were scrapped. Substitutes improvised. Richard slowed construction on the $100 million corporate campus and fast-tracked expansion into the United Kingdom. Mary Kay announced new recruiting bonuses, new sales bonuses. An expanded car program was up and running by March.

That summer, for its three sold-out "Share the Spirit" Seminars, her team decked the Dallas Convention Center in red, white, and blue, with the intention of donating the bunting to the next tenant, the Republican National Convention. Thousands dabbed away tears as Paul Anka sang "My Way," Mary Kay's favorite song. Car keys and fur coats and jewelry and vacations were awarded while women applauded one another for hours. And when all that was over, Mary Kay hosted a breakfast for the National Federation of Republican Women, where Vice President George H. W. Bush and his son Jeb stopped by.

The day after, *CBS Morning News* interviewed the pink Cadillac lady for its color coverage of the convention. Accustomed to charming the press, Mary Kay was nonplussed when offhand comments about the Kennedy assassination ("It's terribly unfair. The man was not a Texan. He was not a Dallasite. He just was passing through") and the Texas School Book Depository ("I think what we should [do] is tear that building down and make a parking lot out of that thing and not have it there for people to remember") turned into a faux pas of national proportions. One made worse when arsonists torched the Texas School Book Depository two days later.

The company tried damage control. Making an exception to the company policy of never contradicting the press, vice president of marketing Dick Bartlett explained that Mary Kay meant Lee Harvey Oswald was the one "passing through." Nobody bought it. Newspapermen pointed out that Oswald lived much of his life in Texas and spent seventeen months in Dallas–Fort Worth prior to the assassination. Editorial writers had a field day denouncing Mary Kay. By week's end, stock was at a new low.

That fall, *Mary Kay on People Management*, her second collaboration with Shook, hit bookstores. Chapters included "Praise People to Success" and "Help Other People Get What They Want—and You'll Get What You Want." On CEO complaints of executive stress, Mary Kay had this to say: "For me the stress was far greater when I had to worry about having enough money to put food on the table, pay the rent, and buy clothes for my children." Full of advice to live by the Golden Rule and to sandwich criticism between two layers of praise, the book held no surprises for anyone who had heard her speak. For everyone else, it read as radical refutation of macho management. By October, *Mary Kay on People Management* was on the *New York Times* and *Wall Street Journal* bestseller lists. Recruitment and stock prices still failed to rise.

Richard canceled the $8 million advertising budget, froze corporate hiring, and sold off seventy-nine acres of the corporate campus site. Mary Kay announced a new incentive program. Decked in diamonds and Kabuki-thick makeup, she hit the hustings yet again. Knowing that women's-page editors would never ask about earnings per share or quarterly reports, she gave long, chatty interviews, admitted to a chemical peel, and alluded to ardent beaus. Much mention was made of her company's inclusion in *The 100 Best Companies to Work For in America.* None of it helped.

Altogether, Mary Kay and Richard owned at least 37 percent of company stock. Along with smaller percentages owned by family, company officers, and company directors, she and Richard controlled about 45 percent of outstanding shares. Enough to make a takeover difficult. But not impossible.

Mary Kay Cosmetics Inc. carried no debt, owned real estate in a red-hot Dallas market, and had well-sited warehouses within easy distance of major metropolitan areas. Its factory, which had effectively eliminated local competition by subsuming the Goodiers' operation, was a model of efficiency, enjoyed exemplary labor relations, boasted one of the best-integrated workforces in the South, and possessed proprietary formulas that guaranteed a steady revenue stream. Its well-regarded skin care accounted for 10 percent of the American market and had never been sold in stores or on television. Its core business had never been franchised.

In the heyday of the hostile takeover, Mary Kay Cosmetics Inc. was a business begging to be bought and broken apart.

CHAPTER TWENTY-ONE

A Pink Palace

In 1985, Richard started playing offense, making plans to take the company private through a leveraged buyout.

For two decades, he had prided himself on paying cash. He had boasted about keeping the company debt-free. He had accumulated impressive assets without mortgaging future earnings. The value of those assets was about to go through the roof.

So he started getting rid of them. The four distribution centers, all on prime commercial real estate, would be sold off and rented back on short-term leases. What was left of the corporate campus site would go next. Then the headquarters building would be sold and rented back on a long-term lease. If everything worked according to plan, many of the company's most valuable holdings would be gone and he and his mother would end up owing hundreds of millions of dollars. Explaining that to Mary Kay was not going to be easy.

Like most leveraged buyouts, this one would depend on borrowed money to repurchase shares. Once the company was private again, incoming moneys could be used to pay off the debt, since there would be no stockholders expecting dividends. That spring, Richard put together a $280 million horse trade that promised stockholders a quick payout plus an IOU: $10 in cash plus subordinated debentures of $8.15 per share paying 14.75 percent a year in interest after the first five years. For a stock that had been trading at around $10 a share, that was considered a can't-miss offer. Analysts were still saying that the glory days of direct selling were over and never coming back. It looked like they might be right: Mary Kay Inc.'s annual earnings were down another 38 percent.

As the deal was being worked out, federal drug agents raided Million Air's hangar in Addison, seizing a twin-engine plane kept there by Joe Bill Bennett, an oilman charged with running a drug-smuggling ring that moved mountains of cocaine and marijuana from south of the border to U.S. distribution points. Rumors flew. Convinced that Richard Rogers was about to get his comeuppance, half of Dallas predicted that he would be investigated next.

He was not, but his LBO was not going smoothly. Son of a mother who increased incentives when she wanted to get something done, Richard sweetened his deal. This time, the offer was estimated at $404 million: $11 in cash plus subordinated debentures of $8.25 paying 15 percent interest after the first five years. The stock inched upward.

Republic National Bank backed out of its agreement to guarantee $45 million. More rumors flew. Dallas busybodies blamed it on the drug connection. *The New York Times* and *The Wall Street Journal* reported that Republic was miffed because Richard had chosen the Bank of New York to head the syndicate behind the LBO. Over two days of heavy trading, the stock price fell. Modest gains made during the last year were wiped out. A stockholders' meeting was set for October.

Before that could happen, the *Dallas Times Herald* ran an investigation on Bennett and his drug-smuggling ring, revealing that Richard had guaranteed an $80,000 loan for Bennett to buy the plane seized in the DEA raid. Other loans made or guaranteed by Richard amounted to more than $250,000. Rumors ramped up as Bennett made wilder and wilder claims to deflect attention from his own charges. Richard was never charged, but Mary Kay's personal fortune now became part of the stake to take the company private. The price of the LBO climbed to somewhere between $450 million and $469 million.

Meetings were set and reset. Orders fell. Production dropped. The company let go of fifty employees, its first layoff. When stockholders met, over 94 percent of those present voted for the buyout. During a fifteen-minute meeting that December, the board of directors rubber-stamped Richard's deal. Mary Kay wept when she heard the news. The millionairess who clipped coupons, hoarded S&H Green Stamps, and saved each ink-smudged rubber band from her daily newspaper delivery thought she was about to lose everything. When the 1985 fiscal year ended, sales and net earnings were down for the second year in a row. Stockholders congratulated themselves on getting out in the nick of time.

Operating income, which measured the company's profit after expenses, had been $41.4 million in 1984, then $28 million in 1985. In 1986, with no real estate sales to buoy the bottom line, it dropped to $12.2 million. Bank payments were rescheduled. As the company struggled to cover the interest on its massive debt, it seemed that Mary Kay may have been right to weep. The high-yield debt securities that financed the LBO were being called zombie bonds.

For the next few years, the company would lose money on paper as a result of carrying so much debt. The Internal Revenue Service would pursue the company for $29 million in taxes on what it said was undeclared equity resulting from accounting practices used in the LBO. The company would battle them in court, finally settling for $3 million in 1991.

By then the LBO would count as another coup for Richard and his mother.

While Mel was alive, everyone pretended that he paid for the Round House and its upkeep. No need for that anymore.

Nor to pretend that the 4,600 square feet of the Round House were still big enough for Mary Kay. Gone were the days when a dozen or so DIQs trooped through for their tea, cookies, and tour. Planning her dream house, Mary Kay had never dreamed she would be hosting three hundred or four hundred women at a time. "It was a tradition that the directors [in qualification] would visit with Mary Kay at home, and by now there were so many of them that the Round House was getting kind of cramped," Erma Thomson explained. At the same time, Mary Kay noticed that her NSDs were moving into huge showplaces. As Thomson said, "She thought she might like to have a place like that too."

Richard was also pressuring her to live someplace bigger. He had long since moved into his own Frank Meier–designed, built-to-order $3.95 million mansion, sited where he could sit on his back terrace and watch golfers struggle with the fourteenth hole at the Bent Tree Country Club. Ben, who had left the company years before, had a house more than twice the size of his mother's, on a lot seven times as big.

So, with the intention of creating a single superluxury complex big enough to satisfy Richard, set a standard for her NSDs, and entertain all those DIQs, Mary Kay bought three high-rise apartments in a new complex near the Galleria. Then she hired Meier again. Interior walls were torn down and renovations underway before she began to think better of it. Thomson remembered her saying, "'I don't want to live up in the air.'" Meier remembered her visiting the site and going to the balcony to admire her new view: "She came back inside and told me, 'Frank, the height makes my poodle nervous.'" And that was the end of that.

Finally, at the end of 1984, with company profits down by double digits and consultants quitting left and right, Mary Kay bought a house under construction in Preston Hollow, the North Dallas neighborhood where property values were rising so fast that ten-year-old mansions were being bought as teardowns. A magnet for moguls, mayors, and sports stars, Preston Hollow had more Horatio Alger winners per square mile than anywhere else in Texas. Dust Bowl refugee turned real estate magnate Ebby Halliday lived there in a 3,710-square-foot house, as did wildcatting corporate raider T. Boone Pickens (8,906 square feet), billionaire businessman H. Ross Perot (8,200 square feet), and Mary C. Crowley (6,725 square feet, not counting the Baptist chapel in the backyard). Competitive nature to the fore, Mary Kay closed on a thirty-room mansion (11,874 square feet) on a one-acre lot.

Designed by local architect Fred Wynn, Mary Kay's stucco château started as a spec house, the most expensive yet seen in Dallas. The real estate company claimed it was nineteen thousand square feet and carried a price tag of $4 million, although it was not and did not. "She got a better price than somebody else because the builder [John Needham] wanted the name," the architect's widow explained. "It never hurts to have a famous client."

Deciding that she would have it finished to order, Mary Kay hired Meier as soon as the title cleared. Crews worked nonstop to have it ready by Seminar. "In the process of doin' the plans, I came to realize it was very poorly built," Meier said. "There were $250,000 worth of things we found that didn't meet the building codes that had to be corrected." Mary Kay pulled out all the stops, adding $1.8 million in finish work. Then she made sure it was pink. "It's not too flashy. It's a very lovely soft pink. It just gives the house a glow," said Mary Kay.

Once more, her house became the talk of the town. People who had never met her could recite its every particular: the forty-foot-high exterior entryway flanked by guardant lions, a twenty-eight-foot-high interior entryway, and a staircase so wide and grand that it looked like the set of a Metro-Goldwyn-Mayer spectacular.

Her new house would have six bedrooms and nine bathrooms (even though her family did not live with her); an en suite master bathroom with a double vanity (shared with her poodle); a concert-size grand piano (even though she didn't play); a swimming pool and colonnade copied from San Simeon (even though she did not swim); a three-car garage (even though she parked out front so passersby would see her Cadillac); five fireplaces (even though they were impossible to use in the Dallas heat); a vaulted ceiling with classical busts around its perimeter (visible only from twenty feet off the ground); a media room (for the woman who called TV "a waste of time"); along with a wine cellar and wet bars (for the teetotaler who never served alcohol).

To fill its quarter-acre interior, she went on a ten-day spree in France, with the company's purchasing agent tagging along to slap shipping labels on whatever antique or artwork caught the boss's eye. "I didn't care if it was Napoleon III or Napoleon XXIX," said Mary Kay, who bought enough to fill a boxcar. Back in Dallas, Janet Winkler, designer for the company's corporate interiors, spent months accompanying the boss to the Dallas Trade Mart to get the rest.

The result was pure Mary Kay. Pastels predominated. Crystal chandeliers were everywhere, including the double-height, seven-hundred-square-foot marble kitchen, which looked big enough to hold the entire Kane Street house where she had grown up. Floral arrangements were everywhere too, made from silk flowers so they would never be wilted or messy. The concert grand was converted into a player piano so Mary Kay could pop in a Liberace tape when she wanted to prank DIQs by pretending she could play.

After the christening of the house with a dinner for the company's top four hundred performers, functions were nonstop. Hosting hundreds at a time in her new great room, Mary Kay would stand on one of its three mezzanine-level balconies to welcome the women looking up to her, then come downstairs to give each of them one-on-one girlfriend time. Toward the end of any event, she would pose in front of the great room's fireplace until every woman got a souvenir snapshot. Her orthopedist warned that standing in high heels was wrecking her knees. Her ophthalmologist warned that camera flashes were ruining her eyes. Mary Kay paid no attention.

When each month's contingent of DIQs traipsed through, Mary Kay continued the tradition of serving spiced tea and warm-from-the-oven cookies, while consultants snuck into the bathroom and swiped a roll of pink toilet paper as a souvenir. On the tours that followed, DIQs oohed and aahed over her double-height bedroom, where an interior staircase led to an en suite office. They bounced on her bed. They saw the desk where she wrote her books. Recalling the story of the young mother who headed to her first Stanley convention with one spare dress to her name, they opened her closet and counted her seventy-nine evening gowns.

Her personal bathroom remained the highlight of any tour. Once again, decor ran to Grecian statuary and gold-plated plumbing. This time, though, the toilet, tub, and sinks were made from semiprecious pink quartz hand carved by a man in Lubbock who had also done Liberace's bathroom. To ensure that DIQs would still be able to pose for their good-luck photos in her tub, Mary Kay had ordered a crystal chandelier to be suspended over this one too. To avoid another violation of building code, Meier waited until the house passed inspection before he complied. But he had a chandelier over the tub before the first DIQs came through.

Zoning regulations were not as easy to get around. Remembering her robberies, Mary Kay petitioned to build a pink guardhouse out front. Neighbors petitioned against it, the zoning board turned down her original proposal, and the press had a field day. Papers throughout the U.S. and Canada ran photos of her Pink Palace—PINK MANSION HAS NEIGHBORS SEEING RED—and stories reprising her robberies. The *Dallas Times Herald* reported the size of the new house as eighteen thousand square feet. *The Dallas Morning News* and Associated Press upped it to nineteen thousand. The struggles of her LBO were buried in the back of the business pages.

Not long before her move, when Dallas was being called the country's "Kidnap Capital," the FBI had advised Mary Kay and other Texas tycoons to keep a low profile, drive an unidentifiable car, avoid strangers, and have a house that could not be easily surveilled. But keeping a low profile was hardly the point of her move, so Mary Kay proceeded to pile on more jewelry—a two-inch pavé diamond heart pendant was her latest favorite—and park her pink Cadillac in front of her Pink Palace where nobody could miss it. Unwilling to give up driving the jumbo pink car with MARY K-I plates, she acquiesced to security detail in a follow car. Then did her best to escape them. Slowing for a yellow light, she would roll to a near stop and gun the engine just in time to streak through before the light turned, with a sotto voce "Lost 'em again!" as her follow car disappeared in the rearview mirror.

Other measures escaped attention. Long before every celebrity had one, she ordered a huge safe room built off the master bathroom. Live-in help, in the person of her old Sixth Ward neighbor Tillie Bass and Tillie's second husband, Lewis Chaney, were housed within shouting distance of her bedroom, in a suite complete with a kitchenette so they would never have to wander out of earshot for a midnight snack.

For herself, Mary Kay kept the freezer stocked with hot dogs and Stouffer's Lean Cuisine. A coupon clipper who insisted on doing her own shopping—"No one else is as motivated to save me money"—Mary Kay could be seen pushing her cart up and down supermarket aisles, alphabetized coupon file in diamond-ringed hand, bodyguard trailing behind. If a store was unable to honor her coupon, she demanded a rebate. "I'm amazed when I see my daughter buy $104 in five minutes, just throwing things in the car. I don't shop that way at all," she said. Marylyn had heard it all before: "I tell her: 'Mother, if I'm ever kidnapped, please don't send coupons.'"

When she saw the bill for feeding the mansion's construction crew, Mary Kay resolved to save money by catering their lunches herself, giving the construction workers pimento cheese with chips and Coke, her own favorites. Groceries and gas were purchased only where S&H Green Stamps were given, because Mary Kay found few pastimes more satisfying than pasting the trading stamps into booklets that could be redeemed for gifts or donated to some worthy cause. "She would drive clear across Dallas to save a dime on a loaf of bread," Doretha Dingler said. "We'd say 'Mary Kay, you're spendin' more on gas than you're savin'!' But she had lived through the Depression."

Despite employing housekeepers, Mary Kay could not restrain her own compulsion to tidy. At headquarters, she would take the sink sponge from the employee lunchroom home so she could wash and disinfect it. She would wipe down counters. "She was the original anticlutter neatnik," Thomson said. When tours of headquarters were scheduled, Mary Kay went through first to ensure all was in apple-pie order. Thomson remembered, "People would have pictures of their families and so on near their desks, but that was not for Mary Kay. She would say, 'This is the Wicked Witch of the West coming through!'" Desk drawers would be heard slamming in response.

At the Pink Palace, employees who lingered after an event would watch Mary Kay bustle through cleanup before anyone could beat her to it. Then, in her own version of an after-party, she would join every-

Mary Kay and Gigi in front of 8915 Douglas Avenue.

one in the kitchen to share a bucket of Kentucky Fried Chicken. Then she would tidy the kitchen too. She could hardly sit still.

Because for all Meier's fixes, the Pink Palace gave her plenty to do. Drywall collapsed. Ceilings leaked. Water seeped through unsealed window frames and ruined silk curtains. A creek running under the house flooded her first floor. "We walked in one time and there were about ten little pots that were catching water that was comin' in," Dingler remembered.

"She hated that house."

But Mary Kay was never one to spend much time at home.

As soon as she moved in, she moved out again, taking a suite at the Anatole Hotel for the duration of back-to-back, sold-out Seminars. That summer, it seemed unthinkable that there could be anything wrong with the company when Mary Kay presented so much glittering pink evidence to the contrary. Her Pink Palace was already one of the must-see sights of Dallas. Kit Konolige profiled "the Dallas dynamo" in *The Richest Women in the World*, alongside Doris Duke, Gloria Vanderbilt, and her friend Ebby Halliday. *People* magazine portrayed her as "a mascaraed Moses" leading her chosen people to the Promised Land. Hundreds of consultants contributed to the fat compilation of recipes called *Cooking with Mary Kay*, which she introduced with two of her favorite jokes: "One Director said the way she calls her family to dinner is 'GET IN THE CAR!!' Another Director said the best thing she makes for dinner is RESERVATIONS!!!" Seminar was more extravagant than ever. Mary Kay gave away more pink Cadillacs and more diamond jewelry.

The minute it was over, she hit the road. Escaping the house that she was already calling "the Pink Elephant," she crisscrossed the country until it was time for her to join that year's Top Ten prize trip. Still complaining that on Stanley Pilgrimages "we got to see somebody's rose garden and that was it," Mary Kay made each year's prize trip more preposterously lavish than the last. "Once you came to the airport with your luggage, you never touched it again," a prizewinner remembered. "All the tips were given for you. Everything was prepaid."

Winners got flights on the Concorde, trips on the Orient Express, private tours of Tuscany. They lolled on private beaches while custom fireworks lit the skies. Rolls-Royces chauffeured them to five-star hotels where they checked into suites the size of apartments, with the biggest and best suite going to that year's top earner. "I was a country girl. I had no idea people lived that way," Dingler, a regular on those trips, remembered. "It was first class all the way."

Husbands were included so there would be no complaints on the home front. Many wore the gold or diamond watches awarded to husbands whose wives were crowned at Seminar. Almost all were already happy recipients of sports cars, a by-product of Mary Kay's advice to their wives: "It's only human nature to wonder, 'What's in it for me?'" Meeting them, Mary Kay would say, "Pat her on the back every day and tell her she's wonderful. She'll make you a rich man."

Always first on the bus, Mary Kay sat in front to greet each couple as they boarded. Later she would join the shopping and sightseeing so everyone could get to know her. At meals, she tried to follow the custom she used for banquets and company events, switching places with each course so everyone had a chance to sit next to her.

That October, Mary Kay and her prizewinners were on a cruise bound for Israel when word came that terrorists had hijacked the nearby MS *Achille Lauro*, taken passengers and crew hostage, and murdered wheelchair-bound passenger Leon Klinghoffer. More hijackings were anticipated. Calling together her cohort, Mary Kay informed them that the ship would be making for Port Said in Egypt, the nearest secure harbor. She had also arranged evacuation to Athens and flights home for anyone who wanted to leave. Then she announced that she had no intention of abandoning ship herself. Hearing that, one and all remained. The next morning, when their ship docked in Port Said beside the rescued *Achille Lauro*, Mary Kay boarded a bus to see the pyramids. Then she went on a camel ride.

Stateside again, sixty-seven-year-old Mary Kay kept it up. Giving interviews. Accepting awards. Enlisting Tillie's help with Thanksgiving for fifty-two of her nearest and dearest. Hosting one function after another at her Pink Palace. Going to her beige office each day. Not slowing down at all.

Crowley was not slowing down either. Her cancer came back, but she didn't miss a beat. She had surgery, put on oversize sunglasses to hide what the treatments did to her face, and got on with running her $500 million business, teaching Sunday School, funding philanthropies, and updating the company cookbook. *Cooking with Love and Butter (or Sometimes Diet Margarine)* would soon enshrine company classics like Mary's Green Goop alongside displayer contributions like Pepsi Chicken, Potato Chip Cookies, and Hot Buttered Lemonade. In less than a year, Crowley's cancer would kill her. But not before she granted more interviews, gave away more money, and listened to adoring displayers belt their rewrite of the title tune from *Mame*: "*Your spe cial fas-ci-na-tion proved to be in-spi-ra-tion-al / We think you're just sen-sa-tion-al, Ma-ry!"*

As Crowley fought end-stage cancer, oversize sunglasses reappeared on Mary Kay too. During a Leadership Conference in Canada, the hemifacial spasm that she called her "charley horse of the face" came back. Scheduling her hospital stay so she would recover in plenty of time for Seminar, Mary Kay headed to Pittsburgh for March 25 surgery with Peter Jannetta, who had pioneered a microvascular decompression technique to relieve the spasms. Within a week, she was complaining about enforced bed rest, giving interviews while she was supposed to be recuperating, making notes for the next management seminars, and ensuring that a Horatio Alger Award would be forthcoming for Jannetta, the kid from South Philly who had done a stint as a Fuller Brush Man to pay his way through the University of Pennsylvania.

Less than a year after the LBO, it seemed as though there had never been a downturn. The company was laying out a long game of international expansion. Stateside recruitment was headed up, which meant that sales would be too. Mary Kay, her company, her products, her books, and her consultants were everywhere. Country radio played "That Big Pink Truck," the novelty number forever after known as "the Mary Kay truck song." Pressed on purple vinyl with a pink label, the Stargem release featured ex–truck driver Leon Smith singing lyrics by Texans Neil Scanlon and Ken Sutherland:

> *The whistles and the winks I get,*
> *Lord, what can I say?*

Actress and author Fannie Flagg's *Fried Green Tomatoes at the Whistle Stop Cafe*, a novel with a Mary Kay storyline, was published with endorsements from Harper Lee and Eudora Welty, spent thirty-six weeks as a *New York Times* bestseller, then became a hit movie with Kathy Bates, fresh off her Academy Award win as Best Actress, playing a consultant. Dumpy and despondent when the story begins, its middle-aged protagonist comes into her own as a Mary Kay consultant. Flagg admitted that the character was based, in part, on her unhappy mother, who dreamed of life as a Mary Kay consultant with a pink Cadillac: "The only thing I could think that would change a woman's life so drastically and so for-the-better is Mary Kay."

Incapable of walking past anyone who called out to her, Mary Kay was in constant conversation with security guards, clerks, shoeshine boys, and random fans. "How are *you* today?" she would ask. If the answer was "Okay" or "Good," she would shake her head, smile, and correct them: "You're GREAT! Fake it 'til you make it!"

Campy and quotable, she was constantly in the public eye, salting beauty advice with Southernisms like "That dog don't hunt," dispensing career counsel in a soft Gulf Coast accent.

Many of the adages, affirmations, and aphorisms that were now being called "Mary Kay–isms" had been borrowed from Crowley, who had borrowed from Mr. Bev's talks at Stanley Home Products, who had borrowed from his own inventions for Fuller Brush, where he had often repurposed the aphorisms of founder Alfred C. Fuller and evangelist Dwight Lyman Moody—plus an idea or two from Baptist minister and *Acres of Diamonds* author Russell Conwell. Borrowings and appropriations and inspirations looped back through over a century of pep talks, sermons, Chautauquas, and camp meetings to be muddled and misquoted by audiences raised on Horatio Alger, Dale Carnegie, and Norman Vincent Peale.

No matter. Mary Kay was now getting the credit. Her edits and epigrams were repeated worldwide:

> "What does she have that you can't have fixed?"
>
> "From fourteen to forty a woman needs good looks;
> from forty to sixty she needs personality, and I'm here
> to tell you after sixty she needs cash."

"When you come to the end of your rope,
tie a knot and hang on!"

"Give yourself something to work toward—constantly."

"Fail forward to success."

"It's not where you start, it's where you finish."

Subcultures and socioeconomic groups jumped on the bandwagon. To MBAs, Mary Kay represented managerial genius. To stay-at-home moms, she stood for validation of traditional roles. To career women, she proved that women could excel as executives. To the Moral Majority, she was a living embodiment of Christian values. To drag queens, she was utterly fabulous. Everyone who had ever felt put down, put-upon, or taken for granted could identify with Mary Kay.

MARY KAY IS EQUAL TO THE AMBITIONS OF AMERICAN WOMEN read the headline on her recruitment brochure, which held a message of self-empowerment that would have done the now-forgotten Mr. Bev proud: "You must believe that you matter. That you are somebody. That you are like no other person in the universe." Accompanying text explained that it could take six to eight years for a consultant to earn $100,000 a year (about $375,000 today). Recruits soon discovered that only NSDs earned those six-figure incomes, that directors averaged under $25,000, and that most consultants averaged under $2,000. But at least the opportunity existed, and that opportunity did not exist in many other places.

At Avon, consultants were still supervised by male managers, not by women who came up through the ranks. James Preston became CEO of Avon in 1988 after following a career path that began with a blind ad in *The Wall Street Journal*. When he found out the advertised job was with "the ding-dong cosmetic company," he threw away the telegram inviting him to interview. When he found out Avon's Fortune 500 ranking, he dug the telegram out of the trash and answered it. With no experience in direct sales or cosmetics, Preston was hired as a supervisor in the Representative Service Department, a stepping stone to the position of division field manager. "I had twenty-five women reporting to me in that first job. They averaged twenty-five years' experience, or 625 years compared to my year or so. Many of them had known the founder of the company, David McConnell," Preston recalled. "Listening to these women—how they talked with representatives, wrote to them, and handled situations . . . that was my basic training." Putting any of those women in charge would have been unthinkable.

Women had few routes to roles like his. Admissions officers of elite MBA programs were not impressed by business experience that was secretarial. At one extreme, the swashbuckling Wall Street culture of the 1980s averred that greed was good and corporate warriors would do well to study Machiavelli, Clausewitz, and Sun Tzu. At the opposite extreme, a sing-along Mary Kay culture handed women a one-hundred-plus-page manual full of advice like "There is no such thing as constructive criticism—only destructive criticism."

"It helped me in my career," said Paulette Schwoebel, who became a consultant in the 1980s while working for the U.S. Army, a company culture as unlike Mary Kay's as any could possibly be. "My career was taking off at the time. I was a grade 9 [the civilian equivalent of a first lieutenant], and I was getting a promotion every year." Schwoebel was married, was raising a young child, and had recently advanced to a junior executive position, where she was expected to wear suits and makeup. When a friend invited her to a beauty show, she went to support her friend and try on makeup, "because I'm not the kind to go to a department store and have people gawk at me. There was a comfort level there, the appeal of being with friends instead of strangers." She bought the line, then signed on to sell. "The women I met almost all admired her [Mary Kay]. Most men did too. She was a millionaire, a success story. . . . She was very professional."

Schwoebel went at direct selling gung ho. "The company was open to everybody: women who never had an opportunity for anything else . . . divorced mothers . . . people had never given them an opportunity or paid attention to them. In Mary Kay they were able to work their way up. Mary Kay herself came from such humble beginnings. The message through the whole company was 'You too can be successful,'" Schwoebel remembered. "Some of those senior directors had overcome their own problems. They had an inner drive. They believed in themselves. I latched on to that."

Schwoebel quit her Mary Kay business after a year—"It's not as easy as they make it look"—but stuck with its management style. "Men tend to only see the negative, the numbers," she explained. "You can't just reprimand somebody and not praise the good part." After earning two master's degrees, one of them at the National War College, and retiring with a civil service grade equivalent to the rank of a general, Schwoebel said, "When you're managing people, if you find the thing that somebody is doing right—and encourage that—it makes a huge difference."

With Mary Kay, encouragement never stopped. She constantly added accolades. There was always another rung to the Ladder of Success, another shot at going from runner-up to queen. Mimicking Mary Kay, NSDs dreamed up promotions that harked back to the heyday of Albert "Fine and Dandy Al" Teetsel. They distributed trophies and show ribbons, awarded their own prizes, and pushed unit leaders to do the same. "I remember attending my first Seminar and the first night we [our unit] had a little dinner. There was lots of recognition. All the top sellers were getting cute little bracelets. I kept waiting for my name to be called," sales director Georgia Baird remembered. "Until it was time for the top person. She [the senior director] called my name and gave me a ruby and diamond ring. It was absolutely beautiful." When Baird took the ring to be sized, she learned it was eighteen-karat gold and worth at least $1,500. "That blew me away," said Baird, who was still selling Mary Kay Cosmetics over forty-five years later. "She got her money's worth from that many times over."

Units gave themselves names like Leading Ladies, Love Locomotives, Barbie Dolls, Kucharski Kickers, Gold-Diggers, Shooting Stars, Blazing Stars, and Lucky Stars. All mimicked Mary Kay's constant communication: circulating newsletters full of favorite recipes and family updates, dispatching thank-you notes, sending cards for birthdays and anniversaries and graduations, writing notes of congratulation when a consultant hit a sales record, writing notes of encouragement when she did not.

That year, the company launched Career Conferences in fourteen cities. Soon they were scheduled in more than forty. To cope with hotel and banquet food, Mary Kay stowed a bottle of Texas Gunpowder, made from dried jalapeños, in her purse; then she hit the road. Making her grand entrance at the "Success Express" Seminar in 1987, Mary Kay rode in on an old-fashioned locomotive. Then she and her Texas Gunpowder hit the road again, now with Career Conferences added to DIQ visits, Leadership Conferences, Jamborees, Seminars, and all the rest. Plus joining her Top Ten winners on their prize trip to Hong Kong.

Sales and recruitment soared. The company was on track to end 1987 ahead of its 1983 high when, on November 9, Richard announced that Mary Kay was stepping down as chairman of the board. Henceforth, her title would be "chairwoman emeritus," effective immediately. Forty-four-year-old Richard would now be chairman, while retaining his position as CEO.

If it was a palace coup, Mary Kay ignored it. She was too busy gearing up for the company's twenty-fifth anniversary. Describing the retirement that never happened, she said: "Well, my son comes along one day and he says, 'Mother, it's time for you to retire and enjoy life.' What he doesn't realize is that I enjoy doing what I do more than anything else. And he went down and made an announcement to our personnel—about two thousand people: 'Mary Kay has retired.' And at that point the women began to cry and the men looked like they'd been hit with a wet fish. And he said, 'No, no, no. She's going to be here every day.' He saw immediately that he'd said the wrong thing. So since that day . . . it's never been mentioned again."

Nothing changed. Through dozens of rallies, appearances, and interviews, Mary Kay retold the story of Richard's announcement with the same details, the same pacing, the same "hit with a wet fish" phrasing. She showed no sign of stopping.

CHAPTER TWENTY-TWO

"Something to Work Toward—Constantly"

In the 1980s, the generation signing up to sell was desperate in a different way from the men who tramped door to door during the Depression or the housewives who held home demonstration parties after the war.

Practicing physicians were buying starter kits. Lawyers and white-collar managers were getting as worked up about their pink-Cadillac prospects as any farmwife or stay-at-home mom. "Mary Kay said that before we publicize it, first let's see how they [the doctors] do," Doretha Dingler remembered. "She made it a rule to not leave your job until you had been with Mary Kay at least six months and it was payin' your bills." But these women had come to the company as a considered career move. Some were getting bumblebee pins and car keys in no time at all.

By 1987, American women were averaging about sixty-five cents for every dollar earned by men and complaining about it more than ever. The younger and the more educated they were, the more they complained. For years, American women had been completing more bachelor's and master's degrees than American men. Just the same, women were paid less at every educational level. A woman who earned a degree like an MD, an MBA, or a JD could expect her lifetime earnings to be at least $1 million less than a man with the same degree.

Gloria Mayfield Banks, who would join the company in 1988, didn't talk about the glass ceiling; she called it the "brick ceiling." Two generations younger than Brownie Wise, Mary C. Crowley, and Mary Kay, her story was not so different from theirs. Banks and her three sisters had grown up in Detroit, where both parents had full-time jobs. Diagnosed as dyslexic in seventh grade, Banks worked hard—"My middle name is work"—earned A+ grades, became a head cheerleader, and paid her way through Howard University. "I worked as a checker in a Safeway grocery store, and I always worked the fast lane because I wanted to play the game with myself of seeing how quickly I could get the line to move." Later, she followed an older sister to Harvard Business School, where she earned her MBA. Along the way, she survived ten years of domestic violence and stints at IBM and Stratus, company cultures not then noted for being welcoming to women.

When a friend invited her to a Mary Kay skin care class, Banks had a divorce in the offing and was nobody's idea of a natural candidate for staging beauty shows. She did not wear makeup, was the single mother of two children in diapers, and held down a full-time job as assistant director of admissions at the Harvard Business School. "I was beyond busy." Nevertheless, she needed money for childcare, and when she heard about the Ladder of Success, its strategy was not lost on her: "In Mary Kay, there's clarity in terms of how much you make. It's a structure that's easy to understand. At IBM, I could sell a $4 million machine and have no idea how much I would be taking home because the structure was so convoluted. If I sell $100 for Mary Kay, I take home $50."

Banks would break company records, drive enough pink cars to fill a parking lot, remarry, create a second career as a motivational speaker, and wind up a multimillionaire. She would dream up a success strategy called Queendom and cofound a corporate event-planning company called Charisma Factor. But first she discovered how hard it could be to sell skin care. At her first beauty show, her total was $7. After that, she balanced sales with recruiting and, within five months, earned her first company car, a red Pontiac Grand Am.

Two and a half years after that first beauty show, she quit her $60,000-a-year job to sell full time. "You hear about a woman out West with eleven kids who's successful. Then you hear about a Harvard MBA who's successful. It's a company culture that reinforces 'If they can do it, you can do it.'"

The company's twenty-fifth anniversary was off to a roaring start. Recruitment was up. Earnings per consultant were higher than ever. The company expanded into Germany. Through its Australian subsidiary, it entered New Zealand. Thailand and Mexico were up next. Citing increases for Avon and Mary Kay Inc., *The Wall Street Journal* reported that direct selling was not dying after all. The company was swimming in cash. Mary Kay was drawing double her pre-LBO corporate salary. Richard was drawing triple. His side hustle, Million Air, had twenty-five franchisees across the U.S. and Canada.

After a three-year hiatus, the company was getting ready to advertise again. In the meantime, there would be no mistaking the face of Mary Kay Cosmetics. On breakfast television, Mary Kay gave a chatty interview to *Good Morning America.* On prime time, she judged the Miss USA pageant when Miss Texas took the crown. When doctors said she needed knee replacements, Mary Kay said the surgeries would have to wait. When doctors told her not to spend so much time in high heels, she told them that was not going to happen either. Nothing was going to interfere with the twenty-fifth anniversary.

Within a week of turning seventy, she gave a speech at the Smithsonian as part of its "The American Entrepreneur Today" series. While in Washington, she presented the Horatio Alger Award to Carol Burnett, hosted a table of consultants who had won a sales contest for the right to sit with her, and sent everyone at the event home with swag bags of Mary Kay Cosmetics.

On that same trip north, she joined fellow members of the Horatio Alger Association's scholarship committee to tour the Milton Hershey School, an orphanage and vocational school in central Pennsylvania where milking cows was still part of the curriculum. Impressed by what she saw as the "solid values" of the students she met there, Mary Kay dreamed aloud of starting an orphanage. Maybe one that could adjoin a retirement home for her directors. Until company executives told her the stock buyback had to be paid off before any orphanages or retirement homes could be built.

She would do all she could to hurry that day. Throwing herself into preparations for the Silver Celebration Seminar, she again commissioned gowns from Victor Costa, the Paris-trained designer whose ruched bodices and crumb-catcher necklines were seen on the likes of Brooke Shields and Ivana Trump. Dallas's "King of Glamour" knew what women wanted.

Born in Houston's Fifth Ward during the Depression, Costa had grown up with his own dreams of Hollywood and the high life. He and Mary Kay understood each other. Let the couture crowd look down their noses at his profitable plus-size clothes and prom dresses, let them call him "the Copycat King"; during the late 1980s, Costa was reported to gross $50 million a year. Besides a bridal collection and *Vogue*-branded sewing patterns, he had a boutique in Bergdorf Goodman, produced a collection exclusive to Saks Fifth Avenue, and whipped up one more for Neiman Marcus.

Nevertheless, early in their acquaintance, Costa came to realize that necklines, hemlines, and almost everything else had to be done the Mary Kay way. No cleavage. No exposed knees. "She had nice legs," Costa remembered. "She had a round back, big bust, no neck. She was short [holding his hand just below his neck], with a bosom that started very high [gesturing to his collarbone]." Skirts had to look slimming and still have enough ease to let her cross the convention center stage. Sleeves had to be long. Beading could not add weight to a gown worn throughout a five-hour awards ceremony. It all had to stand up to hours of hugs.

Escorted by one or more members of the Seminar production team, Mary Kay would arrive at his Dallas office with her fur person tucked under her arm and some little gift—chocolates, cuff links—for Costa.

The girl who had walked to Dow in forty-nine-cent cotton dresses did not stint when it came to Seminar. Mary Kay liked her laces, velvets, and brocades, and she liked them reembroidered, sequined, and beaded. "Price was no object, although I way, *way* undercharged her," Costa said. Materials that passed muster with Mary Kay were dispatched to company headquarters to be tested under stage lights. "She was not pretentious. She was never, *ever* difficult," Costa recalled, too chivalrous to name the clients who were. Decades later, he was still referring to her as "my friend Mary Kay."

Her girls were never going to forget this one. For the anniversary, as sales prize and souvenir, Mary Kay offered an eighteen-inch porcelain doll that showed her in pink fairy-godmother garb, accurate in every detail down to the modesty panel masking the doll's cleavage. Seminar's fashion show would have no fewer than twenty-five American designers. Every single Seminar attendee would get a copy of the "On Silver Wings" verse. Anyone who qualified as Star Consultant during all four quarters of the anniversary year would have her name included on the

Silver Anniversary Collector's Doll, which came with a certificate of authenticity signed by Mary Kay.

commissioned "On Silver Wings" installation, a semiabstract sculpture showing lines soaring heavenward like fighter jets in a zoom climb. That consultant would go down in company history.

All of Dallas readied. According to the press office, twenty-five thousand consultants were coming. Welcoming banners fluttered from downtown streetlights. Ten hotels were fully booked. Restaurants hired extra help. Neiman Marcus stocked up.

A week before the first edition, the special-events team moved into a hotel near the convention center so they could work more or less nonstop. Then Mary Kay, her security detail, her personal assistants, and Gigi the fur person moved into the eighth floor of the Anatole Hotel for the weeks that her staff called "the Mary Kay marathon." Any minute she was not onstage, Mary Kay expected to be at a luncheon, dinner, interview, or unit meeting and she expected to walk in briefed by a folder full of consultants' names, family histories, and sales records. "Her energy amazed us," remembered Jennifer Cook, who was thirty-three years younger. "We were exhausted."

Mary Kay could hardly wait. That Awards Night entrance would be her best yet. Costumed heralds blew a fanfare to begin the evening, a flock of NSDs gowned in silver and black preceded her, then a barouche decked with ostrich plumes and drawn by live horses rolled onstage. Gowned in her own black-and-silver Costa couture, Mary Kay descended from her carriage to deliver her signature line: "Are you ready for the most exciting night of your life?" Maria Matthews, then in her fourth year as a consultant, remembered: "Because it was the twenty-fifth anniversary, everything was, like, on steroids. You know, it was always flashy and beautiful and colorful. . . . The twenty-fifth, because we knew it was something very special, was just extra."

Consultants had plenty of reasons to celebrate. Updates were coming to the product line: nail care, a new fragrance, blemish treatments for the teen market. And, at long last, there would be lipsticks. Because Mary Kay insisted on applying lip color with a brush, these lipsticks were being called limited edition. More would be coming, though. It was inevitable.

The company was changing again. A more visible percentage of award winners were Latina, reward for recruitment efforts that had started long before, when Mary Kay enrolled at Berlitz in an attempt to learn Spanish. "That was just impossible, though; she didn't have the time," remembered Gladys Reyes, who started as Mary Kay's Spanish teacher and wound up as her interpreter. "DIQs would come to Dallas for training and I would do translations for the Hispanic women. Some of them had never traveled before." Reyes spent hundreds of hours standing at Mary Kay's shoulder, repeating her every word. "I *loved* the work and I was happy to do anything in the company—anything but sales," said Reyes. Mary Kay recruited her anyway. Three decades later, Reyes would retire as an independent national sales director.

If the language lessons were less successful, no one seemed to care. Mary Kay could say, "¡Te quiero mucho!" and that was all some women needed to hear. As more Latinas attended Seminar, the company began passing out headsets for simultaneous translations in Spanish. Later that year, when the company opened its wholly owned subsidiary in Mexico, Mary Kay wrote her speech, had Reyes translate it, and then read it in the same accented Spanish she had used for the opening of Argentina eight years before. Struggles to master their language only seemed to endear her to Spanish speakers. When Mary Kay went into a Mexican restaurant and called for a grandfather when she had meant to order a glass of milk, all was forgiven. At least she was trying.

Mary Kay de México would become one of the company's strongest subsidiaries, a foreign market second only to China. In the first three months, three thousand consultants signed up. In years to come, there would be subsidiaries throughout Central and South America, with customers throughout the Western Hemisphere, up to and including Cuba. In the meantime, as conflicts in Central America continued, the stateside segment exploded. Having made their way out of Cuba, El Salvador, Guatemala, Nicaragua, and Panama, more and more Latinas were marching across the convention center stage and straight into their American Dream. To Mary Kay, they were proof that her selling opportunity could change the world.

Seminar weather had been hellish that year. Temperatures averaged around 100 degrees Fahrenheit and hit 105 two days in a row. Seventy-year-old Mary Kay wore wigs and long-sleeved suits throughout.

When the Seminars in Dallas wound up, Mary Kay was due in Toronto to celebrate ten years in Canada and a 60 percent surge in Canadian sales. There she planned to spend another four or five hours standing in high heels on knees that needed to be replaced, while she presented an array of jewelry, furs, and dream vacations, plus the keys to twenty-eight pink Cadillacs, thirty-one pink Buick Centurys, a dozen white Mercury Topazes.

She never made it. The press office announced that she was bedridden with a bad flu. Then it said she was exhausted. Mention was made of August temperatures in Texas. Gerald Allen, head of the international division, flew north instead.

Imprisoned in her Pink Palace by knees that no longer supported her, Mary Kay scheduled videos that would give her a presence in Toronto. At a mini Seminar held for husbands, Mary Kay appeared on-screen to flatter and flirt, telling them: "As men, you're able to see the big picture when perhaps your wife cannot." Then the men sang "The Mary Kay Husband Song," set to the tune of the Oscar Mayer jingle "My Bologna Has a First Name," with verses that included:

'Cause no one in the world today
Can change your life like Mary Kay!

In its business pages, the *Toronto Star* reported the absence of the "goddess of gumption" and "heroine of hustle," then interviewed Allen, who spun the company's mid-1980s "slump" as the side effect of a sales force grown "too big and unwieldy"; claimed that the company righted itself by "trimming 75,000 beauty consultants"; boasted that the company would soon pass $1 billion in sales, and announced that "Mary Kay Cosmetics has the largest number of female employees in North America earning more than $100,000 annually." If that projected $1 billion was an optimistic reference to retail, and thus half the actual earnings, and if those employees were independent contractors, nobody on the business desk of the *Star* seemed to care. The reporter made it clear that he was writing a send-up about silly women who drove pink cars the size of boats.

In Dallas, Mary Kay scheduled knee replacements that would have her in heels before the next Seminar. To save time, she had both legs done at once. "I was horrified that she didn't have anyone to be there with her when she got home from surgery," Thomson remembered. "So even though I usually didn't get Richard involved—he was just as busy as she was—I asked him to talk to his mother about getting a nurse. He went into her office. He came out later and said, 'She doesn't want a nurse.'"

Gritting her teeth through the physical therapy that she called "physical torture," Mary Kay made jokes about "bionic knees," "knee transplants," and "the doctor [who] forgot to put in the WD-40." She planned to make her recuperation an object lesson for her sales force. If she couldn't travel, she could still make phone calls. She could read and sign paperwork. She could write as many notes and cards as ever. Maybe more. By November, she was boasting that her recovery was ahead of schedule. As was everything else. Financials for the anniversary year promised to be nearly 25 percent ahead of the previous year. Mary Kay herself was already deep into travel plans for the new year.

But the old year wasn't over. In December, Berkeley Breathed, who had won that year's Pulitzer Prize for Editorial Cartooning, started a storyline about cosmetics testing on animals in *Bloom County*, his nationally syndicated comic strip. Mary Kay was his villain.

The company lodged a complaint, which delighted Breathed. Newspapers threatened to cancel the strip, which made him happier still. "The issue was ready to explore," he recalled, "and Mary Kay gave me a character and a hook for people's popular imagination. If she hadn't been so silly in her image, it simply wouldn't have worked."

Animal rights protesters demonstrated outside company facilities. Mary Kay sent pink lemonade for their refreshment. *Bloom County* featured a talking penguin at the labs of Mary Kay Inc. with the dialogue bubble "Their products are made from animals . . . tested on animals . . . and sold by salesladies who wear animal fur coats! It's a MARY KAY MASSACRE!!" Mary Kay sent a thank-you note.

"I still have it," Breathed said over twenty years later. "She claimed to be flattered by the attention . . . and crowed about being well-known enough to get mentioned in my strip. She thanked me for choosing her. With an exclamation point. . . . She included a copy of her autobiography, which she mentioned had sold over a million copies. A classic response. If she wasn't going to show any contrition regarding the issue, it was the way to do it. I have to hand it to her."

That May, the company announced a moratorium on animal testing. On June 5, so did Amway. Two and a half weeks later, Avon proclaimed itself the first major cosmetics company to permanently halt animal tests. In July, Revlon banned animal testing. That same month, Procter & Gamble announced grants to fund animal testing alternatives. Several state legislatures introduced bills to outlaw the Draize test, the infamous "blind bunny" test, for cosmetics. Not long after, the company began participating in conferences at the Johns Hopkins Center for Alternatives to Animal Testing and publicizing its development of non-animal safety tests.

The Mary Kay storyline in *Bloom County* was over in a couple of weeks, but people remembered those strips for years. "Some things just come together in the perfect storm of pop culture," said Breathed, who named his next collection *The Night of the Mary Kay Commandos* and thus, in 1989, became responsible for Mary Kay's name making another appearance on bestseller lists.

As the fortunes of Mary Kay Inc. rebounded, Dallas-based BeautiControl made its own comeback. The hillbilly hide tanner's beauty company found one more set of owners: a young couple taking BeautiControl public at the same time that Mary Kay was taking her company private.

Jackie Brown was long gone. When Tri-Chem bought BeautiControl in 1971, she had signed a five-year contract to stay on as CEO, working with a young executive named Richard W. "Dick" Heath. "Dick reminded me of Richard Rogers when he was in front of a crowd," she later wrote. "He revved up the audience with the marketing plan and sent them racing out the door to work harder." Less impressed with the rest of Tri-Chem management, Brown left when her five years were up.

Without her, morale plummeted. Sales did too. By 1980, BeautiControl was losing $400,000 on $1 million in sales and being described as defunct. That year, as Mary Kay Inc. entered its third continent and went from $167 million to $235 million in sales, Dick Heath parted ways with Tri-Chem. No relation to the hide tanner from the holler known as Heath Valley, Heath used $60,000 of his own money and a ten-year, $484,000 loan to buy BeautiControl's remaining assets, then declared that he would rename it Jinger Lee Inc. after his wife. If anyone could revive a dying direct-sales company, it would be her.

Still in her twenties, Jinger Lee Maples Heath already had a life that sounded like one of Paul Harvey's *The Rest of the Story* broadcasts. Born in a small town in West Texas on Christmas Day of 1952, Jinger Lee had parents who married when they were fifteen and sixteen, then split and reunited again and again. Her mother, Ova Wyanell Dodson, had been abandoned by her own mother. Her father, Jack Denzil Maples, had been reared in a brothel before going out on his own at age ten. Her mother sometimes supported the family because her father was sometimes a blackout alcoholic.

Jinger adored her father, who was so good at selling used cars that he had won an award from Ford. "He told me all kinds of things: When you meet somebody, you stare right into the person's right eye, because most people are right-eye dominant. . . . When you have a business lunch, you never order a burger or a sandwich. You order a salad so you can chew real quick and talk. He was a phenomenal salesperson. I am too."

Another dyslexic who turned herself into an A+ student, another compulsive overachiever, Jinger hated not being busy—"I would rather work than do anything"—and kept up a schedule that would kill a horse. She was yearbook editor. She was on homecoming court. When she couldn't afford nice clothes, she sewed her own and won her school's "Best Dressed" award. With money made roguing maize, selling shoes, and helping her dad load car carriers, Jinger paid to have her buck-toothed smile fixed. If Mary Kay's mantra was "You can do it!," Jinger's was "If I can change, you can too."

Jinger, who adored the glamour of the beauty business, met a recently divorced Dick Heath when she was on a college vacation. Nine years later, when he had climbed the corporate ladder and she was working as an interior designer while raising their two children plus the two children from his first marriage, the Heaths sank their life savings into BeautiControl. Recalling long, unglamorous days in hair nets and rubber gloves, Jinger said, "We filled the jars, cleaned the toilets, answered the phones, and wrote the newsletters." To no avail. BeautiControl never rebranded as Jinger Lee Inc. because the Heaths could not afford new packaging or new stationery. By the end of their first year, they had lost $65,000 on $761,000 in sales.

Soon they were so broke that Dick was trying to sell 50 percent of BeautiControl back to Tri-Chem because he couldn't make a $35,000 loan payment. With nothing to lose, Dick let Jinger talk him into revamping the product line based on the "What season are you?" style of color analysis in Carole Jackson's *Color Me Beautiful*, a bestseller that had come out two years before. Companies large and small were already selling women ways to "get their colors done." Undaunted, the Heaths announced themselves "the World's Premier Skin Care and Image Company" and offered consultants training and certification as color analysts, making them eligible to hold free "clinics" for four or five customers at a time.

When word got out that each clinic averaged $250 retail, BeautiControl's consultant count came bounding back. By November of 1983, sales for a single month were $1 million, and Avon, Amway, and Mary Kay were coming up with their own color analyses. Backed by venture capitalists, the Heaths retook control from Tri-Chem. In 1986, when their stock opened at $16 a share, Dick bought Jinger a sixteen-carat diamond ring. *Forbes* called BeautiControl "the next Mary Kay."

Jinger was young, pretty, and happily married to a handsome man. She had an enviable figure—not just compared with Mary Kay's seventy-year-old great-grandmother silhouette but compared with just about anybody's. She ran a 2:50 marathon. She wore Chanel. In 1989, the Heaths traded up from their 6,843-square-foot house in Preston Hollow to a 12,500-square-foot, $22 million mansion with formal gardens laid out along Versailles-inspired allées. Long before *Lifestyles of the Rich and Famous* got around to Mary Kay and her Pink Palace, it did a segment on the *Dynasty*-like digs of Dick and Jinger.

As the Heaths brought BeautiControl back to life, long-dormant disputes reawakened too. Once again, the two Dallas-based direct sellers accused each other of stealing ideas and poaching personnel. Letters from lawyers flew back and forth. Some turned into lawsuits. Irked though she might have been, Mary Kay tried to refrain from public comment. She preferred to be seen as above the fray.

Besides, BeautiControl was small fry. At the end of the 1980s, everyone assumed that Mary Kay was trying to take over Avon.

Undeterred by flops that included its failed $1.1 billion diversification into health care and its fire-sale divestiture of Tiffany & Co., Avon had yet to budge from the old-boy management style that had served it so well in the 1950s.

All kinds of people thought they could do better. As an asset-rich, multibillion-dollar company—albeit one just now realizing that women had entered the workforce—Avon found itself fighting off more than one takeover. Several involved a young executive named John Rochon, who had joined Mary Kay's company in 1980. By 1989, Rochon was vice chairman and putting together bids for Avon. Press coverage of the takeover attempts identified him as a "Mary Kay aide" or "a top Mary Kay executive," which often got abbreviated to "Mary Kay."

"The gal that could make a sale, but never could add up a ticket" had no direct involvement in Avon intrigues, which became byzantine as takeover attempts multiplied. In 1989, for example, Rochon's Argonaut Partners, a holding company within Richmont, another Mary Kay Inc.–affiliated holding company, joined forces with oil heir Gordon Getty and the Fisher family of property developers to form Chartwell Associates, an entity created chiefly for the purpose of acquiring Avon stock.

James Preston, now CEO of what he had once referred to as "the ding-dong cosmetic company," did not get wind of Chartwell's involvement until Chartwell was legally obligated to tell him, by which time it owned over 6 percent of Avon and was well on its way to owning more. Beset by Chartwell, Amway, and other persistent and unwanted suitors, Preston commissioned a full-page ad in *The Wall Street Journal* urging Avon ladies to write to Chartwell in protest of the takeover. In a more practical vein, Avon also implemented a poison pill strategy, hoping to thwart a takeover by limiting further stock acquisition.

For sixteen months, the Street watched Chartwell run rings around Avon. Argonaut split from Chartwell, which effectively doubled the amount the two allies could acquire without triggering Avon's poison pill. Avon sued, accusing Argonaut and Chartwell of staying in cahoots. Argonaut and Chartwell countersued. Avon announced that it would hire Rochon as a special consultant. Rochon announced that he had no intention of quitting his day job in Dallas.

By 1990, Chartwell controlled two seats on Avon's ten-person board. Proxy fights were planned. To please shareholders, Preston announced that he would boost Avon's bottom line by selling some of its stake in Avon Japan. When his buyer backed out, he accused Chartwell, which then owned almost a fifth of Avon, of spoiling the sale. Through it all, Mary Kay remained the marquee name, her headline value outstripping even that of oil heir Gordon Getty.

Mary Kay herself stuck to what she knew best: Motivating women. Accepting awards. In 1989, she was back at the Waldorf Astoria as the only woman among the inaugural inductees into the National Sales Hall of Fame. The year after, she accepted accolades from Baylor University, the Northwood Institute, the General Federation of Women's Clubs, and the Komen Foundation for the Advancement of Breast Cancer Research. Each month, she still sent her checkbook to Richard so he could balance it for her.

When more surgeries curtailed her travels, Mary Kay used that time to assemble a small book as a Christmas gift to directors, compiling quotations and verses like Jessie B. Rittenhouse's "My Wage":

I worked for a menial's hire,
Only to learn, dismayed,
That any wage I had asked of Life,
Life would have paid.

Directors loved it. The next year, Mary Kay made it a sales incentive.

Meanwhile, the Avon acquisition had gone from farce to slapstick. Early in 1991, in an incident known as "Garbagegate," Avon admitted that its law firm had hired private detectives to go through a dumpster behind Richmont, the holding company that managed Argonaut's investments. When Mary Kay Inc. sued Avon for trespassing and industrial espionage, Avon appealed for its right to piece together shredded paper recovered from the dumpster, a right that the court granted as long as Richmont had a representative present during the hundreds of hours that was expected to take.

By April Fool's Day, when *New York* magazine published its coverage of Garbagegate, Chartwell was selling off its Avon stock. In the end, takeover attempts earned the slimmest of profits after paying all the lawyers and investment bankers, who were the only ones to make real money from the years of convoluted corporate raiding.

No matter. Mary Kay headed a company poised to take over the planet. Up until now, the company had been making about 10 percent of its sales from overseas markets, compared with Avon's 50 percent and the even higher percentages at Amway and Tupperware. That was about to change. Addressing the 1991 audience at the World Economic Forum in Davos, Switzerland, company president Dick Bartlett expounded upon improvements to data processing that made Soviet-style central planning obsolete; talked up women and their growing role in the world economy; held forth on recent confabs with political leaders in China, Latin America, Eastern Europe, and the Soviet Union; and foretold a brilliant future for direct selling. That same year, the company launched in Taiwan. Plans were well underway for launches in the former Soviet Union and mainland China, with Bermuda, Brazil, Singapore, and other territories to be scooped up along the way.

Then Richard decided that he'd had enough.

To his mother's horror, Richard semiretired in 1991.

Feeling compelled to make up time "wasted" by surgeries, Mary Kay seemed to be everywhere at once that year: stopping by Fort Huachuca in Arizona to donate five thousand tubes of sunblock to troops due to deploy in Operation Desert Storm; conversing with Betty Ford and Nancy Reagan at a breast cancer fundraiser; attending a Leadership Conference costumed as Mae West; flying to Paris and Rome on the Top Ten Trip, which had been renamed Top Trip because dozens of directors now qualified; jetting to Canada and Bermuda for yet more company confabs; doing press anywhere and everywhere she could.

Richard felt no such compulsion. The twenty-year-old newlywed who had poured body and soul into his mother's start-up was now a twice-divorced forty-eighty-year-old bachelor who shuttled between residences in Aspen and Cabo San Lucas in a Gulfstream III. For whatever business he could not conduct by phone, fax, or Federal Express, he made the occasional stop in Dallas, where day-to-day running of the company was left to forty-year-old Rochon.

Others had already gone. Ben left the company the year that Mel died. Crowley died when she was seventy-three, the birthday that Mary Kay was about to celebrate. Mary Kay's last surviving sibling, Cecil Wagner, died in 1987, the same year that Richard split from his second wife. Pastor Billy Weber was gone by 1988, forced to resign from Prestonwood Baptist after getting mixed up in his own Jimmy Swaggart–style sex scandal. When a member of her staff died, Mary Kay used that as an excuse to move out of her Pink Palace, saying that previous robberies left her too frightened to remain there.

That same year, the company terminated Debi Eyerman, an NSD who had drunk-driven her pink Cadillac off the road one too many times. Fighting dismissal with depositions lurid enough to inspire the *Forbes* headline DEBI DOES DALLAS, Eyerman cited Bartlett's drunk-driving charge and dredged up drug allegations against Richard.

NSDs were retiring too. Ann Sullivan had been the first. Helen McVoy had announced that 1991 would be her last year. More were bound to go. The company now offered a package that included a pension, health benefits, and the title of national sales director emeritus. All the girls who had swapped recipes at the potlucks would soon be gone. All of them were younger than Mary Kay.

Her daughter Marylyn was next. In April, fifty-five-year-old Marylyn went to sleep after a day of shopping and did not wake up. An autopsy showed that she had died of pneumonia. Obits saluted Mary Kay's firstborn as a mother of five, a grandmother of seven, and one of the company's first ten consultants. At the Round House, Mary Kay had a weeping willow planted in Marylyn's memory. Then she went back to work.

Two weeks after Marylyn's death, she learned that one of the women she called her daughters, her NSDs, had been diagnosed with breast cancer. By then, Mary Kay had been to enough fundraisers and banquets to know the statistics by heart: Breast cancer was still the leading cancer in women age thirty-five to fifty-four; breast cancer was still responsible for 10 percent of all cancer deaths; almost a third of the women diagnosed with breast cancer would die of it. She had watched Rena Tarbet, another NSD, go through two mastectomies and six years of aggressive chemotherapy. She knew that Dorothy Zapp, her old Sixth Ward schoolmate, had discovered a lump during a self-exam and undergone a modified radical mastectomy.

And still she was getting letters from women who went to their doctors complaining of pain and fatigue, only to be told that they were depressed or imagining things. Most were not diagnosed until the cancer advanced.

That year, Mary Kay opened Seminar with the announcement of a company-wide initiative against breast cancer. Urging her audience to schedule mammograms and do self-exams, she provided a "cancer room" and mobile mammogram unit at the convention center. She ordered breast palpation simulators so consultants could practice identifying lumps at sales meetings.

Mary Kay had made up her mind to cure cancer.

CHAPTER TWENTY-THREE

"My Legacy Is Assured"

Mary Kay had never been one for luncheons and committee meetings. She lent her name to fundraisers, sat on boards, acted as honorary chair of this or that. Enthroned as Queen of Hearts at a hospital's Mardi Gras fundraiser, she smiled for the cameras. "But it wasn't her way," said Erma Thomson. "She would join a civic organization. She would go to their meetings and not much had been done. That wasn't her way."

Early on, giving had been impromptu. Some would say impulsive. When a consultant in Nashville needed a dialysis machine, Helen McVoy and Mary Kay rounded up donations, stuffed the checks into a briefcase, got on a plane, and emptied the briefcase on the consultant's hospital bed. The consultant got her machine; the company got the front of the Woman's World section in that Sunday's *Tennessean* with the headline CHRISTMAS GIFT: LIFE, WITH LOVE.

The next year, a director in St. Louis decided on "Mary Kay Night at the Ballpark" as a cancer fundraiser. So Mary Kay got on a plane to St. Louis, bobby pinned a Cardinals cap to her wig, and threw out the first pitch. The Cardinals employee delegated to help her practice remembered, "When I handed Miss Mary her glove to wear and the ball, she put the glove on the wrong hand." Fans were charmed anyway. Mary Kay Night became an annual event.

Products were donated to nursing homes. Checks were written for worthy causes, usually for cancer charities. In 1987, Mary Kay was onstage appealing for cancer-research donations when a woman in the audience shucked a newspaper out of its protective plastic sleeve, stuffed in cash, and passed the plastic bag down the row. Soon the bag of money was being passed hand to hand while women rooted through their purses for more. Watching the spontaneous stuffing of cash, the stage crew was sure that no money would make it to the stage. Mary Kay was sure it would.

It did. And with it came new problems. The first was how to recreate a spontaneous gesture. Jennifer Cook explained, "Once Mary Kay had made up her mind to do something, we knew it was going to happen again." At the next year's Seminar, the company distributed what Cook called "cute little donation bags," placed donation boxes around the convention center, and set up a gift-for-donation program that enticed donors with excess inventory like educational tapes and jewelry. "Those ladies love jewelry," said Cook.

The second problem was how to handle all the money coming in. By the early 1990s, as contributions mounted and Mary Kay's cancer initiative gained momentum, it was past time to make the process more structured. "We had been filtering money to a cancer society. As the amount of money increased, the staff was getting concerned," Cook remembered. "We began looking for a more formal way to distribute the funds. First, we needed a doctor to review the grants [applications]. Nobody at headquarters had the ability to really judge them." Setting up a foundation seemed unavoidable. Thomson explained, "She always reacted to what she heard in her office, the women who came to her with their problems." Hence the new foundation would focus on women's cancers.

Mary Kay did not seem to care that, in Dallas, donations to the arts offered the surer route to social status. Over the years, she would make donations to the arts, but those donations were fewer and farther between. Celebrating the company's affluence of the early 1970s, she released one thousand pink balloons with free tickets to the Dallas Symphony attached. Decades later, she allowed the symphony to use her Pink Palace as a showhouse in hopes that the gesture would drum up interest in the house. That time, twelve thousand people bought tickets and the symphony raised a small fortune, but no hoped-for homebuyer appeared.

Unloading the Pink Elephant would take another two years. Selling its contents would take a $1.2 million auction, with profits earmarked for charity. The rigged grand piano went for $9,000 and a pair of vases brought $30,000. The press called it a yard sale anyway.

Now, as company balance sheets recovered from the LBO, pledges to churches grew larger again. In her mid-seventies, the age when Mr. Bev became preoccupied with his legacy, Mary Kay became ever more publicly Christian, ever more visibly active in the Baptist Church. She appeared on *The 700 Club*, evangelist Pat Robertson's talk show on the Christian Broadcasting Network, and flew to California for *Hour of Power*, joining Reverend Robert Schuller at his Crystal Cathedral just south of Disneyland.

The secular world had already anointed her.

In 1993, after passing $1 billion in retail, her company debuted on the Fortune 500. Hailing her as one of the best business leaders in the U.S., a Harvard Business School professor called her company "an opportunity-generating machine." In a *Fortune* profile, the company CEO explained that consultants did not think of themselves as selling cosmetics: "They are selling what we believe to be the premier business opportunity for women today."

That year, the company opened the Mary Kay Museum, something that had been on Mary Kay's to-do list since she first toured the Liberace Museum in Las Vegas. Designed by Frank Meier as an annex to headquarters, the museum included two theaters and exhibition space done up in marble, brass, etched glass, and pricey exotic woods. Admission was free. Seminar gowns were displayed on Mary Kay mannequins with heads modeled from a Mary Kay life mask. Adjacent displays held Career Apparel highlights, including the black wool suit with matching cowgirl hat that started it all. Framed press clippings showed Mary Kay pulling a pink plow to break ground for a distribution center, and Mary Kay in a pink ten-gallon hat posing in front of a pink eighteen-wheeler. Vitrines held decades' worth of makeup palettes, consultant kits, premiums, sales prizes, and golden goblets. "Now I have a place to keep all my stuff," said Mary Kay.

Mary Kay mannequin with head modeled from a Mary Kay life mask.

But maybe that was not enough. To make sure women understood why she started the company, she issued *Pearls of Wisdom*, which would be sold at Seminar. In its two hours of irony-free audio, she retold the origin story of the diamond bumblebees, touted the virtues of singing, and revisited the tale of winning a flounder lamp. Pacing and delivery were pure Mary Kay. One recording used geese as an analogy:

> When a goose falls out of the formation, suddenly it feels a drag and the resistance of trying to fly alone, and it quickly gets back in the formation to take advantage of the lifting power of that bird immediately in front; and when a goose gets tired, it rotates back into the formation and another goose flies to that point position, and the geese in the formation honk from behind to encourage those up front to keep up their speed.

In honor of the company's thirtieth anniversary, the City of Dallas renamed the convention center access road for the duration of Seminar.

Geese made for a smooth transition to "crowing" at success meetings, which segued to an "On Silver Wings" recitation. That, in turn, segued to "World of Dreams," the theme for the thirtieth-anniversary Seminar.

Like most Seminar themes, "World of Dreams" could be interpreted more than one way. Consultants could understand it as an allusion to their "Pink Bubble," that dreamworld where wishes came true and things were as they should be. Businessmen could construe it as a declaration of global ambition.

Up until now, expansion had been opportunistic. An entrepreneur would call from someplace like Australia or Argentina. A director would move. A consultant might recruit on a visit to relatives. Sooner or later, that area would reach a tipping point and Mary Kay would have herself a new market. That had worked well enough before the company became a billion-dollar multinational taking on Avon and Amway. During the 1980s, opportunities were missed. Watching women react to the sight of Mary Kay in Berlin—"First we get freedom, and then we get Mary Kay!"—company executives saw that her charisma was exportable. So was her message.

The year before, only 11 percent of company revenues came from non-U.S. markets. Now, as over thirty-six thousand women came to "World of Dreams," an intentional expansion was about to pay off. Distributors were active in Iceland and Brunei. The company was taking another look at shuttered U.K. operations. Sales were on target to triple in Taiwan. Expansion into mainland China was in the works. Mary Kay Russia was set to open on September 13; product shipments had started eighteen months before the scheduled opening.

The former Soviet Union was primed for the Mary Kay selling opportunity. There, the best private-sector jobs were still men only, women made up most of the unemployed, and any woman who found work was lucky to make $100 a month. Foreign beauty brands were exorbitantly priced; access to them was erratic.

Dispatched to design pink headquarters inside a prime prerevolutionary building in Moscow, Meier looked over the European contractors, concluded "they were all doing sorry work," then decided to have the project done from Dallas. Cargo containers with everything from compressors to snacks for the crew were shipped to Finland, "knowing if we shipped it to Russia, it would disappear off the docks." After materials cleared customs, his handpicked crew jetted from Dallas to Moscow. "These guys were jacks-of-all-trades: electrical, drywall, plumbing, glass, ceiling," Meier remembered. "Some had never flown on an airplane, never gotten outta Dallas." Working from 7:00 a.m. to 7:00 p.m. each day, the Texans became a tourist attraction. "Nobody in Russia works like that," said Meier, comparing his project with one next door "that never made any progress because they were taking vodka breaks every coupla hours."

As the opening of Mary Kay Russia got closer, political discord turned into civil unrest. More of Moscow's infrastructure collapsed. On the Mary Kay project, everything ran ahead of schedule. Meier did not submit plans or worry about building inspectors because the company had hired ex-KGB as "their drivers, their guards, their get-ridders-of-red-tape." On weekends, ex-KGB showed the Texans around Moscow and chauffeured them to dachas in the countryside.

Thirty years to the day after the disastrous opening in Exchange Bank Plaza, Mary Kay Russia opened its Moscow headquarters. According to a PR office fond of serendipitous numbers, the venture started with thirty consultants. Most had been recruited via the kind of help-wanted ads that had started Mary Kay's career at Stanley Home Products. Other Western brands, Nike among them, would run out of product shortly after opening. Mary Kay Russia would not.

A week after the opening, President Boris Yeltsin moved to dissolve the Congress of People's Deputies and the Supreme Soviet; they, in turn, voted to impeach him. Street fighting broke out, tanks moved in. On October 4, Yeltsin ordered the army to shell the House of Soviets. During those final weeks of the Soviet system, at least a hundred people died in Moscow. Hundreds more were wounded. Mary Kay Russia did land-office business.

In 1994, its first full year, Mary Kay Russia made $9 million. The next year, that tripled. By then, the average consultant in Russia was making $300 to $400 a month. Go-getters made five or six times more. Surgeons and physicists signed up. In the U.S., where annual sales averaged around $2,400 or $2,500, consultants could be heard to complain about expenditures of time and effort. In Russia, there were not many complaints. By the end of 1995, Mary Kay Russia was the company's fourth-largest division. A case study coauthored by the company's director of corporate heritage claimed that recognition ceremonies were later staged at the Kremlin, one of the few venues big enough to hold all the women who wanted to be there.

In the U.S., company events were so numerous and well attended that swells of Mary Kay enthusiasm buoyed convention centers and hospitality businesses coast to coast. Inaugurating the main ballroom of the Charlotte Convention Center, hundreds of Mary Kay ladies broke into such a vigorous bunny hop that bits of ceiling rained down on terrified Amway distributors convening below.

Total employment in the traditional job market continued to fall. By 1994, the company had roughly 400,000 consultants in twenty-one countries. About half were under age thirty-five. About two thirds also held a full-time job. And there were still so many signing up. Women like Cynthia Thompson, who got up at 4:00 a.m. each day to deliver *The New York Times* before she left for her job with AT&T, where she sold party-plan pantyhose and Mary Kay Cosmetics on her lunch hour. These were women in pink-collar jobs or, sometimes, white-collar jobs that were not turning out as they had hoped. *The Philadelphia Inquirer* called them "corporate drones in desk jobs." The company preferred to call them "corporate doubters." These were women who came to Mary Kay for more than money.

She had to show them. Next came a commissioned docudrama called *Thinking Like a Woman: The Life and Times of Mary Kay Ash*, to be sold as a video and play in perpetuity at the Mary Kay Museum. Reenactments of her early life, some more factual than others, were used to illustrate the cause and effect of company culture. Before there was a company that gave working mothers a flexible schedule, there was a scared little girl making potato soup for her invalid father. Before there was a product that required regular reorders, there was an eager saleswoman who hit a dead end hawking child psychology books. Before there was a company where women were encouraged to contribute, there was a male manager who shot down great ideas because his star salesperson was "thinking like a woman."

In 1994, after the Dallas Convention Center expanded again, forty thousand women arrived for Mary Kay's "Deep in the Heart [of Texas]" Seminar. Paying their way from as far away as Germany and Japan, overseas consultants joined locals to sing out their own rendition of the theme song:

Big cash you say? Now here's the way:
Sell Mary Kay of Texas!

Because another surgery, this time on her rotator cuff, had not healed in time for Seminar, seventy-six-year-old Mary Kay asked Victor Costa to design arm slings to match her evening gowns, then went through four sessions of Seminar giving one-armed hugs.

"We tried to keep her from working so hard all the time, but everybody knew that was impossible," said Thomson, who would retire that year. When her staff created a Seminar greenroom so she could have a few minutes to rest, Mary Kay decided it was the ideal place to give interviews and connect with more directors.

"I was at Seminar and sitting in the audience with my mother and sister, and these two big burly men in suits came up to me and said, 'Mary Kay would like to see you,'" recalled Craig Hogan, then enjoying national notoriety as "the first guy to earn a pink Cadillac."

"At that time, and I don't imagine it's too different now, women were making seventy-two cents to every dollar that men made. The women got that. . . . It was a compelling and easy story. If I had ten women in a room, three or four would be interested." Ushered into the greenroom for a one-on-one with Mary Kay, Hogan recalled, "There she was, tiny as can be, and she had her shoes off. She came up to my chest.

"She said, 'I have something for you,' and she gave me a beautiful scrapbook. It was frilly and lacy, as you would expect from Mary Kay, about two and a half or three inches thick and full of all the clippings about me and my pink Cadillac. She handed it to me and said, 'Honey, I want to thank you for all the free publicity! We're just so proud of you!'

"I just cracked up."

Collaboration with Bob Shook continued. In 1995, the year that *Publishers Weekly* estimated sales in the self-help category at a fast-growing $279 million, she came out with *Mary Kay: You Can Have It All: Lifetime Wisdom from America's Foremost Woman Entrepreneur.* Announcing that the advance and royalties would go to her cancer charities, Mary Kay timed publication so the book could be sold at Seminar.

Like the two before it, the new book repurposed favorite maxims, familiar anecdotes, and old grudges about male mismanagement. Mary Kay championed flexible hours for working mothers and advocated escape from endless housework. She scolded women for wasting hours watching TV. She shared time-saving tips such as "After you finish the dinner dishes, set the table for breakfast." She called one chapter "Dealing with the Male Ego" and another "Yes, You Can!" She made pronouncements about the company's future: "When I look at our national sales directors and the outstanding directors who are daily joining their ranks, I know my legacy is assured." Boosted by sales of forty thousand copies at Seminar, the book debuted as number three on the *Wall Street Journal* bestseller list in August and went to number one the next week, breezing past *Men Are from Mars, Women Are from Venus* and *Chicken Soup for the Soul.*

At the 1995 Seminar, with the company now in twenty-three countries, "The Greatest Celebration on Earth" opened with a puff of smoke that evaporated to reveal Mary Kay behind the wheel of a pink Cadillac. Climbing out of the driver's seat, she deadpanned: "Would you like to drive one of those?"

In Seminar speeches, Mary Kay spoke of a "mission" in language that paid homage to the God of Abundance. He was the God who honored you as you honored Him: "In doing so [giving to others], you will be blessed beyond measure with all the riches of life. That's living the Mary Kay dream."

That year, as each edition of Seminar ended, she lingered after the last presentation so consultants could shake her hand and have their picture taken with her. She explained that she had never forgotten an event when she stood in line for hours to congratulate a Stanley vice president and shake his hand: "As I got up to him after all that length of time—I was so inspired to be able to shake his hand—he never did even see me. He was looking over my shoulder at how many more there were in the line. I thought, 'If I ever get to be the person with whom they're shaking hands, I'm going to put my attention on that person.'"

As each woman came to the front of the line, Mary Kay would touch her arm or take her hands, study her face, and say something like "I know you will be successful. I can see it in your eyes." Still ignoring ophthalmologists' warnings about camera flashes and orthopedists' warnings about hours of standing in high heels, Mary Kay was dead set that every single consultant who wanted a photo would get one.

Word spread. When the last Seminar in the series wound up, three thousand women were waiting. Each got her snapshot with Mary Kay. It took six hours.

After decades with Home Interiors and Gifts, Don Carter was getting out of his mother's business. In the meantime, he was making another fortune flipping foreclosed properties.

Having inherited his mother's energy along with his share of her billion-dollar company, Carter already had a slew of sidelines, including a professional rodeo, an indoor soccer team, a Rolls-Royce dealership, an offshore drilling company, a freight hauler, and a 1,700-acre cattle spread. Best known was the Dallas Mavericks, the NBA franchise he bought without ever attending a pro game. Millions of basketball fans who had never heard of Mary C. Crowley or her direct-sales empire now knew Carter as the short white man who sat courtside whooping and waving his Stetson whenever the Mavericks were ahead.

In February of 1993, Carter–Crowley Properties scooped up a thirty-four-acre compound owned by a savings and loan that had gone bust. Sited on the Dallas Tollway just north of the Galleria, the Addison landholding included a 599,000-square-foot main structure that offered the largest block of vacant office space in suburban Dallas. Priced at $100 million, the compound had been sitting empty and unfinished for eight years. Carter got it for $22.6 million. Nine months later, he flipped it to the company founded by the woman who had once been his aunt.

Everything about it seemed made to order for Mary Kay, whose headquarters leaseback was set to expire in 1996. Its main building had thirteen floors, her lucky number, covered in three acres of granite that was unmistakably pink. Squint just the right way and the windows looked like a honeycomb, making it irresistible to a workforce schooled in the

Mary Kay Inc.'s 599,000-square-foot headquarters building in Addison, Texas.

symbolism of bumblebees. Inside, an atrium soared four times higher than the atrium of the old headquarters. Its footprint could also accommodate expansion of the Mary Kay Museum, perhaps with room for a pink Cadillac or two.

By the time Mary Kay moved in, the main building had thirteen elevators with buttons shaped like the company's compacts. Columns in the cafeteria were shaped like lipsticks. Receptionists' stations were inlaid with bee-motif marquetry. With its exotic woods and custom finishes, the boardroom on the thirteenth floor was so opulent that, before the year was out, *Dallas: J.R. Returns* was using it for scenes of Texas-style wheeling and dealing.

As the relocation became public, six hotel chains announced construction in Addison. The spur road out front was renamed Mary Kay Way. Finally, in 1995, Mary Kay moved into a thirteenth-floor office that looked much like her last one. The big brass peacock came along. So did the crystal chandelier, the porcelain figurines, the sectional couch, the silk flower arrangements, and the porcelain desk set with its plumed pen.

As it always had, Mary Kay's office door stayed open. "You've always got to be available when they need you," she told directors. Just outside that door, nine or ten or eleven secretaries did their best to keep up.

Texas Monthly knew what got Texans turning pages. Small-town crime. Big-city corruption. Bum Steer Awards. Barbecue. "Best of" lists. "Worst of" lists.

Each issue offered the opportunity to learn afresh that everything was bigger and better in Texas. In 1995, its covers included a close-up of Texas-size cleavage for "Silicone City," an investigation of Houston's breast-based economy. The year's bestselling cover showed the murdered singer Selena in a bedazzled bra, framed by cover lines including "Guns: A Special Report" and "I Shot to Kill." Then, in November of 1995, its cover girl was Mary Kay.

This was no Scavullo glamour-puss or sweet little old lady. Those thin lips were not in a Mona Lisa smile. Her head was not cocked to the side. This Mary Kay looked mad as hell and stood next to a cover line screaming MARY KAY AT WAR! She wore overfancy jewelry with a pale-pink suit that looked like a cake smothered by indigestible amounts of fondant and dragées. Her eyebrows were painted halfway to the hairline of her big, old-timey wig. Every minute of seventy-seven years showed on that face.

The story inside was worse. Using the rivalry between BeautiControl and Mary Kay Inc. as the premise for "Hostile Makeover," writer Skip Hollandsworth cast forty-two-year-old Jinger Heath as the va-va-voom version of Mary Kay for a new generation. He reported that, like Mary Kay, Jinger lived in a multimillion-dollar château in Preston Hollow, made contributions to cancer research, and attended Prestonwood Baptist. He also reported that, unlike Mary Kay, Jinger had a handsome husband ("the kind of good-looking guy one normally sees posing in a tuxedo ad"), a British butler, and a twenty-by-twenty-foot clothes closet that was three stories high.

His Mary Kay was a lonely old lady who pushed her grocery cart through Tom Thumb, trailed by her bodyguard. He quoted a former secretary, who spoke of Mary Kay's "obsession with work." Mary Kay herself admitted that she would never quit: "They'll have to carry me out of the building."

Issues flew off newsstands. For damage control, the company's PR team arranged interviews to capitalize on Mary Kay's campy charm and homespun wisdom. With the excuse of promoting *Mary Kay: You Can Have It All*, which had almost sold out of its initial print run, Mary Kay was booked on *CBS This Morning*, where veteran curmudgeon Harry Smith introduced her with the words "There is no more potent role model for the self-made woman than Mary Kay Ash." Cheered by a live audience full of women in company regalia, Mary Kay talked up her invasion of the former Soviet Union. "The average woman in corporate Russia, if there is such a thing, makes $82 a month. Our present directors over there are making between $5,000 and $11,000 a month. I expect Yeltsin to apply any day," said Mary Kay.

Jackie Brown saw *Texas Monthly* too. Moved to mend fences, she telephoned headquarters and was summoned to what Brown called "the top floor of her ivory tower." As mentor and protégée had their first face-to-face in decades, Mary Kay went on autopilot, telling the potato soup story, launching into legends of the company's founding. Then she seemed to catch herself. Just as fast, talk turned to reminiscences. Mary Kay asked, "If you had it to do all over again, would you answer my newspaper ad?" Brown answered, "In a heartbeat."

Brown thought that Mary Kay looked lonely. "It was sad, it was all she had left. Her son had left the business. . . . She was one of the ten best-known names in the world and there she was trapped in her ivory tower." Asked to autograph the *Texas Monthly* cover, Mary Kay refused, giving Brown an inscribed copy of her latest book instead. She told Brown to stop by and see herself on the Wall of Fame in the Mary Kay Museum downstairs. The two parted with a hug.

Long after, Brown would slip in and out of the present tense—"Mary Kay holds a grudge" and "Mary Kay is . . ."—when she talked about Mary

Kay. Fifteen years after their last meeting, she would publish a memoir called *Ask ME About Mary Kay.* For her author photo, Brown posed as a blond in a pink suit holding a poodle.

Age seventy-seven, Mary Kay rose at 5:00 a.m. to clock her "nine-day workweek." Never stingy with self-improvement tropes, she not only encouraged consultants to join her in "the Five O'Clock Club" but also personally telephoned new members at 5:30 a.m. to chirp encouragement. She had to let them know that they could do it too. She just had to.

Each morning, she spent twenty-seven minutes getting dressed. That included twenty-one minutes listening to self-improvement tapes while she put on her false lashes and a full face of makeup that looked like the full face of makeup she had been putting on for three decades. Application was every bit as virtuosic as it had been in 1980, when she failed to fool a celebrity panelist on *To Tell the Truth* because "her makeup is more artistically applied."

Work, though, was never far away. Besides the bat phone connecting her bedroom office to Jennifer Cook's desk at headquarters, Mary Kay had tape recorders stowed in her dressing room, kitchen, and car, plus a miniature tape recorder in her purse, so she could make use of "otherwise idle" time by giving dictation.

Many had tried to convince her to hire a chef. Bill Besse, on her security staff, was the latest to lose the battle. Every morning, she fixed herself breakfast in the Round House kitchen, which had been remodeled with pale-pink Formica that matched the company packaging. Then she packed a lunch to take to the office. If there were no company functions that night, she would be back in her pink kitchen to make herself dinner.

The drive to work was a different story. There was no more gunning through yellow lights to shed her security detail. Around the time that gas stations had given up S&H Green Stamps, Mary Kay had given up driving herself to work. Now security chauffeured her while she spent the twenty-minute commute giving dictation or listening to audiobooks like Zig Ziglar's *How to Be a Winner* and Michael LeBoeuf's *Working Smart: How to Accomplish More in Half the Time.*

Arriving at her thirteenth-floor office by late morning, she handed off the tote bag of work that she had taken home the night before. Settling in behind her oversize partners desk, Mary Kay kicked off her heels, put on the slippers stowed in her bottom right desk drawer, and got to work.

Time not spent in business meetings was spent on business calls. Over and above scheduled conferences and interviews, her staff fielded about sixteen thousand telephone calls a year from people certain that Mary Kay would want to hear what they had to say. She also tried to call six directors each day "for no reason," keeping conversations personal but short. Applying "the controlled rush" she advised her girls to use, Mary Kay was shameless about making excuses to get off the phone. "I'm on my way out the door" was a favorite. Long chats were time wasted.

Long lunches were time wasted too. Mary Kay would take out the jalapeño cornbread or the chicken breast and salad she had packed that morning and close her office door. "Men were always trying to get her to go to lunch," Thomson recalled, explaining that Mary Kay watched her weight and could not abide the length of business lunches. "But she didn't want to go to lunch with people. She liked to work."

If she could read at the same time, so much the better. There were so many company communications to study, so many women to encourage. *Applause*, the in-house magazine, still published commission totals of the highest earners, a list that now went on for pages, with hundreds of names crammed onto each page. Weekly newsletters had to be read too, along with NSD newsletters and all the collateral from all those overseas markets.

Then there was correspondence. Mary Kay received at least 18,500 pieces of mail a year (some estimates went as high as 7,000 a month); she still expected each to be answered within twenty-four hours. On her birthday, an extra 10,000 or so cards, letters, and little gifts would arrive. She replied on pink stationery, sometimes with a verse like

You're one of the nicest people
that I have ever known,
For you make others happy
in a way that's all your own.

Mary Kay herself originated more mail than ever. Each typed letter of congratulation—"You are the bright and shining star among our star consultants"—would be signed by Mary Kay. Every consultant got a Mary Kay–designed birthday card from the company in a facsimile of Mary Kay's handwriting. If the birthday girl was high in the company hierarchy, she got a present too. Added to that were Mary Kay's own handwritten notes of condolence, notes of encouragement, and extra notes of congratulation.

Any trip, any event, any visit anywhere generated more notes, more cards, more correspondence. Mary Kay held herself to "the three-foot rule": If she came within three feet of someone, she said something to them. Entering an elevator meant acknowledging everyone in it, then responding if they spoke to her. That, in turn, often imposed an obligation to follow up with a note of thanks, encouragement, or advice. Many ended with some variation on "Please keep in touch!"

On the lookout for more ways to connect, Mary Kay was now experimenting with the internet. While Avon readied a direct-to-consumer website that would bypass Avon ladies, Mary Kay imagined a web that would drive business to her girls. Waiting for the boys downstairs to work that one out, she hosted AOL online chats that promised to teach "how to build your own business."

When everyone else's workday ended, Mary Kay took her tote bag of take-home work and climbed into her limo. Back in her pink kitchen, she might indulge in a hot dog or two from the hoard in her freezer. Then came more work. In between, so automatic that she no longer noticed them, were housekeeping rituals. Each day, for example, she would straighten a different closet or dresser drawer until she had gone through the entire house, at which point she would start over again. According to Mary Kay, those were the habits that kept a home company-ready at all times. Planning what to wear the next day, she would consult a closet where everything was color coded and perfectly aligned. If she wanted matching jewelry, she might get out Magic Markers and turn her diamonds into rubies or emeralds or sapphires. On another night, nail polish remover would turn them back again.

No day ended without "the Six Most Important Things," a rite she had followed for half a century. According to a story that had long been a staple of self-help literature, in 1918, PR man Ivy Lee promised steel magnate Charles Schwab that executives would increase their output by listing and ranking six goals for the next day; when they did, the results so impressed Schwab that he gave Lee a check for $25,000. Positive that the Six Most Important Things could help women as much as the Five O'Clock Club, Mary Kay included the technique in her autobiography, where Shook updated the story with snappy dialogue, made Lee an efficiency expert, and upped the payout to $35,000.

Mary Kay wrote down the six things she wanted to accomplish. Then she ranked them. Toughest went top, easiest went bottom. The next day, tasks would be tackled in order. Anything unfinished went to the top of the next day's list.

Once that was done, it was lights-out. At home, she was in bed before eleven. At five the next morning, she would be ready to tackle her list.

CHAPTER TWENTY-FOUR

"The Idealization"

On February 26, 1996, as her company closed on $1 billion wholesale, Mary Kay had a stroke that left her unable to speak. Few knew it was not her first. During the last year, her latest book, *Mary Kay: You Can Have It All*, had made it to the *New York Times* and *Wall Street Journal* bestseller lists, selling out of its initial 250,000-copy print run. She had driven a pink Cadillac onto the convention center stage, moved into pink headquarters with fourteen acres of office space, expanded her museum, started online chats, braved the *Texas Monthly* cover, and watched her company open in China. She had dispatched more phone calls, cards, letters, faxes, and emails than ever. As recently as January, she had urged 6,500 women at a sold-out Leadership Conference in San Antonio to "work like crazy." She herself had worked through pregnancies, rheumatism, shingles, brain surgeries, knee replacements, eye surgery, and shoulder surgery.

This time would be different. Interviews were canceled. She no longer came to headquarters. She did not speak at a sold-out Leadership Conference in April. She missed her own induction, that year's only woman, into *Fortune*'s National Business Hall of Fame. A company spokesperson declined specifics, saying that Mary Kay was eager to return to work.

In the meantime, the company was doing fine without her. Pink

Cadillacs, diamond bumblebees, and over-the-top Seminars gave Mary Kay Cosmetics brand recognition galore. The line of succession was in place. In 1981, Mary Kay had concluded her autobiography with a chapter called "Leaving a Legacy," which gave her blessing to Richard as chief executive officer and designated her NSDs as "the Mary Kays of the future." Year after year, she had praised those NSDs "forward to success," telling them, and anyone else who would listen, how well they would do at continuing her company.

Her saying so made it so. When she did not appear at Seminar that summer, NSDs stepped in. There would be no gleeful Mary Kay making a grand entrance on a whirling carousel or in a horse-drawn carriage, but prayers were read, speeches given, and winners hugged. More car keys than ever were conferred, more prizes presented. Newspapers reported her absence under headlines like MARY KAY WOMEN CARRY ON THE DREAM. The Associated Press quoted a director saying, "More and more it made us aware that all of us are Mary Kay, and we must continue her dream even when she can't be there."

Months passed. Without Mary Kay to open territory, the company continued its juggernaut through Eastern Europe. Without Mary Kay as main attraction, company conferences continued to sell out. Without Mary Kay to raise funds, the Mary Kay Ash Charitable Foundation debuted as a 501(c)(3) funding the fight against women's cancers. Without Mary Kay to charm interviewers, the company got as much media attention as ever. She remained a mandatory mention in any tale of improbable success against impossible odds. Her life story appeared in *Success After Forty: Late Bloomers Who Made It Big* alongside the life stories of Abraham Lincoln and Mother Teresa. She was the only woman included in *Forbes Greatest Business Stories of All Time.*

After ten years of record sales, Seminar expanded again in 1997. All five editions of "The Incredible Journey"—Pearl added to Diamond, Emerald, Ruby, and Sapphire—sold out. NSDs again took over emcee duties. When it came time for the candlelight ceremony, the audience held electric candles while performers launched into the contemporary Christian hit "Carry Your Candle."

Hold out your candle for all to see it.
Take your candle, and go light your world.

As the music reached its crescendo, the backdrop of flickering candles parted, and there, propped on a mobile platform, was Mary Kay.

The tiny figure opened her arms. As the audience leaped to its feet and screamed, she smiled, gave a little wave, gestured toward her heart, and blew kisses. An NSD read the message Mary Kay had approved: "It is true, I did see the dream! I did see the vision! I did provide you the vehicle, and for thirty-four years I have watched with such pride, because you just took my dream and this opportunity and ran with it."

After that, she had planned one last surprise. For weeks, she had been practicing something to say at Seminar. When the words wouldn't come, she mouthed "You can do it!" instead.

As Estée Lauder's company had done under similar circumstances, Mary Kay's company turned her office into a shrine.

Every silk flower stayed where she had left it. The life-size brass peacock, souvenir of that long-ago jaunt to Mexico with Mel, remained on its roost. Slippers were still stowed in the bottom desk drawer. Mirrored vitrines displayed dozens of porcelain figurines—Belleek, Boehm, Cybis, Lladró—that had been gifts from Mel and grateful NSDs. On her oversize partners desk, her ostrich-plume pen remained at the ready. Outside her office door, on a counter inlaid with bee-motif marquetry, the company sold Kodak disposables so visitors could take souvenir photos.

Confined to the Round House, Mary Kay spent hour after hour watching videos of company functions that took place without her. New products were presented for her inspection. Meetings of the Mary Kay Ash Charitable Foundation were conducted in her living room, where a wigged, suited, jeweled, and made-up Mary Kay weighed in via hand gestures and eye movements. She listened attentively as long lists of consultants' awards and achievements were read. No longer able to get girlfriend time with Mary Kay, aspiring members of the Millennium Club were promised "your name on a plaque presented to Mary Kay herself and a permanent part of the Mary Kay Museum."

Friends, most often NSDs or former assistants, came by to take her to lunch. Until another stroke put her in a wheelchair and those outings had to stop. "It's important for me to present a good image. When the time comes that I can no longer do that, I'd be a liability to the company instead of an asset," she had written years before. A wheelchair was not the Mary Kay image.

Youth choirs, church choirs, and the company choir came to sing. Other visitors were encouraged to read the Bible aloud; most found that when they tried to stop, Mary Kay would tap the Good Book to let them know they could do a little more. Ministers came to pray. Family made visits. An ex-marine at the front door kept out everyone else.

For her birthday in 1998, NSDs gave her a casting of *The Cross of the Millennium*, the same present that the pope received the year before. The foot-high acrylic sculpture, which superimposed a resurrected Christ over the crucified Christ, was moved into her bedroom—positioned to be Mary Kay's last sight on earth. That same year, in honor of its thirty-fifth anniversary, the company produced a gilt-edged tract called *From Our Hearts: 13 Stories of Compassion, Perseverance and Hope*, a sampling of stories that had been circulating at Seminar and sales meetings for years. Recounting ordeals that included incarceration and the death of a child, women wrote of how they had found support from "the Mary Kay family," "the Mary Kay culture," and "the Mary Kay world."

The company was going gangbusters.

While Mary Kay was active, the worldwide consultant count hovered between 400,000 and 450,000. Not long after, it was close to 750,000. A quarter of company revenues now came from international markets. Russia was setting records. As were other countries where good lipsticks and good jobs had been in short supply.

The year before Mary Kay's stroke, the company was in twenty-four markets. The year after, it was in the Czech Republic and Ukraine and had a factory in Switzerland. Launches in Brazil and the Netherlands followed; then came El Salvador, Hong Kong, Kazakhstan, the Philippines, and Slovakia. By the time those opened, the company was building distribution centers and hiring support staff for its rollout in Poland. Keys to pink Cadillacs (or pink Toyotas, pink Mercedes, black Saabs, black Volvos, or silver BMWs) were being given out all over the globe.

China had not been easy. By government edict, cosmetics sold in China had to be manufactured in China, which meant committing to an $8 million Hangzhou factory before so much as a single jar of skin cream was sold. Avon and Amway had gotten an earlier start. So had start-ups based in China and Taiwan, many pushing gadgets more outrageous than anything any wind whistle–selling nineteenth-century Yankee huckster ever dared dream up. By the time Mary Kay China opened in 1995, citizens unwise to the ways of capitalism were being bilked left and right. Pyramid and Ponzi schemes abounded. The central government, responding to years of complaints, finally denounced direct selling as demonic. In April of 1998, China outlawed the entire industry.

By September, Mary Kay China was back in business, thanks to lobbying by the U.S. government; appeals from Amway, Avon, and other U.S. direct sellers; and modifications to the Mary Kay business model. "God first, family second, career third" was now translated as "Principles first, family second, career third" to sound better to communist ears. Obeying the letter of local law, the company opened retail stores and offices so consultants would have a venue for beauty shows. Seminar-style rallies, proscribed as cultlike by the People's Republic, were held in Hong Kong.

The internet had been difficult in a different way. In the mid-1990s, direct sellers like Avon saw the web as their way to sell without a sales force. Direct sellers who took the opposite approach, like Mary Kay Inc., ran into problems that ranged from a sales force intimidated by the internet to consultants who launched sites with overstated and illegal product claims.

Those problems started to be solved in 1997, when the company coaxed more consultants online by selling turnkey websites for $35—no technical expertise required. All the consultant needed was access to a computer, an item that the company happened to be offering as a sales prize. Before the end of the program's first year, over ten thousand consultants had purchased personal websites. Two years after that, the company debuted Mary Kay InTouch, a platform making it possible for a consultant to work her Mary Kay business at any hour of the day or night. On the main website, marykay.com, online shoppers could browse and buy; then their transaction was routed to the closest registered consultant. Or the shopper could type in her zip code, find a drop-down menu of nearby consultants, and take her pick. By 2000, the company was claiming that half its orders originated on the internet. The next year, the Direct Selling Association, a trade group that had been watching the internet wreak havoc on its industry, gave the company its Industry Innovation Award.

Seminar continued to sell out. Each summer, women who would have been pariahs at other beauty companies crowded the convention center: women who had aged out of their nine-to-five jobs, women gripping the harnesses of service dogs, women using walkers or wheelchairs or crutches or canes, overweight women who relied on mobility scooters to cover the center's two million square feet, Muslims in hijabs, Pentecostals in ankle-length skirts, former nuns who dressed like lay sisters, pregnant women with bellies so swollen they looked like they might give birth any minute.

And when those women arrived at Seminar prepared to be inspired to the point of tears, the NSDs did not disappoint. Although no one could milk a line like "I believe for every drop of rain that falls, a flower grows" quite like Mary Kay, the NSDs had perfected their own unhurried delivery and meaningful pauses. When an NSD started in on the lyrics of an old Diana Ross hit at 1999's "It's Your Turn!" Seminar, thousands of purses could be heard clicking open as tissues were taken out for the "It's my turn to start from number one" that everyone knew was coming.

No one was allowed to forget Mary Kay, though. Thanks to years of archived audio and video, she always seemed to be smiling down from the Jumbotron or just offstage commenting on the proceedings. Not a day of Seminar went by without her.

Nor did she stop selling books. In 2000, Mary Kay appeared on the cover of *Living a Rich Life*, a company-sponsored hardcover full of financial advice that covered everything from how to read a stock table to how to calculate the cost of procrastination. In addition to lessons on computing a debt-to-income ratio, readers were reminded that three out of five adults living in poverty were women and learned that women earned seventy-four cents for each dollar earned by men.

The same year, the company's corporate heritage director launched a project nicknamed "Chicken Soup for the Mary Kay Soul," published as *Paychecks of the Heart: 113 Inspiring Stories About Living the Principles of Mary Kay Ash.* Proceeds went to the Mary Kay Ash Charitable Foundation, which was giving away $500,000 a year and now broadening its mission to support survivors of domestic violence. "Over the years, so many women had come to her office with those stories," Erma Thomson explained. "This was something she had heard again and again."

As the financial meltdowns of the late 1990s sent more Asian and Latin American women to the company, consultants who had never met the flesh-and-blood Mary Kay found new ways to express their fervor. A consultant in Tajikistan spent hundreds of hours hand-knotting a traditional Tajik carpet patterned with Mary Kay's face and mailed it to the museum, where it joined dozens of similar tributes. Throughout China, college women revered Mary Kay as a sage who had shown the way to balance family and career. Thousands competed for Mary Kay Scholarships. Dozens made a self-financed pilgrimage to Seminar in Dallas.

Accolades grand, small, and strange continued. Historian H. W. Brands profiled her in *Masters of Enterprise* alongside the likes of John

Carpet made by Tajikistan consultant Nadija Abdullaeva, given to Mary Kay in 2000.

Jacob Astor, Andrew Carnegie, and Walt Disney. Lifetime, the "Television for Women" cable network, called Mary Kay the most influential businesswoman of the twentieth century. Now writing about her reverentially, *Texas Monthly* named Mary Kay "Salesman of the Century." The Women's Museum installed her in its "Unforgettable Women" hall. The Women's Chamber of Commerce of Texas honored her as one of the century's most influential women. In due course, each honor was memorialized in the Mary Kay Museum and posted on the company website, much as it would have been if Mary Kay were still writing her thank-you notes.

The sales pitches, the slogans redacted from Frank Stanley Beveridge and Mary C. Crowley, the uncorrected assumptions in newspapers and magazines, and the ghostwriter's elisions and exaggerations, were becoming codified. Years later, John Rochon, who was responsible for the day-to-day running of the company, would boast: "The idealization of the person was completely in my control. Mary Kay never made a mistake after she left the company."

Then came the return of the prodigal.

By the summer of 2001, Mary Kay's health problems had multiplied. In the five years since his mother's stroke, Richard had retained the title of chairman and kept abreast of goings-on at Richmont Corp., which acted as a holding company for the family's investments. Otherwise, he remained at a remove. The last time *The Wall Street Journal* name-checked Mary Kay's financial genius son had been in 1996, when its real estate column ran an item about his pricey new vacation house in Aspen. It was no secret that Mary Kay wanted him back at the office.

On June 26, that's what she got. "I have decided to resume 'hands on' leadership of Mary Kay Inc.," Richard wrote to employees. "During recent months, Mother has been clear in her hope and encouragement of my return to a leadership role in the company we founded together almost forty years ago. Honoring her wish is the right and only decision for me, giving her comfort and peace of mind that Mary Kay Cosmetics will remain a private family-held enterprise."

Rochon was out. Richmont would be dismantled. There would be no further investment in corporate caterers, muffin franchisers, Dirt Devil vacuum cleaners, or their like. Richard's letter explained that his decisions were "in no way related" to his mother's health. A day or two later, a company spokeswoman assured everyone that eighty-three-year-old Mary Kay was "in good health for her age."

A few weeks after, Richard opened Seminar with "Well, Mom, you got your wish. I'm back." The audience, who had given him a standing ovation before he said a word, shrieked. Staying on message, Richard reassured attendees that Mary Kay Inc. would concentrate on its core mission: providing opportunities for women. "Mother's dream ministers to the welfare of humankind," he told them. It was what they wanted to hear.

To the press reporting Richard's return, a company executive explained that Mary Kay was a mother figure. Rounding out the business-is-personal angle, he explained that the price of entering the corporate world was "spending time with family" and "flexibility about family needs"; then he segued into family legacies established when daughters of consultants became consultants themselves. All of it made a neat tie-in to Velocity, a line aimed at customers' teenage daughters that was set to launch in September.

Mary Kay's own family fit right in. "Praised forward to success" since birth, Richard's son Ryan was going into the family business. Consultants had been introduced to Ryan when he was a tuxedoed, towheaded little boy standing on the Seminar stage next to his grandmother. When he was seven, that grandmother gave him an inscribed copy of *Mary Kay on People Management*, telling him that he would need to learn its lessons for the day when he became president of the company.

Like his father, Ryan attended a prestigious prep school and applied to Southern Methodist University. Unlike his father, he was accepted at SMU, finished a summa cum laude degree in finance, and graduated with the highest GPA in his class. Following an appropriate interval at another firm, he joined the company as a financial analyst. A year later, he added duties as vice president of the Mary Kay Ash Charitable Foundation and began doing more public speaking. Businesspeople inside and outside the company respected Ryan, who was clean-cut, well-mannered, and smart as could be. Older consultants cooed when they saw him. His grandmother could not have planned it any better.

She had not stopped there. Years before, Mary Kay had specified that her body be cremated and her ashes interred next to Mel's at Sparkman–Hillcrest. She had approved the inscription, left instructions about her funeral, outlined a memorial service, and decided who should be invited. She knew what songs she wanted sung. She knew who she wanted to sing them. She'd thought of everything.

CHAPTER TWENTY-FIVE

"The Face of Business for Women"

She had been speechless and housebound for more than five years, her health in further decline since the start of summer. By November, directors were emailing each other with word that "she was not herself anymore." Finally, at four thirty in the afternoon on November 22, 2001, that year's Thanksgiving Day, Mary Kay died at home from natural causes related to her strokes.

Her press office was prepared. The announcement of her death made most six o'clock news broadcasts, all the late-evening news shows, and all the morning papers. PINK EMPIRE CHANGED THE FACE OF BUSINESS FOR WOMEN read the front page of the next day's *Dallas Morning News*, trotting out the old saws about the poverty of the Sixth Ward and how she "dreamed of becoming a physician." *Women's Wear Daily* said she started her company a month after leaving Stanley Home Products. Her *New York Times* obit, promoted on the paper's front page, was headlined MARY KAY ASH, WHO BUILT A COSMETICS EMPIRE AND ADORED PINK, IS DEAD AT 83. Inside, a half page described her as "the high priestess of pink," called her "once divorced and twice widowed," and captioned a photo "Below, she drove a pink Cadillac at a seminar late last month."

With statistics supplied by the company, media announced that

Mary Kay Inc. had done $2.4 billion retail in 2000, with a 17.1 percent increase in sales that outpaced the rest of the cosmetics industry. Reports rounded off its workforce to 3,600, over and above 850,000 consultants in thirty-seven countries, adding that Mary Kay awarded leases to over ten thousand pink Cadillacs and anointed 151 "Mary Kay Millionaires." Noncompany estimates calculated her personal fortune at $98 million, over two thirds of it in company stock. Her 1993 will left Ben a million dollars in cash, forgave any outstanding loans to Richard, and divided the remainder of her property into thirds among Richard, Ben, and Marylyn's children. Richard was executor; his son Ryan would later become coadministrator of the family trust.

Suspending send-ups of the feisty little lady in the big pink car, a flurry of analysis and reevaluation hailed Mary Kay as an innovator, uncommonly canny entrepreneur, and early advocate of women's rights—although close reading showed that attitudes about working women may not have changed as much as headlines claimed. One reporter took company-generated boilerplate about Lula's long hours running the café and changed it to "her mother worked as a waitress," as if unable to imagine a woman in any other role. Writing as though the gender pay gap were a thing of the past, a *Dallas Morning News* editorial sought to put Mary Kay's life in context with "One must consider what life was like for women in business in the years before 1963, and what it has become since." By 2001, it had become three female CEOs in the Fortune 500 and women earning an average of seventy-six cents on the dollar compared with men.

Obits noted that Mary Kay was survived by two sons, sixteen grandchildren, twenty-eight great-grandchildren, and one great-great-grandchild. As she had planned, her remains were cremated and interred at Sparkman–Hillcrest, the cemetery that held Dallas celebrities Greer Garson, Mickey Mantle, and former sister-in-law Mary C. Crowley. Three husbands were there already: Charlie Weaver, near his sister; George Hallenbeck, near his jogging route; and Mel Ash in the mausoleum, where Mary Kay now joined him.

The interment was private. A bronze plaque spoke of "her God-given mission" and "inspiring thousands of women around the world," wording she had approved long before.

Her memorial service was announced for Wednesday, November 28, at 2:00 p.m. at Park Cities Baptist Church.

When the day came, the weather could not have been worse. Through the night, freezing rain slicked roads. Through the morning, sleet alternated with snow. Skies were dark. Driving was impossible. Pink Cadillacs arrived anyway. News vans got to the church early to stake out stand-ups. Company-chartered buses ferried NSDs from company-reserved rooms at the DoubleTree. Employees, including the pink-robed Mary Kay Choir, rode company buses from the pink headquarters in Addison.

Inside, the nave of Park Cities looked like the setting for a sales crusade. Its sanctuary was pink, its rafters inscribed with the kinds of buoyant Bible verses that Mary Kay might have worked into one of her talks. "For by grace are ye saved through faith: It is the gift of God." "Serve the Lord with gladness: Come before His presence with singing." Poster-size portraits of Mary Kay—head tilted to the side, platinum wig, ivory suit, white diamonds—were placed near entrance and pulpit. A string orchestra, a grand piano, and the black-robed Park Cities choir filled the front of the church, which was banked in ferns and flower arrangements.

Richard, Ben, and Ben's wife sat in the front pew. Arrayed around them were grandchildren and great-grandchildren. Next came the honorary daughters, Mary Kay's 150 NSDs, who had been FedExed invitations to the memorial and the NSD reception to follow. All had traveled at their own expense. Many wore pink. Honoring her mentor with one diamond bumblebee, an NSD bracelet, two rings, and a mink, Pamela Shaw later wrote, "Everything I wore, she either had given me or I had bought with Mary Kay money." Afterward, several would ad-

Richard Rogers speaking at the Park Cities Baptist memorial.

journ to Neiman Marcus for stress-release shopping in their mentor's memory.

Hundreds of long-tenured employees, including former personal assistants Jennifer Cook and Erma Thomson, filled other pews. With them were representatives of Dallas's old guard, including real estate mogul Ebby Halliday and Crowley's son, Don Carter.

Bad weather or not, weekday or no, this was an event to honor Mary Kay; the service started on time. The Park Cities pastor spoke first, followed by Reverend Robert Halsey, a Methodist minister who did not meet Mary Kay until after her stroke. "She was a saint," said Halsey, tearing up as he talked about bringing his youth choir to visit the Round House. Richard spoke next. "She believed anyone could be successful in life with enough encouragement and praise," he said. "I know for sure she practiced that belief on me."

Looking rich, fit, and twenty years younger than she could possibly be, Dalene White, consultant number one, went next. White reminisced about the company's first Christmas party, when she arrived early to see a wigless Mary Kay in housecoat and slippers. That got a laugh. She got another laugh when she talked about her old friend's compulsions for dyeing shoes and clipping coupons, adding, "Greasy hamburgers and Mexican food took precedence any day over a gourmet meal."

Next came Rena Tarbet, an NSD with a reputation as one of the company's best speakers. Tarbet was known for wringing emotion from her audience. Today was no different. She spoke of how she and Mary Kay cried together over Tarbet's mastectomies, then cried again over the death of Mary Kay's daughter. Tarbet got her laugh when she reminded them of the time Mary Kay's skirt fell off at Seminar. "Well, you've seen it all," said Mary Kay.

Grandson Ryan Rogers spoke last, telling anecdotes from his childhood and assuring everyone that the public Mary Kay and the private Mary Kay were one and the same.

As hymns, Mary Kay had selected "It Is Well with My Soul," "Well Done, My Child," "Amazing Grace," and "How Great Thou Art." The company choir sang a setting of "On Silver Wings" that used a recording of Mary Kay speaking the verse. After benediction, the service wound up with three of her favorites: "My Way," "Onward, Christian Soldiers," and, as recessional, "I've Got That Joy, Joy, Joy, Joy," the old Sunday school round that had been the source for "I've Got That Mary Kay Enthusiasm." As it was sung, company veterans joined in and clapped along.

The next year, her company posted record profits.

During the worldwide recession of 2002, wholesale climbed to $1.6 billion. In a U.S. hard-hit by the September 11 attacks and the collapse of the dot-com bubble, business flourished. In Argentina, the Argentine Great Depression pushed sales up 15 percent. Even when distribution logistics condensed thirty-seven international markets to thirty-three, the worldwide consultant count climbed to 900,000. Russia was booming. So was China.

And Mary Kay was back as a cultural icon. Now fair game in ways that she had not been as an octogenarian stroke victim, she became the heroine of CBS's high-camp *Hell on Heels: The Battle of Mary Kay*, which opened with a *Citizen Kane*–style montage that included wrinkled lips whispering, "Rosebud." As a tall, slim, and reclusive Mary Kay, Oscar winner Shirley MacLaine tossed and turned inside her Pink Palace boudoir, her irreclaimable Rosebud revealed to be a lipstick shade. In the next montage, MacLaine delivered the Mary Kay-ism "I go to bed every night as Elizabeth Taylor and I wake up as Charles de Gaulle," while sequin-clad chorus boys curvetted across the Seminar stage and an emcee belted, "Put on your makeup and wake up to who you can be!" *The Dallas Morning News* pronounced *Hell on Heels* "a big pink valentine to Mary Kay."

Once again, direct selling ran opposite or, as analysts liked to say, "countercyclical" to the rest of the economy. Once again, women were latching on to party-plan selling. Companies old and new profited from parties for crafts, clothes, candles, sex toys, jewelry, wine, and anything else that could be sold from someone's living room. Billionaire Warren Buffett made headlines when Berkshire Hathaway paid a reported $900 million for Pampered Chef, a party-plan seller founded by another mother frustrated in her search for work with flexible hours. Press coverage of the trend usually began by questioning whether direct selling was still relevant and finding that it was, particularly for women. Teachers were still a gold mine.

Reporting the surge in party-plan selling, *The New York Times* interviewed a working mom who explained that she had quit her position as partner in a consulting firm because long workdays kept her from her children. Whereupon she started selling Shaklee. In affluent suburbs

On the company's fortieth anniversary in 2003, Mattel released a limited-edition "Mary Kay Star Consultant Barbie," complete with red jacket and Ladder of Success pin.

north of New York City, the *Times* found "four Mary Kay representatives who are successful enough to drive the company's signature pink Cadillac" among 920 Mary Kay consultants in Westchester County.

A few firms had faded away after the departure of their quirky, charismatic founders. World Gift closed soon after Dick Kelly sold the business and retired. After his death in 1999, the $1 billion empire that Dave Longaberger built on collectible baskets was sold and resold while women who had been counting on collectible baskets to fund their retirements watched that dream die. "Big Basket," Longaberger's seven-story mimetic headquarters, stood empty for years before being bought by a hotelier with plans to make it a luxury destination, only to be foiled by COVID-19 and the market for luxury tourism in central Ohio.

Others in the old guard seemed headed the way of the tea wagons. Stanley Home Products had become StanHome and merged with Enesco, a giftware company, before becoming a subsidiary of erstwhile nemesis Fuller Brush. After selling BeautiControl to Tupperware, Dick Heath spent four years as a Tupperware executive, then did three years as CEO of Home Interiors before that company closed.

For a while, Avon made money in spite of itself. In 1999, "the company for women" had named its first female CEO. Not long after, Avon tried another end run around Avon ladies by launching beComing, a brand aimed at brick-and-mortar stores like Sears and JCPenney; management was confident that Avon ladies would cross-promote the new line without compensation.

Meanwhile, Mary Kay Inc. doubled down on the internet. By 2003, the company claimed that 85 percent of its revenues originated with the online sales of one million consultants spread over thirty-three (or, depending on the month, thirty-four) markets. Sales in foreign markets continued to rise, sign of a soon-to-come day when the company would be more or less evenly divided between North America, Latin America, Europe, and the Asia-Pacific. As Ryan later explained: "We've seen the value of the business opportunity play out in emerging markets where the standard of living isn't as great as the U.S." Saluting four years of record results and the company's fortieth anniversary, fifty-three thousand Seminar attendees, including flag-waving foreign directors, sang "We Are the World," changing its lyrics to "We are the world, we are the women."

Global expansion notwithstanding, the company remained as full of totems and traditions as ever. Audio and video of Mary Kay played every day of every Seminar. An NSD introduced every Awards Night with Mary Kay's line "Are you ready for the most exciting night of your life?" and got the same auditorium-shaking affirmation. Mary Kay's long-departed and ill-tempered fur person Gigi was commemorated as both Christmas ornament and piggy bank. A heart-shaped pink tub at company headquarters ensured DIQs would still have their good-luck photo op.

Appropriating buzzy phrases like *social selling*, *social commerce*, and *social sharing*, the company launched digital gizmos galore: virtual makeovers, virtual catalogs, QR codes linked to videos, online wish lists. Most were not much used until the COVID-19 pandemic put a pause on beauty shows. When that happened, the company came up with a $30 digital-only starter kit and added more apps. Halfway through shutdown, it opened Suite 13, a three-dimensional "showroom" designed for the virtual reality headsets that almost nobody owned yet. Two years of Seminars were conducted virtually. Mary Kay ladies tweeted, posted on Facebook, pinned on Pinterest, uploaded tutorials to YouTube and Instagram, and went about their business by scrolling touchscreens.

The internet also accelerated a backlash.

The company became a flashpoint for people fed up with direct selling. Anti–Mary Kay chat rooms, threads, blogs, Facebook pages, and YouTube videos abounded. Liquidator sites and eBay vendors dumped product at a discount. Trolls coined *hunbot* and *Kaybot* for direct sellers who started conversations with "Hun, let me tell you about . . ." Former consultants sounded off about absurd amounts of work. They complained about pressure to invest in inventory.

Chief among them was ex-consultant Tracy Coenen, who began her *Mary Kay Sucks* blog in 2006 and, four months later, rebranded it as the website *Pink Truth*. Under pseudonyms like "SuzyQ" and "Raisinberry," ex-consultants contributed commentary on all matters Mary Kay, from being conditioned by a dysfunctional family ("Anybody who throws you a bone gets strong loyalty and support") to directors' suits ("a weird plaid that looks like upholstery"). Husbands griped. "I figured, since signing up with a starter kit didn't really cost that much ($100) and we had recently moved about three hours away from our hometown (because of my job), and she was staying home and taking care of our young boys, I thought it would [*sic*] probably wouldn't be 'that bad' for her to get out and do something," wrote one. Coenen, who had once aspired to a career as a prison warden, published news of NSD comings and goings, company contracts, and links to downloads of *Applause*.

That pushed her site to the top of Google searches and made it a source for legacy media, notably "The Pink Pyramid Scheme: How Mary Kay Cosmetics Preys on Desperate Housewives," a 2012 cover story in *Harper's Magazine* that ticked through seven thousand words of decades-old complaints about direct selling. Using a first-person narrative, Virginia Sole-Smith described directors dangling dreams of pink cars and lucrative careers while strong-arming recruits into bigger and bigger inventory buys. One interviewee, sourced through *Pink Truth*, accumulated "over $15,000 in credit card debt and a basement full of unsold products," which she sold at a loss or threw away before getting a divorce attributed to "the whole Mary Kay thing." The story noted the company's inability to guarantee how much a consultant could earn, expenses that consultants assumed as independent contractors, the infinitesimal percentage who made six-figure incomes, and a business model that made recruiting a lucrative downline the only sure way to make big money. Mary Kay was no longer around to send a thank-you note.

Similar investigations followed, most citing *Harper's*, *Pink Truth*, or both. MARY KAY PREYS ON WOMEN made a killer headline on forbes.com, the online edition of a magazine that had deified Mary Kay during her lifetime. On National Public Radio, a former consultant complained about the social pressures inherent in party-plan selling and the pressure to overbuy inventory; as a counterpoint, the company's head of compliance reminded the audience that Mary Kay Inc. had a 90 percent buyback policy for unsold inventory, a fact unreported in most of the exposés.

Backlash or no, direct selling wasn't going anywhere.

In 2012, the year that mainstream media did most of its Mary Kay exposés, direct selling in the U.S. climbed to $31.6 billion, a 5.9 percent increase over the previous year. Roughly three quarters of those sellers were women.

Best efforts to the contrary, Avon was back to selling through Avon ladies when beComing became another write-off, initiating a decades-long decline during which the onetime Wall Street darling was divided, sold, and resold. While that was going on, the rest of the category boomed. Aspirants to Avon's former preeminence included Arbonne from Switzerland and Natura from Brazil. Utah-based Nu Skin published annual reports with billion-dollar sales figures and record earnings per share. Using direct selling to sign up customers for electricity, natural gas, and solar energy, Texas-based Ambit Energy grew 20,000 percent in its first three years. Superintending a scented-wax empire from a suburb of Boise, Idaho, Scentsy saw year-over-year increases of more than 100 percent. LuLaRoe took its polyester leggings business from zero to $2.3 billion in four years. Jewelry maker Stella & Dot could measure revenues in the hundreds of millions before it was a decade old. Sounding like so many moms before her, a Stella & Dot stylist, then reigning as Mrs. America, said, "It really gives the flexibility to work more from home and be closer to my children all while supplementing a great income to support my family."

Outselling them all was "wellness," a catchall category for supplements, weight-loss regimens, and the kind of cure-alls that Nutri-Bio and Abundavita once peddled. As before, outrageous claims produced outrageous profits. Just as the Mary Kay media storm was dying down, activist investor William Ackman made a billion-dollar bet against Herbalife, denouncing the MLM as "the best-managed pyramid scheme in the world." When the ensuing stink subsided, nearly four years later, twenty million Americans were involved in MLMs and a former MLM owner was president. Herbalife went about its business while billionaires who had been bullish on its stock, including Carl Icahn, made a bundle. Ackman moved on.

As years passed, less outrage was directed at Mary Kay and her company. In 2015, on the Mary Kay–themed *20/20* exposé "The Secrets of the Sell," ABC News reporter Rebecca Jarvis interviewed three young, chipper, Cadillac-driving consultants, then interviewed four less-than-chipper former consultants. One of the ex-consultants complained: "I may have to go to eight, nine, ten people before I get somebody who agrees to have a skin care class."

In the end, *20/20* went the way of *60 Minutes* before it. The segment wrapped with smiling women in sparkly gowns shimmying on the Seminar stage as Jarvis's voice-over concluded: "You don't have to see much of Mary Kay Seminar to see that these women are getting a lot more out of the experience than commissions: the camaraderie, the fun, and, for some, the pink Cadillac. How hard would you be willing to work for all that? That's for you to decide."

When the company made news, it was often for beneficence. While the effective altruism movement swept Silicon Valley, Mary Kay Inc. never wavered in its allegiance to the movement's spiritual forebearer: Arthur Frederick Sheldon's "He Profits Most Who Serves Best." The Mary Kay Ash Foundation distributed over $1 million a year in grants for cancer research, pointedly favoring projects led by women. Funds went to women's shelters, support of the National Domestic Violence Hotline, and campaigns against digital dating abuse. Acreage was reforested. Landfill eliminated. Renewable energy powered the headquarters, factory, and distribution center. A social media campaign nudged girls toward careers in math, science, and technology. Mary Kay China sponsored programs that repaired cleft palates, financed scholarships for women, and underwrote collectives for female entrepreneurs.

In the decade after the exposés, the name of Mary Kay Ash went back to being shorthand for pluck and perseverance; her story made for compulsory inclusion in collections like *Dreams That Built America*, *Entrepreneurs Who Changed History*, and *Great Second Acts*. In the universe of how-to and self-improvement publishing, it seemed impossible to put out a book like *Secrets of Superstar Sales Pros* or *Reaching Beyond Excellence* without at least one quotation from Mary Kay. *The Barefoot Executive*, written by a mother who said she was forced to become an entrepreneur because she was unable to find a job with flexible hours, quoted Mary Kay Ash alongside Leonardo da Vinci.

Marketing and management primers alike paid tribute. When the Wharton School published *Lasting Leadership: What You Can Learn from the Top 25 Business People of Our Times*, Oprah Winfrey and Mary Kay were the only women to make the cut. *The Harvard Business Review* ranked her as a "superboss" alongside the likes of Ralph Lauren and George Lucas. Business schools cranked out case studies that sounded like they came from the company's PR department; Harvard Business School titled one

"Mary Kay Inc.: Enriching Women's Lives While Embracing Change" and introduced it with the Mary Kay-ism "When you reach an obstacle, turn it into an opportunity."

At last, in 2023, Ryan Rogers became president and CEO of the company founded by his father and grandmother, just as Mary Kay had told him he would. *Forbes* described the company he took over as being "in more than forty markets" with a worldwide sales force exceeding 3.5 million.

As the company celebrated its sixtieth year, women in the U.S. averaged eighty-two cents for every dollar earned by men.

ACKNOWLEDGMENTS

This biography got its start over twenty-five years ago, when I was researching Mary Kay Ash and her company for my first book, *Color Stories: Behind the Scenes of America's Billion-Dollar Beauty Industry.*

As I learned more about her, I found that Mary Kay lived a life intertwined with history that had been largely ignored. Integrating that history would present the perfect opportunity for nontraditional storytelling: borrowing from Studs Terkel, I wanted to let her life be defined by its intersection with the lives around her. And, on a technical level, Mary Kay had a story begging to be written in vernacular language that could close the distance between subject and reader.

Taking me at my word, Nancy Milford, executive director of the Leon Levy Center for Biography, awarded me a Leon Levy Fellowship for the 2009–2010 academic year. I used the appointment, funds, and time to contact as many of Mary Kay's contemporaries as I could. In the end, I did so many interviews—I quit counting after the first two hundred—that I can't list them all. Some subjects sent short but revelatory texts or emails. Others were generous with documentary evidence and multiple interviews. Among my key sources: Georgia Hall Baird; Gloria Mayfield Banks; Cliff Barrows; Edward L. Berthold; Bill Besse; Lee and Wanda Bower; Berke Breathed; Jackie Brown; Jennifer Bickel

Cook; Victor Costa; Thomas Damigella; Doretha Dingler; Judith Eckman Duke; Evalyn (Mrs. LeNaire) Eckman; Robert "Bob" Eckman; Mr. and Mrs. George Foristall; Fred Goodwin Sr.; Theodore R. "Ted" Hallenbeck, PhD; Ebby Halliday; Jinger Heath; Craig Hogan; Joyce Jutkus; Richard E. "Dick" Kelly; Denise Kucharski; Elizabeth "Libby" Weatherford Lee; Joan B. Marcus; Frank L. Meier; Jennifer Skemp O'Grady; Arthur Pearson; Ken Pearson; Audrey Peel; Homer Perkins; Brian Regensburger; Michael Regensburger; Gladys Reyes; Evan Richardson; Paulette Flowers Schwoebel; Bob Shook; Anne Sloan; Dan Squires; Barbara Sunden; Erma Thomson; Kathy Villarreal; and Don Zapp.

When other subjects refused interviews, their reasons often proved equally informative, a list that includes Judith and Mel Einsidler, Leona Rogers, and Pamela Shaw. "Mary Kay Representative Number One," Dalene White, invited me to stay at her ranch but, before I was able to accept, signed a nondisclosure agreement with Mary Kay Inc. Nevertheless, I benefited from her off-the-record advice about book titles and sources.

At MECA in Houston, Armando Silva, Emily Zermeno, and Alice Valdez gave me a private tour of the former Dow School, sharing what they had learned during renovations of the building. Nova Lemons tracked down Dallas documents. Baylor University's Cassy Burleson, PhD, and Marlene S. Neill, PhD, introduced me to Emma Weidmann, who interviewed Maria Matthews.

Writing a book that depends so heavily on public records would have been impossible without help from archivists, librarians, administrators, and other keepers of the flame, a list led by Robert McKean and Victoria L. Connor at Stanley Park of Westfield, Jim Hundemer and Yolanda Sauceda at the Houston Independent School District, Paula Bosse at the Dallas Public Library, Elaine Sokolowski at the Peoria Public Library, Michael Wassmer of the Mary Kay Corporate Communications Team, Paula Robinson at Duke University's Fuqua School of Business Library, Lisa May at the Archdiocese of Galveston–Houston, Brittany Rose at the Texas Baptists Historical Collection, Amy Robinson at the Direct Selling Association, librarians at John H.

Reagan High School (now Heights High School), Ellen Holt-Werle at the DeWitt Wallace Library at Macalester College, Steve Greenberg at Coe College, Peter Weis at Northfield Mount Hermon School, Tom Nguyen at the Old Sixth Ward Neighborhood Association, AnnElise Golden at Harris County Archives, Diana Treviño at St. Joseph Catholic Church in Houston, Jim Sigmund and Jane Ledbetter at the Cypress Historical Society, members of the Tyrone Area Historical Society, Norma Chaires at New York University's Archives Collection, Debra P. Brookhart at the American Legion Library Division, Kate Hanson Plass at Longfellow House, Sara Wilson at the University of North Texas Oral History Program, Emily Hughes and John Goplen at Watkins 1868, Linda Gross at the Hagley Museum and Library, Peter Liebhold at the National Museum of American History at the Smithsonian Institution, and Kay Peterson at the Archives Center of the Smithsonian Institution.

Very early in this project, I benefited from reading "The Peddler's Progress," the PhD dissertation of Walter Friedman, later published by Harvard University Press as *Birth of a Salesman*; Friedman was the first to show how selling's can-do culture consolidated the culture at-large. Likewise, I had the advantage of watching Laurie Kahn's *Tupperware!* on PBS's "American Experience," which told a story that was greater than the sum of its parts.

During my year at the Leon Levy Center, I was grateful for the kindness of Shelby White, cofounder David Nasaw, director Brenda Wineapple, and my fellow fellows: Vanda Krefft, John Matteson, Wendy Lesser, Helen Decker, and Lars Kokkonen. Afterward, I benefited from an extended stay at the Wertheim Study, thanks to Jay Barksdale at the New York Public Library.

Heading the list of friends who lent their time and expertise: Penny Clement, who went to Texas and tracked down records that nobody else could find, and her husband, Rob Clement, who read an early draft and gave me a businessman's perspective. CaSandra Cossey, Evelyn Cossey, Natasha Simon, Nadine Stewart, Diana Liu, Marylue Durff, George Haywood, and Ann Krcik gave opinions, edits, and emotional support.

Xioadan Zhang introduced me to Ting Yuan, who explained how Mary Kay is regarded in China, especially among college women. A day job at Avon headquarters in Manhattan helped me understand differences among direct selling's corporate cultures. An apartment in Hell's Kitchen put me in proximity to the Lloyd Sealy Library at John Jay College, with its unrivaled collection of works relating to frauds, swindles, and Ponzi schemes.

In 2012, my agent, David McCormick, pitched this book to Rick Kot, executive editor at Viking Penguin. When the project then proceeded to hit one delay after another—a long list that includes COVID-19—both men practiced their own versions of "praise forward to success" to get me to the finish line. After Rick retired, Camille LeBlanc inherited the project and proceeded to roll up her sleeves and put publication back on track. I'm grateful to Camille and her colleagues—copy editor Hilary Roberts, production editor Nicole Celli, book designer Daniel Lagin, publicist Yuleza Negron, associate publisher Kate Stark, subsidiary rights manager Bridget Gilleran, marketer Chantal Canales—for going above and beyond the call of duty. Elizabeth Yaffe solved the problem of a tricky book title with her genius cover design.

As this book goes to press, direct selling and multilevel marketing are once again inspiring outrage. Much is being written about direct selling, much of it has an agenda, and much of it is inaccurate. Here, I hope you find work that is neither pro nor con.

At face value, this is the first biography of an icon who founded an outrageously successful and secretive business with its own language, manners, and customs. Beyond that, this book also offers a first look at the golden age of direct sales, a forgotten chapter of American history. Finally, it's a Texan tall tale of second chances and self-invention, a look at the twentieth century's Land of Opportunity and its great American Dream.

NOTES

INTRODUCTION: SEMINAR, JULY 1992

1 **By 1969, she is:** Mike Antich, "General Motors Celebrates 50 Years with Mary Kay," *Automotive Fleet*, April 1, 2019, automotive-fleet.com/328408/pink-is-the-color-of-success-trophies-on-wheels.

1 **Dolly Parton has the script:** Mark Caro, "Gaudy Appearance Is for Fun; Dolly Is for Real," *Omaha World-Herald*, April 12, 1992.

2 **Magazine covers ask:** Cover, *Ladies' Home Journal*, June 1991; Mary Kay Ash, *Mary Kay* (Harper & Row, 1981), 83.

2 **She runs sales contests:** Morris L. Mayer, *Direct Selling in the United States: A Commentary and Oral History* (Direct Selling Education Foundation, 1996), 36.

2 **While Macy's files:** Daniel Gross and the editors of *Forbes*, *Forbes Greatest Business Stories of All Time* (John Wiley & Sons, 1996), 242; "The Fortune 500 Includes 14 Area Companies," *Fort Worth Star-Telegram*, March 31, 1993 (based on 1992 sales).

2 **she celebrates these:** Margaria Fichtner, "The Miracle of Mary Kay," *Miami Herald*, October 3, 1982; "Mary Kay: The Cosmetic Empire," posted September 13, 2024, by Biography, YouTube, 45 min., 3 sec., youtube.com/watch?v=ZoiFiicfo30.

2 **This morning, well before:** "Mary Kay Seminar Soars to a Record 32,000," Southwest News Wire, July 20, 1992.

2 **about 70 percent:** Wendy Zellner, "Mary Kay Is Singing I Feel Pretty," Bloomberg News Service, December 2, 1991.

3 **average sales of $2,400 a year:** John A. Quelch and Nathalie Laidler, "Mary Kay Cosmetics, Inc.: Asian Market Entry," Harvard Business School Case 9-594-023, 2009.

3 **they will watch women:** "Mary Kay Seminar Soars to a Record 32,000."

3 **"When Mary Kay comes out":** Barbara Sunden, interview with the author, June 3, 2024.

3 **At seventy-four, she still looks:** *60 Minutes*, "The Pink Panther," aired October 28, 1979, on CBS, cbsnews.com/video/the-pink-panther.

4 **"She is not the rah-rah":** Maria Matthews, interview with Emma Weidmann, May 25, 2024.

CHAPTER ONE: THE CHANGE-OF-LIFE BABY

5 **Younger than her closest sibling:** On the certificate of live birth filed in 1918, Lula gives her age as thirty-four at the time of the birth; on a birth certificate filed in 1943, she lists it as thirty-two.

5 **Scheme after scheme:** "County Court," *Beaumont Enterprise,* January 8, 1904; "Garnishments," *Beaumont Enterprise,* January 2, 1905.

6 **Headed by an Ohio-born:** *Directory of the City of Houston 1913* (Morrison & Fourmy, 1913).

6 **Thus far, its greatest success:** Houston Hot Well, "Special Chicken Dinner Every Sunday 50¢," *Houston Post,* June 20, 1915. A news article mentions that "Grand Secretary Gilbert was entertained . . . and a chicken dinner at the Houston Hot Well hotel"; "U.C.T. Officers Conferred," *Houston Post,* July 18, 1916.

6 **The plan was for Lula:** Houston Hot Well had at least two other married couples before the Wagners' arrival. See "Wanted—Man and Wife to Take Charge of Houston Hot Well Hotel," classified ad, *Houston Post,* February 5, 1912; "Houston Hot Well Hotel: Hostelry Is Gaining in Popularity," *Houston Post,* September 19, 1915.

6 **Texas was dotted:** Janet Valenza, *Taking the Waters in Texas* (University of Texas Press, 2000).

7 **Baseball teams came:** Monte Cely, "Early 20th Century Major League Baseball in a Central Texas Town," PowerPoint presentation, January 2009.

7 **In Cypress, Connable:** Gregg Eckhardt, "The Hot Wells Hotel and Spa," Edwards Aquifer Website, accessed April 13, 2011, edwardsaquifer.net/hotwells.html.

7 **French filmmaker Gaston Méliès:** Frank Thompson, *The Star Film Ranch: Texas' First Picture Show* (Republic of Texas Press, 1996).

7 **teetotaling Baptist burgs:** *The Heritage of North Harris County* (North Harris County Branch, American Association of University Women, 1977).

7 **Forecasting a future:** Houston Hot Well, "Houston's Pleasure and Health Resort," *Houston Post,* July 31, 1910.

8 **the chief adornment:** Mary Kay, "Mary Kay as a baby," Facebook, May 18, 2010, facebook.com/photo?fbid=395570037170&set=a.395569877170&locale=gl_ES.

10 **Later, Mary Kay's father:** 'Mary Kathlyn Wagner' (1943). *Certified copy of birth certificate for Mary Kathlyn Wagner, 16 August 1943.* Application number 24727. Harris County, Texas. On Mary Kay's corrected birth certificate, filed in 1943, Lula gives his birthplace as Missouri and changes his name to Edward Alexander Wagner.

10 **Alex and his brother Conrad:** John Edward Weems, "The Great Galveston Hurricane of 1900: A Historical Overview," *Handbook of Texas,* 1952, updated March 15, 2016, tshaonline.org/handbook/entries/galveston-hurricane-of-1900.

10 **The two were married:** "Marriages," *Beaumont Enterprise,* January 4, 1902. Both of Mary Kay's parents were known to give different ages on different occasions. On Cecil's birth certificate, Lula lists her age as nineteen. 'Cecil DeWitt Wagner' (1905). *Certified copy of birth certificate for Cecil DeWitt Wagner, 11 May, 1905.* Application number 941711. Jefferson County, Texas.

10 **Cecil DeWitt followed:** 'Cecil DeWitt Wagner.' *Birth certificate.*

10 **After they had been married:** May 15, 1904, per archdiocese records. Lisa May, director of archives and records, Archdiocese of Galveston-Houston, email to the author, June 2, 2014.

11 **Lula's father had been:** "County Democratic Convention," *Liberty Vindicator,* June 22, 1900.

11 **Even getting elementary schools:** Frederick Eby, *The Development of Education in Texas* (Macmillan, 1925), 169.

11 **But no one went:** Eby, *Development of Education in Texas,* 224, 230–31.

11 **The teachers were homesick:** "Memorable Moments of Houston Retired Teachers Bicentennial Year," unpublished oral histories, Houston Independent School District Professional Library.

12 **In Cypress, Mary Kay's sisters:** "History of CFISD," Cypress-Fairbanks Independent School District, accessed December 4, 2009, cfisd.net/aboutour/history.html.

12 **There, a lone teacher:** John Bernard Sullivan, "A Historical Perspective of the Cypress-Fairbanks Independent School District, Houston, Texas, 1884–1984" (PhD diss., Southern Illinois University, 1988), 37.

13 **Mary Kay told people:** Gaylon Finckley Hecker and Marianne Odom, *Growing Up in the Lone Star State* (University of Texas Press, 2021), 32.

13 **If people confused:** Mary Kay made it a policy never to correct the press.

13 **In the fall, Spanish influenza:** "Drastic Action to Halt Epidemic," *Houston Post,* October 10, 1918.

13 **Even Juergen's Saloon:** "Juergen's Hall Community Center," Clio, accessed May 29, 2025, theclio.com/entry/ 80143. Juergen's business survived as a general store and meeting place.

13 **In a legal feud:** The Hot Well Development Company had long been fighting on multiple legal fronts. See, for example, "Local Courts," *Houston Post*, December 1, 1917; "Ninth Civil Appeals," *Houston Post*, April 25, 1919; National Reporter System, *The Southwestern Reporter*, vol. 211 (West Publishing Co., 1919), 960–68.

14 **In January of 1920:** United States Bureau of the Census, *Fourteenth Census of the United States: 1920* (U.S. Government Printing Office, 1922).

14 **Soon after she arrived:** 'James D. Cross' (1919). *Certified copy of death certificate for James D. Cross, 21 October 1919.* Application number 30151. Liberty County, Texas.

14 **Then Great-Grandmother Cross:** 'Julia Cross' (1919). *Form for use of widows of soldiers who are in indigent circumstances, 17 November 1919.* Application number 36276. State of Texas.

14 **Cotton prices plunged:** "Table 9, American Upland Cotton: Prices Received by Farmers," in *Prices Received by Farmers, United States 1908–55* (U.S. Department of Agriculture, 1956).

14 **That year, as America's population:** United States Census Bureau, "History of Urban and Rural Areas," last revised September 3, 2024, census.gov/about/history/historical-censuses-and-surveys/census-programs-surveys/geography/urban-and-rural-areas.html.

CHAPTER TWO: "YOU CAN DO IT!"

15 **Awash in oil money:** *High Spots in Houston Public Schools* (Board of Education, November 24, 1927).

16 **Houston became known:** Sharon G. Larkin, "Texas Central Railroad" unpublished demographic study, 1986, Houston Independent School District Archives.

16 **Other fathers had all kinds:** City directories for 1920–33: Morrison & Fourmy Co., *Houston City Directory* (R. L. Polk); United States Bureau of the Census, *Fourteenth Census of the United States: 1920* (U.S. Government Printing Office, 1922).

16 **Peck Kelley, still years:** Martin Donell Kohout, "The Life and Legacy of Jazz Pianist Peck Kelley," *Handbook of Texas*, December 5, 2006, updated November 17, 2020, tshaonline.org/handbook/online/articles/fke80.

16 **Mexicans were starting:** United States Bureau of the Census, *Fourteenth Census of the United States: 1920*, Houston Ward 6, Harris, Texas, roll T625_1815, page 10B, enumeration district 96.

16 **end of the Wagners' block:** 'Old Sixth Ward Historic District' (1977). *National Register of Historic Places nomination form, 23 March 1977.* United States Department of the Interior, National Park Service.

16 **Alex agreed to pay:** Old Sixth Ward Neighborhood Association, "2111 Kane; Lot 10, Block 407," accessed April 12, 2013, drive.google.com/file/d/1cjmSuEUQ3_ykfo634kOMgbVGeYtTbX-x/view.

16 **Built in 1890:** '2111 Kane Street, Old Sixth Ward' (2017). *Certificate of appropriateness, 23 February 2017.* HPO file number 170224. Houston Archaeological & Historical Commission. houstontx.gov/planning/Commissions/docs_pdfs/hahc/reports_ACTION_2017/FebAction/B8_2111_Kane_Alt_Addition_ACTION.pdf; '2111 Kane Street, Old Sixth Ward' (2021). *Certificate of appropriateness, 17 November 2021.* HPO file number 2021_0315. Houston Archaeological & Historical Commission. houstontx.gov/planning/Commissions/docs_pdfs/D10_2111_Kane_St_Solar_Panels_Final.pdf.

18 **Daisy, turning thirteen:** City directories for 1920–33: Morrison & Fourmy Co., *Houston City Directory.*

18 **His years at the Hot Well Hotel:** "Leased Hot Wells Hotel," *Houston Post*, April 8, 1917. Wagner was known to bill himself as the man in charge of the enterprise.

18 **He would run:** Morrison & Fourmy Co., *Houston City Directory*, 102.

19 **the divorce granted in April of 1926:** "Fifty-Fifth District Court," *Houston Chronicle*, April 18, 1926.

19 **her parent remarried:** "Marriage Licenses," *Houston Chronicle*, June 24, 1928.

19 **Mary Kay would say that:** John C. Henderson, "The History of Sanatorium, Texas: A Tuberculosis Treatment Center," *Handbook of Texas*, 1976, updated March 30, 2020, tshaonline.org/handbook/entries/sanatorium-tx.

19 **Even in the 1920s:** Henderson, "History of Sanatorium."

19 **To this day:** I heard this rumor repeatedly during 2009 when I walked the Sixth Ward and interviewed locals, and I later heard it in off-the-record interviews; however, I was unable to find any corroborating evidence.

19 **She kept her job:** City directories for 1920–33: Morrison & Fourmy Co., *Houston City Directory.*
20 **would be no more proprietorships:** "Mary Kay Ash—1978 Horatio Alger Award Recipient," posted September 21, 2015, by Horatio Alger Association, YouTube, 5 min., 5 sec., youtube.com/watch?v=hMu5hS7E2Jw.
20 **sometimes pile goods:** Gaylon Finckley Hecker and Marianne Odom, *Growing Up in the Lone Star State* (University of Texas Press, 2021), 34.
20 **With a mother working:** When sources refer to Lula's fourteen-hour days, they are counting only the hours that the café was open. Mary Kay repeatedly described her mother as leaving for work at 5:00 a.m. and returning at 9:00 p.m. See Hecker and Odom, *Growing Up*, 35.
21 **In 1994, a company biopic:** Allen Mondell and Cynthia Salzman Mondell, *Thinking Like a Woman* (Mary Kay Inc., 1994).
21 **Lula told the little girl:** Mary Kay Ash, *Mary Kay* (Harper & Row, 1981), 3.
21 **A childhood friend said:** Mondell and Mondell, *Thinking Like a Woman.*
21 **Hell-bent on catching up:** The city issued bonds for $3 million in 1924, $4 million in 1926, and another $4 million in 1928. See William A. Young Jr., *History of the Houston Public Schools, 1836–1965* (Gulf School Research Development Association, 1968), 39; *A Review of Work and Progress in the Houston Schools, Part I: The Building Program of the Houston Independent School District (1924–1930)* (Board of Education of the Houston Independent School District, 1937), 4.
23 **An ambitious principal:** It did not remain free. By 1932, the charge for kindergarten at Dow was three dollars for five-year-olds, four dollars for underage children.
23 **The resulting twenty-six rooms:** *Review of Work and Progress*, 22–23.
23 **The old teachers' entrance:** Observations of the author, visit to MECA (Multicultural Education and Counseling Through the Arts) in the former Dow School, December 9, 2009.
23 **Houston's schools had initiated:** *Review of Work and Progress*, 27.
23 **"the habit of success":** *High Spots*, 17.
24 **An only child:** Don Zapp, interview with the author, November 19, 2009; Dorothy's brother Don was not born until the Zapps moved out of the Sixth Ward.
24 **Dorothy's mother played:** Ash, *Mary Kay*, 13.
24 **"Mary Kay's circumstances":** Mr. and Mrs. George Forristall, interview with the author, January 19, 2010.
25 **In old age:** Ash, *Mary Kay*, 13–14.
25 **In Mary Kay's mind:** "Mary Kay: The Cosmetic Empire," posted September 13, 2024, by Biography, YouTube, 45 mins., 3 sec., youtube.com/watch?v=ZoiFiicfo30.
25 **Sat at the lunch counter:** Ash, *Mary Kay*, 2–3.
25 **As her company became:** "Mary Kay: The Cosmetic Empire."
26 **the sort of good Christian woman:** Julia Sweeney, "Thanksgiving Is for Family," *Dallas Times Herald*, November 23, 1975.
26 **With the Zapps gone:** Hecker and Odom, *Growing Up*, 35; Ash, *Mary Kay*, 14.
26 **Tillie Bass, an older girl:** Hecker and Odom, *Growing Up*, 37.
26 **as Mary Kay reached:** Robert Willard McAhren, "Making the Nation Safe for Childhood: A History of the Movement for Federal Regulation of Child Labor, 1900–1938" (PhD diss., University of Texas, 1967); Kriste Lindenmeyer, *A Right to Childhood: The U.S. Children's Bureau and Child Welfare, 1912–46* (University of Illinois Press, 1997).
27 **By 1930, the census:** Comparisons of United States Bureau of the Census, *Twelfth Census of the United States: 1900* (U.S. Government Printing Office, 1901); United States Bureau of the Census, *Fourteenth Census of the United States*; United States Bureau of the Census, *Fifteenth Census of the United States: 1930* (U.S. Government Printing Office, 1931–32).
27 **"Probably it is not generally":** Frank M. Black, "The Growth of the Houston High School," unpublished monograph, 1923–24, filed 1969, Houston Independent School District Archives.
28 **Lula got her:** Hecker and Odom, *Growing Up*, 35.
28 **She molded herself:** *Handbook for Principals and Teachers of the Junior and Senior High Schools* (Board of Education of the Houston Independent School District, 1937). The handbook reiterates messages found in multiple *Houston Post* editorials, features, and news stories in 1931–32.
29 **Tributes to Cloverine's curative powers:** Richard and Judy Dockrey Young, eds., *Ozark Tall Tales: Collected from the Oral Tradition* (August House, 1989), 64–65.

29 **But the ingredient most responsible:** This distribution strategy represented instant buyer gratification, since most retailers obligated the buyer to submit proofs of purchase before receiving a premium (e.g., in the second half of the nineteenth century, Babbitt's Best Soap mailed color lithographs upon receipt of soap wrappers).

29 **Mary Kay signed on:** "History of Wilson Chemical Company," Tyrone Area Historical Society, accessed March 17, 2010, tyronehistory.org/faq–WCCo.html.

31 **Mary Kay heard rhetoric:** American Legion, *American Legion School Award (an Educational Activity for Legion Posts)*, brochure giving presentation speeches, 1939.

32 **Begun as a way:** Debra P. Brookhart, American Legion Library Division, email to the author, February 15, 2013.

32 **Mary Kay won her medal:** Bess W. Scott, "Schools: Legion Medals Are Awarded Honors Pupils," *Houston Post*, May 29, 1932.

CHAPTER THREE: CONFIDENCE

33 **In Houston, an education:** Maricruz Garza, Public Information Office, Houston Independent School District, email to the author, December 14, 2009.

33 **The year she was born:** "Views of State Superintendent [Benjamin M.] Baker," *University of Texas Bulletin*, no. 1824 (April 25, 1918): 842.

33 **did not have a freestanding:** Frank M. Black, "The Growth of the Houston High School," unpublished monograph, 1923–24, filed 1969, Houston Independent School District Archives. As early as 1878, the city had a school for boys that charged a four-dollar monthly tuition, putting it beyond the means of anyone who was not already upper-middle class.

34 **Houstonians rebuilt on the site:** *High Spots in Houston Public Schools* (Board of Education, November 24, 1927), 13.

34 **By 1932, over fifty-seven:** [Texas] State Board of Education, *Texas Statewide School Adequacy Survey* (Works Progress Administration, 1937).

35 **That lasted until October:** Convict Record Ledgers, convict no. range B 067401–073300, vol. 1998 /038-165, Texas State Library and Archives Commission, Austin.

35 **Civic boosters advertised:** Anne Sloan and the Houston Heights Association, *Houston Heights* (Arcadia Publishing, 2009), 31.

35 **Boys had the option:** *The Pennant 1933* (Senior Class of John H. Reagan Senior High School, 1933), "Reagan Cadet Corps."

35 **For girls, the counterpart:** Libby Lee, interview with the author, December 26, 2009.

36 **"She worked them pretty hard":** Bob Tutt, "Houston Endowment's Creekmore Dies at 87," *Houston Chronicle*, February 6, 1993.

36 **Red Coat practices:** Lee, interview with the author.

36 **Worn with a flannel skirt:** Anne Sloan, interview with the author, December 21, 2009.

36 **Because the Red Coats:** Lee, interview with the author.

37 **Immaculately turned out:** Betty T. Chapman, "Houston Has Marched to Growing Parade of High School Drill Teams," *Houston Business Journal*, November 12, 2010.

38 **She was there:** "12,000 Attend Shrine Dance," *Houston Post*, February 23, 1933.

40 **Oratorical contests were fiercely:** Robert A. Caro, *The Path to Power* (Alfred A. Knopf, 1982), 206–14.

41 **After years of frenzied growth:** John Bernard Sullivan, "A Historical Perspective of the Cypress-Fairbanks Independent School District, Houston, Texas, 1884–1984" (PhD diss., Southern Illinois University, 1988), 39.

41 **Students blamed the Depression:** Kingsley Davis, *Youth in the Depression* (University of Chicago Press, 1935).

41 **In an autobiography:** Mary Kay Ash, *Mary Kay* (Harper & Row, 1981), 15.

41 **If it had not:** "Makes School Record," *Houston Post*, May 20, 1934.

41 **The daughter of an executive:** "Reagan Red Coats Install," *Houston Post*, May 20, 1934.

41 **A bubbly brunette:** "Popular," *Houston Post*, May 20, 1934.

42 **On Friday night:** "City Graduate Rites Tonight," *Houston Post*, June 1, 1934.

42 **Despite the start:** "1733 [*sic*] Graduate at Exercises," *Houston Post*, June 2, 1934.

CHAPTER FOUR: SELL TEN, GET ONE FREE

45 **Mary Kay called him:** Mary Kay Ash, *Mary Kay* (Harper & Row, 1981), 15.

45 **Mary Kay's exact contemporary:** Libby Lee, interview with the author, December 26, 2009.

46 **People regarded him:** Mr. and Mrs. George Forristall, interview with the author, January 19, 2010.

48 **fifty-one hours a week:** Mary Elizabeth Pidgeon, *Women in the Economy of the United States of America* (U.S. Government Printing Office, 1937), 30–42.

48 **That fall, just before:** "House Belonging to C. B. Hastings Burns on Sunday," *Liberty Vindicator*, November 11, 1936.

48 **a favorite of gamblers, dope dealers, and the vice squad:** "L-Men Visit Buccaneer Grill," *Houston Post*, January 13, 1937; "Man Charged in Wounding at Grill Here," *Houston Chronicle*, March 8, 1937.

48 **The gambler who owned the Grill:** "Dope Dealer Hunted in Spot Slaying of Salibo," *Houston Post*, July 23, 1937.

50 **Most insurance companies:** Ruth Shallcross, *Should Married Women Work?* (National Federation of Business and Professional Women's Clubs, 1940).

50 **Americans agreed that the U.S.:** "The Fortune Quarterly Survey: VI," *Fortune*, October, 1936. To obtain results that would "faithfully duplicate in microcosm the opinions and preferences of the nation's 75,000,000 adults," the magazine commissioned Roper to conduct personal interviews with 4,500 Americans, with each section of the country represented according to population distribution, men and women represented equally, and adults above and below the age of forty represented equally.

50 **A 1937 Department of Labor:** Pidgeon, *Women in the Economy*, 7.

50 **In places like Pennsylvania:** Bureau of Women and Children, *Industrial Home Work in Pennsylvania Under the N.R.A.* (Pennsylvania Department of Labor and Industry, 1935), 1–4.

51 **But everyone knew that women:** "The Salesman's Wife," Edward Bok, *Salesmanship*, November 1916. Trade literature portrayed women as gullible fools.

52 **the early 1930s, a Department:** Pidgeon, *Women in the Economy*, 50.

53 **pews were crammed:** See unpublished multipage statistical tables beginning (before Quarles's tenure) with "Table I: Church Membership and Church Property of Union Baptist Association, Year Ending Sept. 30, 1928" and continuing through "Minutes of the One Hundred and Fifth Annual Session of Union Baptist Association (1945)," compiled by Union Baptist Association; and Brittany Rose, email to the author, November 18, 2010. Although in a 1979 *New York Times* interview Mary Kay recalls Quarles attracting over 900, that did not happen until the early 1940s, when, according to the statistical tables of the Union Baptist Association, Quarles revived membership from its 1938 low of 281.

53 **"The fundamentals of various":** "Executive Memories: My Summer Job," *New York Times*, June 10, 1979.

53 **In a 1995 interview:** "How I Learned to Sell," *D Magazine*, October 1, 1995.

53 **As her prize possessions:** Mrs. Sam Whelchel, "The Family of an Automobile Worker," unpublished manuscript, Folklore Project, Life Histories, 1936–39, U.S. Work Projects Administration, Federal Writers' Project, Library of Congress, Washington, D.C., loc.gov/item/wpalh000568.

54 **"We can do without":** Thomas Chandler Haliburton, *Sam Slick; The Clockmaker* (1835; repr., Philadelphia: T. B. Peterson, 1899), 16.

54 **When Blake came back:** Morris L. Mayer, *Direct Selling in the United States: A Commentary and Oral History* (Direct Selling Education Foundation, 1996), 36.

CHAPTER FIVE: ACRES OF DIAMONDS WITHIN REACH

55 **The Yankee peddler:** Richardson Wright, *Hawkers and Walkers in Early America* (J. B. Lippincott, 1927), 28; Alfred C. Fuller, as told to Hartzell Spence, *A Foot in the Door* (McGraw-Hill, 1960), 58, 66–68.

55 **Scotsman Thomas Hamilton:** Thomas Hamilton, *Men and Manners in America* (Philadelphia: Carey, Lea & Blanchard, 1833), 126.

55 **In 1879, *How 'Tis Done*:** Bates Harrington, *How 'Tis Done* (Syracuse: W. I. Pattison, 1879).

56 **other forms of salesmanship:** Walter A. Friedman, "John H. Patterson and the Sales Strategy of the National Cash Register Company," *Business History Review* 72, no. 4 (1998).

56 **A trade association formed:** "Direct Selling Timeline," *Direct Selling Journal*, accessed February 3, 2025, dsa.org/direct-selling-journal/direct-selling-timeline.

56 **Federal Trade Commission issued:** Earl Lifshey, "FTC's Fair Trade Practice Rules," in *Door-to-Door Selling: The Factual Story of a Little Known but Rapidly-Growing $7 Billion Industry* (Fairchild Publications, 1948), 15.

56 **The company that would dominate:** Fuller, as told to Spence, *Foot in the Door*, 43–56.

58 **"The trainers told us":** Billy Graham, *Just as I Am*, rev. ed. (HarperCollins, 2011), 36.

58 **The future evangelist:** Graham, *Just as I Am*, 38.

58 **After graduation, their careers:** Torburn P. Meyer, "Direct-to-Home Selling, with Special References to the Jewel Tea Company, Inc." (master's thesis, University of California, 1930), 14.

58 **Like their sisters:** There was even a trade publication that catered to "ladies desirous of earning money during their spare time." See Mail Order News Corporation, "The 'Pin Money' Magazine," *Mail Order News* (Newburgh, N.Y.), July 15, 1913.

58 **The professional door-to-door:** Early trade literature promoted phrenology and linked physiognomy to personality. See Grant Neblo, "Character Analysis," *Salesmanship*, December 1916: "No wishy washy character ever had a jaw square from the ear down."

58 **Other companies might have:** *Keystone Krew Kronikle*, 1912, Stanley Home Products Collection, Archives Center, National Museum of American History, Smithsonian Institution, Washington, D.C.; Maria Russell, "A Legacy of Generosity," *Jacksonville Free Press*, March 26, 2020, jacksonvillefreepress.com/annie-malone-a-legacy-of-generosity.

59 **The first in her family:** A'Lelia Bundles, *On Her Own Ground* (Scribner, 2001); A'Lelia Perry Bundles, *Madam C. J. Walker* (Chelsea House, 1991).

59 **Decades before a diamond-decked:** "Wealthiest Negro Woman's Suburban Mansion," *New York Times*, November 4, 1917. The 1917 article reported Villa Lewaro as having thirty-four rooms, while subsequent stories from the same newspaper reported thirty-five rooms.

59 **"I had to make":** "Annie Malone and Madam C. J. Walker: Pioneers of the African American Beauty Industry," National Museum of African American History & Culture, accessed March 27, 2025, nmaahc.si.edu/explore/stories/annie-malone-and-madam-cj-walker-pioneers-african-american-beauty-industry.

59 **Just before World War II:** Lifshey, *Door-to-Door Selling*, 5.

61 **Or she no longer:** Or she could have been embarrassed by the negative connotations of Grolier, encyclopedias, and subscription book sales, which had been targets of industry reform. See "Subscription Field Faces 'Clean-Up,'" *New York Times*, October 2, 1950; John D. Morris, "F.T.C. Complaint Accuses Grolier," *New York Times*, July 13, 1971.

61 **During an interview in 1995:** "How I Learned to Sell," *D Magazine*, October 1, 1995; Morris L. Mayer, *Direct Selling in the United States: A Commentary and Oral History* (Direct Selling Education Foundation, 1996), 36; Lewis Leary, *The Book-Peddling Parson* (Algonquin Books, 1984); Richardson Wright, *Hawkers and Walkers in Early America* (J. P. Lippincott, 1927), 53.

62 **Mary Kay was among:** Gregory A. Dixon, *Acres of Diamonds: The Russell Conwell Story* (Impact Communications, 2005); Howard P. Chudacoff, "Success and Security: The Meaning of Social Mobility in America," in *The Promise of American History: Progress and Prospects*, ed. Stanley I. Kutler and ed. Stanley N. Katz (Johns Hopkins University Press, 1982). Proceeds from Conwell's pamphlet and readings are credited with funding Temple University in Philadelphia.

62 **All that and heaven too:** Russell H. Conwell, *Acres of Diamonds* (Harper & Brothers, 1915), 18.

62 **Men who would have scorned:** Homer Perkins, interview with the author, September 18, 2009.

62 **In one Depression-era study:** S. S. Hoover, "Ban House-to-House Selling? Yes!," *Rotarian*, April 1939.

63 **"Salesmen of the doorbell variety":** Hoover, "Ban House-to-House Selling?"

63 **Thus, on November 16, 1931:** Shenandoah Grant Lynd, "No Soliciting Allowed," in *Law in the Western United States* (University of Oklahoma Press, 2000), 390–98.

63 **Few could resist the likes:** Lifshey, *Door-to-Door Selling*, 19.

64 **A staple of direct selling:** James M. Rock, "A Growth Industry: The Wisconsin Aluminum Cookware Industry, 1893–1920," *Wisconsin Magazine of History*, Winter, 1971–72.

64 **To pitch them:** Mayer, *Direct Selling*, 22.

64 **Wear-Ever Aluminum issued charts:** Lifshey, *Door-to-Door Selling*, 40. The FTC would later

cite Wear-Ever for misleading health claims. See "The Aluminum Cooking Utensil Inc.," in *Federal Trade Commission Decisions*, vol. 54 (U.S. Government Printing Office, 1960), 1643–47.

64 **"The idea was to persuade":** Norman Vincent Peale, *Enthusiasm Makes the Difference* (Fawcett Crest Books, 1969), 508–10.

65 **As vice president at Fuller:** Perkins, interview with the author; Bruce W. Manternach to Homer Perkins, August 16, 1976, Stanley Home Products Collection, box 1, Archives Center, National Museum of American History, Smithsonian Institution, Washington, D.C.

65 **Beveridge, known to all:** Fuller Brush sales were trending downward, and in 1932 the company would post a net loss. See "Hercules Powder Reports Big Gain," *New York Times*, January 27, 1934.

66 **A lot of the old:** Joan B. Marcus, *To Better Your Best* (Stanley Home Products, 1981), 14–17.

66 **Mr. Bev was taking on:** Sierra Jimenez, "The Ups and Downs of the Fuller Brush Co.," *Fortune*, October 1938. The article quotes government figures giving the industry a total wholesale value of $50 million in 1923 and $42 million in 1935.

66 **In what twenty-first-century:** Clive Howard, "The Stanley Way of Making Money," *Coronet*, January 1951.

66 **After two years:** "Financial History Notes, Undated," Stanley Home Products Collection, box 11, folder 9, Archives Center, National Museum of American History, Smithsonian Institution, Washington, D.C.

66 **"is paying 40":** "Salary and Bonus Notes, Undated," Stanley Home Products Collection, box 11, folder 8, Archives Center, National Museum of American History, Smithsonian Institution, Washington, D.C.

66 **In Maine, a new salesman:** Perkins, interview with the author; M. R. Turner, "Stanley's 46th Anniversary 1931–1977," *Stanley Standard*, Fall 1977; Marcus, *To Better Your Best*, 64–66.

67 **prior to the party plan:** "Company Comparisons, 1933–1945," Stanley Home Products Collection, Archives Center, box 20, folder 7, National Museum of American History, Smithsonian Institution, Washington, D.C. In 1942, sales hit $5,486,547.

67 **"pleasant, profitable part-time":** For examples of recruitment ads, see classifieds under "Female (Miscellaneous)," *Dallas Morning News*, May 26, 1942; and "Female (Miscellaneous)," *Dallas Morning News*, November 11, 1942.

67 **Next to ads:** "WANTED—White Girl to Work in Sandwich Factory," "Female (Miscellaneous)," *Dallas Morning News*, September 1, 1942.

67 **His description of work:** C. B. Eckman, "Attention Teachers and Students," "Female (Miscellaneous)," *Dallas Morning News*, May 29, 1942.

CHAPTER SIX: AN ALLIGATOR BAG

70 **She would be there:** Homer Perkins quoting Frank Stanley Beveridge during interview with the author, September 18, 2009.

70 **As Mary Kay remembered it:** Mary Kay Ash, *Mary Kay* (Harper & Row, 1981), 97.

70 **"Those three days changed":** Ash, *Mary Kay*, 97.

70 **The length and rhythm:** Kenneth O. Brown, *Holy Ground: A Study of the American Camp Meeting* (Garland, 1992); Ellen Eslinger, *Citizens of Zion: The Social Origins of Camp Meeting Revivalism* (University of Tennessee Press, 1999).

71 **"Rally! Rally! Rally!":** Perkins, interview with the author.

71 **Four decades after:** Ash, *Mary Kay*, 98.

73 **In 1943, he introduced:** Joan B. Marcus, *To Better Your Best* (Stanley Home Products, 1981), 42.

73 **The Golden Rule:** Edward J. Samuel, *The House of Stanley*, privately published booklet, Stanley Home Products Collection, Archives Center, box 5, National Museum of American History, Smithsonian Institution, Washington, D.C.

73 **Mary Kay recalled that one:** Sandra Mardefield, "Incentive Interview: Mary Kay Ash," *Incentive*, January 1996.

74 **"They know how to sell":** Perkins, interview with the author.

74 **There were slogans:** "Advertising Materials, 1935–1982," Stanley Home Products Collection, Archives Center, box 5, folder 1, National Museum of American History, Smithsonian Institution, Washington, D.C.

74 **Linking one snappy saying:** Perkins, interview with the author.

75 **champion of morality:** Marcus, *To Better Your Best*, 2; "Honor in Business," in *Catalog of Copyright Entries, part 1, group 2* (U.S. Government Printing Office, 1914), 992.
75 **He spoke with a nonroyal:** Perkins, interview with the author.
76 **Sitting in the back:** Paul Rosenfield, "The Beautiful Make-Up of Mary Kay," *Saturday Evening Post*, October 1981.
76 **"An alligator bag":** Ash, *Mary Kay*, 99.
76 **Eager to put:** Morris L. Mayer, *Direct Selling in the United States: A Commentary and Oral History* (Direct Selling Education Foundation, 1996), 28.
79 **"You also had to be":** Perkins, interview with the author.
79 **"You are not selling brushes":** Marcus, *To Better Your Best*, 63.
79 **One beginner, who had decided:** Perkins, interview with the author.
81 **Practicing "Tell somebody":** Kristin McMurran, "Mary Kay Ash," *People*, July 29, 1985.
81 **If a woman decided:** Perkins, interview with the author.
82 **time that Mary Kay made:** Marcus, *To Better Your Best*, 150–53.
82 **"And wouldn't you know":** Ash, *Mary Kay*, 99.
83 **Mary Kay was giving:** Judy Lunn, "The Dallas Cosmetic Empress Who Keeps a 38,000-Member Sales Force in the Pink," *Houston Post*, January 28, 1978.
84 **"Once I worked terribly hard":** "Mary Kay Ash Interview," posted October 3, 1980, by Foggy Melson's Breakdown, YouTube, 2 min., 6 sec., youtube.com/watch?v=NGQg_NraKpc.
84 **In any case, Perkins:** Perkins, interview with the author.
86 **At the Rice Institute:** "Dorothy Zapp, Rice Senior, Named Duchess to Huntsville Ball," *Weimar Mercury*, February 10, 1939.

CHAPTER SEVEN: "S-T-A-N-L-E-Y, STANLEY ALL THE TIME"

87 **Leaving a child:** "Baby Farming," Adoption History Project, updated February 24, 2012, pages.uoregon.edu/adoption/topics/babyfarming.html. The term remained in use through the first half of the twentieth century (e.g., Angelo Patri, "Co-Operative Plan Provides Nursery," *Commercial Appeal* [Memphis], October 12, 1950).
87 **The War Manpower Commission:** "Services for Children of Working Mothers in War Time," Office of Civilian Defense Publication 3625, 1943, fraser.stlouisfed.org/title/services-children-working-mothers-war-time-9567.
87 **In weekly radio broadcasts:** Associated Press, "Flanagan Hits Child Neglect," *Atlanta Constitution*, December 1, 1943; Ann Cottrell, "Priest Assails Mothers' Jobs in War Plants," *New York Herald Tribune*, December 1, 1943.
88 **Pundits predicted a generation:** William M. Tuttle Jr., *"Daddy's Gone to War"* (Oxford University Press, 1993), 88.
88 **During the lead-up to war:** Homer Perkins, interview with the author, September 18, 2009. Perkins described his encounter with a federal official in charge of gas allotments, who told him there was "no such category" as direct selling. Perkins said, "He had no conception that there were 200,000 or 300,000 making a living going door to door."
88 **She allowed two minutes:** Mary Kay Ash, *Mary Kay* (Harper & Row, 1981), 87.
89 **"I needed a method":** Mary Kay Ash, interview by Donald L. Caruth, November 4, 1974, No. OHB3, p. 2, University of North Texas Oral History Collection, Denton, Tex. At the beginning of the transcription, Caruth says the first interview is taking place on November 7; however, I have followed the archive label of November 4.
89 **Her youngest child:** Richard Rogers, interview by Donald L. Caruth, November 11, 1974, No. OHB4, pp. 25–26, University of North Texas Oral History Collection, Denton, Tex.
90 **Instead, Stanley's seven tenets:** "The Stanley Seven-Point Plan," undated, Stanley Home Products Collection, box 6, folder 6, Archives Center, National Museum of American History, Smithsonian Institution, Washington, D.C.
91 **And it worked:** Clio Associates, *Frank Stanley Beveridge: The Man and His Legacy* (Frank Stanley Beveridge Foundation, 2002), videocassette, 41 min.
92 **some versions of this story:** Ash, *Mary Kay*, 64–65.
92 **In the 1981 autobiography:** Ash, 105.
92 **One version had university officials:** Ash, 105.

92 **neither alleged alma mater:** Jean Palmquist and Iqbal Haider, University of Houston, conversations and emails with the author, August 20 and September 4, 2014; Ana Bernard, Rice University, email to the author, August 18, 2009. It's also possible that she enrolled and had to drop out before completing a semester.

93 **By 1941, magazines:** "Boom in Babies," *Life*, December 1, 1941.

93 **In 1943, U.S. fertility:** Tuttle, *"Daddy's Gone to War,"* 26.

93 **Black markets sprang up:** Catherine Mackenzie, "A Black Market in Babies, Too," *New York Times*, February 18, 1945.

93 **When one Houston couple:** "National Affairs," *Newsweek*, January 22, 1945.

93 **Like his mother before him:** Rogers, interview by Caruth, 22.

94 **Wife and children:** Enlistment Record for Julius B. Rogers Sr., 19 January 1944, Electronic Army Serial Number Merged File, ca. 1938–46 (Enlistment Records), National Archives, Washington, D.C., aad.archives.gov/aad/record-detail.jsp?dt=893&mtch=1&tf=F&q=rogers+julius+b&bc=sl,fd&rpp=10&pg=1&rid=7405168.

94 **In 1945, the year:** Division of Vital Statistics, "Table 1: Marriages, Divorces, and Rates," in *100 Years of Marriage and Divorce Statistics United States, 1867–1967* (National Center for Health Statistics, 1973), cdc.gov/nchs/data/series/sr_21/sr21_024.pdf.

95 **The financial bounty:** Julius B. Rogers Sr., Final Payment Work Sheet, 3 November 1945, D.D. Voucher 21993, U.S. War Department.

CHAPTER EIGHT: "SALESMEN ARE NOT BORN, BUT MADE"

96 **At five feet four:** Edward L. Berthold, interview with the author, December 2, 2010.

96 **Foremost among them:** "Area Sales," Stanley Home Products, 1944, Norman Squires Collection, series 3, Archives Center, National Museum of American History, Smithsonian Institution, Washington, D.C.

96 **Born in Apollo:** "Address of Joseph L. Beck at the Beck Reunion in 1906," Family Trees, Ancestry.com, accessed February 1, 2011.

97 **Reversing custom, a housewife:** John Sherman Wright, "The Development of Policies Affecting the Marketing Operations of the Jewel Tea Company, Inc., 1901–1951" (PhD diss., Ohio State University, 1967), 70–73, 178–79. As Wright points out, the premiums acted as advertising and their distribution tended to ensure customer continuity.

97 **By 1917, Jewel:** "The Jewel Way," *Jewel*, June 1926; Wright, "Development of Policies," 51, table 2.

97 **For all this:** "Jewel Way"; Wright, "Development of Policies," 50–54, 237–38.

98 **Company literature showed:** *Working for Jewel* (Jewel Tea, 1927), 9.

98 **Then World War I came:** Wright, "Development of Policies," 50–54.

98 **A relative recalled:** Evalyn Eckman, interview with the author, November 30, 2010.

98 **Promoted and transferred to Illinois:** Grand Lodge of Illinois archivist, interview with the author, November 5, 2010. Eckman was a member of Mount Joliet Lodge number 42, listed as a sales manager for Fuller Brush Company, elected on August 24, 1923, initiated on September 7, 1923, passed on September 21, 1923, and raised on December 7, 1923 (the "third degree" that made him a Master Mason).

98 **His picture appeared:** Autopoint, "Big Business Says Merry Christmas," *Chicago Tribune*, December 14, 1930.

99 **"My life is proof":** Alfred C. Fuller, as told to Hartzell Spence, *A Foot in the Door* (McGraw-Hill, 1960), 1.

99 **Next best was boasting:** Fuller, as told to Spence, *Foot in the Door*, 3–4.

99 **Homilies and inspirational messages:** Fuller, as told to Spence, 190.

99 **Learning every motivational maxim:** "South Park Methodist; Leader: Mr. C. B. Eckman of Chicago," *Hartford Courant*, January 1, 1927; Eckman, interview with the author.

99 **Fuller's gloss on the gospel:** Fuller, as told to Spence, *Foot in the Door*, 190.

100 **Added to all those:** Fuller, as told to Spence, 199–203.

101 **"He also loved to tell jokes":** Berthold, interview with the author.

102 **He went without her:** City directories for 1937–43: *Polk's Peoria City Directory* (R. L. Polk). For a while, the family gathered for weekend dinners, "possibly for the sake of the children," according to Bob Eckman in an email to the author, March 20, 2011.

102 **His wife divorced him:** Berthold, interview with the author.

102 **As an area manager:** "Seaboard," 24 May 1945, Stanley Home Products Collection, Archives Center, National Museum of American History, Smithsonian Institution, Washington, D.C.

103 **The two couples:** Eckman, interview with the author.

103 **Eckman's own father:** United States Bureau of the Census, *Twelfth Census of the United States: 1900* (U.S. Government Printing Office, 1901). C.B. was nine, his stepmother twenty-four, his father forty-one.

103 **Believing that a little:** Edward L. Berthold, letter to the author, January 5, 2011.

103 **"My father died":** Berthold, interview with the author.

104 **Leaving Electrolux for:** Berthold, letter to the author.

105 **Eckman explained how much:** "The Frank Stanley Beveridge Homestead," Stanley Park of Westfield, accessed September 17, 2009, no longer available, stanleypark.org/gallery/frank-stanley-beveridge-homestead-westfield.

105 **the fifty-five-year-old:** 'Mrs. Mary Rogers and C. B. Eckman' (1946). *Certified copy of marriage license for Mrs. Mary Rogers and C. B. Eckman, 3 August 1946.* Application number 68067. Dallas, Texas.

106 **"He [Eckman] spent":** Judith Eckman Duke, letter to the author, December 28, 2010.

106 **Another grandchild referred:** Bob Eckman, email to the author, March 20, 2011.

106 **"Never missed a day":** Berthold, interview with the author.

106 **Responsible for the entire state:** "The Beautiful Windsor," Imperial Club, accessed January 20, 2011, imperialclub.info/Yr/1940/index.htm.

106 **she advertised that autumn:** Classified advertisement, *Dallas Morning News*, November 30, 1946.

107 **"This often makes it possible":** Mary Kay Ash, *Mary Kay* (Harper & Row, 1981), 67.

107 **"I found that when":** Ash, *Mary Kay*, 67.

107 **"You do well":** Mary Kay Ash, *Mary Kay: You Can Have It All* (Prima, 1995), xiii.

107 **She would open:** *And Stirred with Love* (Mary Kay Inc., 2002), 313.

108 **Now that the war:** Clippings, Stanley Home Products Collection, box 5, folder 3, Archives Center, National Museum of American History, Smithsonian Institution, Washington, D.C.

108 **At the start of his:** Stanley Home Products Collection, box 1, folder 2, Archives Center, National Museum of American History, Smithsonian Institution, Washington, D.C.

108 **Most lasting were the lessons:** Arthur Frederick Sheldon, "The Philosophy of Service," *Rotarian*, February 1921.

108 **Sheldon taught that service:** "Arthur Frederick Sheldon: He Made a Motto," *Rotarian*, February, 1976; session of Tuesday Morning, June 14th, *Proceedings of the 1921 Rotary Convention*, accessed June 21, 2011, rotaryfirst100.org/leaders/sheldon/images/sheldonspeech.jpg.

108 **Customers would gravitate:** "Arthur Sheldon: He Made a Motto," *Rotarian*, February 1976.

110 **And when those lessons landed:** A. F. Sheldon, *The Fuller Manual of Fundamentals on Service and Man Building* (Fuller Correspondence Service, 1922). Other direct sellers soon had equivalents. Jewel Tea, for example, put together "twelve little books" called *The Mackintosh System of Selling: Working for Jewel* (Jewel Tea, 1927), 21.

110 **Written in a style:** Sheldon, chapter 24, lesson 12, in *Fuller Manual of Fundamentals*, 1.

110 **Dale Carnegie's *How to Win*:** Undated manuscript carbon, Stanley Home Products Collection, box 6, folder 6, Archives Center, National Museum of American History, Smithsonian Institution, Washington, D.C.

110 **Now, besides sales manuals:** "$101,000 Given to Honor Mac Grad Elmer Nyberg," *Mac Weekly* (Macalester College, Saint Paul, Minn.), October 6, 1961.

110 **Practicing what he preached:** "From the Little Red School House," Brownie Wise Papers, 1938–68, series 2, Archives Center, National Museum of American History, Smithsonian Institution, Washington, D.C; "$101,000 Given." ("His 'Little Red Schoolhouse' articles and various publications have had circulations in the millions.")

111 **put on a boiled shirt:** Photo attached to Eckman, email to the author.

112 **"The mood of the Centennial":** Ebby Halliday, interview with the author, July 31, 2009.

112 **From 1940 until August:** "County Population Estimate Goes Up," *Dallas Morning News*, November 8, 1946. And no sooner did the Chamber of Commerce issue that figure than, within months, it began revising upward again—guessing at a population increase of 50 percent or

better—and apologizing that the original figure hadn't accounted for the heads of households still living in temporary quarters until their families arrived or the 13,000 veterans' families on the waiting list for public housing.

113 **By May 14:** Last Will and Testament of Clarence Blair Eckman, filed 2 June 1947, Probate Court, Dallas County, Texas, case no. 27347.

CHAPTER NINE: THE GOD OF ABUNDANCE

115 **LeNaire, at least:** Judith Eckman Duke, letter to the author, December 28, 2010.

116 **That same Tuesday:** "Rites Arranged for C. B. Eckman," *Dallas Morning News*, June 3, 1947.

117 **Maybe she was not wearing:** Nadine Stewart, email to the author, November 30, 2010.

117 **Fulfilling wifely duties:** Evalyn Eckman, interview with the author, November 30, 2010.

119 **a top Stanley dealer:** "U.S. Individual Income Tax Return 1947," 1948, Brownie Wise Papers, 1938–68, box 1, Archives Center, National Museum of American History, Smithsonian Institution, Washington, D.C. Wise listed herself as a full-time, self-employed Stanley dealer with an income of $1,549.23.

119 **There would be as many:** "Stanley Home Products Builds $60,000 Addition for Storage," *Dallas Morning News*, January 31, 1951.

119 **Years afterward, when she:** Mary Kay Ash, *Mary Kay* (Harper & Row, 1981), 50.

120 **a "Program of Self-Analysis":** "The Stanley Seven-Point Plan," undated, Stanley Home Products Collection, box 6, folder 6, Archives Center, National Museum of American History, Smithsonian Institution, Washington, D.C.

121 **Norman Vincent Peale:** Norman Vincent Peale, *A Guide to Confident Living* (World's Work, 1913; repr., Touchstone Books, 2007), 167.

121 **a chapter of her autobiography:** Ash, *Mary Kay*, 50.

121 **When there weren't enough parties:** Audrey Peel, interview with the author, April 28, 2011.

121 **"One by one, my problems":** Ash, *Mary Kay*, 51.

122 **On June 7, 1949:** Joan B. Marcus, *To Better Your Best* (Stanley Home Products, 1981), 109.

122 **Eckman had done his job:** "Sales," Stanley Home Products Collection, box 7, folder 10, Archives Center, National Museum of American History, Smithsonian Institution, Washington, D.C.

123 **Legend credits the genesis:** Marcus, *To Better Your Best*, 94–95.

124 **After stocking the park:** "Carillon Tower," Stanley Park, accessed May 23, 2025, stanleypark.org/facilities/carillon-tower.

124 **Trying to keep:** Michael Regensburger, interview with the author, 2011.

124 **Bequeathed to the public:** Marcus, *To Better Your Best*, 95–96.

125 **Because no other company:** Brownie Wise, a former Stanley dealer, would imitate the setting—down to the pavilion and wishing well—when she opened Tupperware Home Parties headquarters in Kissimmee, Florida, in 1954.

125 **Wearing a boutonniere:** Marcus, *To Better Your Best*, 101–3.

125 **During those three:** Kenneth B. Miller, "Stanley Home Products, Inc.: A Study of Its Current Public Relations Policies with Recommendations for a Future Program" (master's thesis, Boston University, 1958).

125 **Piling into buses:** "The Stanley Pilgrim," 1948, Brownie Wise Papers, 1938–68, series 2, Archives Center, National Museum of American History, Smithsonian Institution, Washington, D.C.

126 **They heard that Stanley:** Clive Howard, "The Stanley Way of Making Money," *Coronet*, January 1951.

126 **If they knew where:** Observation of the author, visit to Stanley Park, November 15, 2010.

126 **Joining hands, the pilgrims:** Marcus, *To Better Your Best*, 98.

127 **Mr. Mac would reappear:** "The Stanley Pilgrim," 1948, Brownie Wise Papers, 1938–68, series 2, Archives Center, National Museum of American History, Smithsonian Institution, Washington, D.C.

127 **"People do respond":** "The Stanley Pilgrim," 1948, Brownie Wise Papers, 1938–68, series 2, Archives Center, National Museum of American History, Smithsonian Institution, Washington, D.C.

127 **Toward the end of those:** "The Stanley Pilgrim," 1948, Brownie Wise Papers, 1938–68, series

2, Archives Center, National Museum of American History, Smithsonian Institution, Washington, D.C.

128 **"We want every one":** Marcus, *To Better Your Best*, 103.

128 **One year, when her branch:** Ash, *Mary Kay*, 15–16.

128 **It was a dark:** "Sleet, Freezing Rain Glaze Dallas Streets," *Dallas Morning News*, January 18, 1949.

129 **"With doubt and dismay":** Berton Braley, "Opportunity," Poemist, accessed April 4, 2025, poemist.com/berton-braley/opportunity.

129 **"You never knew":** Peel, interview with the author.

129 **this would be the one:** Morris L. Mayer, *Direct Selling in the United States: A Commentary and Oral History* (Direct Selling Education Foundation, 1996), 12–13.

129 **Besides its half-size:** Mary C. Crowley, *You Can Too* (Power Books, 1980), 37–40.

129 **"It was a bitterly cold":** Ash, *Mary Kay*, 121–23.

129 **The Sunday school teacher told:** Crowley, *You Can Too*, 37–40.

130 **"The two of us":** Crowley, 38.

130 **"If Don and Ruthie":** Crowley, 16.

131 **Next, she got herself:** Mary C. Crowley, *Think Mink!* (Fleming H. Revell, 1976), 31.

131 **They wed in 1948:** Crowley, *You Can Too*, 33–34.

132 **CPA or not:** Alfred C. Fuller, as told to Hartzell Spence, *A Foot in the Door* (McGraw-Hill, 1960), 70.

132 **"The idea of selling":** Crowley, *You Can Too*, 38.

132 **"I really wasn't always":** Crowley, 39.

133 **"Everyone wants to be":** Jackie Brown, interview with the author, November 15, 2009.

133 **Soon they would be:** In *Think Mink!*, published in 1976, Crowley disingenuously revealed two of Mary Kay's never-mentioned marriages, first by referring to her as "Mrs. Eckman," then by adding, "Later, Mary Kay married my brother and moved away from Dallas and I had some of her people in my unit, too." In her own autobiography, published in 1981, Mary Kay fondly recollected her friendship with Crowley but neglected to mention their family ties.

CHAPTER TEN: "A HOUSE IS NOT A HOME"

134 **"A house is not a home":** Mary C. Crowley, *You Can Too* (Power Books, 1980), 38.

134 **Back at Maple Springs Drive:** City directories for 1940–58, *Worley's Greater Dallas City Directory* (John F. Worley Directory Co.).

134 **When census takers came:** United States Bureau of the Census, *Seventeenth Census of the United States: 1950* (archives.gov/1950census, 2022), Dallas, Dallas County, Texas.

135 **On June 9, 1950:** 'Alfred L. Miller v. Lila Rose Miller' (1950). *Certified copy of divorce certificate for Alfred L. Miller v. Lila Rose Miller, 27 February 1950.* Application number 40258. Dallas, Dallas County, Texas; "Ninety-Fifth District Court," *Dallas Morning News*, March 1, 1950.

135 **he had been employed:** City directories for 1940–58, *Worley's Greater Dallas City Directory.*

135 **She thought about doing:** Jon Anderson, "In the Pink," *Chicago Tribune*, February 14, 1991.

135 **This would be her last:** Evalyn Eckman, interview with the author, November 30, 2010.

135 **In 1950, when sales:** "The Brush Man," *Time*, January 16, 1950.

135 **When *Time* magazine:** "Brush Man."

136 **In any of those:** "Consumer Income," in *Current Population Reports* (U.S. Department of Commerce, 1953). Women's income—more than men's—also varied downward if they were nonwhite or living in a rural area.

136 **When a hostess was shown:** Stanley Home Products, "I Like Being a Stanley Party Hostess," *Life*, September 25, 1950.

136 **The following January:** Clive Howard, "The Stanley Way of Making Money," *Coronet*, January 1951.

136 **In 1951, Mr. Bev:** Lazo & White, "Stanley Advertising Evaluation, Volumes I and II" (submitted in 1953), Stanley Home Products Collection, box 11, folders 16–17, Archives Center, National Museum of American History, Smithsonian Institution, Washington, D.C.

137 **Miller was all in favor:** "New Cases Filed," *Dallas Morning News*, December 15, 1950.

137 **Mary Kay was left:** "Dayton Locals," *Liberty Vindicator*, November 30, 1950.

137 **the twenty-eight-page paean:** *A Guide to Homemaking* (Stanley Home Products, 1952).

138 **On March 8, 1952:** 'Vernon Ross Schumacher and Marylyn Yvonne Rogers' (1952). *Marriage license of Vernon Ross Schumacher and Marylyn Yvonne Rogers, 8 March 1952.* Marriage license number 168634. Harris County, Texas.

139 **Some used the slogan:** Stanley Home Products, "Stanley Offers Opportunity for Women," *Life*, April 23, 1951.

139 **"Earn cash in your spare":** "Waitresses Over 200 Pounds," Female Help—Miscellaneous 16D, *Fort Worth Star-Telegram*, April 13, 1947.

140 **Miss O'Brien herself:** At a speech made in 1951, when she was named president of Stanley Home Products; "Corporate Records, 1940–1999," Stanley Home Products Collection, Archives Center, box 2, folder 3, National Museum of American History, Smithsonian Institution, Washington, D.C.

140 **"The handles fell off":** Mary Kay Ash, interview by Donald L. Caruth, November 4, 1974, No. OHB3, p. 42, University of North Texas Oral History Collection, Denton, Tex.

140 **Stanley offered her three chances:** Ash, interview by Caruth, 3–4.

140 **Crowley, who would later write:** Mary C. Crowley, *Pocketful of Hope* (Home Interiors & Gifts, 1981), 136.

141 **The next year, Stanley's slogan:** "Advertising Materials, 1935–1982," Stanley Home Products Collection, Archives Center, box 5, National Museum of American History, Smithsonian Institution, Washington, D.C.

141 **That January, Mary Kay:** 'Mary Kathlyn Miller v. Alfred L. Miller' (1953). *Certified copy of divorce certificate for Mary Kathlyn Miller v. Alfred L. Miller, 30 March 1953.* Dallas, Dallas County, Texas.

141 **People described him:** Dick Kelly, interview with the author, October 7, 2009.

142 **Later she summed up:** Ash, interview by Caruth, 5.

142 **Kelly remembered taping:** Rosalie McGinnis, "Stories About People Help Sell World Gifts," *Dallas Morning News*, July 23, 1967.

142 **"I began to think":** E. Richard Kelly, *Everyday Is a Gift* (pub. by author, 2005), 144.

143 **Crowley later claimed:** Mary C. Crowley, *Think Mink!* (Fleming H. Revell, 1976), 50.

143 **Kelly disagreed, claiming:** Kelly, interview with the author.

143 **She began by recruiting:** Morris L. Mayer, *Direct Selling in the United States: A Commentary and Oral History* (Direct Selling Education Foundation, 1996), 12–13.

CHAPTER ELEVEN: STORYTELLER

144 **subdivision called Freeway Manor:** Details of the original September 2, 1955, transaction are noted on a subsequent sale. See Deed of Sale from Mary K. Weaver to John H. Rizer, March 5, 1964, Harris County Deed Records, vol. 5448, p. 164.

144 **World Gift specialized:** Christock llc, "7" Hand Painted Wooden Windmill Dutch Holland World Gift Co Volendam W19," eBay, accessed January 25, 2025, ebay.com/itm/196037622637.

145 **When a fresh shipment:** E. Richard Kelly, *Everyday Is a Gift* (pub. by author, 2005), 155.

145 **Crowley wanted her displayers:** Mary C. Crowley, *You Can Too* (Power Books, 1980), 34.

145 **A displayer for World Gift:** Kathy Villarreal, interview with the author, October 22, 2009.

145 **Back in Dallas:** Dick Kelly, interview with the author, October 7, 2009; Kelly, *Everyday Is a Gift*, 154.

145 **"I'm the guy":** Kelly, interview with the author; Kelly, *Everyday Is a Gift*, 161–62.

146 **that was all it took:** Rosalie McGinnis, "Stories About People Help Sell World Gifts," *Dallas Morning News*, July 23, 1967.

146 **"Everywhere I went":** Kelly, interview with the author.

146 **Hostess parties became:** Mary Kay Ash, interview by Donald L. Caruth, November 4, 1974, No. OHB3, p. 6, University of North Texas Oral History Collection, Denton, Tex.

146 **Noticing that her gift shows:** Kelly, interview with the author.

147 **her territory accounted:** Ash, interview by Caruth, 6–7.

148 **On those trips:** Kelly, interview with the author.

148 **Gulf Freeway was:** Louis Blackburn, "Here's a Tour of Gulfgate, One of America's Wonders," *Houston Post*, September 14, 1956; Burton Chapman, *Telephone Road, Texas* (Baxter Press, 2007), 81.

149 **While Mary Kay endured:** "Houston's 1954 Parade of Homes to Be Launched Officially Today," *Houston Chronicle*, September 5, 1954.

150 **For direct selling, this:** "Exclusive 'East of Main' Site Picked for Parade of Homes," Glenbrook Valley, accessed March 29, 2010, no longer available, glenbrookvalley.com/amenities/?action=picture&itemId=734285.

150 **while her chickens:** "Lowe's Electric All Electric Home," Arch-ive, accessed April 2, 2010, no longer available with same content, arch-ive.org/archive/lowes-all-electric-home.

151 **She would fly:** World Gift Company, "If You Have a Flair for Interior Decorating and Like Foreign Gifts," *Chicago Tribune*, April 22, 1962.

151 **She had seen:** Ash, interview by Caruth, 71.

151 **Mary Kay wasn't too clear:** Richard Rogers, interview by Donald L. Caruth, November 11, 1974, No. OHB4, p. 11, University of North Texas Oral History Collection, Denton, Tex.

151 **Coverture was both:** Elizabeth York Enstam, "The Evolution of Women's Rights in Texas: A Historical Overview," *Handbook of Texas*, 1976, updated March 31, 2021, tshaonline.org/handbook/online/articles/jsw02.

152 **That lasted until Kelly:** Kelly, interview with the author.

152 **World Gift was now:** "Gains Are Noted in Direct Selling," *New York Times*, June 7, 1955.

152 **Forward-thinking publications:** Karon Kehoe, "Custom-Made Job . . . Direct Selling," *Charm*, pre-1965 reprint, cited in Small Business Administration, *Small Business Bibliography*, no. 39, August 1965.

153 **Stanley's advertising in *Life*:** Stanley Home Products, "Personal to Women," *Life*, May 4, 1953.

154 **During routine orientation:** "Unit Orientation," May 18, 1948, Brownie Wise Papers, 1938–68, series 2, Archives Center, National Museum of American History, Smithsonian Institution, Washington, D.C.

154 **Stanley pilgrims tossed pennies:** Bob Kealing, *Tupperware Unsealed* (University Press of Florida, 2008), 150.

154 **In 1953, New York:** Kealing, *Tupperware Unsealed*, 95–96.

156 **A *Life* photo essay:** "Life Goes on a Big Dig," *Life*, May 3, 1954.

156 **In March of 1955:** Ludwig Bemelmans, "My Craziest Tour of Paris," *Coronet*, March 1955.

156 **In 1956, *Life*:** "A Wealth of Wishes," *Life*, August 13, 1956.

156 **As Tupperware parties:** Kealing, *Tupperware Unsealed*, 103.

156 **On April 17, 1954:** "How Brownie Wise Whoops Up Sales," *Business Week*, April 17, 1954.

156 ***Cosmopolitan*'s profile:** Jon Whitcomb, "Sunshine Cinderella," *Cosmopolitan*, April, 1957.

156 **Wise wrote a book:** Brownie Wise, as told to Maurice Marshall, *Best Wishes, Brownie Wise* (Podium, 1957), flap copy; Steven Kelman, "Productivity and the Placebo Effect," *Federal Computer Week*, October 10, 2012, hks.harvard.edu/publications/productivity-and-placebo-effect.

157 **In January of 1958:** Kealing, *Tupperware Unsealed*, 196.

157 **Calling his new boss:** Michael Regensburger, interview with the author, 2011.

157 ***A week so luxurious:*** Stanley Home Products, "Paris Holiday" (1958).

158 **Getting wind of her plan:** Kelly, *Everyday Is a Gift*, 169–72.

158 **Next, Crowley secured:** Mary C. Crowley, *Think Mink!* (Fleming H. Revell, 1976), 54.

158 **She then signed:** Crowley, *Think Mink!*, 56.

158 **"a way in which God":** Crowley, 15.

158 **The new company's first commandment:** Mary C. Crowley, *Pocketful of Hope* (Home Interiors & Gifts, 1981), 308.

159 **"Women had to wait":** Homer Perkins, interview with the author, September 18, 2009.

160 **She was on the road:** Paul Rosenfield, "The Beautiful Make-Up of Mary Kay," *Saturday Evening Post*, October, 1981.

160 **Soon that same sister-in-law:** "Think Mink!," *Stanley Standard*, November 1957. Stanley was using the slogan at least a month before Crowley launched her company.

CHAPTER TWELVE: "A GOLDEN DOOR MARKED 'MEN ONLY'"

161 **Out in California:** Morris L. Mayer, *Direct Selling in the United States: A Commentary and Oral History* (Direct Selling Education Foundation, 1996), 14–15.

161 **An incessant "Ding Dong":** Although Dreher did not launch the "Ding Dong" campaign until 1958, it established its elegant Avon Lady earlier, as shown in the 1955 fragrance advertisement on page 162.
163 **Kelly then had:** Dick Kelly, interview with the author, October 7, 2009.
164 **In a full page:** "World Gift Company, Inc. to Formally Open New Brook Hollow Quarters November 20 from 12–7 pm," *Dallas Morning News*, November 19, 1959.
164 **In her two-paragraph bio:** "World Gift Company, Inc. to Formally Open New Brook Hollow Quarters."
164 **From then on:** Mary C. Crowley, *You Can Too* (Power Books, 1980), 54.
165 **God was on her side:** Crowley, *You Can Too*, 69.
165 **Pursuing the most aggressive:** Mary C. Crowley, *Think Mink!* (Fleming H. Revell, 1976), 75–78.
166 **She also kept her Cadillac:** Mary Kay, "Mary Kay with her dog, Rags. Mary Kay loved dogs and owned several including two poodles named Monet and Gigi," Facebook, May 18, 2010, facebook.com/photo/?fbid=395570097170&set=a.395569877170&locale=gl_ES.
166 **At Kelly's suggestion, Mary Kay:** Kelly, interview with the author.
166 **When she wasn't on the road:** Mary Kay Ash, interview by Donald L. Caruth, November 4, 1974, No. OHB3, p. 42, University of North Texas Oral History Collection, Denton, Tex.
167 **In an interview:** Paul Rosenfield, "The Beautiful Make-Up of Mary Kay," *Saturday Evening Post*, October, 1981.
168 **He did not stay:** Theodore Hallenbeck, email to the author, August 25, 2009.
168 **Lee Bower and his wife:** Lee and Wanda Bower, interview with the author, December 7, 2010.
169 **"Make no small plans":** "Earl Shoaff's Millionaire Maker Secret Revealed!," posted August 20, 2023, by Dustin Grant, YouTube, 41 min., 23 sec., youtube.com/watch?v=Viyw9-iVqLM.
169 **As practiced in the mid-twentieth:** *Director's Manual* (Mary Kay Cosmetics, 1973), section 12, 4. By the twenty-first century, the terms *multilevel marketing* and *direct selling* were often used interchangeably.
169 **continued like a chain letter:** The key distinction was primarily selling product versus primarily selling a franchise. In the 1970s, the Federal Trade Commission would characterize this selling model as "inherently deceptive," calling "recruitment with rewards unrelated to product sales, is nothing more than an elaborate chain letter device in which individuals who pay a valuable consideration with the expectation of recouping it to some degree via recruitment are bound to be disappointed." See "Koscot Interplanetary Inc., et al," in *Federal Trade Commission Decisions*, vol. 86 (U.S. Government Printing Office, 1976), 1,106–92.
170 **Putting principle into practice:** Reference Division, Beverly Hills Public Library, email to the author, November 4, 2009; Glenna Dunning, History/Genealogy Department, Los Angeles Public Library, email to the author, October 28, 2010.
170 **Scorning the kind:** "Nutri-Bio Company Schedules Seminars," *Arizona Republic*, January 23, 1963.
170 **In large-circulation magazines:** Nutri-Bio, "Better Nutrition," *Life*, May 25, 1959, 12.
170 **Touted by TV star:** "Bob Cummings Show—Winston Cigarettes Ad (Sponsor)," posted April 10, 2010, by Gregory May, YouTube, 12 sec., youtube.com/watch?v=IfX-96juc14; "Look at . . . Laugh at . . . 'Love That Bob,'" *Fort Worth Star-Telegram*, September 17, 1961.
171 **Nutri-Bio's claims:** U.S. Department of Health, Education, and Welfare, Food and Drug Administration, "HEW-R80," news release, November 27, 1961.
171 **More misleading claims:** Bob Cummings, *Stay Young and Vital* (Prentice-Hall, 1960).
171 **Drug Administration was seizing:** Science Service, "Head of FDA Calls Food Faddism Biggest Racket in the Health Field," *York Daily Record*, November 26, 1963; "In the United States District Court for the District of Oregon, United States of America, Libelant," *Corvallis Gazette-Times*, June 27, 1962; Associated Press, "U.S. Seizes Pills; Calls Labels False," *New York Times*, November 28, 1961.
171 **Hallenbeck was out of work:** Kelly, interview with the author.
171 **On May 5, Hallenbeck:** George A. Hallenbeck, "A Particular Type of Man," *Dallas Morning News*, May 5, 1963.
172 **Kelly claimed he considered:** Kelly, interview with the author.
172 **Kelly was planning something:** Ash, interview by Caruth, 8. For an example of how the company later sold distributorships, see World Gift, "World Gift Is Coming to North West Texas!," *Amarillo Globe-Times*, October 3, 1967.

172 **Having invested $500:** Kelly, interview with the author.
172 **Mary Kay admitted that:** Ash, interview by Caruth, 9.
172 **In one retelling:** Paul Rosenfield, "The Beautiful Make-Up of Mary Kay," *Saturday Evening Post*, October 1981.
173 **In a 1970s version:** Ash, interview by Caruth, 12.
173 **She did not mention:** Crowley, *Think Mink!*, 78.
174 **That night, the shoebox:** Ash, interview by Caruth, 29–30.
174 **More than once, she had:** BeautiControl, "Not Responsible," *Dallas Morning News*, January 15, 1954.
174 **Dark, who had inherited:** Ash, interview by Caruth, 14.
174 **Mary Kay took the formulas:** Richard Rogers, interview by Donald L. Caruth, November 11, 1974, No. OHB4, p. 13, University of North Texas Oral History Collection, Denton, Tex.
174 **Mary Kay then found:** David Preziosi, "Exchange Park: Dallas' Cutting Edge Development of the 1950s," CandysDirt.com, December 9, 2021, candysdirt.com/2021/12/09/exchange-park-dallas-cutting-edge-development-of-the-1950s.
175 **But Hallenbeck had grown up:** "Crimson Trackmen Smother Cornell," *Coe College Cosmos* (Cedar Rapids), May 28, 1936.
175 **Back in Cedar Rapids:** "Two Healthiest at Franklin High," *Gazette* (Cedar Rapids), May 26, 1928.
175 **He had played:** "Only a Breather," *Gazette* (Cedar Rapids), December 9, 1945.
175 **He prided himself:** Bower interview with the author, December 7, 2010.
175 **Until Hallenbeck had:** Mary Kay Ash, *Mary Kay* (Harper & Row, 1981), 3.
175 **Hallenbeck had so many irons:** Rogers, interview by Caruth, 8.
175 **For years, she had called:** Rogers, interview by Caruth, 9.

CHAPTER THIRTEEN: FRIDAY THE THIRTEENTH

177 **That would be the official:** Horatio Alger Association, "Horatio Alger Award Nomination Packet," accessed February 13, 2025, horatioalger.org/wp-content/uploads/2023/05/Horatio-Alger-Award-Nomination-Packet.pdf; Daniel Gross and the editors of *Forbes* magazine, *Forbes Greatest Business Stories of All Time* (John Wiley & Sons, 1996); "Business Leaders," *Washington Post*, May 12, 1988.
177 **That story would be cited:** John Strengrevics under the supervision of John P. Kotter, "Mary Kay Cosmetics, Inc.," Harvard Business School Case 9-481-126, 1981; Mukul Pandya and Robbie Shell, *Nightly Business Report Presents Lasting Leadership: What You Can Learn from the Top 25 Business People of Our Times* (Wharton School, 2005).
178 **a favorite fairy tale:** Kris Thoma, "In the Pink," *Pensacola News Journal*, October 22, 2006. "The Greatest Female Entrepreneur" honorific was conferred by Baylor University in 2003.
178 **Dick Kelly said:** Dick Kelly, interview with the author, October 7, 2009.
178 **When she opened her bills:** E. Richard Kelly, *Everyday Is a Gift* (pub. by author, 2005), 273–74.
178 **The gravestone listed:** George Arthur Hallenbeck, U.S., Find a Grave Index, 1600s–Current, accessed January 21, 2025, findagrave.com/memorial/145881631/george_arthur_hallenbeck.
178 **name she used when:** 'Mary Kay, Inc.' (1963). *Articles of incorporation of Mary Kay, Inc., 26 August 1963.* Corporation Division, Secretary of State of Texas.
179 **Ben told her:** Mary Kay Ash, interview by Donald L. Caruth, November 4, 1974, No. OHB3, pp. 22–23, University of North Texas Oral History Collection, Denton, Tex.
179 **"Richard became my business partner":** Ash, interview by Caruth, 21.
180 **After leaving the all-male:** Ash, interview by Caruth, 1–5.
180 **Later, Richard recalled:** Richard Rogers, interview by Donald L. Caruth, November 11, 1974, No. OHB4, p. 23, University of North Texas Oral History Collection, Denton, Tex.
180 **At boarding school:** Rogers, interview by Caruth, 23.
180 **That was why:** Rogers, interview by Caruth, 15.
181 **With that settled:** Mary Kay Ash, *Mary Kay* (Harper & Row, 1981), 31.
181 **Supposedly she countered:** "Sylvia Schaefer, Obituary," *South Florida Sun-Sentinel*, May 28, 2013.
183 **breaking up the:** Ash, *Mary Kay*, 36.

183 **She was not the first:** Mary Lisa Gavenas, *Color Stories* (Simon & Schuster, 2002), 45–51, 133–36.
184 **"Everybody has skin":** Paulette Schwoebel quoting Mary Kay Ash in an interview with the author, August 20, 2009.
184 **After each show:** Doretha Dingler, *In Pink* (Brevin, 2012), 12–13.
184 **"When a woman applies":** *Director's Manual* (Mary Kay Cosmetics, 1968, rev. 1973).
186 **Once it was on:** Jackie Brown, *Ask ME About Mary Kay* (Strategic, 2010), 37.
186 **Because it caused redness:** Sue Young, *The Heart of a Leader* (iUniverse, 2009), 32–33.
186 **The packaging was pale pink:** Ash, interview by Caruth, 54–55.
186 **The saleswoman who:** Mary Kay Cosmetics Inc., *Simulated Beauty Show*, 1972, LP.
186 **She also pointed out:** Ash, interview by Caruth, 54.
187 **Beauty by Mary Kay opened for:** "Mary Kay: The Cosmetic Empire," posted September 13, 2024, by Biography, YouTube, 45 min., 3 sec., youtube.com/watch?v=ZoiFiicfo30.
187 **Inventory rested resplendent:** Ash, interview by Caruth, 32.
188 **The only good-luck gift:** Mary Kay Global (@marykayglobal), "Meet Oscar the Ivy! Oscar was gifted to Mary Kay Ash in 1963 in celebration of starting Mary Kay. She loved her plants so much she named them! Oscar started with six leaves in a tiny pot and has been flourishing ever since," Instagram, August 16, 2022, instagram.com/marykayglobal/p/ChVTdCeLOAH.
188 **In the issue of *Vogue*:** Fashion Tress, "Are You Woman Enough for a Wig?," *Vogue*, September 15, 1963.
188 **At her first, sales totaled:** Ash, interview by Caruth, 30–31.
188 **was thirty-two-year-old:** Helen Mundell, "Mary Kay Opens Career Doors for Women," *Ithaca Journal*, July 13, 1990.
190 **Visiting Houston for Thanksgiving:** Ash, *Mary Kay*, 34.

CHAPTER FOURTEEN: "PRAISE FORWARD TO SUCCESS"

191 **"We kept the wigs":** Mary Kay Ash, interview by Donald L. Caruth, November 4, 1974, No. OHB3, p. 33, University of North Texas Oral History Collection, Denton, Tex.
191 **Wigs were not yet sold:** Richard Rogers, interview by Donald L. Caruth, November 11, 1974, No. OHB4, p. 33, University of North Texas Oral History Collection, Denton, Tex.
191 **Each consultant was equipped:** Sylvia Schaefer, *All About Wigs* (Fashion Tress Inc., 1962), 28.
191 **Until then, wigs:** Rogers, interview by Caruth, 32.
192 **Richard followed the example:** Rogers, interview by Caruth, 34.
192 **In October, the company's first:** Rogers, interview by Caruth, 36.
192 **But the wig business:** Rogers, interview by Caruth, 34–35.
192 **Once bought, a wig:** "Wigs: Mary Kay Shares Déjà Vu," *Mary Kay Foundation Blog*, November 2, 2016, accessed July 22, 2018, no longer available.
192 **After which Richard:** Rogers, interview by Caruth, 34–35.
192 **With an eye to winning:** Mary Kay Fashion Wig and Beauty Shows, "Earn $500," *Dallas Morning News*, December 3, 1963; Jackie Brown, interview with the author, November 15, 2009; Jackie Brown, *Ask ME About Mary Kay* (Strategic Book Group, 2010), 3–13.
193 **"She was glossy":** Brown, *Ask ME About Mary Kay*, 6.
194 **A ranch-bred rodeo queen:** "Miss Marjorie Boren Weds Eugene Brewer," *Chattanooga Daily Times*, August 27, 1950; Yolanda Alvardo, "Biz Whiz High on Motivation in Profitable Cosmetics World," *Lansing State Journal*, July 8, 1979.
194 **"I remember how proud":** Mary Kay Ash, *Mary Kay* (Harper & Row, 1981), 174.
194 **"Everybody wants to be like":** Brown, interview with the author.
195 **In 1931, Mr. Bev's first:** Joan B. Marcus, *To Better Your Best* (Stanley Home Products, 1981), 17.
195 **That night, Richard:** Brown, *Ask ME About Mary Kay*, 25–28; Brown, interview with the author.
195 **Later she would write:** Brown, *Ask ME About Mary Kay*, 45.
196 **Heading home to Arkansas:** Brown, 31–44.
196 **time for the January:** Brown, 48–50.
197 **When consultants tried:** Doretha Dingler, *In Pink* (Brevin, 2012), 50.
198 **"When I met her":** Erma Thomson, interview with the author, August 18, 2014.
199 **Then he promoted himself:** This promotion was mentioned in a later story about another

promotion. See "Mary Kay Cosmetics Elevates Management," *Dallas Morning News*, January 19, 1968.

199 **His mother and brother:** Ash, interview by Caruth, 22–23.

200 **"Pretend that everyone":** "Mary Kay: The Cosmetic Empire," posted September 13, 2024, by Biography, YouTube, 45 min., 3 sec., youtube.com/watch?v=ZoiFiicfo30.

200 **Gone were the days:** Ash, *Mary Kay*, 32–33.

200 **Instead of a closet-size:** Mary Kay, "Mary Kay in her new office in Dallas in 1967," Facebook, May 18, 2010, facebook.com/photo/?fbid=395570327170&set=a.395569877170&locale=gl_ES.

201 **Every week, she typed:** "Mary Kay: The Cosmetic Empire."

201 **"In that culture":** Doretha Dingler, interview with the author, November 9, 2018.

201 **She decorated the new cinder:** Mary Kay, "Mary Kay hosts the first Seminar on Sept. 13, 1964. The event was held in the Company warehouse. Mary Kay personally cooked chicken for 200 people as well as orange Jell-O salad which melted in the September heat," Facebook, May 18, 2010, facebook.com/photo/?fbid=395570297170&set=a.395569877170&locale=gl_ES.

202 **"She stood up and praised":** Brown, interview with the author.

203 **Beneath the headline:** Mary Kay, "Mary Kay with her sons, Richard Rogers (left) and Ben Rogers (right), proudly highlight the Company's first-year growth. This photo appeared in The Dallas Morning News on Sept. 20, 1964," Facebook, May 18, 2010, facebook.com/photo/?fbid=395570302170&set=a.395569877170&locale=gl_ES.

CHAPTER FIFTEEN: THAT MARY KAY ENTHUSIASM

205 **Convinced it was counterproductive:** Dale Carnegie, *How to Win Friends and Influence People* (Simon & Schuster, 1936), 3.

205 **Later, a company manual:** *Director's Manual* (Mary Kay Cosmetics, 1968, rev. 1973), section 16, 10.

206 **In November of 1963:** Deed of Sale from Mary K. Weaver to John Q. Atchley and Phaona Mae Atchley, 8 November 1963, Harris County Deed Records, vol. 5326, p. 179.

206 **Four months later, she sold:** Deed of Sale from Mary K. Weaver to John H. Rizer, 5 March 1964, Harris County Deed Records, vol. 5448, p. 164.

206 **At one point, the company:** Mary Kay Ash, interview by Donald L. Caruth, November 11, 1974, No. OHB3, p. 86, University of North Texas Oral History Collection, Denton, Tex.

206 **Look what happened:** Bob Kealing, *Tupperware Unsealed* (University Press of Florida, 2008), 194–220.

207 **In theory, they should:** Alice MacDonald under the supervision of John A. Quelch, "Mary Kay Cosmetics, Inc.: Marketing Communications," Harvard Business School Case 9-583-068, 1983.

207 **So far, her biggest addition:** Ash, interview by Caruth, 58.

207 **She pushed consultants:** Ash, interview by Caruth, 26–27.

208 **The problem of managing:** Direct Selling Association, "Code of Ethics," accessed March 28, 2025, dsa.org/consumerprotection/code-of-ethics.

209 **"Even if she falls":** Ash, interview by Caruth, 53.

209 **To Mary Kay's mind:** Richard Rogers, interview by Donald L. Caruth, November 11, 1974, No. OHB4, pp. 18–20, University of North Texas Oral History Collection, Denton, Tex.

209 **Likewise, she instituted:** Kay Longcope, Boston Globe Syndicate, "Top Saleswoman Tells How and Why," *Manhattan Mercury*, March 18, 1982.

210 **"As a teacher with":** Sue Young, *The Heart of a Leader* (iUniverse, 2009), 5.

210 **"You got married":** Doretha Dingler, interview with the author, November 9, 2018.

210 **"Women had no opportunities":** Jackie Brown, interview with the author, November 15, 2009.

211 **One of them, Ouida Caldwell:** Eline de Bruijn, "Richardson Woman, 92, Still Selling Mary Kay Products After 50 Years," *Dallas Morning News*, March 4, 2016.

211 **Later, Helen McVoy said:** Longcope, "Top Saleswoman."

211 **"mostly as a lark":** Grady Phelps, "$100,000 Saleswoman," *Corpus Christi Caller-Times*, May 9, 1977.

212 **There and then:** Longcope, "Top Saleswoman."

212 **Stocking them was expensive:** Rogers, interview by Caruth, 37–38.

212 **sales went up $20,000:** Mary Kay Ash, *Mary Kay* (Harper & Row, 1981), 33.
213 **"Don't waste dollar time":** A frequent Mary Kay-ism cited by Teresa McUsic for the *Fort Worth Star-Telegram.* See "Mary Kay Ash Tells How to Do Them Both," *Corpus Christi Caller-Times,* October 15, 1995.
213 **"I remember having":** Georgia Hall Baird, interview with the author, May 31, 2024.
214 **Each received an engraved:** Brown, interview with the author; Jackie Brown, *Ask ME About Mary Kay* (Strategic Book Group, 2010), 170–71.
214 **Kelly claimed that Mary Kay:** Dick Kelly, interview with the author, October 7, 2009.
215 **Not long after, Ash popped:** Brown, *Ask ME About Mary Kay,* 185–90.
215 **Two days before:** Brown interview with the author.
215 **made the front page:** John Rutledge, "Masked Gunmen Tie Up and Rob Woman Executive," *Dallas Morning News,* December 27, 1965.

CHAPTER SIXTEEN: THURSDAY-NIGHT HALLMARK CARDS

217 **Mel made his bar mitzvah:** Accessed May 3, 2012, ftmeade.army.mil/museum/archives/Archive_BW_CMTC_2.html.
217 **Families vacationed in Bermuda:** Passenger list for *Queen of Bermuda,* Hamilton, Bermuda, to New York, 26 November 1937, New York Passenger Lists, 1820–1957, ancestry.com.
217 **Never the kind of peddler:** 'Ash Medical Supply' (1936). *Application for account number, November 20, 1936.* U.S. Treasury Department; Central TV Sales, "A Very Merry Christmas," *Fort Lauderdale News,* December 24, 1957.
218 **In 1945, he was back:** Indictment, *U.S. v. Melville J. Eschwege, Alias M. J. Ash and M. Jerome,* November 5, 1945, No. 1969, F.D.C. No. 15584 (District of Columbia).
218 **She returned the favor:** Mel Einsidler, comment to the author, December 3, 2010.
218 **almost no one did:** Jackie Brown, *Ask ME About Mary Kay* (Strategic Book Group, 2010), 190.
218 **Mel shaved a few years:** Marcia Smith-Durk, "Mel Ash Is Mary Kay's 'Chairman,'" *Dallas Times Herald,* November 4, 1979.
218 **After Mel's death:** First Amended Inventory, Appraisement, and List of Claims and Order, filed 23 March 1983, Estate of Melville J. Ash, case no. PR-80-02664-CP3, Probate Court, Dallas County, Texas.
218 **his less gallant moods:** Brown, *Ask ME About Mary Kay,* 191.
218 **Later, after their honeymoon:** Mary Kay Ash, *Mary Kay* (Harper & Row, 1981), 47–48.
219 **"In those early days":** Erma Thomson, interview with the author, August 18, 2014.
219 **"Mel was the sweetest":** Georgia Hall Baird, interview with the author, May 31, 2024.
219 **The subject of previous:** Smith-Durk, "Mel Ash Is Mary Kay's 'Chairman.'" Like his wife, Mel tended to omit marriages, leading the *Dallas Times Herald* to write: "From the time his wife died [1933] until Mel married Mary Kay, he said he enjoyed his bachelor life."
219 **Despite telling reporters:** Smith-Durk, "Mel Ash Is Mary Kay's 'Chairman.'"
219 **Buttering up the old lady:** Smith-Durk, "Mel Ash Is Mary Kay's 'Chairman.'"
219 **Usually the gift:** Ash, *Mary Kay,* 167.
219 **Mary Kay liked that one:** "Talking to a Texan," *Marshall News Messenger,* January 5, 1986. The bear was reincarnated later in the 1980s.
219 **Mel was allowed:** Julia Sweeney, "Mary Kay Ash: Two Worlds," *Dallas Times Herald,* May 14, 1975.
220 **"she was really happier":** Thomson, interview with the author.
220 **Mary Kay liked Tex-Mex:** Mary Brown Malouf, "Hot Dish," *Dallas Observer,* January 18, 1996.
220 **In contrition, the two:** Sweeney, "Mary Kay Ash."
220 **Because Ash wanted:** Thomson, interview with the author.
221 **"She had one of those":** Thomson, interview with the author.
221 **Producing pictures torn:** Hugh Moffett, "Ideas in Houses: Round Home Moored to a Hill," *Life,* August 5, 1966.
221 **"still holding on":** Dick Kelly, interview with the author, October 7, 2009.
221 **She insisted, for example:** Frank Meier, interview with the author, August 12, 2009.
221 **"She put tremendous trust":** Frank Meier, interview with the author.
222 **Mary Kay would ask:** Mary Kay Ash, interview by Donald L. Caruth, November 4, 1974, No. OHB3, p. 62, University of North Texas Oral History Collection, Denton, Tex.

223 **To the husbands:** Ash, *Mary Kay*, 71.
225 **"I decided that":** Morris L. Mayer, *Direct Selling in the United States: A Commentary and Oral History* (Direct Selling Education Foundation, 1996), 29.
225 **"She [the consultant] would":** Ash, interview by Caruth, 41.
225 **Her first company-wide initiative:** Ash, *Mary Kay*, 17–18.
225 **Richard thought the whole thing:** Richard Rogers, interview by Donald L. Caruth, November 25, 1974, No. OHB4, p. 131, University of North Texas Oral History Collection, Denton, Tex.
225 **With all the pomp:** "Mr. and Mrs. T.V. Tips Were Honored," *Carollton Chronicle*, October 19, 1967.
225 **Winners got a big:** "Mary Kay: The Cosmetic Empire," posted September 13, 2024, by Biography, YouTube, 45 min., 3 sec., youtube.com/watch?v=ZoiFiicfo30.
226 **she had become a speaker:** Brown, *Ask ME About Mary Kay*, 83.
227 **"a colossal fit":** Brown, 201.
227 **At ten that Friday:** Brown, 231–37. In her book, Brown alludes to Friday the thirteenth being bad luck; however, that Friday fell on April 15.
227 **Twisting the knife:** During the 1960s, Brown sometimes changed the spelling of the company name. See Beauty-Control, "Hide Tanner's Process," *Dallas Morning News*, April 9, 1967.

CHAPTER SEVENTEEN: "NEXT YEAR, YOU'LL DO EVEN BETTER"

229 **The next day was Saturday:** Jackie Brown, *Ask ME About Mary Kay* (Strategic Book Group, 2010), 244.
229 **Mary Kay's lawyer:** *Mary Kay Inc. v. J. Brown et Vir*, case no. DC-66-04628, 162nd District Court (Texas), May 24, 1966.
229 **BeautiControl's Diamond Deb:** Brown, *Ask ME About Mary Kay*, 338–39.
230 **BeautiControl even had:** Brown, 137, 273–74.
230 **Beginning in the summer:** Brown, 299.
230 **All kinds of people came:** Dick Kelly, interview with the author, October 7, 2009.
230 **the suits' second year:** 'Ramona Rochelle' (1967). *Certified copy of death certificate for Ramona Rochelle, 9 March 1967.* Application number 29862. Texas Vital Statistics Unit.
231 **Mary Kay's remaining directors:** Doretha Dingler, interview with the author, November 9, 2018; Doretha Dingler, *In Pink* (Brevin, 2012).
231 **Monthly directors' meetings:** Julie Benell, "Tasty Recipes Are Swapped When These Directors Meet," *Dallas Morning News*, April 24, 1969.
231 **Doretha Dingler, a regular:** Dingler, interview with the author.
231 **Forty years later:** Jinger Heath, interview with the author, October 14, 2009.
232 **"Some years ago there lived":** Mary Kay Inc., "Beauty and the Beasts," *Family Circle*, May 1970.
232 **During the first year:** Mary Kay Cosmetics Inc., *Annual Report*, 1975.
232 **Early in the proceedings:** Jackie Brown, interview with the author, November 15, 2009.
232 **In private, she might complain:** Erma Thomson, interview with the author, August 18, 2014.
232 **In public, she would turn:** Matthew Schifrin, "Investing: Peeking Inside LBOs," *Forbes*, June 13, 1988. Although Mary Kay did not allow her company to reveal her age, Schifrin points out that it was publicly available information listed on the 10-K reports filed annually.
233 **sixty-three-year-old:** Mary McDowell, *Never Too Late* (Harvest House, 1981); KOSA-TV, "Mary McDowell: Mary Kay Sales Director," 1978, Texas Archive of the Moving Image, accessed January 10, 2025, texasarchive.org/2013_01465.
234 **"You can teach school":** McDowell, *Never Too Late*, 67.
234 **she would be enthroned:** Kay Y. Bell, "Never Say Never: It's Not Too Late," *Pensacola Times*, November 2, 1983.
234 **Up until January 1:** Elizabeth York Enstam, "The Evolution of Women's Rights in Texas: A Historical Overview," *Handbook of Texas*, 1976, updated March 31, 2021, tshaonline.org/handbook/online/articles/jsw02.
235 **"We've found that":** Mary Kay Ash, *Mary Kay* (Harper & Row, 1981), 157.
235 **Sometimes the only birthday card:** Mary Kay Ash, interview by Donald L. Caruth, November 11, 1974, No. OHB3, p. 95, University of North Texas Oral History Collection, Denton, Tex.
235 **Pink slips were warm:** Dingler, *In Pink*, 16–17.
236 **She briefed consultants:** Mary Kay Cosmetics Inc., *Booking, Coaching & Recruiting*, 1972, LP.

236 **"These words have worked":** Mary Kay Cosmetics Inc., *Simulated Beauty Show*, 1972, LP.

236 **Mary Kay advised:** *Director's Manual* (Mary Kay Cosmetics, 1966, rev. 1973).

236 **The meeting should start:** Mary Kay Cosmetics Inc., *Simulated Beauty Show*; Mary Kay Cosmetics Inc., *Booking, Coaching & Recruiting*.

236 **As consultants arrived:** Mary Kay Cosmetics Inc., *Tunes for Toppers: Sing Along with the Vickeroos*, 1972, LP.

237 **Following a tradition:** Ash, interview by Caruth, 95.

238 **Keeping track of all this:** Thomson, interview with the author.

238 **Within minutes of meeting:** Erma Thomson, interview by Caitlin Chegwiddden, January 22, 2019, No. 1943, p. 7, University of North Texas Oral History Collection, Denton, Tex.

238 **By the third Seminar:** "Beauty by Mary Kay Seminar," *Longview News-Journal*, September 26, 1966.

238 **The next year, she distributed:** Bill Rives, "Views," *Denton Record-Chronicle*, September 22, 1968.

239 **In direct selling, where:** In 1985, a Harvard Business School case study gave company turnover as 80 percent per year, estimating Avon at 150 percent and Tupperware at 100 percent. Alice MacDonald under the supervision of John A. Quelch, "Mary Kay Cosmetics, Inc.: Marketing Communications," Harvard Business School Case 9-583-068, 1983.

239 **Lest any driver miss:** "New Home of Mary Kay Cosmetics," *Dallas Morning News*, August 20, 1967.

239 **In 1967, Mary Kay Inc.:** Richard Rogers, interview by Donald L. Caruth, November 25, 1974, No. OHB4, pp. 75–76, University of North Texas Oral History Collection, Denton, Tex.

239 **It had invented:** "Subsidiary of Mary Kay Will Double Its Plant," *Dallas Times Herald*, July 29, 1973.

240 **A consortium had already offered:** Mary Kay Ash, *Mary Kay on People Management*, 1985 paperback ed. (Warner Books, 1984), 175.

240 **Koscot's pitch was more:** Thomas Thompson, "Dare to Be Great!," *Life*, May 28, 1971.

240 **His miracle ingredient:** "Mink Oil," Cosmetics and Skin, updated August 13, 2018, cosmeticsandskin.com/fgf/mink.php.

241 **"Mr. Enthusiasm" favored outfits:** Wayne King, "Glenn Turner: A Franchiser with Flamboyance," *New York Times*, January 13, 1972.

241 **Cartwheeling twin dwarfs:** Nancy Imperiale, "Twin Dwarfs Were Huge Part of Turner's Sensational Act," *Orlando Sentinel*, June 29, 2003.

241 **Missing the irony:** At the end of 2019, the claim was still on a *Wikipedia* entry for Koscot, despite a link that led directly to the May 28, 1971, cover of *Life* showing *Jesus Christ Superstar*.

241 **Turner was a huckster:** Rogers, interview by Caruth, 67–68.

241 **At the end of 1967:** Rogers, interview by Caruth, 68.

241 **Mary Kay formally named herself:** "Mary Kay Cosmetics Elevates Management," *Dallas Morning News*, January 19, 1968.

242 **Excerpts from a speech:** "Feminine Opportunity Increasing Rapidly," *Dallas Morning News*, January 18, 1968.

242 **Despite her impatience:** "Club Activities," *Dallas Morning News*, April 11, 1968; "Club Activities," *Dallas Morning News*, June 5, 1968.

243 **Just before Easter:** "Mary Kay Files 195,000-Share Stock Offering," *Dallas Morning News*, April 13, 1968.

243 **With the IPO underway:** Rogers, interview by Caruth, 105–9.

243 **On August 8, 1968:** 'Lula Wagner' (1968). *Certified copy of death certificate for Lula Wagner, 8 August 1968.* Application number 57266. Texas Vital Statistics Unit.

243 **After a lifetime:** Inventory and Appraisement, filed October 21, 1968, Estate of Lula V. Murphy, case no. 101,049, Probate Court, Harris County, Texas.

243 **On regular visits:** Ash, *Mary Kay*, 132–33.

244 **Mary Kay sometimes said her:** Documents vary. The 1900 census gives Lula's birth year as 1882. Mary Kay's first birth certificate gives Lula's birth year as 1883, although the Texas Registrar of Vital Statistics could locate no record of Lula's birth in 1883 in response to requests made in 2009 and 2010. Lula's death certificate lists a birth date of 1884. Mary Kay's delayed birth certificate assumes a birthdate of 1885, and Lula's 1941 marriage license assumes a birth date of 1886.

CHAPTER EIGHTEEN: A PINK CADILLAC

245 **Shares opened near $12:** Richard Rogers, interview by Donald L. Caruth, November 11, 1974, No. OHB4, p. 81, University of North Texas Oral History Collection, Denton, Tex.

245 **The next morning:** "$1.8 Million: Mary Kay Collects on Stock," *Dallas Morning News*, August 30, 1968.

245 **photo of grinning investment bankers:** "Mary Kay Goes," *Fort Worth Star-Telegram*, August 30, 1968.

245 **On September 13:** "Land Bought by Mary Kay," *Dallas Morning News*, September 13, 1968.

245 **A few weeks later:** "Mary Kay's Net Doubles," *Dallas Morning News*, October 18, 1968.

246 **With everything going:** Rogers, interview by Caruth, 77–81.

246 **Having established the stock's:** "Mary Kay Talks Acquisition Bid," *Dallas Morning News*, November 27, 1968.

246 **By the time the contract:** "Mary Kay Buys Supplier for $7.5 Million in Stock," *Dallas Morning News*, December 10, 1968; John Tubb, "Local Market Falls Off," *Austin American-Statesman*, December 15, 1968.

246 **With Cosmetic Creations signed:** Rogers, interview by Caruth, 81.

246 **while his former partners:** "Mary Kay Buys Site," *Dallas Morning News*, December 24, 1968.

246 **His next round:** Rogers, interview by Caruth, 82.

246 **The new 108,000-square-foot:** Rogers, interview by Caruth, 87–91.

247 **Mary Kay believed:** Mary Kay Ash, interview by Donald L. Caruth, November 4, 1974, No. OHB3, p. 26, University of North Texas Oral History Collection, Denton, Tex.

247 **Within a decade:** Mary Kay, "Mary Kay at the opening of the North Central Training and Distribution Center in Illinois in 1975," May 18, 2010, Facebook, facebook.com/photo/?fbid=395570602170&set=a.395569877170&locale=gl_ES.

247 **"Each time we'd try":** Frank Meier, interview with the author, August 11, 2009.

247 **company found a dainty bulldozer:** "Boudoir Pink," *Atlanta Journal*, November 4, 1970.

247 **Months later, when that center:** "Tyler Roses to 'Bomb' Atlanta, Ga.," *Tyler Morning Telegraph*, June 1, 1971; "Mary Kay Inc. Opens Plant," *Atlanta Constitution*, June 3, 1971.

247 **when the company had outgrown:** Henry Woodhead, "Think Pink," *Atlanta Constitution*, March 16, 1973.

248 **It also had:** Rogers, interview by Caruth, 110–15.

248 **In private, Mary Kay griped:** Ash, interview by Caruth, 92.

248 **Papers there ran headlines:** Nancy Dexter, "Tanning Her Hide Made Millions," *Age* (Melbourne), February 23, 1971.

248 **From the company's first:** Ash, interview by Caruth, 66.

248 **When the North Texas chapter:** "Executive Receives Honor," *Dallas Morning News*, April 3, 1969.

248 **He preferred press:** "$5 Million Firm Headed by Youth, 24," *Fort Worth Star-Telegram*, January 19, 1968.

249 **"was datin' all the girls":** Meier, interview with the author.

249 **In 1969, she celebrated:** "Jack Wittrup," askART.com, accessed July 31, 2025, askart.com/artist/Jack_Wittrup/117909/Jack_Wittrup.aspx.

250 **Instead, driving her new Cadillac:** Mary Kay Ash, *Mary Kay: You Can Have It All* (Prima, 1995), 199.

251 **"Our small office":** Erma Thomson, GenerationsLestWeForget, accessed August 11, 2014, no longer available, generationslestweforget.com/amazing-excerpts/thompson-erma-excerpt.

251 **More recently, multilevel:** Zig Ziglar, *Zig* (Doubleday, 2002), 147.

251 **When she read out:** Yvonne Pendleton, *Paychecks of the Heart* (Mary Kay Inc., 2000), 45–46.

252 **Offering bumblebees in three:** Later, a double-wide, 3.5-carat bee was conferred on top-level retirees.

252 **"Aerodynamics have proven":** Joan Rice, "Honey Bee . . . Mary Kay's as Popular as Her Cosmetics," *Akron Beacon-Journal*, October 23, 1977.

254 **"If we awarded":** Ash, *Mary Kay: You Can Have It All*, 203.

254 **Mary Kay kept right on:** Mary Kay Ash, *Mary Kay* (Harper & Row, 1981), 81.

254 **When Marabel Morgan's:** Marabel Morgan, *The Total Woman* (Fleming H. Revell, 1973).

254 **After he left, Mary Kay:** James Ewell, "Founder of Cosmetic Firm Bound, Robbed of Jewelry," *Dallas Morning News*, August 23, 1974.
254 **the stolen jewels were:** Associated Press, "Texas Robbery: $53,000 in Gems," *Des Moines Tribune*, August 23, 1974.
255 **"Really, three recruits":** Doretha Dingler, interview with the author, November 9, 2018.
256 **Her next totem:** Kay Longcope, Boston Globe Syndicate, "Company Based on Golden Rule, Belief in Women," *Manhattan Mercury*, March 18, 1982.
257 **By the mid-1970s:** Rogers, interview by Caruth, 53, 56.
257 **Unusual for a U.S. beauty:** Ash, interview by Caruth, 89–90.
257 **A few more shades:** Ash, interview by Caruth, 89.
258 **she was decked in diamonds:** Don Stokes, "Mary Kay: It's a Way of Life," 1977, Texas Archive of the Moving Image, accessed May 26, 2025, texasarchive.org/2013_00628.
258 **After acquiring all:** Pendleton, *Paychecks of the Heart*, 236–38.
258 **Twenty years later:** "Odds and ends," *Wall Street Journal*, April 18, 1991.
259 **After joining the company:** Margaria Fichtner, "In the Pink," *State* (Columbia, S.C.), November 14, 1982.
259 **Instead, directors shared:** Alice MacDonald under the supervision of John A. Quelch, "Mary Kay Cosmetics, Inc.: Marketing Communications," Harvard Business School Case 9-583-068, 1983.
260 **castle he had been building:** Troy Herring, "Glenn Turner's Castle," *Winter Park/Maitland Observer*, January 12, 2018.
260 **Founded in 1964:** Wallace Turner, "Lawsuits Threaten Millionaire Promoter of Pyramid Sales," *New York Times*, February 19, 1973.
261 **In 1972, a pilot:** Associated Press, "Jet Hits Ice Cream Parlor, Killing 22 in Sacramento," *New York Times*, September 25, 1972.
261 **The year after, Patrick died:** "William Patrick Is Killed in California Air Crash," *New York Times*, June 10, 1973.
261 **Securities and Exchange Commission brought:** Michael C. Jensen, "S.E.C. Lays Fraud to Holiday Magic," *New York Times*, June 29, 1973.
261 **Losing a battle:** *Annual Report of the Federal Trade Commission for Fiscal Year Ended June 30, 1932* (U.S. Government Printing Office, 1932), 239–40.
261 **Jan and Frank Day sold:** Morris L. Mayer, *Direct Selling in the United States: A Commentary and Oral History* (Direct Selling Education Foundation, 1996), 15.
261 **Fuller Brush sales had been:** "Jobs: A Good Man Is Hard to Find—So They Hire Women," *Time*, November 4, 1966.
261 **Led by executives:** Charles L. Hinkle and Esther F. Steinman, "Case 26: Mary Kay Cosmetics, Inc.," in *Cases in Marketing Management: Issues for the 1980s* (Prentice-Hall, 1984).
261 **While Richard kept:** "Business: Avon Calling," *Time*, December 4, 1978.
262 **In 1967, she had taken:** Brownie Wise Papers, 1938–68, series 1, 4, 5, 6, Archives Center, National Museum of American History, Smithsonian Institution, Washington, D.C.
262 **Afterward, the first woman:** Laurie Whitmore, "Brownie Wise Dies at Home," *Orlando Sentinel*, September 25, 1992.

CHAPTER NINETEEN: HORATIO ALGER STORIES

264 **"We had a price increase":** "Lessons of Leadership: Flying High on an Idea," *Nation's Business*, August 1978.
265 **"Australia is about where":** Julie Jensen, "Never Too Old to Feel Beautiful," *Quad City Times*, October 8, 1974.
265 **In between, she squeezed in:** "Locals," *New Washington Herald*, May 5, 1977.
266 **Told that she could:** Alice MacDonald under the supervision of John A. Quelch, "Mary Kay Cosmetics, Inc.: Marketing Communications," Harvard Business School Case 9-583-068, 1983.
266 **"round-cornered offices":** Frank Meier, interview with the author, August 11, 2009.
268 **In 1975, Crowley:** "Hall of Fame," Direct Selling Association, accessed May 25, 2025, dsa.org/events/awards-program/hall-of-fame.
268 **Taking action to dispel:** "Who We Are," Horatio Alger Association, accessed May 25, 2025, horatioalger.org/who-we-are.

268 **Mary C. and Mary Kay:** Jon Anderson, "Add 14 Chapters to Horatio Alger's Story," *Chicago Tribune*, May 24, 1978.

269 **In her acceptance:** "Mary Kay Ash—1978 Horatio Alger Award Recipient," posted September 21, 2015, by Horatio Alger Association, YouTube, 5 min., 5 sec., youtube.com/watch?v=hMu5hS7E2Jw.

269 **To make her point:** Mary C. Crowley, *Women Who Win* (Fleming H. Revell, 1979), 110–11.

269 **She funded a $2.5 million:** "Crowley," KXAS-TV (Fort Worth, Tex.), June 19, 1986, digital .library.unt.edu/ark:/67531/metadc2218249/m1/?q=mary%20kay%20ash.

269 **"Sometimes we would be":** Cliff Barrows, interview with the author, October 1, 2009.

270 **She hired the handicapped:** Mary C. Crowley, *You Can Too* (Power Books, 1980), 99–106.

270 **She started a Christmas tradition:** Joe Taylor, "Shopping Spree II," *Dallas Times Herald*, August 7, 1975.

270 **Or how she supported:** Mary C. Crowley, *Pocketful of Hope* (Home Interiors & Gifts, 1981), 83.

270 **Thus, in the spring:** Mary Kay Ash, *Mary Kay* (Harper & Row, 1981), 143–49.

272 **Refusing to endorse:** Kay Longcope, Boston Globe Syndicate, "Company Based on Golden Rule, Belief in Women," *Manhattan Mercury*, March 18, 1982.

272 **Profiling her, *Reader's Digest*:** Roul Tunley, condensed from *Shreveport Magazine*, "The Sweet Smell of Success," *Reader's Digest*, November, 1978.

272 ***Business Week* put her:** "The 100 Top Corporate Women," *Business Week*, June 21, 1976.

272 **She told interviewers:** Longcope, "Company Based on Golden Rule."

273 **the only place big enough:** Mary Kay, "Mary Kay with an independent sales force member in 1974," Facebook, May 18, 2010, facebook.com/photo/?fbid=395570597170&set=a.395569877170&locale=gl_ES.

273 **Women patted feathered:** "WSB-TV Mary Kay Ash, 1980," posted February 8, 2023, by Foggy Melson's Breakdown, YouTube, 2 min., 6 sec., youtube.com/watch?v=NGQg_NraKpc.

274 **As she did every year:** One year, for example, the blouses to be worn with directors' suits were stipulated as pink for director, ivory for senior director, and teal for future nationals who had five or more offspring directors. See Ash, *Mary Kay*, 160.

275 **"Her senseless death":** Ash, *Mary Kay*, 54.

275 **Fed up with all that:** Carol Edgar, "The Hot Pink Empire of Mary Kay Ash," *Texas Monthly*, April, 1979.

275 **Mary Kay had a similar:** *60 Minutes*, "The Pink Panther," aired October 28, 1979, on CBS, cbsnews.com/video/the-pink-panther.

278 **According to the version:** Ash, *Mary Kay*, 112–13.

278 **"I told CBS":** Cindy Creasy, "Pink Lady Proves She's Right on Track," *Richmond Times-Dispatch*, November 9, 1979.

278 **Local television presented:** "Mary Kay Solar," KXAS-TV (Fort Worth, Tex.), November 27, 1979, digital.library.unt.edu/ark:/67531/metadc1130608/m1/?q=mary%20kay%20cosmetics.

279 **"She couldn't believe":** Erma Thomson, interview with the author, August 18, 2014.

279 **J. Ben Rogers had died:** Inventory and Appraisement, filed December 16, 1977, Estate of J. Ben Rogers, Sr., docket no. 148,993, Probate Court, Harris County, Texas.

279 **Ex-husband Charlie Weaver:** 'Charles William Weaver' (1980). *Certified copy of death certificate for Charles William Weaver, 15 December 1980.* Application number 93867. Dallas County, Texas.

279 **Mary Kay stayed home:** Thomson, interview with the author.

280 **Aside from joint holdings:** First Amended Inventory, Appraisement, and List of Claims and Order, filed March 23, 1983, Estate of Melville J. Ash, case no. PR-80-02664-CP3, Probate Court, Dallas County, Texas.

280 **Four days later:** 'Melville Jerome Ash' (1980). *Certified copy of death certificate for Melville Jerome Ash, 7 July 1980.* Application number 51358. Texas Vital Statistics Unit.

CHAPTER TWENTY: "REACH OUT AND TOUCH"

281 **Mel was pronounced:** 'Melville Jerome Ash' (1980). *Certified copy of death certificate for Melville Jerome Ash, 7 July 1980.* Application number 51358. Texas Vital Statistics Unit.

281 **His funeral was at Northway:** "Deaths, Funerals A-1," *Dallas Morning News*, July 8, 1980.

281 **Thanks to deployment:** James E. Adams, "Cadillacs and Cosmetics Mix at Mary Kay Meeting," *St. Louis Post-Dispatch*, July 10, 1980.

281 **Addressing an audience:** Elaine Viets, "Reach Out and Touch," *St. Louis Post-Dispatch*, July 20, 1980.

283 **One newspaper called her:** Marilynn Marter, Knight News Service, "Mary Kay: A Queen Bee in Constant Flight," *Arkansas Gazette*, August 24, 1980.

283 **Fiscal 1980 could come:** Alice MacDonald under the supervision of John A. Quelch, "Mary Kay Cosmetics, Inc.: Marketing Communications," Harvard Business School Case 9-583-068, 1983.

283 **Citing statistics that sounded:** Mary Eckardt, "Mary Kay Cosmetics: 'More Exciting Than a Honeymoon,'" *Sheboygan Press*, August 1, 1980; Alice MacDonald Court under the supervision of John A. Quelch, "Mary Kay Cosmetics, Inc.: Marketing Communications," Harvard Business School Case 9-583-068, 1983.

283 **When Richard invited her:** Erma Thomson, interview with the author, August 18, 2014.

283 **Asked if she might marry:** Kristin McMurran, "Mary Kay Ash," *People*, July 29, 1985.

283 **"The letters I get":** Margaria Fichtner, "The Miracle of Mary Kay," *Miami Herald*, October 3, 1982.

284 **A consultant who exceeded:** MacDonald, "Mary Kay Cosmetics, Inc."

284 **As the workload grew:** Thomson, interview with the author.

284 **Unable to meet:** Don Stokes, "Mary Kay: All Your Tomorrows," 1980, Texas Archive of the Moving Image, accessed March 31, 2025, texasarchive.org/2013_00629.

285 **By the time the final:** Don Stokes, "Mary Kay Cosmetics: Capture the Vision," 1981, Texas Archive of the Moving Image, accessed March 31, 2025, texasarchive.org/2010_00144.

285 **Prompted by the profile:** John Strengrevics under the supervision of John P. Kotter, "Mary Kay Cosmetics, Inc.," Harvard Business School Case 9-481-126, 1981.

286 **A countdown clock:** Mary Kay Ash, *Mary Kay* (Harper & Row, 1981), 193.

286 **gushing profile of "profits powerhouse":** Howard Rudnitsky, "The Flight of the Bumblebee," *Forbes*, June 22, 1981.

287 **She let the NSDs:** Doretha Dingler, interview with the author, November 9, 2018.

287 **Shooting in Scavullo's:** Evan Richardson, interview with the author, September 29, 2014.

287 **the magazine ran the same:** Paul Rosenfield, "The Beautiful Make-Up of Mary Kay," *Saturday Evening Post*, October 1981.

288 **Then she met Bob Shook:** Robert Shook, interview with the author, November 6, 2017; Bob Shook, email to the author, November 5, 2017; *Encyclopedia.com*, "Shook, Robert L. 1938–," accessed January 10, 2025, encyclopedia.com/arts/educational-magazines/shook-robert-l-1938.

289 **The book opened:** Ash, *Mary Kay*, 1–9.

289 **One chapter gathered:** Ash, 172–90.

289 **"the richest ghostwriter":** Shook, interview with the author.

289 **"If we sell a million":** Thomson quoting Richard Rogers, interview with the author.

289 **Mary Kay did her best:** Mary Kay, "Mary Kay gets some rest between stops on the 1991 book tour for her autobiography. Mary Kay's two-month book tour included several major cities across the United States," Facebook, May 18, 2010, facebook.com/photo/?fbid=395570822170&set=a.395569877170&locale=gl_ES. The publication date was 1981, not 1991, as noted in the post.

289 **Major newspapers ran:** Harper & Row, "You've Gone Pretty Far for a Woman," *Chicago Tribune*, December 7, 1981.

290 **She did dozens:** "KRTV Mary Kay Ash, 1962," posted August 12, 2020, by Montana Historical Society, YouTube, 10 min., 22 sec., youtube.com/watch?v=z-NnQdcyFv0.

290 **A week might have:** Erma Thomson, interview with the author, August 18, 2014.

290 **"Even clothes were agony":** Thomson, interview with the author.

290 **Wearing the same:** "KTVI-TV2 DONAHUE Mary Kay Cosmetics. V-Cord 2 Color Recording," posted November 5, 2021, by Obsolete Video, YouTube, 40 min., youtube.com/watch?v=8e0ImnTjuXg.

291 **Then she flew home:** Thomson, interview with the author.

292 **Without going into details:** Kay Longcope, Boston Globe Syndicate, "Company Based on Golden Rule, Belief in Women," *Manhattan Mercury*, March 18, 1982.

292 **Declaring, "I can't have":** Longcope, "Company Based on Golden Rule."

293 **Ebby Halliday remembered:** Ebby Halliday, interview with the author, July 31, 2009.

293 **with Mary Kay heading up:** Helen Parmley, "Church Raises $10 Million," *Dallas Morning News*, November 9, 1983.

293 **As its twentieth year began:** Alice MacDonald Court under the supervision of John A. Quelch, "Mary Kay Cosmetics, Inc.: Marketing Communications," Harvard Business School Case 9-583-068, 1983.

293 **In celebration, employees:** Jennifer Skemp O'Grady, interview with the author, September 20, 2009.

293 **Later a *New York Times*:** Grace Gluek, "Capturing C.E.O.'s for Posterity," *New York Times Magazine*, December 3, 1989.

293 **end of the first fiscal:** *Mary Kay '82* (Mary Kay Inc., 1983).

293 **Over breakfast with:** Shari Spires, "Mary Kay Ash: Cosmetics Superstar," *Palm Beach Post*, January 11, 1983.

294 **Mary Kay stayed on message:** Napoleon Hill Foundation, "Some of you may remember Mary Kay Ash, founder of Mary Kay cosmetics company. Did you know she was a devout follower of Napoleon Hill's philosophy? In 1983, she delivered a speech at the Napoleon Hill Gold Medal Award ceremony," posted January 19, 2020, Facebook, facebook.com/NapoleonHillFoundation/posts/some-of-you-may-remember-mary-kay-ash-founder-of-mary-kay-cosmetics-company-did-/10158016188282138.

294 **Planning the company's twentieth:** Mary Kay, "Mary Kay at the 20th Anniversary Seminar in 1983. Mary Kay's message to the independent sales force in the Seminar brochure read, 'I don't have a crystal ball, so I can't read the future. But over the years, I have learned to read people,'" Facebook, May 18, 2010, facebook.com/photo/?fbid=395570817170&set=a.395569877170&locale=gl_ES.

294 **Beneath, she added:** Treasures to Behold, "Wedgewood [*sic*] Pink 1983 Jasperware Mary Kay Cosmetics 6.5 Inch Plate," eBay, accessed March 27, 2025, ebay.com/sch/i.html?_nkw=mary+kay+commemorative+plate+wedgewood&_.

294 **came *The Mary Kay Guide*:** The Beauty Experts at Mary Kay Cosmetics, *The Mary Kay Guide to Beauty* (Addison-Wesley, 1983), 8.

294 **A Book-of-the-Month:** "Best Sellers," *New York Times*, January 15, 1984.

295 **Based on past performance:** Richard and Mary Kay had noted the drawbacks of operating a public company years earlier. See Richard Rogers, interview by Donald L. Caruth, November 11, 1974, No. OHB4, pp. 94–101, University of North Texas Oral History Collection, Denton, Tex.

295 **A front-page analysis:** "Party at Mary Kay Not Too Lively as Recruiting Falls Off," *Wall Street Journal*, October 28, 1983.

297 **Making an exception:** Ed Bark, "Official Explains What Mary Kay Meant," *Dallas Morning News*, August 23, 1984.

297 **Richard canceled the $8 million:** Steve Brown, "Mary Kay Scraps Plans for Complex," *Dallas Morning News*, November 3, 1984.

CHAPTER TWENTY-ONE: A PINK PALACE

299 **The four distribution centers:** "Mary Kay Cosmetics: Financial Results," Business Wire, January 31, 1985.

299 **Then the headquarters:** "Mary Kay Announces Sale of Headquarters," *Dallas Morning News*, February 9, 1985.

299 **That spring, Richard:** Edwin A. Finn Jr., "Mary Kay Gets Buyout Offer from Managers," *Wall Street Journal*, May 31, 1985.

300 **Analysts were still saying:** John Crudele, "Mary Kay to Go Private Again," *New York Times*, May 31, 1985.

300 **As the deal:** Associated Press, "Arrests of Eight Smash Drug Ring," *Tyler Courier-Times*, May 30, 1985.

300 **Son of a mother:** "Mary Kay Buyout," *New York Times*, July 2, 1985.

300 **Meetings were set:** "Mary Kay Cosmetics Resets Date of Special Meeting of Shareholders," Business Wire, November 8, 1985.

301 **During a fifteen-minute meeting:** Associated Press, "Mary Kay Cosmetics Becoming Private Firm," *Chicago Tribune*, December 4, 1985.

301 **The high-yield debt securities:** Marcia Parker, "Mary Kay in the Pink; Company's Putting On a New Face," *Pensions & Investment Age*, November 2, 1987.

301 **The Internal Revenue Service:** Keli Flynn, "The Legacy of Mary Kay Cosmetics: Empowering Women Through Beauty," *Handbook of Texas*, October 1, 1995, updated October 18, 2023, tshaonline.org/handbook/entries/mary-kay-cosmetics.

301 **"It was a tradition":** Erma Thomson, interview with the author, August 18, 2014.

302 **Ben, who had left:** "In Dallas: Zeta Alumnae Home Tour Slated Friday," *Marshall News Messenger*, April 2, 1978.

302 **Thomson remembered her saying:** Thomson, interview with the author.

302 **Meier remembered her visiting:** Frank Meier, interview with the author, August 11, 2009.

302 **Designed by local architect:** Alice Wynn, interview with the author, May 4, 2009.

302 **The real estate company:** Jann Kelso, "Heard & Overheard," *Dallas Morning News*, December 30, 1984.

303 **"She got a better price":** Wynn, interview with the author.

303 **Deciding that she:** Meier, interview with the author.

303 **"It's not too flashy":** Marylyn Schwartz, Dallas Morning News Syndicate, "New Mary Kay House Is in the Pink," *Waukesha County Freeman*, August 28, 1985.

303 **Her new house would have:** Candy Evans, "Mary Kay Ash Home Bites the Dust, R.I.P.," Candys Dirt.com, March 14, 2017, candysdirt.com/2017/03/14/mary-kay-ash-home-bites-dust-r-p.

303 **"I didn't care":** Schwartz, "New Mary Kay House."

304 **The concert grand:** Jennifer Cook—Author, "Like most women who climb the ladder of success to the top in Mary Kay, National Sales Director Mona Butters never meant to become a Beauty Consultant when she first learned about the products," Facebook, July 17, 2023, facebook.com/photo.php?fbid=591530553116726&id=100067793589253&set=a.416066103996506.

304 **After the christening:** Marylyn Schwartz, Dallas Morning News Syndicate, "A Cosmetics Queen Reigns Supreme in a $5 Million Manse," *Chicago Tribune*, August 18, 1985.

304 **Her ophthalmologist warned:** Thomson, interview with the author.

304 **They snuck into:** Jennifer Cook—Author, "This week I had the pleasure of going down memory lane with a good friend and co-worker at Mary Kay Inc., Gail Harris. Gail worked at Mary Kay from 1979-1985, and then she rejoined the staff in 1992 to 2019," Facebook, July 31, 2022, facebook.com/photo/?fbid=197598192616536&set=a.416066103996506.

304 **they opened her closet:** Kit Konolige, *The Richest Women in the World* (Macmillan, 1985), 107.

305 **decided to suspend a crystal:** Meier, interview with the author.

305 **Remembering her robberies:** KXAS-TV (Fort Worth, Tex.), "Ash Guard House," July 9, 1985, digital.library.unt.edu/ark:/67531/metadc1237808/m1/?q=mary%20kay%20ash.

305 **upped it to nineteen thousand***:* Schwartz, "Cosmetics Queen Reigns Supreme."

305 **Not long before her move:** Allen Pusey, *Dallas Times Herald*, "Kidnapping-Prevention Course Captivates Them?," *Clarion-Ledger* (Jackson, Miss.), March 22, 1980.

305 **Unwilling to give up:** Bill Besse, interview with the author, June 17, 2014.

305 **Slowing for a yellow light:** Jennifer Cook, interview with the author, May 10, 2021.

305 **Long before every celebrity:** Wynn, interview with the author.

306 **If a store was unable:** Jennifer Cook, *Pass It On* (Brown Books, 2021), 101–2.

306 **"I'm amazed when I see":** Marty Primeau, "Mary Kay Ash," *Dallas Morning News*, August 28, 1983.

306 **"She would drive":** Doretha Dingler, interview with the author, November 9, 2018.

306 **At headquarters, she would:** Thomson, interview with the author.

307 **Then she would tidy:** "Mary Kay Ash's Pink Mansion," *Mary Kay Foundation Blog*, accessed July 22, 2018, marykayfoundation.org.

307 **A creek running:** Cook, *Pass It On*, 103–4.

307 **"We walked in":** Dingler, interview with the author.

308 **Kit Konolige profiled:** Konolige, *Richest Women in the World*, 107–12.

308 ***People* magazine portrayed:** Kristin McMurran, "Mary Kay Ash," *People*, July 29, 1985.

308 **Hundreds of consultants contributed:** *Cooking with Mary Kay* (Mary Kay Cosmetics, 1985).

308 **Still complaining that on:** Jon Anderson, "In the Pink," *Chicago Tribune*, February 14, 1991.

308 **"Once you came to the airport":** Gloria Mayfield Banks, interview with the author, December 30, 2009.

308 **"I was a country girl":** Dingler, interview with the author.

308 **Many wore the gold:** Mary Bland Armistead, "Mary Kay Way Fun—and Prosperous," *Roanoke Times*, October 31, 1979.

308 **Meeting them, Mary Kay:** "Mary Kay: The Cosmetic Empire," posted September 13, 2024, by Biography, YouTube, 45 min., 3 sec., youtube.com/watch?v=ZoiFiicfo30.

309 **That October, Mary Kay:** Doretha Dingler, *If the Pink Shoe Fits* (Brevin, 2013), 70–72.

309 **She had surgery:** Diane Jennings, "Mary Crowley," *Dallas Morning News*, November 17, 1985.

309 **soon feature company classics:** Mary C. Crowley, *Cooking with Love and Butter* (Home Interiors and Gifts, 1986), 13, 86, 131, 265.

309 **Crowley's cancer would kill her:** Jennings, "Mary Crowley."

310 **During a Leadership Conference:** Rob Salem and Rita Zeckas, "Back in the Saddle Again for Sutton Place Dien-Dins," *Toronto Star*, April 25, 1986.

310 **Pressed on purple vinyl:** Katy Bee, "Radio & Records," *Tennessean* (Nashville), July 17, 1987.

311 **Flagg admitted that the character:** Heather Burke, Mary Kay Independent Beauty Consultant, "Did you know that Mary Kay Ash and Fannie Flagg, author of 'Fried Green Tomatoes at the Whistle Stop Cafe,' were big fans of each other? Please read this excerpt from author Fannie Flagg's speech at our 1992 Emerald Seminar. And of course, enjoy the original recipe!," Facebook, July 12, 2020, facebook.com/photo.php?fbid=2631365317107047&id=2070600596516858&set=a.2070615923181992.

312 **Recruits soon discovered:** "Mary Kay Finds Incentives That Pay Off," *Chemical Week*, May 13, 1981.

312 **James Preston became CEO:** Morris L. Mayer, *Direct Selling in the United States: A Commentary and Oral History* (Direct Selling Education Foundation, 1996), 64–65.

313 **"There is no such thing":** *Director's Manual* (Mary Kay Cosmetics, 1966, rev. 1973).

313 **"It helped me":** Paulette Schwoebel, interview with the author, August 20, 2009.

314 **"I remember attending":** Georgia Hall Baird, interview with the author, May 31, 2024.

315 **To cope with hotel:** Doretha Dingler, *In Pink* (Brevin, 2012), 84.

315 **Describing the retirement:** *CBS This Morning*, February 27, 1992.

315 **Through dozens of rallies:** She told the same story to a *Chicago Tribune* reporter, almost verbatim. See Anderson, "In the Pink."

CHAPTER TWENTY-TWO: "SOMETHING TO WORK TOWARD—CONSTANTLY"

316 **"before we publicize it":** Doretha Dingler, interview with the author, November 9, 2018.

317 **Gloria Mayfield Banks, who would:** Gloria Mayfield Banks, interview with the author, December 30, 2009.

317 **After that, she balanced:** Gloria Mayfield Banks, conversation with the author, May 12, 2025.

318 **The company was swimming:** Matthew Schifrin, "Peeking Inside LBOs," *Wall Street Journal*, June 13, 1988.

318 **His side hustle:** Victor E. Sasson, "Aircraft Bases Still Flying High," *Record* (Hackensack, N.J.), June 19, 1988.

318 **On prime time, she judged:** "The Eyes of the Beholder," *Dallas Morning News*, February 8, 1988.

318 **she gave a speech:** Sharon Warren Walsh and Mark Potts, "Giddyap!," *Washington Post*, April 19, 1988; "Business Leaders," *Washington Post*, May 12, 1988.

319 **Impressed by what she saw:** Sue Young, *The Heart of a Leader* (iUniverse, 2009), 75–76, 94.

319 **Let the couture crowd:** Mimi Swartz, "The Fantasy World of Victor Costa," *Texas Monthly*, September 1987.

319 **early in their acquaintance:** Victor Costa, interview with the author, June 27, 2011.

321 **Then Mary Kay, her security:** "Event," *Dallas Times Herald*, July 29, 1990. Mary Kay took over the eighth floor so often that the Anatole decorated and named a suite in her honor.

321 **"Her energy amazed us":** Jennifer Cook, interview with the author, May 10, 2021.

321 **NSDs gowned in silver:** "Mary Kay 25th Anniversary Silver Celebration!," posted February 20, 2017, by Honeydew Wilkins, YouTube, 3 min., 52 sec., youtube.com/watch?v=ycMqwjr3Qb4.

321 **"Because it was the twenty-fifth":** Maria Matthews, interview with Emma Weidmann, May 25, 2024.

322 **"That was just impossible":** Gladys Reyes, interview with the author, March 1, 2010.

322 **Mary Kay could say:** "Mary Kay: The Cosmetic Empire," posted September 13, 2024, by Biography, 45 min., 3 sec., YouTube, youtube.com/watch?v=ZoiFiicfo30.

323 **At a mini Seminar:** Canadian Press, "Makeup Hubbies Must Adjust," *Fort McMurry (Alberta) Today*, August 22, 1988.

323 **In its business pages:** Pat Brennan, "What's a Mary Kay Party Without Its Head Cheerleader?," *Toronto Star*, August 18, 1988.

324 **"I was horrified":** Erma Thomson, interview with the author, August 18, 2014.

324 **Gritting her teeth:** Young, *Heart of a Leader*, 74, 82, 93.

324 **The company lodged:** Berke Breathed, email to author, August 18, 2009.

324 **Mary Kay sent pink lemonade:** Jon Anderson, "In the Pink," *Chicago Tribune*, February 14, 1991.

325 **a talking penguin:** Berke Breathed, *The Night of the Mary Kay Commandos* (Little, Brown, 1989), 72.

325 **"I still have it":** Breathed, email to author.

326 **Still in her twenties:** Jinger Heath, interview with the author, October 14, 2009; Jinger Heath, *Positively You!* (Golden Books, 1998).

326 **Jinger adored her father:** Heath, interview with the author.

328 ***Forbes* called BeautiControl:** William P. Barrett, "See Dick and Jinger Sell," *Forbes*, August 7, 1989.

328 **She ran a 2:50 marathon:** Colleen O'Connor, "High Profile: Jinger Heath," *Dallas Morning News*, April 9, 1989.

328 **In 1989, the Heaths:** Karen Eubank, "Beauty Magnate's Former Preston Hollow Luxury Home," CandysDirt.com, accessed January 10, 2025, https://candysdirt.com/2020/06/27/beauty-magnates-former-preston-hollow-luxury-home; Candy Evans, "Dallas Real Estate News: Claire Dewar Is the Happiest Agent in Town—Ginsberg-Heath Estate on Park Lane, Sold, Closed, Finally!," CandysDirt.com, accessed January 10, 2025, https://candysdirt.com/2012/03/05/dallas-real-estate-news-claire-deware-happiest-agent-town-4707-park-lane-sold-closed.

328 **Long before *Lifestyles*:** "Television," *Dallas Morning News*, April 18, 1984.

329 **"The gal that could make a sale":** Richard Rogers, interview by Donald L. Caruth, November 11, 1974, No. OHB4, p. 9, University of North Texas Oral History Collection, Denton, Tex.

329 **Beset by Chartwell:** Avon, "An Open Letter from Avon: Enough Is Enough," *Wall Street Journal*, November 17, 1989.

329 **In a more practical vein:** Avon Products v. Chartwell Associates L.P., 907 F.2d 322 (2d. Cir. 1990), casemine.com/judgement/us/59148993add7b04934504a77.

330 **Early in 1991:** Associated Press, "Beauty Wars Turning Ugly," *Oshkosh Northwestern*, March 14, 1991.

330 **When Mary Kay Inc. sued:** James C. Hyatt, "Avon Lady's Visit to Trash Dumpster Yields Court Accord," *Wall Street Journal*, March 19, 1991.

330 **Addressing the 1991 audience:** "Mary Kay President Foresees Worldwide Burst in Direct Selling," Business Wire, February 5, 1991.

331 **Feeling compelled to make up:** Anderson, "In the Pink"; "Williams Attends Cancer Program," *Tyler Morning Telegraph*, October 10, 1990; Jennifer Cook—Author, "Recently, I published Mona Butters' memories from her Mary Kay career. Having observed Mary Kay for 20 years and spent personal time with her, Mona also shared these lessons she learned from Mary Kay by watching her actions," Facebook, July 17, 2023, facebook.com/photo.php?fbid=595245982745183&id=100067793589253&set=a.416066103996506.

332 **Fighting dismissal with depositions:** Lisa Gubernick, "Debi Does Dallas," *Forbes*, September 3, 1990.

332 **Her daughter Marylyn:** Staff Reports, "Cosmetic Magnate's Daughter Dies," *Dallas Times Herald*, April 30, 1991; Associated Press, "Mary Kay Ash's Daughter Found Dead," *Dallas Morning News*, April 30, 1991.

332 **She knew that Dorothy Zapp:** Mr. and Mrs. George Forristall, interview with the author, January 19, 2010. Because she remarried after the death of her first husband, Dorothy's full name would have been Dorothy Zapp Forristall Brown.

333 **She ordered breast palpation:** Forristall, interview with the author.

CHAPTER TWENTY-THREE: "MY LEGACY IS ASSURED"

334 **Enthroned as Queen of Hearts:** Condensed from *Women's Wear Daily* and *W*, "Eye," *Fort Worth Star-Telegram*, March 10, 1985.

334 **"But it wasn't her way":** Erma Thomson, interview with the author, August 18, 2014.
334 **The consultant got her machine:** Virginia Keathley, "Christmas Gift: Life, with Love," *Tennessean* (Nashville), December 20, 1970.
334 **The next year, a director:** Michael Wassmer, Mary Kay Corporate Communications, email to the author, May 17, 2021.
334 **The Cardinals employee:** "The Day Mary Kay Pitched to the St. Louis Cardinals," *Timeless Treasures* (blog), August 31, 2015, mktimelesstreasures.weebly.com/red-jackets.html.
335 **Mary Kay was onstage:** Wassmer, email to the author, May 17, 2021.
335 **Mary Kay was sure:** Denise Kucharski, interview with the author, May 25, 2021.
335 **Jennifer Cook explained:** Jennifer Cook, interview with the author, May 10, 2021.
335 **"She always reacted":** Thomson, interview with the author.
336 **Celebrating the company's affluence:** "Subsidiary of Mary Kay Will Double Its Plants," *Dallas Times Herald*, July 28, 1973.
336 **Decades later, she allowed:** Ebby Halliday, interview with the author, July 31, 2009.
336 **That time, twelve thousand people:** Stacey Freedenthal, "Hundreds Brave Rain for Final Mary Kay Tour," *Dallas Morning News*, June 1, 1992.
336 **Unloading the Pink Elephant:** Kyle Pope, "For Sale: Versailles Look-Alike; Condition: In the Pink; Has Garage," *Wall Street Journal*, February 11, 1994.
336 **Selling its contents:** Associated Press, "Pink in the Black," *Daily Advocate* (Greenville, Ohio), May 11, 1994.
336 **appeared on *The 700 Club*:** Crystal Cathedral, "Mary Kay Speaks Live, In-Person This Sunday!," *Los Angeles Times*, March 17, 1994; "Mary Kay's Golden Year Full of History & Vision," posted January 9, 2014, by CBN—The Christian Broadcasting Network, 3 min., 44 sec., youtube.com/watch?v=ChzPiXV-5AI.
336 **In 1993, after passing:** Jim Fuquay, "Fortune Just Out of Reach," *Fort Worth Star-Telegram*, March 31, 1993.
336 **Hailing her as one:** Alan Farnham, "Mary Kay's Lessons in Leadership," *Fortune*, September 20, 1993.
336 **In a *Fortune* magazine profile:** Farnham, "Mary Kay's Lessons in Leadership."
337 **Vitrines held decades' worth:** Nancy Kruh, "Memories in Pink," *Dallas Morning News*, August 12, 1993.
337 **To make sure women understood:** Mary Kay Ash, *Pearls of Wisdom*, 40th anniv. special ed. (Mary Kay Inc., 2002), two CDs.
338 **Watching women react:** Dianne H. B. Welsh and Yvonne Pendleton, "Direct Selling Worldwide: The Mary Kay Cosmetics Story," *International Journal of Family Business* 3, no. 1 (2006): 61–68.
339 **only 11 percent:** John A. Quelch and Nathalie Laidler, "Mary Kay Cosmetics, Inc.: Asian Market Entry," Harvard Business School Case 9-594-023, 2009.
339 **Dispatched to design:** Frank Meier, interview with the author, August 11, 2009.
340 **average sales of $2,400:** Extrapolated from productivity figures given for 1986 through 1992 in Exhibit 1, John A. Quelch and Nathalie Laidler, "Mary Kay Cosmetics, Inc.: Asian Market Entry," Harvard Business School Case 9-594-023, 2009.
340 **A case study coauthored:** Welsh and Pendleton, "Direct Selling Worldwide."
340 **Inaugurating the main ballroom:** Doug Smith, "Bunny-hoppers Have the Joint Jumping," *Charlotte Observer*, March 28, 1995.
341 **Women like Cynthia Thompson:** Mike Mills, "Taking the Office Home with Them," *Washington Post*, September 21, 1994.
341 ***The Philadelphia Inquirer* called them:** Kyle York Spencer, "Mary Kay Women on Corporate Careers: Goodbye Is All She Wrote," *Philadelphia Inquirer*, January 7, 1996.
342 **"We tried to keep her":** Thomson, interview with the author.
342 **"I just cracked up":** Craig Hogan, interview with the author, January 19, 2010.
342 **In 1995, the year:** Mary Kay Ash, *Mary Kay: You Can Have It All* (Prima Lifestyles, 1995).
343 **Boosted by sales:** "Best Selling Books," *Wall Street Journal*, August 9, 1995.
343 **He was the God:** "Our Mission," *Paula's Power Performers*, accessed July 27, 2025, mkpaula.com/our-mission.
343 **she had never forgotten:** "Mary Kay: The Cosmetic Empire," posted September 13, 2024, by Biography, YouTube, 45 min., 3 sec., youtube.com/watch?v=ZoiFiicfo30.

343 **As each woman:** Yvonne Pendleton, *Paychecks of the Heart* (Mary Kay Inc., 2000), 322.
344 **After decades with Home Interiors:** Brendan M. Case, "Focus on Upscale Direct Sales Was Costly for Home Interiors & Gifts," *Dallas Morning News*, May 2, 2008.
344 **Having inherited his mother's energy:** Carlton Stowers, "Sports Too Nice to Be Successful?," *D Magazine*, January 1996.
344 **Carter got it:** Steve Brown, Dallas Morning News Service, "Mary Kay Puts Beleaguered Building in the Pink," *Chicago Tribune*, February 5, 1995.
345 **the boardroom on the thirteenth:** "The Mary Kay Boardroom Lands on Prime-Time Television," Mary Kay Inc., January 1, 1996, newsroom.marykay.com/news/the-mary-kay-boardroom-lands-on-prime-time-television.
346 **"available when they need you":** Doretha Dingler, interview with the author, November 9, 2018.
346 **Using the rivalry:** Skip Hollandsworth, "Hostile Makeover," *Texas Monthly*, November 1995.
347 **With the excuse of promoting:** "Mary Kay Ash, Mary Kay Cosmetics, Discusses How She Got Started in the Business," *CBS This Morning*, November 28, 1995.
347 **Jackie Brown saw *Texas Monthly*:** Jackie Brown, interview with the author, November 15, 2009.
347 **Mary Kay asked:** Jackie Brown, *Ask ME About Mary Kay* (Strategic Book Group, 2010), 381.
347 **"It was sad":** Brown, interview with the author.
348 **Fifteen years after:** Brown, *Ask ME About Mary Kay*, back cover.
348 **Never stingy with self-improvement:** Mary Kay Ash, *Mary Kay* (Harper & Row, 1981), 88–89.
348 **That included twenty-one minutes:** Kristin McMurran, "Mary Kay Ash," *People*, July 29, 1985.
348 **Mary Kay had tape recorders:** Ash, *Mary Kay*, 88–89.
348 **Bill Besse, on her security:** Bill Besse, interview with the author, June 17, 2014.
349 **She also tried to call:** Sandra Mardefield, "Incentive Interview: Mary Kay Ash," *Incentive*, January 1996.
349 **"Men were always trying":** Thomson, interview with the author.
350 **Mary Kay–designed birthday card:** Mardefield, "Incentive Interview."
350 **Mary Kay held herself:** Pendleton, *Paychecks of the Heart*, 328.
351 **If she wanted matching:** Jennifer Cook, *Pass It On* (Brown Books, 2021), 102.
351 **Positive that the Six:** Ash, *Mary Kay*, 79–80.

CHAPTER TWENTY-FOUR: "THE IDEALIZATION"

352 **On February 26, 1996:** Jennifer Cook, *Pass It On* (Brown Books, 2021), 17.
352 **her latest book, *Mary Kay*:** "Best Sellers," *New York Times*, August 27, 1995; Associated Press, "Mary Kay Founder Dies," CBS News, November 22, 2001, cbsnews.com/news/mary-kay-founder-dies.
352 **She had driven a pink:** "Our History," Mary Kay, accessed March 28, 2025, marykayglobal.com/our-history.
352 **As recently as January:** Kelley Shannon, Associated Press, "Cosmetics Guru Mary Kay Ash Inspires Sales Leaders with Talk," *Monitor* (McAllen), January 12, 1996.
352 **She did not speak:** Associated Press, "Ailing Chief Still Mary Kay's Spiritual Force," *Chicago Tribune*, August 11, 1996.
352 **She missed her own induction:** "Buick Manager to Accept Honor on Behalf of Durant," *Flint Journal*, April 24, 1996.
353 **Mary Kay had concluded:** Mary Kay Ash, *Mary Kay* (Harper & Row, 1981), 202–6.
353 **Year after year, she had:** Morris L. Mayer, *Direct Selling in the United States: A Commentary and Oral History* (Direct Selling Education Foundation, 1996), 29.
353 **Newspapers reported her absence:** Associated Press, "Mary Kay Women Carry On the Dream," *El Paso Times*, July 28, 1996.
353 **"More and more it made":** Katie Fairbank, Associated Press, "Being 'Mary Kay,'" *Kerrville Daily Times*, August 18, 1996.
353 **Without Mary Kay to raise:** Michael Wassmer, email to the author, May 17, 2021; "Our History," Mary Kay Ash Foundation, accessed March 27, 2025, marykayashfoundation.org/who-we-are/our-history-timeline. Mary Kay signed the papers establishing the foundation the week before her stroke.

353 **Her life story appeared:** Allan Zullo with Bill Hartigan, *Success After 40* (Andrews McMeel, 1997).

353 **She was the only woman:** Daniel Gross and the editors of *Forbes* magazine, *Forbes Greatest Business Stories of All Time* (John Wiley & Sons, 1996).

353 **NSDs again took over:** "Mary Kay Seminar 1997—Incredible Journey," posted January 13, 2020, by Honeydew Wilkins, YouTube, 4 min., 15 sec., youtube.com/watch?v=dPEH7BxB-6Y.

354 **An NSD read:** Doretha Dingler, *In Pink* (Brevin, 2012), 134.

354 **When the words:** Some women swear that they heard the words distinctly. See Yvonne Pendleton, *Paychecks of the Heart* (Mary Kay Inc., 2000), 153; "Mary Kay: The Cosmetic Empire," posted September 13, 2024, by Biography, YouTube, 45 min., 3 sec., youtube.com/watch?v=ZoiFiicfo30.

354 **As Estée Lauder's company:** Estée Lauder Companies, "Take a Tour: Mrs. Estée Lauder's Office," Facebook, June 20, 2017, facebook.com/watch/?v=1712108688818307.

354 **Slippers were still stowed:** "Mary Kay Ash Office Tour | Mary Kay Inc. Corporate Headquarters," posted January 10, 2023, by Mary Kay, YouTube, 5 min., 15 sec., youtube.com/watch?v=bO4shRAvMPw.

354 **Outside her office door:** Observations of the author, July 1999.

354 **New products were presented:** Jennifer Cook, interview with the author, May 10, 2021.

354 **Meetings of the Mary Kay Ash:** Dingler, *In Pink*, 132–33.

355 **Friends, most often:** Doretha Dingler, interview with the author, November 9, 2018; Cook, interview with the author.

355 **"It's important for me":** Ash, *Mary Kay*, 205.

355 **Youth choirs, church choirs:** Bill Besse, interview with the author, June 17, 2014; Dingler, interview with the author.

355 **Other visitors were encouraged:** Sue Young, *The Heart of a Leader* (iUniverse, 2009), 96–97.

356 **Avon and Amway had gotten:** John A. Quelch and Nathalie Laidler, "Mary Kay Cosmetics, Inc.: Asian Market Entry," Harvard Business School Case 9-594-023, 2009.

356 **In April of 1998:** Craig Smith and Ian Johnson, "Beijing, Fearing Fervor, Bars the Door Against Direct Marketers," *Wall Street Journal*, April 22, 1998.

356 **By September, Mary Kay China:** Bloomberg News, "Mary Kay to Resume Sales in China," *Toronto Star*, September 5, 1998.

357 **the program's first year:** Laura Klepacki, "Reaching Out, a Byte at a Time," *Women's Wear Daily*, April 17, 1998.

357 **the Direct Sellers:** "Industry Innovation Award," Direct Sellers Association, accessed February 12, 2025, dsawebsite.gtacns.com/awards/industry-innovation-award.

357 **Each summer, women:** Observations of the author, July 1999.

357 **When an NSD:** Observations of the author, July 1999.

358 **In 2000, Mary Kay:** Sharon Morgan Tahaney, *Living a Rich Life* (Forbes Custom Publishing, 2000).

358 **the company's corporate heritage:** Pendleton, *Paychecks of the Heart*, 18; Laura Klepacki, "The Evolving World of Mary Kay," *Women's Wear Daily*, April 6, 2001.

358 **"Over the years, so many":** Erma Thomson, interview with the author, August 18, 2014.

358 **A consultant in Tajikistan:** Observations of the author, July 2009.

358 **Throughout China, college women:** Ting Yuan, interview with the author, September 2009.

358 **Historian H. W. Brands profiled:** H. W. Brands, *Masters of Enterprise* (Simon & Schuster, 1999).

359 **Lifetime, the "Television for Women":** "Texas Women's Hall of Fame: Mary Kay Ash," Texas Woman's University, updated February 5, 2020, twu.edu/twhf/honorees/mary-kay-ash.

359 **Now writing about her reverentially:** "The Best of the Texas Century—Business: Salesman of the Century," *Texas Monthly*, December 1999.

359 **The Women's Museum installed:** "Mankiller to Be Featured in 'Unforgettable Women' Exhibit," *Tulsa World*, March 6, 2000.

359 **"The idealization of the person":** Joseph Guinto, "Not So Pretty in Pink," *D Magazine*, March 2004.

360 **By the summer of 2001:** Laura Klepacki, "Mary Kay Heir Returns," *Women's Wear Daily*, July 6, 2001.

360 **name-checked Mary Kay's financial:** "Private Properties," *Wall Street Journal*, June 14, 1996.

360 **It was no secret:** Guinto, "Not So Pretty."

360 **"I have decided to resume":** Klepacki, "Mary Kay Heir Returns."

360 **Rochon was out:** John Kirkpatrick, "Mary Kay Chief to Break Up Investment Firm," *Dallas Morning News*, June 29, 2001.

360 **Richard's letter explained:** Kirkpatrick, "Mary Kay Chief to Break Up Investment Firm."

360 **A day or two later:** Kirkpatrick, "Mary Kay Chief to Break Up Investment Firm."

360 **"Mother's dream ministers":** Sudeep Reddy, "Pursuing the Dream; Mary Kay CEO Exhorts Faithful at Convention," *Dallas Morning News*, July 27, 2001.

361 **All of it:** David Koenig, Associated Press, "Mary Kay Cosmetics Looks to Teens in Bid to Stay Young Itself," *Merced Sun-Star*, September 13, 2001.

CHAPTER TWENTY-FIVE: "THE FACE OF BUSINESS FOR WOMEN"

362 **By November, directors:** Sue Young, *The Heart of a Leader* (iUniverse, 2009), 93; Doretha Dingler, interview with the author, November 9, 2018.

362 **Her press office:** PR News Wire, "Mary Kay Ash, Founder of Mary Kay Inc., Passes Away," news release, November 22, 2001.

362 **PINK EMPIRE CHANGED:** Joe Simnacher, "Cosmetics Icon Mary Kay Ash Dies; Pink Empire Changed the Face of Business for Women," *Dallas Morning News*, November 23, 2001.

362 ***Women's Wear Daily* said:** WWD Staff, "Remembering Mary Kay Ash," *Women's Wear Daily*, November 26, 2001.

362 **Her *New York Times* obit:** Enid Nemy, "Mary Kay Ash, Who Built a Cosmetics Empire and Adored Pink, Is Dead at 83," *New York Times*, November 23, 2001.

363 **Her 1993 will:** Last Will and Testament of Mary Kay Ash, July 23, 1993, filed January 10, 2002, Estate of Mary Kay Ash, Probate Court, Dallas County, Texas, case no. PR-02-00100-2.

363 **One reporter took:** David Koenig, Associated Press, "Mary Kay Ash Remembered at Dallas Service," *Monitor* (McAllen, TX), November 29, 2001.

363 **Writing as though:** "Mary Kay Ash: She Led the Way for Generations of Women," *Dallas Morning News*, November 24, 2001.

363 **What it had become:** Bureau of Labor Statistics reference desk, telephone call with the author, March 25, 2025; "Women CEOs in Fortune 500 Companies, 1995–2023," Pew Research Center, January 14, 2015, pewresearch.org/chart/women-ceos-in-fortune-500-companies.

363 **As she had planned:** Find a Grave database, memorial pages for Greer Garson (memorial ID 2465), Mickey Mantle (memorial ID 1239), and Mary Elizabeth Weaver Crowley (memorial ID 74577178), accessed March 25, 2025, findagrave.com.

363 **Three husbands were there already:** Find a Grave database, memorial pages for Charles William Weaver (memorial ID 74577179), George Arthur Hallenbeck (memorial ID 145881631), and Melville Jerome Ash (memorial ID 7041521), accessed March 25, 2025, findagrave.com.

364 **When the day came:** Tiara M. Ellis, "Here Comes Winter," *Dallas Morning News*, November 28, 2001.

364 **Its sanctuary was pink:** "Capital Projects," Park City Baptist Church, accessed January 15, 2025, pcbc.org/capitalprojects.

364 **Poster-size portraits:** Mary McKee, "Friends Recall Wit, Compassion; Mary Kay Ash 1918–2001," *Fort Worth Star-Telegram*, November 29, 2001.

364 **All had traveled:** "Remembering Mary Kay Ash—written on Nov. 29, 2001; recorded in Nov. 29, 2024," posted November 29, 2024, by Pamela Shaw, YouTube, 30 min., 43 sec., youtube.com/watch?v=7cexDx4QnZg; Pamela Shaw, "A Tribute to Mary Kay," accessed January 10, 2025, unitnet.com/servlet/newsServlet?method=getArticle&id=393752&jspURL=/jsp/news/article.jsp&ntype=2.

366 **Tarbet got her laugh:** Joe Simnacher, "'She Was a Saint'; Family, Friends, Workers Pay Tribute to Abilities, Love of Mary Kay Ash," *Dallas Morning News*, November 29, 2001.

366 **Grandson Ryan Rogers:** Young, *Heart of a Leader*, 95.

366 **As hymns, Mary Kay:** Observation of the author, memorial program posted at the Mary Kay Museum, March 2025.

366 **After benediction, the service:** Simnacher, "'She was a Saint.'"

366 **During the worldwide recession:** Mary Kay Inc. Corporate Communications, "2003 Fact Sheet," 2003.

367 **In Argentina, the Argentine:** Libby Estell and Jeanie Casison, "Don't Cry for Me, Argentina," *Incentive*, April 2002.

367 **Now fair game:** "Hell on Heels: The Battle of Mary Kay 1/10," posted August 30, 2008, by machinegunkelly111, YouTube, 9 min., 45 sec., youtube.com/watch?v=_8-tBuUVSYg.

367 ***Dallas Morning News* pronounced:** Ed Bark, "'Hell on Heels' Is a Big Pink Valentine to Mary Kay," *Dallas Morning News*, October 6, 2002.

367 **Companies old and new:** Ellen L. Rosen, "In Business: Another Home-Shopping Network," *New York Times*, August 25, 2002.

367 **Billionaire Warren Buffett:** Dennis Rodkin, "Pampered Chef Owner Goes on House Diet," *Chicago*, April 25, 2011; Bob Kaiser, "A Mom with Vision and Drive Joins Buffett," *South Florida Sun Sentinel*, September 29, 2002.

367 **Reporting the surge:** Rosen, "In Business."

368 **World Gift closed:** Dick Kelly, interview with the author, October 7, 2009.

368 **After his death in 1999:** Dave Ghose, "The Longaberger Basket Case," *Columbus Monthly*, April 19, 2017.

368 **"Big Basket," Longaberger's:** Kent Mallett, USA Today Network, "Plans Scrapped to Turn Longaberger Basket Building into Hotel," *Newark Advocate*, January 17, 2021.

368 **had become StanHome:** "Remembering Stanley Home Products," *Republican* (Springfield, Mass.), September 4, 2019.

369 **After selling BeautiControl:** Bloomberg News Service, "Tupperware to Buy BeautiControl," *News-Press* (Fort Myers), September 21, 2000.

369 **"the company for women":** Dana Canedy, "Opportunity Re-Knocks at Avon; Passed Over Before, a Woman Is Named Chief Executive," *New York Times*, November 5, 1999.

369 **management was confident:** Observations of the author during beComing organizational meetings in the summer of 2001 and beComing launch in September of 2001.

369 **By 2003, the company:** Mary Kay Inc. Corporate Communications, "2003 Fact Sheet."

369 **As Ryan later explained:** Elie Ofek et al., "Mary Kay Inc.: Enriching Women's Lives While Embracing Change," Harvard Business School Case 9-522-004, 2022.

369 **Saluting four years of record:** Staff Reports, "Business Roundup," *Casper Star-Tribune*, August 24, 2003; "MK Seminar 2003 Highlights Part 1," posted April 9, 2011, by Pnkshdw, 9 min., 3 sec., YouTube, youtube.com/watch?v=ikhxDCJHSGw; "MK Seminar 2003 Highlights part 2." posted April 9, 2011, by Pnkshdw, YouTube, 7 min., 45 sec., youtube.com/watch?v=Xh71mue2TFU.

369 **An NSD introduced:** Observations of the author, July 1999 and July 2009.

369 **Mary Kay's long-departed:** Finks Finds, "Mary Kay Ash Pink Gigi Poodle Glass Christmas Ornament with Display Stand and Box," eBay, accessed January 25, 2025, ebay.com/itm/116413637275.

369 **A heart-shaped pink tub:** Mary Kay Linge, "How the Founder of Mary Kay Went from Single Mom to Billion-Dollar Beauty Queen," *New York Post*, October 2, 2021, nypost.com/2021/10/02/how-mary-kays-founder-went-from-single-mom-to-billion-dollar-beauty-queen.

370 **Halfway through shutdown:** "A Digital Transformation: Mary Kay Launches Immersive Virtual Experience Platform Suite 13," Mary Kay Inc., April 15, 2021, newsroom.marykay.com/media/a-digital-transformation-mary-kay-inc-launches-immersive-virtual-experience-platform-suite-13.

370 **Trolls coined *hunbot*:** Kaitlyn Tiffany, "The Internet Is Starting to Turn on MLMs," *Atlantic*, December 17, 2020.

370 **Chief among them:** "About Pink Truth," *Pink Truth*, accessed March 26, 2025, pinktruth.com/about-pink-truth.

370 **Under pseudonyms like:** Raisinberry, "The Twisted Sisterhood of Mary Kay," *Pink Truth*, August 22, 2023, pinktruth.com/2023/08/22/the-twisted-sisterhood-of-mary-kay.

370 **"a weird plaid":** Tracy, "Sales Director and NSD Suits," *Pink Truth*, accessed January 17, 2022, pinktruth.com/2022/01/17/sales-director-and-nsd-suits-2022.

370 **Husbands griped:** Tracy, "A Frustrated Mary Kay Husband," *Pink Truth*, accessed April 19, 2022, pinktruth.com/2022/04/19/a-frustrated-mary-kay-husband.

370 **Coenen, who had once aspired:** Tracy Coenen, "About the Author," Amazon, accessed January 10, 2025, amazon.com/stores/Tracy-Coenen/author/B001JSHG4A?ref=ap_rdr&isDramIntegrated=true&shoppingPortalEnabled=true.

370 **That pushed her site:** Virginia Sole-Smith, "The Pink Pyramid Scheme," *Harper's*, August 2012.

371 **Using a first-person narrative:** Sole-Smith handled company background with sentences that included: "In 1938, Mary Kay Ash, a twenty-year-old Army wife raising three children alone in Houston, began selling books and housewares for Stanley Home Products." In 1938, Mary Kay was not an army wife (her husband entered in 1944), her third child had not been born (Richard came in 1943), she was not selling Stanley (which did not allow women until 1939), and Stanley sold no books and few items that could be classified as housewares.

371 **MARY KAY PREYS:** Helaine Olen, "Mary Kay Preys on Women," *Forbes*, July 20, 2012, forbes.com/sites/helaineolen/2012/07/20/mary-kay-preys-on-women.

371 **In 2012, the year:** Gillian Wee and Zohair Siraj, Bloomberg News Service, "Mary Kay Cosmetics Billionaire Drives Pink Escalade," *Akron Beacon Journal*, August 9, 2013.

371 **Best efforts to the contrary:** Lawrence Hrebiniak et al., "Changes Needed at Avon Are More Than Cosmetic," *Knowledge at Wharton*, April 25, 2012.

371 **Aspirants to Avon's former preeminence:** Kari Hamanaka, "Arbonne's Makeover," *Orange County Business Journal*, August 15, 2021; Lauren Silva Laughlin, "Avon Pays a Price for Age in Brazil Tie-Up," *Wall Street Journal*, May 22, 2019.

372 **Utah-based Nu Skin:** "Annual Reports," Nu Skin, accessed March 26, 2025, ir.nuskin.com/financial-information/annual-reports.

372 **Using direct selling to:** Ambit Energy Corporate Communications, Inc. "500 Recognizes Ambit Energy as America's Fastest Growing Private Company," August 24, 2010.

372 **Superintending a scented-wax empire:** Zach Kyle, "Scentsy Still Smells Success," *Idaho Statesman*, May 4, 2014.

372 **LuLaRoe took its polyester:** Rebecca Davis O'Brien, "Lawsuits Mount Against LuLaRoe, Maker of Colorful Women's Leggings," *Wall Street Journal*, January 19, 2018.

372 **Sounding like so many moms:** Yu Shing Ting, "Stella & Dot," *Honolulu Star-Advertiser*, October 31, 2012.

372 **Mary Kay media storm:** Rupert Neate, "Herbalife CEO Accused of Running 'Ponzi Scheme,'" *Guardian*, December 21, 2012.

372 **billionaires who had been bullish:** Samantha Chang, "Billionaire Bill Ackman Dumps Herbalife, Ending 5-Year War Betting Against It," *Investopedia*, June 25, 2019, acceinvestopedia.com/news/billionaire-bill-ackman-dumps-herbalife-ending-5year-war-betting-against-it.

372 **Mary Kay–themed *20/20* exposé:** "Mary Kay Secrets of the Sell," posted August 18, 2021, by Pink Truth, 14 min., 5 sec., YouTube, youtube.com/watch?v=20aMjt0xSn8.

373 **While the effective altruism movement:** Robert McMillan and Deepa Seetharaman, "How a Fervent Belief Split Silicon Valley—and Fueled the Blowup at Open AI," *Wall Street Journal*, November 22, 2023.

373 **Mary Kay Ash Foundation distributed:** "Cancer Research," Mary Kay Ash Foundation, accessed March 26, 2025, marykayashfoundation.org/what-we-do/cancer-research.

373 **Funds went to women's shelters:** Mary Kay Inc., "More Education Is Needed to Help Teens and Young Adults Stand Up to a New Epidemic: Digital Dating Abuse," PR Newswire, October 30, 2017; "Our History," Mary Kay Ash Foundation, accessed March 26, 2025, marykayashfoundation.org/who-we-are/our-history-timeline.

373 **Acreage was reforested:** "Mary Kay Announces 2023 Reforestation Projects and Celebrates 15 Years of Positive Community Impact with the Arbor Day Foundation," Mary Kay, June 22, 2023, newsroom.marykay.com/media/mary-kay-announces-2023-reforestation-projects-and-celebrates-15-years-of-positive-community-impact-with-the-arbor-day-foundation.

373 **Mary Kay China sponsored:** "Mary Kay China's Sponsored Programs & Funds," Mary Kay Global, accessed March 26, 2025, marykayglobal.com/wp-content/uploads/2022/12/Foundations-China.pdf.

373 **her story made for compulsory:** Alan C. Elliott, *Dreams That Built America* (Thomas Nelson/HarperCollins Christian, 2022); DK Publishing, *Entrepreneurs Who Changed History* (DK, 2020); Marlene Wagman-Geller, *Great Second Acts* (Mango, 2018).

373 **In the universe:** Gerhard Gschwandtner, *Secrets of Superstar Sales Pros* (McGraw-Hill, 2007); Jim Mathis, *Reaching Beyond Excellence* (Advantage Media Group, 2006).

373 **written by a mother:** Carrie Wilkerson, *The Barefoot Executive* (Thomas Nelson/HarperCollins Christian, 2011).

373 **When the Wharton School:** Mukul Pandya and Robbie Shell, *Nightly Business Report Presents Lasting Leadership: What You Can Learn from the Top 25 Business People of Our Times* (Wharton School, 2005).

373 **ranked her as a "superboss":** Steve Rosenbush, "What Your CEO Is Reading: Dawn of the Superboss," *Wall Street Journal*, December 25, 2015.

373 **Business schools cranked out:** Ofek et al., "Mary Kay Inc."

374 **At last, in 2023:** Business Wire, "Grandson of Legendary Entrepreneur Mary Kay Ash to Lead Global Cosmetics Giant," news release, November 1, 2022; Cheryl Hall, "Mary Kay's Ryan Rogers Out to Prove His Legendary Grandmother's DNA Still Present," *Dallas Morning News*, October 17, 2023.

374 ***Forbes* described the company:** "Mary Kay" (Forbes Profile [2022]), *Forbes*, accessed January 13, 2025, forbes.com/companies/mary-kay.

374 **women in the U.S. averaged:** Rakesh Kochhar, "The Enduring Grip of the Gender Pay Gap," Pew Research Center, March 1, 2023, pewresearch.org/social-trends/2023/03/01/the-enduring-grip-of-the-gender-pay-gap.

CREDITS

Page 8: Collection of the author.

Page 9: Courtesy of Amegy Bank.

Page 12: Courtesy of Cy-Fair School District.

Page 17: Courtesy of Woodson Research Center, Fondren Library, Rice University.

Page 22: MSS0054-B66-01, courtesy of Houston Public Library, Digital Archives.

Page 26: [Building and Land Assessment Card; 0051920000010] courtesy of Harris County Tax Assessor-Collector, Harris County Archives, Houston, Texas.

Page 30 (top): Courtesy of Tyrone Area Historical Society and Museum.

Page 30 (bottom): Collection of the author.

Page 34: Collection of the author.

Page 36: Collection of the author.

Page 39: Collection of the author.

Page 40: Collection of the author.

Page 42: Collection of the author.

Page 47: Collection of the author.

Page 52: Collection of the author.

Page 57: Collection of the author.

Page 60 (top): Jean Blackwell Hutson Research and Reference Division, Schomberg Center for Research in Black Culture, The New York Public Library.

Page 60 (bottom): Madam Walker Family Archives, collection of the Smithsonian National Museum of African American History and Culture, gift of A'Lelia Bundles.

Page 61: Madam Walker Family Archives, collection of the Smithsonian National Museum of African American History and Culture, gift of A'Lelia Bundles.

Page 74: Courtesy of the Stanley Park of Westfield, Massachusetts, Inc.

Page 101: Courtesy of Evalyn Eckman.

Page 104: Courtesy of Evalyn Eckman.

Page 109 (top, bottom): Collection of the author.

Page 117: Courtesy of Evalyn Eckman.

Page 124: Courtesy of the Stanley Park of Westfield, Massachusetts, Inc.

Page 139: Courtesy of the Stanley Park of Westfield, Massachusetts, Inc.

Page 155 (top, bottom): Brownie Wise Papers, Archives Center, National Museum of American History, Smithsonian Institution.

Page 160: Collection of the author.

Page 162: Avon Products, Inc. records (accession 2155), Manuscripts and Archives Department, Hagley Museum and Library, Wilmington, Delaware.

Page 163: Courtesy of Dick Kelly.

Page 168: Courtesy of George T. Henry Archives, Coe College.

Page 185 (top, bottom): Division of Home and Community Life, National Museum of American History, Smithsonian Institution, gift of Mary Kay Inc.

Page 242: Collection of the Dallas History & Archives Division, Dallas Public Library.

Page 249: Photograph by Skeeter Hagler, collection of the Dallas History & Archives Division, Dallas Public Library.

Page 253: Division of Home and Community Life, National Museum of American History, Smithsonian Institution, gift of Denise Kucharski.

Page 259: Collection of the Dallas History & Archives Division, Dallas Public Library.

Page 264: Photograph by Skeeter Hagler, collection of the Dallas History & Archives Division, Dallas Public Library.

Page 265: Courtesy of glabarre.com—George H. LaBarre Galleries, Inc.

Page 267: Photograph by Bob Jackson, collection of the Dallas History & Archives Division, Dallas Public Library.

Page 276 (top, bottom): Photograph by John Mazziotta, collection of the Dallas History & Archives Division, Dallas Public Library.

Page 291: Courtesy of glabarre.com—George H. LaBarre Galleries, Inc.

Page 296: Copyright © *Atlanta Journal-Constitution*, courtesy of Special Collections and Archives, Georgia State University Library.

Page 307: Barry Lewis/Alamy Stock Photo.

Page 320: Collection of the author.

Page 337: Collection of the author.

Page 338: Photograph by Barry McCoy.

Page 345: Photograph by Barry McCoy.

Page 359: Collection of the author.

Page 365: Erich Schlegel/ZUMA Wire.

Page 368: Collection of the author.

INDEX

Page numbers in italics refer to photos and illustrations.